Rock and Popular Music in Ireland: Before and After U2

Noel McLaughlin and Martin McLoone

IRISH ACADEMIC PRESS

DUBLIN • PORTLAND, OR

First published in 2012 by Irish Academic Press

2 Brookside,	920 NE 58th Avenue, Suite 300
Dundrum Road,	Portland, Oregon,
Dublin 14, Ireland	97213-3786 USA

© Noel McLaughlin and Martin McLoone 2012

www.iap.ie

British Library Cataloguing in Publication Data
An entry can be found on request

McLaughlin, Noel.
  Rock and popular music in Ireland before and after U2.
  1. Popular music—Ireland—History and criticism. 2. Rock
music—Ireland—History and criticism. 3. Rock
musicians—Ireland—History—20th century.
  I. Title II. McLoone, Martin.
  781.6'4'09415'09045-dc23

ISBN: 978 0 7165 3076 3 (cloth)
ISBN: 978 0 7165 3077 0 (paper)

Library of Congress Cataloging-in-Publication Data
An entry can be found on request

Typeset by FiSH Books, Enfield
Printed and bound by CPI Group (UK) Ltd, Croydon, CR0 4YY

This book is dedicated to Molly and Robert McLaughlin
and to the late Noel Rankin

In memory of John McLoone, who actually preferred Josef Locke

Contents

Acknowledgements

First of all we both must thank the many interviewees for being so generous with their time and memories: Rab Braniff, Eamonn Creen, Kev Cully, Dave Fanning, Malcolm Gerrie; the late Bill Graham, Jackie Hayden and Niall Stokes at *Hot Press*, Gregory Gray, Nigel House at Rough Trade Records on Talbot Road, Terri Hooley, Jim Lockhart, Reggie Manuel, Neil McCormick, Barry McIlheney, Fachtna O'Ceallaigh, Jimmy Page, John Reynolds, Simon Reynolds, John Waters and Ian Wilson. Many of you spoke with the erudition of seasoned cultural theorists and gently subverted the idea that practitioners and journalists of different hues are bereft of a critical self-consciousness about their work.

A special note of thanks must go to our colleagues in both popular music studies and particularly in Irish popular music studies: Ian Biddle, Sean Campbell, Simon Frith, Ian Inglis, Dave Laing, Andy Linehan, John O'Flynn, Tony Purvis and Gerry Smyth. As well, a huge thank you must go to Lisa Hyde at Irish Academic Press.

We are extremely grateful to Matt McGee for the cover image of Windmill Lane, Dublin and to Andrew Campbell for the cover design.

Noel McLaughlin would like to thank Rob Proni (for the debates about nations and nationalism) and the staff at the Westbourne Tavern in London W2 for taking in a writing academic. Thanks also to Claude Ashmore, Tristan Hazell, Richard Thomas, Caitlin Lees and Marlies Luktenhues as well as to my students over the years on Popular Music and Film at Northumbria University for their rich ideas and enthusiasm: Stephanie Allum, Shaun Deehan, Beth McGarvie, Anna McNab, Michael Waugh and Chris Wells.

A very particular thanks must go to my colleagues in the Film and Television Studies' '101 suite' at Northumbria University: Ysanne Holt, Peter Hutchings, Elizabeth Kramer, James Leggott and Alison Peirse.

Also, special thanks to John Adams, Joanna Braniff, John Braniff, Robert Braniff, Mick Clarke, Pamela Church Gibson, Sarah Gilligan, John Hill and to colleagues, past and present – Elayne Chaplin, Tobias Hochscherf, Russ Hunter and Jamie Sexton – who were kind enough to read and offer useful comments on draft chapters.

Last, but by no means least, I offer a huge thank you to my partner, best friend and so much more, Maria Trkulja.

Martin McLoone would like to thank the Centre for Media Research at the University of Ulster for continuing support and especially my colleagues Richard Ekins and Ciara Chambers for their stimulating information and ideas about popular music.

Yet again, special thanks go to Cindy, Katie, Maeve and Grainne.

List of Illustrations

Foreword

'Imagine there's no countries / It isn't hard to do'

So wrote John Lennon – the child of an Irish grandfather, as this book reminds us in its opening pages – in one of the late twentieth century's most admired songs.

For many young musicians of the 1950s and 1960s, rock music seemed the way to escape the oppressive national identity imposed by regimes such as those of 'actually existing socialism' in Eastern Europe. From another perspective, postmodern approaches to questions of personal identity have suggested that individuals can chose from multiple identities at different times and in different relationships, with national identity as just one 'pick and mix' option. The work of both Zygmunt Bauman and Amartya Sen seems to offer such a scenario.

The appealing utopian call for a post-national (or a-national) identity – with its own musical cues – however, has generally proved to be just that, utopian. For every band that sought to escape the surly bonds of nationalism, there have been more who undertook to remake national identity, whether through the *rock nacional* of Argentina, the sinister turbo-folk of Milosevic-era Serbia or the almost unlimited varieties of folk-rock or own-language rap from every continent.

But if these are international, even global, trends, each national situation has its own aesthetic, cultural and political contours, its own negotiations between old and new, indigenous and foreign. In this book, Noel McLaughlin and Martin McLoone have set out to discover and define the Irish milieu of those contours and negotiations, and how they have been registered in the music of a series of gifted singers and bands, both well-known and less known, losers as well as winners in the commercial music business.

The book, and the history it narrates, has myriad themes. But if there is a primary one, it is stated by Phil Chevron who recalls that in the 1970s, Dublin (post) punk band The Radiators From Space became aware that they were an 'Irish rock band'. As the book demonstrates, there have been many ways to become such a beast, including some that the musicians involved were unaware of.

If we discount John Count McCormack, the most internationally successful musicians from Ireland before U2 have probably been The Chieftains. A product of the revival of traditional music, a curious mixture of cultural policy (as in Eastern Europe) and cultural industry (as in Greenwich Village and Soho), The Chieftains have played on – and off – the 'Irishness' recognized in myriad Irish pubs around the world and in the touring productions of Riverdance and its successors and imitators.

The Chieftains, then, are unequivocally 'Irish'. But what of U2, the centrepiece of this book? The authors succinctly present the enigmatic issue – 'U2 ... are a conundrum. What other global rock band can be read both as the sound of pre-colonial racial authenticity *and* of global imposition?'

It is easy for their international stadium rock audiences to not hear U2 as Irish. As McLaughlin and McLoone point out, even some of their academic fans seem to assimilate them into a deracinated pantheon of anthemic rock. This contrasts with the reception of Elvis Presley and The Beatles, their predecessor megastars. They were heard as transnational, but also as American or English/Liverpudlian. This simultaneous avowal and disavowal of Anglophonic identity was captured by the Brazilian singer and songwriter Caetano Veloso when he described listening to The Beatles as a teenager:

> To a mind that has evolved within the circumference of Portuguese, English is as strange as any language could be to a human being. And its abiding presence, far from mitigating that strangeness, often only intensifies it ... From hearing so many songs whose sounds became familiar even as their meaning remained obscure ... we became inured to English as a gibberish that is part of life, without requiring any effort on our part to make it intelligible.

U2 came to their full pomp in the age of neo-liberal globalization – which had its Irish analogue, the Celtic Tiger, as the rampant Irish economy of the 1990s was dubbed. It was an age when global English was more pervasive – it's a good bet that Brazilian teenagers of the 1980s could understand, or sing along with U2 lyrics. Perhaps counter-intuitively, this is why their Irish dimension may be less obvious to many fans. But the book redresses that balance by acutely and persuasively teasing out this key feature of their work.

The authors are also attentive to the 'metatext' of the music they discuss, the melange of media words and images that frame the sounds. Noel McLaughlin and Martin McLoone are experts in the cinema of Ireland, and are able to extend and diversify their narrative by reference to music in the movies.

Their exposé of the generally woeful (and sometime wilful) misperceptions of Irish rock to be found in the British music press had this English writer wincing with embarrassment. This is not only a question of racial prejudice – although several shaming examples are quoted here – but one of perspective. For the conservative mainstream discourse of 'the centre' (in popular music, Anglo-America), a band from the periphery (be it Ireland, Australasia or Sweden) is either stereotyped by its origins, or naturalized into honorary Anglo-Americanism, in which case key features of its work may be repressed, as with The Virgin Prunes. It is salutary to be reminded that, *pace* Bob Geldof's image in mainland Britain, in the late 1970s The Boomtown Rats eloquently and belligerently voiced the frustrations of young Ireland. Equally important is the insight about the differing political effects of punk in England and Scotland on the one hand, and in Northern Ireland on the other, where the music played the role of an original 'community relations council', a point that is underlined by reference to the film *Shellshock Rock*.

The admonition of the English music press is presented alongside an acute analysis of *Hot Press*, the long-established Irish media institution that has had no comparable magazine almost anywhere since *Rolling Stone* lost its radical edge – except perhaps for the French periodical *Les Inrockuptibles*. While acknowledging the staunch role of the magazine in championing U2, the book is also critical of the 'river of sound' ideology that underlies much of its writing about Irish music.

In sum, here is a book to inform both Irish and non-Irish readers about a fascinating range of musical practices and expressions, but also one that will provoke thought and debate about the vectors of national identity that inform popular music of all kinds and all places.

Dave Laing
October 2011

Introduction:
Authenticity and Hybridity

One of the recurring myths about the Irish is that they possess a natural proclivity for music and song. This is an enduring national stereotype and has been a feature of colonial discourse about Ireland that can be traced back to the Norman invasions of the twelfth century. 'This race is inconstant, changeable, wily, and cunning', writes Giraldus Cambrensis in 1187. 'It is an unstable race, stable only in its instability, faithful only in its unfaithfulness.'[1] Elsewhere, he writes: 'It is indeed a most filthy race, a race sunk in vice, a race more ignorant than all other nations.'[2] And yet, famously, Cambrensis also observed:

> The only thing to which I find that this people apply a commendable industry is playing upon musical instruments, in which they are incomparably more skilful than any other nation I have ever seen. For their modulation on these instruments . . . is . . . lively and rapid, while the harmony is both sweet and gay.[3]

Cambrensis also warned against being too seduced by this wonderful facility with music. In his account of the conquest of Ireland, he notes: 'As this people are easily moved to rebel . . . they will have to be ruled with great discretion . . . the craft of this people is more to be feared than their prowess in arms.'[4] The prescient Cambrensis may well here have anticipated The Clancy Brothers, Christy Moore and The Wolfe Tones, identifying and then cautioning against the Irish rebel song, one of the country's more enduring musical traditions.

However, this powerful link between the Irish and natural musicality (along with other considerably less attractive traits) was finally consolidated in the Victorian era at the height of British imperial power and influence.[5] Irish music by this stage was constructed as a specific ethnic category based on the assumption that there was an identifiably Irish musical style that existed as an expression of the people, a reflection of their innate feelings and sensibilities. Music, in other words, became a feature of 'race', taking on properties for the colonizer that appeared to transcend the passage of time and that remained fixed and unchanging. The identification of the (native) Irish with natural musicality had proceeded apace during the eighteenth and nineteenth centuries within the Protestant Anglo-Irish Ascendancy as antiquarian inquiry and preservation identified and homogenized the various musics of Ireland, effectively categorizing these as 'ethnic' music. By the late nineteenth century, as Gerry Smyth has usefully pointed out, this musical trait became 'Celtic'. Under the influence of 'two principal fountainheads', Ernest Renan in France and Matthew Arnold in England, this creative trait or 'spirit' became Ireland's defining quality, a recompense for their indolence and lack of enterprise (funnily enough, a negative trait also found in the writings of Cambrensis). In Arnold's vision, Smyth observes caustically, 'the Celts were ideally suited to entertain the English after a hard day at the empire'.[6]

This idea of an Irish national musical tradition was, however, embraced in the eighteenth and nineteenth centuries by Irish nationalism itself, latterly as a response to the tradition of negative stereotyping to be found in British music-hall caricatures and popular imagery.[7] From as afar back as Cambrensis, Ireland's musical heritage had been designated a symbol of her difference from the colonial power, and Irish nationalism accepted this. Thus, if the idea of a national musical trait had been imposed originally on Ireland and the Irish from the outside, it has now become internalized and today bears the traces of a particular nationalist political and cultural history. As we shall see, in countless ways aspects of the legacy of Cambrensis (on musicality) have been accepted by Irish scholars and writers (such as Seán O'Riada, Mícheal O' Súilleabháin and John Waters) and the presumption of Irish natural musicality informs much of wider contemporary commentary on Irish music and artists – Sinéad O'Connor's natural, unadorned voice (and her 'fiery Irish temper'), the 'banshee-style wailing' of Dolores O'Riordan, U2's 'Irish spirit' and so on. This 'organic paradigm' informs both musical evaluation and music production and is the governing principle that underpins both colonial and national discourse on Irish culture in the contemporary post-colonial context.

In post-colonial theory, this appropriation of the 'gaze' (or 'ear') of the colonizer has been much commented on and has been the subject of much debate.[8] In one sense, it seems to call into question even the very legitimacy of a 'national' resistance to outside cultural domination because the national itself is only recognized through, and is already deeply imbued with, the ideologies of the oppressor, especially, and most debilitatingly, in its acceptance of colonialism's essentialist definitions of difference. As Seamus Deane argues in relation to this process: 'The moment you have stabilised your identity you have done part of the job of the imperial system.'[9]

On the other hand, post-colonial theory does seem to open up the possibility of 'strategic essentialism' which, drawing on the definition first articulated by Gayatri Spivak, Katya Gibel Azoulay argues, 'does not preclude alliances between different social groups; nor does it presume that communities are bounded, fixed or that "race" is an essence shared by all members of any given group'. It might be poor philosophy, she contends, but 'at least strategic essentialism does register the politics of commitment'.[10] In the Irish context, this point is argued forcefully, again by Seamus Deane. Attacking what he calls the 'promiscuous embrace of pluralism' as an empty response to imperialism's essentializing discourse, he contends: 'Therefore, while I would accept the need for a recognition of diversity, I don't at the same time say that because things are diverse, because things are so infinitely complex or apparently infinitely complex, there can be no supervening position, that you can't have a political belief or a religious belief.'[11]

This strategic mobilization of imperialism's own discourse is echoed by Nigerian novelist Chinua Achebe, writing about a symposium he attended in Dublin in 1988. Africans, he argues, 'chose English not because the British desired it, but because, having tacitly accepted the new nationalities into which colonialism had grouped us, we needed its language to transact our business, including the business of overthrowing colonialism itself in the fullness of time'.[12] There is in this formulation a clear echo of that descendant of Cambrensis' Irishman, Shakespeare's Caliban. In *The Tempest*, Caliban says to Prospero, 'You taught me language; and my profit on't/Is, I know how to curse' and he reserved most of his best curses for the man who usurped his island. The play was first performed in 1611 just as the second conquest of Ireland was being completed in the Plantation of Ulster. In the confrontations between Caliban and Prospero, the play rehearses some of the settler/native tensions implicit in a process of cultural denigration. Shakespeare describes Caliban as 'a savage and deformed beast' though it is clear that until Prospero took over his island and told him otherwise, he had a higher regard for himself and felt 'mine own king'. Perhaps then, when Caliban talks about his isle being 'full of noises/Sounds and sweet airs, that give delight and hurt not' he does so to disguise his own discordant anger.

In terms of music, these essentialist notions (strategic or otherwise) which underlie dominant conceptions of 'Irishness' (and which are most characteristically applied to Irish traditional music) give rise to two contrasting worldviews. On one hand, they can be seen as ideologically conservative and analytically restrictive, privileging 'nature' over culture and alluding to a deep essence of Irishness that withstands historical change. In this way, the music tends to conjure up and support a view of Ireland that lies in a dim and distant past, wedded to an archaic world no longer relevant to modernity – its needs and pleasures as well as its discontents. On the other hand, the need to mark difference, especially in the global discourse of popular music, might also require the strategic mobilization of aspects of this Irishness precisely to identify and mark out a space in the global 'noise' where local sounds and voices might be heard and articulated (and where a firm political belief or sense of cultural identity might be asserted). The contradiction here represents a considerable epistemological, theoretical and political conundrum and has informed both cultural practice and critical discourse in Ireland for much of the last century.

Post-colonial theory does, however, signpost approaches to these issues that may have considerable critical potential and which are particularly appropriate to a discussion of popular music. For Luke Gibbons, arguing for a new way of thinking through the conundrum, the key lies in a 'postcolonial Enlightenment'. In the broader enlightenment project, he argues, the assumption was that peripheral and minority cultures – tradition in the broadest sense – will succumb to, or would be advised to succumb to, the modernizing logic of metropolitan progress. However, traditional culture, far from being the preserve of backwardness and conservatism, can and should (and should have) offered an important break to the excesses of modernization. Discussing the Belfast Harp Festival of 1792 he notes:

> That the harp had already moved centre stage to the United Irishmen's cultural politics was clear from its adoption as the emblem of the new

movement in October 1791, with the rousing motto: 'It is new strung and shall be heard.' According to the manifesto for the Harp Festival, 'the spirit and character of a people are (intimately) connected with their national poetry and music', and the harp was a resonant image of such national sentiment.[13]

The ancient music of Ireland, and especially the harp, so beautifully (even if subversively) played in the presence of Cambrensis in the twelfth century, came to symbolize the revolutionary potential of tradition. 'The Harp Festival', Gibbons continues, 'may be seen from one point of view as the end of an era, a valediction to the old Gaelic order, but amid the revolutionary strivings of the 1790s, it also presaged a new beginning, a resurgent alternative vision of Irish society.'[14] For militant Republicanism in the 1970s and afterwards, the political potential of traditional music to offer resistance (and build communities of resistance) was an important factor in its own cultural politics. Discussing the changes that traditional music in Belfast went through during the years of the Troubles, Martin Dowling has observed that if the playing of and listening to traditional music had once been a shared experience across the sectarian divide (he instances many prominent Protestant musicians) then this changed with the outbreak of sectarian strife:

> The occasions for sharing traditions became, if not physically impossible, then highly inconvenient if not downright dangerous. The cultural activism that accompanied a reawakened republican movement made good use of traditional music. Set lists that survive from the early 70s at gigs in Belfast show how an evening's music typically progressed from Irish traditional material and anodyne Anglo-American folk song to the more blood-soaked extreme of contemporary political balladry.[15]

This 'politicizing' of the music was also resisted and contested by many of its adherents. Peter McNamee, quoting from broadcaster and traditional music collector Ciarán MacMathúna, summarized one contemporary view of the process: 'the music was held up to a middle-class, urban-based ridicule during the 1950s and '60s... having weathered that storm, there was then a danger of it being subjected to political pressures in the 1970s, subsumed as an adjunct to Republicanism'.[16]

Of course, the colonizing culture today is no longer that of the imperialist nation states of the eighteenth and nineteenth centuries (though Ireland's long historical interface with Britain provides fertile ground for applying post-colonial theory to revision and/or reassertion of the dominant narratives of this relationship).[17] Rather, the imperializing presence now is global capitalism, manifested in cultural terms by the United States, 'the cultural-electronic Goliath of the universe'.[18] But if post-colonial theory has turned its perspective onto the narratives of resistance from within the colonized, prising open the supposed closed spaces of essentialist nationalism, it has also suggested a more complex relationship between the centre and the periphery than is offered by a 'cultural imperialism' paradigm. Thus, for example, it can be argued that in the stultifying and conservative Ireland of the 1930s–1950s, the images and pleasures of popular American cinema or the urban rhythms of jazz music were positively liberating (and, not surprisingly, both of these popular forms were subjected to a long campaign of cultural denigration led by the Catholic Church). In these cases, the power of global culture was instrumental in prising open the cultural sterility of an overly essentialist national culture.[19] Furthermore, global capitalism today works not by 'homogenizing' world culture but rather through 'niche marketing' and the marketing of 'difference'. As Sharma et al. would have it, the 'coolie has become cool'[20] (and one of the features of Irish music and dance was that the Irish 'coolies' became the coolest ethnicity on the world stage in the 1990s). This can have the effect of releasing local energies and local cultures (albeit to feed a voracious marketplace) which themselves lay dormant under the weight of a nationalist hegemony. Thus a new relationship between the periphery and the centre (now the local and the global) has developed 'in which the local should be seen as a fluid and relational space, constituted only in and through its relationship to the global'.[21] If peripheral cultures inhabit this space, then they do so in complex and contradictory ways, feeding into and out of the global in a mutually sustaining manner, even if the power relationship is so obviously weighted against them. Thus the potential for a culture of resistance which can challenge the definitions of identity imposed by the global (and by extension, offer a challenge to the existing power relationship) lies not in a retreat back into the very essentialist narratives which have been part of the oppression in the first place, but in the exploitation of the site of contact between the local and the global. In cultural terms, this has meant the validation of forms of hybridity that grow out of the 'liminal spaces' provided at this intersection, offering a critical perspective on both.[22]

In this formulation, hybridity is 'other' to essentialism and, without essentialism, hybridity could not exist, could not be recognized. As Jan Nederveen Pieterse argues:

> Hybridity as a point of view is meaningless *without* the prior assumption of difference, purity, fixed boundaries. Meaningless not in the sense that it would be inaccurate or untrue as a description, but that, without an existing regard for boundaries, it would not be a point worth making. Without reference to a prior cult of purity and boundaries, a pathos of hierarchy and gradient of difference, the point of hybridity would be moot.[23]

The literature in support of the idea of a hybrid culture is now vast and the result is that the post-colonial debate often appears merely to celebrate hybridity as an end in itself and offers no critical approach to discrimination and evaluation. Much of this literature has in fact moved away from analysing texts altogether in favour of a more discursive approach to the process rather than the products of hybridity.

This book looks broadly at fifty years of Irish rock and popular music (and, next to cinema and television, this is the form of popular culture most associated with Schiller's American electronic Goliath). We attempt to redress the critical imbalance by considering in detail some key hybrid musical texts themselves from a range of Irish artists who have explored the borderlands, hinterlands and heartlands of Irish music and identity. In doing so, we hope to assess also the ways in which these inhabit the spaces between 'Irishness' and the global culture of rock music. We want to consider these texts as forms of hybridity, to locate them in their sociocultural contexts, looking at the discourse about them (especially in Ireland) and to assess their strategies and achievement against the post-colonial concerns we have outlined. Our selection of texts cannot, of course, be comprehensive and our book is offered neither as a history nor a survey of the last half-century of Irish rock and pop.[24] It is the ambition of this book to offer detailed textual and contextual analyses of artists and performers who raise interesting questions about the nature of rock and popular music, as well as about the construction of Irishness within such a global form. Inevitably, in attempting to realize this ambition, we have had to make a choice in regard to whom we select and whom we exclude. Part of the problem is the sheer volume and quality of music production in Ireland over the last half-century; to do justice to all of this music, in the detail that we are proposing, would be impossible in one relatively short volume. We are conscious, therefore, that there are significant omissions in our discussions and we are particularly regretful that many of these omissions are artists and bands that we both value and enjoy.

The narrative here is informed by our subjective judgement of what are the most interesting, the most challenging and, in the end, the most successful musical hybrids. Our starting point has been to choose texts that mobilize recognizably 'Irish' idioms and styles but which attempt to marry these to a more mainstream global rock sound. Central to the book, however, is the band U2, which dominates the story of Irish rock like a colossus, Ireland's very own electronic Goliath, both loved and loathed in equal measure because of this dominance. Our approach to U2 is to look at the ways in which they signal 'Irishness' in their music and performance but also to consider the ways in which they have challenged these expectations by attaching themselves to other musical and performance indicators. We also consider some Irish artists who, despite considerable artistic achievements, are largely unknown or, at best, have remained stubbornly cult or marginal in their appeal (Granny's Intentions, Skid Row, Mellow Candle, Gregory Gray, The Virgin Prunes).

In the final analysis, our discussion is motivated by the observation that, relative to size of population and to the economic strength of the local market, Irish rock and popular music has enjoyed a disproportionately large presence on the global market, especially since the 1980s. The choice of artists and texts is, therefore, also guided by our own predilection for music which challenges, subverts and critiques orthodox notions of Irishness in music. Of course, in this regard it could be argued that more conspicuously 'pop' bands, like Boyzone and Westlife, through their very *popularity*, have challenged dominant notions of what constitutes 'authentic' Irish music. They clearly demonstrate that metropolitan pop music can be produced from the regional, national or cultural periphery and this is obviously a significant achievement, but in doing so they have also reinforced and reproduced, rather than challenged, those very metropolitan norms. As Simon Frith has argued: 'Culture as transformation...must challenge experience, must be difficult, must be *unpopular*...the utopian impulse, the *negation* of everyday life, the aesthetic impulse that Adorno recognised in high art, must be part of low art too.'[25] This is why we focus on Sinéad O'Connor over and above other Irish women performers, because we see in her work a subversion of – even a detonation of – the dominant female archetype in Irish music.

The methodology employed in this discussion varies, however, depending on the artist and the context, embracing cultural history, discourse analysis of the ways in which Irish music has been constructed and framed, textual analysis of both music and performance and analysis of the issues about representation and identity to which these give rise. The argument is supported by original interviews with key protagonists in Irish rock culture: journalists, broadcasters, musicians and management, such as the late Bill Graham of *Hot Press* (who was interviewed on a number of occasions); Fachtna O'Ceallaigh (who is Sinéad O'Connor's manager and was the manager of The Boomtown Rats when they emerged originally in 1977); Jim Lockhart of Horslips and Ian Wilson, producer of 'The Dave Fanning Show' at the time of U2's emergence. These sometimes lengthy interviews, conducted between 1995 and 2011, gave our subjects the opportunity to reflect on the critical concerns outlined and to describe their working practices. We hope that these interviews add nuance to the broader debates about the sometimes contradictory interface of rock, popular music and Irishness. The book also draws heavily on key scholarly writings in the field of popular music studies, cultural studies, Irish studies and the now burgeoning field of Irish popular music studies.

The last point is significant. Irish cultural discourse has been dominated over the last two decades by debates about the definitions and meanings of 'Irishness' and Irish culture (in both its 'indigenous' and its 'diasporic' forms). Fuelled initially by the rapid modernization of the Irish economy from the 1960s onwards and the great social and cultural upheavals that this entailed they were given added charge by the political crisis and violence in Northern Ireland from the 1970s to the 1990s. Since the mid-1990s these cultural debates widened in response to the rapid growth (and subsequent collapse) of the Irish economy in the South, the peace process and political accommodation in the North and a new awareness of the Irish diaspora originally announced by President Mary Robinson in her inaugural address in 1991. These are, in the main, extremely sophisticated and complex (if sometimes very acrimonious) debates but they have neglected, until fairly recently, to deal with popular music in any meaningful way. This has now changed and in the last ten years there has been a growth in studies that have looked at this most popular of contemporary cultural forms and has asked searching questions about underlying assumptions. The essentialist assumptions that are still all too central to the dominant discourse on Irish rock music, however, seem rather bland and crude in comparison to the wider debate. We hope that the discussions here, informed by these wider cultural controversies and contributing to this new concern with popular music in Ireland, will extend the parameters of the debate while marking and celebrating real cultural achievements that have so often been denied a space in the national narratives of Irishness.

NOTES

1. Giraldus Cambrensis, *The History and Topography of Ireland*, edited by Thomas Wright, trans. Thomas Forester (London: H.G. Bohn, 1863), Book 3, Chapter 21.
2. Ibid., Chapter 19.
3. Ibid., Chapter 11.
4. Giraldus Cambrensis, *The Conquest of Ireland*, edited by Thomas Wright, trans. Thomas Forester (London: H.G. Bohn, 1863), Chapter 37.
5. L.P. Curtis, Jr, *Apes and Angels: The Irishman in Victorian Caricature* (Newton Abbot: David & Charles, 1971); Mervyn Busteed, 'Songs in a Strange Land: Ambiguities of Identity amongst Irish Migrants in Mid-Victorian Manchester', *Political Geography*, 17, 6 (1998), pp.73–8.
6. Gerry Smyth, *Music in Irish Cultural History* (Dublin: Irish Academic Press, 2009), p.85.
7. Curtis, *Apes and Angels*.
8. Albert Memmi, *The Coloniser and the Colonised* (Boston, MA: Beacon Press, 1957); Gayatri Chakravorty Spivak, 'Can The Subaltern Speak?', in Cary Nelson and Lawrence Grossberg (eds), *Marxism and the Interpretation of Culture* (Urbana and Chicago, IL: University of Illinois Press, 1988), pp.271–313; David Lloyd, *Anomalous States: Irish Writing and the Post-Colonial Moment* (Durham and London: Duke University Press, 1993); Timothy D. Taylor, *Global Pop: World Musics, World Markets* (New York and London: Routledge, 1997); Georgina Born and David Hesmondhalgh (eds), *Western Music and Its Others: Difference, Representation, and Appropriation in Music* (Berkeley and Los Angeles, CA: University of California Press, 2000); Colin Graham, *Deconstructing Ireland: Identity, Theory, Culture* (Edinburgh: Edinburgh University Press, 2001); Richard Middleton, 'The Real Thing? The Specter of Authenticity', in Richard Middleton, *Voicing the Popular: On the Subjects of Popular Music* (New York and London: Routledge, 2006), pp.199–246.
9. Seamus Deane, 'Canon Fodder: Literary Mythologies in Ireland', in J. Lundy and A. MacPóilin (eds), *Styles of Belonging: The Cultural Identities of Ulster* (Belfast: Lagan Press, 1992), p.28.
10. Katya Gibel Azoulay, 'Experience, Empathy and Strategic Essentialism', *Cultural Studies*, 11, 1 (1997), p.102.
11. Deane, 'Canon Fodder', p.32.

12. Chinua Achebe, 'The Song of Ourselves', *New Statesman and Society*, 9 February 1990, p.32.
13. Luke Gibbons, *Edmund Burke and Ireland* (Cambridge: Cambridge University Press, 2003), p.230.
14. Ibid., p.233.
15. Martin Dowling, *Folk and Traditional Music and the Conflict in Northern Ireland: A Troubles Archive Essay* (Belfast: Arts Council of Northern Ireland, 2009), p.10.
16. Peter McNamee (ed.), *Traditional Music: Whose Music?* (Belfast: Institute of Irish Studies, 1991), p.vi.
17. Deane, 'Canon Fodder'; Lloyd, *Anomalous States*; Colin Graham, ' "Liminal Spaces": Post-Colonial Theories of Irish Culture', *Irish Review*, 16 (1994), pp.29–43; Graham, *Deconstructing Ireland*; Luke Gibbons, *Transformations in Irish Culture* (Cork: Cork University Press, 1996).
18. Herbert Schiller, 'Living in the Number 1 Society', *Gazette*, 60, 2 (1998), p.181.
19. Kevin Rockett, 'Aspects of the Los Angelesation of Ireland', *Irish Communication Review*, 1 (1991), pp.18–23; Martin McLoone, *Irish Film: The Emergence of a Contemporary Cinema* (London: BFI, 2000); Martin McLoone, *Film, Media and Popular Culture in Ireland: Cityscapes, Landscapes, Soundscapes* (Dublin: Irish Academic Press, 2008).
20. Sanjay Sharma, John Hutnyk and Ashwani Sharma (eds) *Dis-Orienting Rhythm: Politics of the New Asian Dance Music* (London: Zed Books, 1996), p.1.
21. Kevin Robins, 'Tradition and Translation: National Culture in its Global Context', in John Corner and Sylvia Harvey (eds), *Enterprise and Heritage: Crosscurrents of National Culture* (London: Routledge, 1991), p.35.
22. Born and Hesmondhalgh, *Western Music*; Iain Chambers, *Border Dialogues: Journeys in Postmodernity* (London: Routledge, 1990); Iain Chambers, *Migrancy, Culture, Identity* (London: Routledge, 1993); Robin Cohen, *Global Diasporas: An Introduction* (London: Routledge, 1997); Paul Gilroy, *The Black Atlantic: Modernity and Double Consciousness* (London: Verso, 1993); Paul Gilroy, *Darker than Blue: On the Moral Economies of Black Atlantic Culture* (Cambridge, MA: Harvard University Press, 2010); Kobena Mercer, *Welcome to the Jungle: New Positions in Black Cultural Studies* (London: Routledge, 1994); Deanna Campbell Robinson, Elizabeth Buck and Marlene Cuthbert, *Music at the Margins: Popular Music and Global Cultural Diversity* (London: Sage, 1991); Pnina Werbner and Tariq Modood (eds), *Debating Cultural Hybridity: Multi-Cultural Identities and The Politics of Anti-Racism* (London: Zed Books, 1997); Robert J.C. Young, *Colonial Desire: Hybridity in Theory, Culture and Race* (London: Routledge, 1994); Graham, ' "Liminal Spaces" '; McLoone, *Film, Media and Popular Culture*.
23. Jan Nederveen Pieterse, 'Hybridity, So What? The Anti-Hybridity Backlash and the Riddles of Recognition', *Theory, Culture and Society*, 18, 2–3 (2001), pp.219–45.
24. For more general histories, see Mark J. Prendergast, *The Isle of Noises: Rock and Roll's Roots in Ireland* (Dublin: O'Brien Press, 1987); Vincent Power, *Send 'Em Home Sweatin': The Showbands' Story* (Dublin: Kildanore Press, 1990); Tony Clayton-Lea and Richie Taylor, *Irish Rock: Where it's come from, where it's at, where it's going* (Dublin: Gill & Macmillan, 1992); Daragh O'Halloran, *Green Beat: The Forgotten Era of Irish Rock* (Belfast: Brehon Press, 2006). For more scholarly accounts, see Gerry Smyth, *Noisy Island: A Short History of*

Irish Popular Music (Cork: Cork University Press, 2005); Smyth, *Music in Irish Cultural History*; Sean Campbell and Gerry Smyth, *Beautiful Day: Forty Years of Irish Rock* (Cork: Atrium Press, 2005); John O'Flynn, *The Irishness of Irish Music* (Farnham: Ashgate, 2008).

25. Simon Frith, *Performing Rites: On the Value of Popular Music* (Oxford: Oxford University Press, 1996), p.20.

PART 1
Before...

1

The Emergence of Irish Popular Music

On the RTÉ website there is an interesting piece of archive footage of The Beatles' first visit to Ireland on 7 November 1963 when they played two concerts at the Adelphi cinema and caused a minor riot in the centre of Dublin.[1] The film shows the band arriving at a busy Dublin airport and being introduced to interviewer Frank Hall. From the beginning, issues to do with Ireland and Irishness are fore-grounded in the exchanges. 'We've a tour of Guinness' brewery lined up', jokes the tour manager, and when George Harrison is introduced to Hall as 'the Irishman', John Lennon can be heard interjecting in the background, 'Hey, listen we're all Irish.' He was, after all, arriving in his grandfather's hometown.

Hall then conducts a short, rather ramshackle interview with the four Beatles in competition with aircraft noise in the background and a clearly distracted and disengaged George Harrison in the fore-ground. As well as the inevitable (for the time) questions about their hairstyles, the 'Liverpool Sound' and their appeal to the young female population in particular, the interview comes back to the issue of their Irishness. 'About your Irish background', Hall begins. 'Yeah', Paul McCartney picks up the point, 'we've all got a bit, except for Hymie on the end there' – a reference perhaps to Ringo Starr's supposed Jewish roots. Despite the obvious Irishness of Lennon and McCartney's names, it emerges that Harrison has the closest Irish connections. He is distracted from the interview because he is looking out for his mother who has come to Ireland to see the band play and to visit her 'hundreds of cousins and relatives', as Harrison puts it.

It is an interesting exchange, right at the beginning of The Beatles' success, because the Irishness of the band is rarely touched on in subsequent narratives. Perhaps the Liverpudlian scriptwriter Alun

Owen (who accompanied them to Dublin) drew on his knowledge of The Beatles' Irish heritage when he constructed the character of John McCartney (Wilfred Bramble), Paul's Irish Republican grandfather in the film *A Hard Day's Night* (directed by Richard Lester, 1964). And, of course, in the aftermath of Bloody Sunday in Derry in 1972, both Lennon ('The Luck of the Irish' and 'Sunday Bloody Sunday') and McCartney ('Give Ireland Back to the Irish') wrote and recorded polemical songs about Ireland. For the most part, however, The Beatles story rarely dwells on this aspect of their background and at best it is merely an incidental detail in the overall Beatles narrative.

However, in terms of popular music in Ireland, it is an interesting and revealing exchange, suggesting contrasting and even contradictory narratives about Ireland and its relationship to rock and pop. Looking back at this interview nearly half a century later, what is striking is the fact that Hall displays, or affects, all the bemusement of an old fogey confronted with the very latest product of modernity which is a puzzle to, as he puts it, 'some of us older people, especially in Ireland'. It is almost as if we today are witnessing that moment when Ireland, at least in terms of popular culture, finally entered the twentieth century, to much general bemusement. Now it must be said that this is a narrative that does command a degree of support. Ireland's entry into urban, industrial modernity originally had been as an integral part of the United Kingdom (or as a colony of England) and her withdrawal from the union in 1922, reinforced by neutrality during the Second World War, effectively meant that the country had withdrawn from this British definition of modernity and was preparing to rejoin on its own national terms. In the interim, Ireland's culture, dominated by essentialist definitions of Irishness and patrolled by a vigilant and intrusive Catholic ethos, had drifted from the mainstream, existing in a space circumscribed by protectionism and censorship.

Although the conditions for Ireland's re-engagement with the modern world had been laid down a few years before in a new economic strategy that was designed to open up the economy for international investment it was a slow process that, by 1963, had so far provided little that was tangible to Ireland's young people and nothing that could be called a youth subculture. Ireland's music, it seemed, was as dormant as the rest of its culture, dozing quietly on the sidelines as the rock 'n' roll revolution proceeded apace elsewhere. The Beatles' arrival in the dozy capital (and in Belfast the next day) woke the place up and provided the impetus for the new 'beat group' scene to emerge both north and south of the border. As Daragh O'Halloran argues, it was the 'one key event…[that] defiantly announced the arrival of beat music to these shores'.[2]

It is a popular interpretation, no doubt, but perhaps it does not tell the whole story. For one thing, scenes very similar to the excitement generated in Dublin were played out all over the world in the first few years of The Beatles' ascendancy (including the crowds, public disruption and sometimes, as in Dublin, riotous frenzy on the streets). It is doubtful, therefore, if Ireland was, in fact, so very different from anywhere else. As George Harrison famously expressed it, 'The Beatles saved the world from boredom', and while Ireland undoubtedly offered its own particular brand of boredom, the impact that The Beatles had was more in tune with global rather than local trends. The most industrially advanced and most musically connected country in the world, the United States, succumbed to The Beatles in just as spectacular a manner a few months later, in February 1964, and versions of Frank Hall's bemused interview were enacted from New York to Los Angeles throughout the weeks that followed.

What is also interesting about The Beatles' encounter with Ireland is the sense of 'coming home' which is implied in some of the exchanges. Harrison's mother Louise used The Beatles' concert as an excuse to meet up with her relatives and George later went off to meet the Dublin cousins he had last seen on a family visit to the city in the 1950s.[3] Clearly implicit in the exchanges is a sense of national pride in the return of 'some of our own', even if 'some of our own' here are the grandchildren and great-grandchildren of Irish emigrants. In fact, the narrative of the returning 'emigrant' as harbinger of a young, modern culture was played out earlier that year when John F. Kennedy visited Ireland in June. In providing the rest of the world with the television pictures of Kennedy's enthusiastic reception in his ancestral home, the recently established Irish television service grew up in public and relayed to a global audience the news that a new, modern era had begun in the ancient homeland. When Frank Hall interviewed The Beatles for Irish television in November of the same year (just two weeks before Kennedy was assassinated in Dallas), the impact of the new economic strategy was already being felt and the effect that new telecommunications media were having on the traditional rhythms of Ireland was already well acknowledged. The Beatles merely tapped into these changes and drew attention to a new-found energy and confidence that was already there. The Beatles were far from being the ambassadors of a new modernity; their rapturous reception in Ireland was merely the latest stage of a <u>new national narrative that had already begun.</u>

1. 'Saving Ireland from boredom' – The Beatles arrive in Dublin Airport, November 1963 (© RTÉ Stills Library)

In the Dublin airport interview, there is some discussion about the 'Mersey Sound' that dominated the British (and Irish) charts throughout 1963 and, of course, in the end, The Beatles brought with them a new sound that seemed to represent a paradigm shift in popular music. However, the general ambience of 'coming home' and returning to 'lost roots' that lies behind the emigrant story in general and here, in The Beatles' first encounter with Ireland in particular, now looks prescient when viewed through the filter of Irish Studies in the 2010s. It presaged that new awareness of diasporic culture in general that was announced by Mary Robinson in 1991 and which would become the motivation for the development of academic Irish Studies in the last decades of the century. An important aspect of this was an attempt to map and assess Irish influence on the development of contemporary popular music in a broader sense.

This new awareness would reach some kind of fruition in the whole 'bringing it all back home' thesis[4] and provides the context of much contemporary writing about Ireland, diasporic culture and popular music.[5] The metaphor here is that of a journey – as Nuala O'Connor puts it, drawing on the work of one of Ireland's most famous exiles: 'For several centuries now Irish music has been on the move, carried in the hands and voices of the Irish people... and... inevitably wound its way back home again, as if to bear out that cyclical impulse at the heart of Irish artistic expression, the "commodious vicus of recirculation", as Joyce thought of it.'[6] In this formulation, The Beatles represented the latest stage of this journey, returning to Ireland with a form of popular music that already bore the characteristics of two great diasporas in the United States: black African and Irish.

There is a similar narrative in U2's film *Rattle and Hum* (Phil Joanou, 1988) which begins with the band performing a live version of The Beatles' 'Helter Skelter' and then moves to a long aerial shot travelling towards the Irish coastline from the sea. This is followed by a montage sequence of images of Dublin: the River Liffey, the city's docklands and surrounding streets. These are accompanied on the soundtrack by the sparse guitar ballad 'Van Diemen's Land' sung by the Edge, a song inspired by Fenian poet and later Boston *Pilot* newspaper editor, John Boyle O'Reilly. A significant figure in Irish history, O'Reilly was one of the leaders of the 1848 Rising that followed the Great Famine and, as a journalist in the United States in later life, he was a vocal campaigner for equality between whites and blacks. The song's narrative follows 'an Irish felon' and his deportation to the penal colony, Van Diemen's Land (modern Tasmania) in the wake of the Famine, a fate that befell O'Reilly.[7] Together the imagery and the two opening songs evoke the complex routes of the Irish diaspora and the city's place as a launch pad for waves of (enforced) Irish emigration: The Beatles and Irish-England, O'Reilly, Irish-Australia and Irish-America.

However, even if one accepts that The Beatles and their music represented in some deep and distant way the culture of the Irish diaspora working through a Joycean 'recirculation', is it still fair to say that their arrival in Ireland represented the birth of contemporary Irish rock music? Again, this is more debatable than it might first appear, because by 1963 there were already two thriving contemporary music cultures in Ireland – the showbands and the traditional music/folk scene – that had kick-started the popular music business already: two cultures, indeed, that The Beatles were well aware of. The values, ideologies and underlying assumptions that informed these music cultures were to impact on the emerging rock music scene in important ways – sometimes positively, sometimes negatively – and these characteristics were already well established by the time The Beatles came to town in 1963.

THE SHOWBANDS

> We had a kind of showband where egos weren't involved and people weren't getting uptight over small things. I played the guitar, sax, drums; we all swapped instruments and had a good time. (Van Morrison)[8]

> Showbands have destroyed some of the finest musicians in the country... (Phil Lynott)[9]

The Beatles' visit to Dublin in 1963 was sandwiched between the release in Ireland of 'She Loves You' in September and 'I Want to Hold Your Hand' in December. Both reached number two in the Irish charts and both were significantly kept from the top spot by Brendan Bowyer and The Royal Showband (with, in September, 'Kiss Me Quick', a cover of an Elvis Presley song first released on his 1962 album, *Pot Luck*, and in December with 'No More', a cover of a song from Presley's 1961 film soundtrack, *Blue Hawaii*).

The fact that both songs were Elvis Presley covers, sung by Elvis Presley imitator Brendan Bowyer, is significant. The negative view of the showbands, especially by the rock generation emerging at the time, and by the dominant rock narrative since, is that they were a sorry imitation of the 'real thing' – an ersatz culture that embarrassingly still dominated in Ireland even in the age of The Beatles, an indication of Ireland's backwardness and lack of hip credibility. But the story may be slightly more complex than that.

Two years earlier, The Beatles had opened for The Royal at the Liverpool Empire Theatre. Bowyer later admitted that, although he could see that they were talented, he couldn't see them being much of a success. He did encourage them, though. He told Vincent Power that after the gig he met the fresh-faced McCartney eating a bag of chips in the car park and admiring The Royal's Mercedes wagon. As Power tells it, Bowyer 'declined the offer of a chip, put a reassuring hand on McCartney's shoulder and advised that if The Beatles stuck together they could do well'.[10] Whatever the truth of the car park encounter, the story illustrates well the relative position of the two bands in 1961 and demonstrates the strength of the Irish live music circuit represented by the showbands at the time. (The Royal's manager, T.J. Byrne, put the night in historical perspective, however, when he told Power: 'We walked out the door that night to become the biggest thing in Ireland. The Beatles walked out to become the biggest thing in the world.'[11])

In 1961, while The Beatles were playing for a couple of hundred punters in the Cavern, The Royal were playing to 2,400 at the Ritz in Manchester.[12] Ireland, in other words, had a successful live music scene that generated excitement across the length and breadth of the home country and well into the Irish heartlands of urban Britain. The Beatles did not, therefore, arrive in Ireland to a blank musical slate, nor were they unaware of the musical culture of Ireland at the time. Even if we accept that their first visit was an important catalyst for the nascent beat-group scene, they came into a country that already had a substantial live popular music scene that attracted young audiences in their thousands. This scene generated an enormous income for the most successful bands, like The Royal, who vied with The Beatles for chart success in Ireland in a way that few other local acts were doing elsewhere with the same consistency.

Showbands had first begun to appear in Ireland from the mid-1950s, slowly displacing from the ballrooms the big band orchestras that largely delivered for young people at the time a brand of music that was little changed from that of their parents' generation. The first showband is generally agreed to have been The Clipper Carlton from Strabane, which was formed originally in 1949–50. By the mid-1950s the band had evolved a formula that included a mix of big band swing and popular American country, laced with some vaudeville and general entertainment tomfoolery (the 'show' element of the act). From 1956 onwards, the set also included the new musical sounds of early rock 'n' roll and as the scene expanded subsequent showbands developed a more top twenty repertoire (and as a consequence dropped the variety or vaudeville aspect of the 'show'). The success in the 1950s of 'The Clippers', as they became known, was extraordinary and lucrative and laid the basis for the explosion of showbands into the 1960s. It also laid the foundation for both a popular music *industry* as well as a popular music *culture* in Ireland. 'The Clippers notched up an impressive string of firsts in the mid '50s', argues Vincent Power on the point, 'first to appoint a manager and road manager, first to introduce percentages, first to play with relief bands, first to tour America, first to buy a custom-built coach, first to distribute publicity photographs and postcards, and first to print their own headed notepaper'.[13] The Royal Showband followed the pattern, deepening and refining the process with even greater success, and in 1962 adding their own significant first to the list as the first Irish pop band to make a record when Bowyer's singing partner in The Royal, Tom Dunphy, recorded the 'country and Irish' classic 'Come Down the Mountain Katie Daly'.

2. Introducing Ireland to sex, drugs and rock 'n' roll – Brendan Bowyer and The Royal Showband (Brent Archive)

By 1965, showbands dominated the live music scene with hundreds of bands criss-crossing the country to fill engagements in thousands of rural and urban ballrooms, playing to audiences often numbered in the thousands. Despite this huge success the showbands leave a mixed historical legacy, veering from near idolatry from their supporters to scorn and disdain from their enemies. Smyth is particularly puzzled by the venom with which the showbands are recalled from the main proponents of Ireland's rock culture – the critics from *Hot Press* magazine or rock stars such as Bono, Bob Geldof and Phil Lynott, for example: 'the showbands have been, and by and large continue to be, regarded as representatives of a benighted past which modern Ireland in all its sophistication has happily left far behind', he argues with some ironic amusement.[14]

A number of reasons for this antipathy suggest themselves. The showbands were seen as mainly a rural phenomenon, touring the country playing the popular hits of the period in provincial ballrooms and remote rural dancehalls to mainly small-town and farming young people. The Royal's recording debut, 'Come Down the Mountain Katie Daly', encapsulated this culture and represented the height of agricultural 'naffness' for the emerging urban young, on the lookout for a more authentic urban sound to represent their new-found freedom and ambition (though, it must be said, by the mid-1960s most urban centres, including Dublin, had their own large showband venues). In part as well, their very commercial success was a problem. The flurry of entrepreneurialism in and around the showband scene – pioneered by The Clippers and developed by the elite bands of the 1960s – gave the showband scene the feel of commercial exploitation. As well as a rural/urban divide, therefore, there was also an art/commerce dichotomy. And as they didn't perform their own compositions they were seen as emblematic of an earlier performance mode that existed on mediocrity and mimicry. The argument was summed up by Mark J Prendergast:

> In the beginning you had the showband and very little else. The idea was that Irish audiences wanted entertainment first and last. The showbands dominated every town and city in Ireland. From the early sixties they made fortunes from live appearances, playing 'covers' of standard hits and English Top Thirty material rather than original material... With their vast resources they controlled the dissemination of popular music throughout the country. Records were a secondary thing to the showband since it was the live event that generated money. Artistic integrity and creativity were subsumed under the primary motive of profit.[15]

Prendergast suggests that somehow making records – or having the inclination to make a record – was a more noble aspiration than playing to a live audience. It seems a bit odd, to say the least, that playing live to an Irish audience is considered more 'commercial' and less 'artistic' than signing to a multinational record company and making a commodity to sell in the global marketplace. And anyway, as we have seen, The Royal pioneered recording in Ireland and most of the top showbands quickly followed The Royal into the recording studio. Niall Stokes, the founding editor of Ireland's leading rock magazine, *Hot Press* is, however, unapologetically adamant: 'I'm not into revisionism on showbands. They operated a stranglehold and in a way that stifled people's creative instincts. There were a lot of people in good rock 'n' roll bands who were bought out by the showbands, put on good salaries in return for being in a mobile jukebox.'[16]

Showbands were seen as a threat to 'creativity'. They were convention-bound, manufactured and formulaic in opposition to the more natural and spontaneous creativity of rock and beat groups. Stokes continues: 'They operated business practices which were in many ways reprehensible. The main one was soaking up publishing money, not providing proper accounting, not paying royalties on recordings. It was a corrupt scene with the moguls buying stuff into the charts. Corruption was endemic and business practices were sloppy at best, dishonest at worst.'[17] There is little doubt that there was much exploitation and downright chicanery going on in the ball-room culture of the time – too much money was being made for it to have been otherwise. It is, nonetheless, something of a contradiction to criticize the showband scene for being blindingly commercial and savagely corrupt while suggesting that the organization of the beat scene or rock promotion generally was a bastion of scrupulous behaviour and benign business practice. Van Morrison, one of the beat groups' first heroes, has spent a career writing and singing songs about the corruption and commercialism of the beat/rock scene both locally and internationally, which traded on 'cool' the better to 'rip you off with a smile/And it don't take a gun'.[18]

Another explanation for the critical hostility towards the show-bands was that their mode of performance seemed to operate within the codes and conventions of light entertainment and show business variety, so despised within 'serious' rock circles. Again, Stokes elaborates:

> The bands themselves were gimmicky. The number of utterly naff attempts at doing something remotely 'stylish' or 'challenging' were

[margin note: Stokes 1994]

legendary in themselves. The best example of this process was in the early 1970s, Magic and His Magic Band, and all it was, was this guy who had come out in a space-suit covered in flashing lights! It was the archetypal Irish showband definition of what popular music was – a very bad interpretation of a glam rock act and just aesthetically poverty-stricken and crass.[19]

And again, things may not have been as simple as all that. Alan Dee started his career playing the organ in the beat group The Chessmen but then decamped when the band evolved into a showband (adding a brass section, presumably to pitch for the bigger money available on the showband circuit). He set up his own experimental beat group The Light and remembers a slightly different atmosphere in the sweaty beat clubs than that which Stokes alludes to. 'By 1967 all gigs were pitched towards the "happening" during the set – something wild at the end of the gig to cause alarm. Every group had a gimmick. Explosions, weird clothes or whatever would be the order of the day.'[20] The values of showmanship and spectacle were essential components of both the beat and the showband scene and arguably these became even more important to the emerging rock scene as it moved on from rhythm and blues and into psychedelia by the late 1960s.

Both Prendergast and Stokes regard the showband scene as boring, dull, unadventurous, show biz and derivative and driven by crass commercial imperatives. Even more sympathetic observers, like Campbell and Smyth, see the showbands as a crossbred 'Frankenstein monster'.[21] The showbands, in other words, were Neanderthals to the beat groups' Homo sapiens, and in history's evolutionary process they lost out to the latter's bigger brain and greater imagination and creativity. Thus a commercially imposed and inauthentic showband scene was superseded by an authentic rock culture, the familiar story of the (good) hip kids winning out against the (bad) straights. Like Neanderthals (and the dinosaurs before them), history required their demise before things could move on.

However, showbands were, paradoxically, part of a *similar* process to that which gave rise to Ireland's developing local rock scene. The showband period marks the first incursion of a popular music culture within Ireland and maybe the dominant view of the rock fraternity, living too close in time and space, misjudges, misunderstands and *misrecognizes* this. For one thing, the showband scene did provide a context for what even Stokes enigmatically referred to as 'those certain things that happened in and around the ballrooms that wouldn't have appealed to the moral guardians and other solid citizens'.[22] In some senses, then, while the showband now appears to be somewhat 'old-fashioned', the rise of showband culture does mark Ireland's entry into a mass-mediated, youth-centred popular culture – the first encounter in Ireland between a localized music scene and the post-Elvis international pop culture. Just as the (albeit heavily censored) cinema provided some relief from the stultifying strictures of 'official' Catholic culture, so it could be argued that the showbands brought to the youth of rural and provincial Ireland the same kind of liberating hedonism that was associated with other forms of imported culture. Whether the rock fraternity wants to admit it or not, the showbands introduced Ireland to sex and drugs and rock 'n' roll (even if a lot of this was hidden from the parish priest who loaned out the hall).

What Stokes and Prendergast articulate in a *historical* perspective is the feeling of the younger urban fan *at the time* for whom the showband scene was anathema. A slightly younger generation comprised this scene and was generally made up of musicians and fans with a different type of investment in the sounds and styles arriving via radio and television. Their commitment, at least in the earlier period, was to a rock culture based around the playing of rhythm and blues so that a kind of intra-generational shift saw the younger demographic rebel against even Elvis and first-phase rock 'n' roll. Thus, while Bowyer and his Elvis imitations clearly *was* rock 'n' roll, this generation viewed post-US Army Elvis as being too commercial. As Stokes notes: 'My major feeling of hostility to the whole showband era is to do with the music as these bands were throwing out third-rate cover versions.'[23]

They were also regarded by the younger beat groups as derivative musicians who depended on a 'safety in numbers' playing philosophy: in order to play beat material, these showbands often had to drop the brass section, which was taken to expose their musical shortcomings. For young beat guitar virtuosi it raised questions about instrumental skills and 'feel'.

One of the most vitriolic critics of the showbands was Bob Geldof, who paints a picture of a very different musical scene emerging in the coffee bars and record shops around his middle-class Co. Dublin suburbs. 'I listened for hours to Sonny Terry's harmonica imitations of train whistles', he writes in his autobiography. 'The talk was of people whose very names said something: Muddy

Waters, Howlin' Wolf, Blind Lemon Jefferson, Mississippi John Hurt, Son House and Robert Johnson. It was not long before indigenous acoustic blues became a point of snobbery with us.'[24] When he returned to Dublin to set up his own band in the mid-1970s, Geldof was to seek out again the vitality and the authentic experience of the early R&B sound. As with their rhythm and blues counterparts in Britain, Irish musicians were adapting the 'authentic' sounds and styles of black America – their 'raw' libidinal and primitive iconographies and meanings – to local circumstances.

However, the appropriation of this exotic 'other' arguably had different implications in the Irish context. The Irish, unlike the British, have a long history of colonization, of themselves being oppressed, rendered inferior and 'othered' as primitive in a process that began with Cambrensis. However, as Lauren Onkey has argued, aside from the black appropriation of Irish song forms in the formation of the blues, the Irish adoption of black styles was not to work in the opposite direction, with black American artists forging cross-racial alliances through the appropriation of conspicuously Irish idioms. There is, Onkey writes, 'no parallel trope of African Americans comparing themselves to the Irish, one indication of how much the Irish were associated with anti-African American sentiments in the United States'.[25] Thus, the Irish were to sit in an odd hinterland caught between the two poles of exotic racial 'other' and white appropriator. As we shall see the adoption, and synthesis, of forms and styles heard and read as black and the attempt to establish different types of cross-racial solidarity between Irish and black will re-emerge throughout the overall narrative of Irish rock as one of its enduring attempts at authenticity.

The dominance of the profit motive and the overt commercialism of the showbands did not, therefore, fit the ideologies of authenticity intrinsic to the kind of music and subcultural Bohemia that Geldof describes. The beat scene, again appropriating patterns of resistance learnt from black America, was also viewed at the time as a 'minor rebellion' against conservative Ireland and attracted the scruffy nonconformists to their tight and smoky venues. The historical significance of the scene, then, is that it was the first *subculture* centred on specifically popular musical identification, structured around sounds, styles and 'attitude'.

Sub-culture [margin annotation]

Bob Geldof's description of his boring teenage years in middle-class suburban Dublin probably best captures what it was about the emerging rock culture that attracted the generation that followed

The Beatles' visit to Dublin and Belfast. 'At fourteen, nothing interested me', he writes. '...In the long holidays I'd wake late and
masturbate, finally rising at 1 or 2 pm, exhausted. I liked clothes, I
liked The Rolling Stones, The Who and The Small Faces...All I
liked doing was reading.' When he went down with his mates to
Murray's record store to listen to the R&B sounds of the 'blues' he
was rescuing himself from a kind of adolescent boredom that was
surely universal at the time. With characteristic honesty, Geldof
understands that this escape from boredom into the music of black
America was also something of a pose in itself. 'If a singer wasn't
black and at least ninety, you could forget it.'[26]

There is much evidence of overlap among musicians. Many later
respected Irish rock musicians began their careers in showbands,
such as Van Morrison in The Monarchs, Henry McCullough in The
Skyrockets and Rory Gallagher in The Fontana. Conversely, many
musicians who began 'promising' careers in rock 'n' roll groups
resorted to the showband for commercial reasons, which gave rise to
certain tensions between 'art' and 'commerce' referred to earlier.
Recollecting the time they opened for The Royal Showband, Bowyer
describes The Beatles as a 'mini-showband' themselves as they were
playing similar songs to showbands. The fact that they were on the
same bill showed that they were, at least, within the same subculture
or inhabited the same paradigm. Bowyer recalls a familiar history,
common to most rock stars of his generation, in Britain as well as in
Ireland, which suggests these conflicting scenes were closer than is
often credited:

> We started in 1957...the only way we could hear rock 'n' roll was on
> Radio Luxembourg, and we didn't have a television yet, so another
> place to encounter that was in the local picture-house in Waterford. I
> was just the right age for that, late teens, and it blew me
> away...'Jailhouse Rock'...That's basically, what started it all.[27]

As with Cliff Richard and Tommy Steele in England, or Johnny
Hallyday in France, Bowyer was adopting the sounds, styles and
performance modes associated with Elvis Presley. Presley is still
regarded as the first great rock 'n' roll innovator, the artist who
brought about a paradigm shift in popular music generally. And yet,
Elvis himself (like the early Beatles and Stones) was a copyist. As
Dick Hebdige has argued, 'to say that Elvis was a mimic is not to
diminish his talent or his achievement'.[28] Great mimics, in other

words, can also be great innovators and it is in this spirit that Bowyer and the showband culture he dominated might better be judged. Conditions in Ireland in this respect, while particular, were not terribly different to those being experienced in the rest of Europe. Bowyer mimicking Presley represented locally the increasingly global 'spirit' of rock 'n' roll performance. The emerging beat scene still needed similar global sounds and poses to imitate and engage with – they just did it differently.

This involved a certain amount of subcultural exclusivity (as articulated by the likes of Bob Geldof) with a value based on the importance of rare records (Murray's record shop in Dun Laoghaire, the record collection of Van Morrison's dad, or the access that young British bands had to the imported music and relayed music stations of American servicemen in Hamburg, Frankfurt and Heidelberg). Radio operated as a 'secret ceremony' and black musics as exotic, as taboo, as 'other'. The preference was for 'raw' over 'cooked' sounds. All of these were a means of marking one's difference from the tastes and identities of the 'undiscriminating' majority. Showbands were seen as the ultimate 'other' against which the rock scene defined itself. Their superficial, unoriginal and undiscerning pop values became the defining characteristic of that which was to be *resisted*, and thus the concept of *authenticity* was established as an informing principle in Irish rock culture.

By 1963, the question of authenticity was, however, already a major concern in the traditional music and folk scene in Ireland and it is interesting to consider the ways in which the assumptions and values of folk interacted with the new spirit abroad in Ireland in the early 1960s to add another layer to the story of Irish rock. For one of the main underlying narratives of this story is the way in which the different musical styles influenced and even cross-fertilized one another and provided an underpinning set of values for the differentiation of *Irish* rock music from other *national* examples of the form, the better to give it a presence in the *global* soundscape.

TRADITIONAL MUSIC AND THE FOLK REVIVAL

When, in 1962, Paddy Moloney assembled the group of musicians that became the first line-up of The Chieftains, he did so specifically to make a record rather than to play live music. 'I knew exactly what

I wanted to achieve. I said to myself I want to mix this in such a way so it won't be just reels, jigs and hornpipes. I wanted to create a different flavour of music with songs and airs. Some of my ideas of blending tin whistle harmonies had been with me since my child-hood...It was music I always wanted to put out on an album.'[29] Although (at age 24) Moloney was already a veteran of the live music scene and the new band rehearsed by playing together for six months before recording, he was drawing a distinction between music as a live event and music as a recorded form. His choice of instruments and players and his process of mixing and blending, even sequencing, were decisions dictated by the desire to record in a studio. When that album, simply called *The Chieftains*, was released in 1963, the same year The Beatles arrived in Dublin, it established a number of things. First, of course, it introduced to the world the group itself that for nearly fifty years now, with Moloney at its head, has maintained its position as Ireland's premier traditional music ensemble, going through a number of personnel changes and experi-menting with an array of other sounds and cultures in the process. Second, it confirmed the slow but steady resurgence of traditional music in Ireland that, linked to the international revival of interest in folk and ethnic music generally, rescued the music from neglect and disdain. Third, of course, as a record, it introduced the traditional to the modern, the ancient tunes to the new technologies of the studio and in doing so ensured the survival of traditional music *through* subjecting it to evolution and change.

Moloney had worked previously with composer Seán O'Riada in the latter's 'folk' orchestra, Ceoltóirí Cualann, which was launched in 1960 with a 'recital' (in formal attire) at the Shelbourne Hotel, an important staging post in the music's journey back from obscurity. O'Riada, a classically trained composer with a distinctly modernist, avant-garde sensibility, had already experimented with orchestral arrangements of traditional music in an attempt to marry high 'art' and popular musical forms – to bridge the gap between the European tradition and the indigenous Irish form. In the soundtrack to the film, *Mise Éire* (George Morrison, 1959) O'Riada managed to both re-energize and reconfigure traditional music while at the same time reinforcing its link to Irish nationalism. The soundtrack music of the film proved to be a popular success, establishing O'Riada as a bold innovator and demonstrating to a wider public (and espe-cially the record-buying public) the enormous range and emotional power of traditional music.

3. 'Internationalizing Irish tradition' – The Chieftains in New York (Corbis)

O'Riada is, however, an intensely contradictory figure in the concatenation of forces that defined the music scene in Ireland at the cusp of the 1960s. For example, despite his penchant for experiment and innovation he argued an essentialist 'folk' position against the emergence of new types of leisure, music and social relations coming in from the outside. Talking about traditional music specifically, he argued that 'it is one of the few things left we can call our own'. He reserved his greatest contempt for those in Ireland who would deny the centrality of the music to Irish identity:

> There are some who sneer at it; they are the ignorant and the stupid, slavish lackies of foreign traditions, servile lapdogs who lick the crumbs which fall from the stranger's table. Let nobody say that our traditions are inferior to those of any other country. They are our traditions, and they suit us best . . . It is precisely because of their suitability that they have survived so long, in the face of so much opposition, from our own people and also from our oppressors . . .

The music, however, is the outward symbol of an inner essence that is wholly unique and by ignoring the music the people of Ireland run the risk of descending into a kind of national and spiritual poverty:

'Our way of life, and our customs, are being thrown out in favour of an alien materialism . . . Our nation that was bought with blood is being sold, spiritually as well as physically, before our eyes, by our own people. This is a great evil, a great madness.'[30]

O'Riada here invokes the spirit of Douglas Hyde's 1892 address, 'The Need to de-Anglicise Ireland', which initiated the Gaelic cultural revival of the late nineteenth century and which similarly chastized the Irish people for drifting from the purity of their Gaelic traditions. Without these traditions, Hyde had argued, the Irish would become 'a nation of imitators . . . alive only to second-hand assimilation'.[31] O'Riada similarly perceives Irish traditional music in these essentialist terms, as the expression of fundamental Irish identity and any other music as the impoverished workings of alien culture. To realize his primordial vision, though, O'Riada was happy to experiment with the styling of traditional music and to employ the techniques of the contemporary, the better to validate and preserve the past. Like the United Irishmen's harp, O'Riada's music was 'new strung', the better to be heard. Interestingly, as well, we can see in O'Riada's language some of the rhetoric encountered in rock discourse about the showbands – the sense of imposition from the outside, the crass commerciality of this imposition and the soul-destroying lack of originality and creativity that it all portends. Authenticity can, indeed, take on strange manifestations.

O'Riada, however, was talking in the 1960s and not the 1890s, as Hyde had been, and his strident attack on the 'alien materialism' of imported culture was rather out of step with the spirit of the times. Perhaps he felt that such highly charged rhetoric was necessary, given the parlous condition of traditional music in Ireland in the 1950s when he first took up the cause. In Dublin, especially, it was 'driven deep underground', according to John Glatt. It was seldom performed in public and effectively banned from pubs, existing mostly in private sessions organized by a small coterie of players. In the country it survived only in small isolated pockets.[32] There was both an element of class snobbery and youthful indifference in this situation. As folk music collector and RTÉ broadcaster Ciarán MacMathúna recalled: 'In my time . . . middle-class people laughed at this kind of music, when it was considered just good enough for the countryside . . . city people and the middle class didn't like it and didn't want to know.'[33] And Seán Keane, later to join The Chieftains, remembers what it was like to be young in Dublin in the late 1950s and to be involved with traditional music: 'Our music was often scorned at as *culchie* music for tinkers... To be seen carrying a fiddle around made you look like a sissy.'[34] Real men in Dublin at that time, it seemed, rocked.

O'Riada set out to make the music respectable again to the middle classes in the first instance, hence the Shelbourne concert and the formal attire. Later he was to popularize the music through the radio show he hosted after the success of the Ceoltóirí Cualann concerts, completing the circle for an underlying revival that had begun with the invention of portable sound recording on tape ten years earlier.

MacMathúna and fellow broadcaster Séan MacRéamoinn (who wrote the script for *Mise Éire*) were central figures in the revival of Irish traditional music in the 1950s. Both worked for Radio Éireann and, armed with the latest in recording equipment, they traversed rural Ireland with sound recordists capturing performances by traditional musicians for archival purposes. Thus from the mid-1950s onwards, in an important process of archive retrieval, the tunes and performances of older players were preserved for posterity. MacMathúna and MacRéamoinn began to broadcast these original 'field recordings', introducing to the airwaves, as they saw it, a more authentic version of the music, and a more regionally diverse kind as well, in place of the bland céilí band style that had been developed for radio before this. The modern technology of the mass media came to the rescue of the traditional form and the groundwork had been laid for the great revival of the music that reached an important moment in O'Riada's score for *Mise Éire* in 1959 and the Shelbourne concert the following year. The success of the Ceoltóirí Cualann performances with the Shelbourne audiences was rewarded with a series broadcast on Radio Éireann, and O'Riada quickly became the main polemicist for the music and its importance to national culture.

However, the disdain in which the urban middle classes held traditional music was not the only problem that the revival had to confront. O'Riada's 'slavish lackies of foreign traditions' also included the urban working class and the young in general, who at this time – like the young Bowyer in Waterford and the young Morrison in Belfast – were tuning into the American black music and the emerging rock and roll that was found on obscure foreign radio stations. For leisure they were dancing to (or playing in) the showbands rather than céilí bands (though Morrison, through his mother's interest in singing, was well aware of the traditional music of the McPeake family in Belfast). Undoubtedly, O'Riada's radio programmes helped in this matter, popularizing the music and making it more clearly part of the national soundscape. But, in itself, this would not have given the music the kind of 'hip' cachet that Elvis had and which it needed if it were to appeal to the young, especially the urban young. This is why it is important to note that the revival, instigated by people like MacMathúna and MacRéamoinn and promoted so assiduously by O'Riada and Ceoltóirí Cualann, coincided with another revival that was to have just such a cachet with the young – the international folk revival with its emphasis on traditional song and balladry and its growing political disenchantment with contemporary consumer culture.

Irish musical traditions, especially in their ballad form, were already playing an important role in this folk revival. In 1962, as O'Riada's orchestra played on radio and as Paddy Moloney formed and rehearsed The Chieftains in Dublin, Bob Dylan was writing the anthems of the new folk movement in New York, picking up tunes from The Clancy Brothers who, at the time, were playing and singing Irish ballads around the clubs of Greenwich Village. The debt is one that Dylan himself readily acknowledges (even if he was unaware of his role in the process identified earlier as a kind of Joycean recirculation). 'What I was hearing pretty regularly...were rebellion songs and those really moved me', he says of his time listening to The Clancy Brothers and Tommy Makem as well as other Irish performers in the White Horse Tavern on Hudson Street:

> All through the night they would sing drinking songs, country ballads and rousing rebel songs that would lift the roof. The rebellion songs were a really serious thing. The language was flashy and provocative – a lot of action in the words, all sung with great gusto...They weren't protest songs though, they were rebel ballads...even in a simple, melodic wooing ballad there'd be rebellion waiting around the corner...The rebel was alive and well, romantic and honorable...I was beginning to think I might want to change over.[35]

Mick Moloney argues that in these Irish songs and music we can find both a particular history of the Irish but also a narrative of struggle that could resonate much more widely:

> Distilled from contexts both tragic and uplifting, these songs convey the complex, evolving experience of this emigrant population through three centuries: the oppression, famine, and poverty that pushed the

Irish west across the ocean; a deep and abiding longing for the Ireland they left behind; a profound sense of sadness for loved ones lost and also a celebration of new loves found. They tell of the backbreaking task of survival...the battles waged for fair treatment and fair pay for the work done by these immigrants on railroads, on canals and in mines, construction and factories...[36]

Dylan realized, however, that 'the Irish landscape wasn't too much like the American landscape' and that he would have to find his own way towards being this rebel singer, but the influence of the Irish tradition is all too evident. He visited England in 1962 and experienced the British folk scene which itself had been built on the reproduction of similar Irish, Scottish and English ballads. Right across the new folk revival the key term was authenticity and Irish traditional music and the songs of Ireland's political struggle in particular were considered the most authentic, especially among the left-leaning intellectuals of the new folk revival.

In 1963, Dylan released *The Freewheelin' Bob Dylan*, which established him, the Greenwich Village folk scene and acoustic guitar-based folksongs as key markers of a new international youth subculture, driven by the idea of the romantic rebel and committed to a kind of music that could provide an alternative to the commercial pop of the charts. In an introduction to one of the tracks on *Freewheelin'*, 'Bob Dylan's Blues', he articulates the core message of folk authenticity: 'Unlike most of the songs nowadays that have been written uptown in Tin Pan Alley, that's where most of the folk songs come from nowadays, this is a song, this wasn't written up there, this was written somewhere down in the United States.'

Just as pubs in England had done a few years earlier, pubs in Ireland began to open up spare rooms and empty basements to the folkies and a new network of venues for playing and listening to music was established. More pubs began to embrace traditional music as well, or offered traditional music on alternative nights to the folk nights, and as its popularity grew traditional music found a new listening audience in the hip young drinkers of the new Bohemia. The congruence of the traditional music revival and the folk revival, and their coterminous rise with the beat group scene in urban centres, was to create a particular musical flourishing in the 1970s in Ireland (as we shall see) but, in the 1960s, the result was the slow emergence of a new youth scene that linked the Irish traditional with the internationally hip – with considerable interplay between both. However, as we have also seen, there was a considerable ideological battle going on as well, about definitions and values that different musics were supposed to represent.

The success of Ceoltóirí Cualann's radio broadcasts led to O'Riada being invited to write and present a series of fifteen lectures, subsequently published as *Our Musical Heritage* which became a seminal text for scholars of Irish music. O'Riada defined the Irish musical tradition as 'untouched, unWesternised, orally transmitted music which is still to my knowledge the most popular type of music in this country'.[37] Despite a long and violent history of colonial contact, Ireland is taken to have retained all 'her individual characteristics' and the only structural similarity the music has is a vague one to Arabic music. O'Riada argues that Irish culture has remained unaffected by the Renaissance, colonialism, the Industrial Revolution and any other forms of cultural exchange brought about by the onset of capitalism. As he explains, 'Foreign bodies may fall in, or be dropped in, or thrown in, but they do not divert the course of the river, nor do they stop it flowing; it absorbs them, carrying them with it as it flows onwards.'[38]

Any potential contact is simply absorbed but does not alter the course of tradition. The metaphor of the river – which is central to this organic paradigm – suggests that Irish music is not artefact – the product of society, culture and human endeavour – but rather is something natural and enduring. Indeed the river is a powerful metaphor that appears again and again in certain types of nationalist discourse and will reappear again in later discussion about Irish music. It is a compelling metaphor that seeks to link Irish music with both nature and time immemorial. It might be noted, though, that there is a downside to this. Helen O'Shea, for example, locates a considerable negative aspect to this formulation within traditional music ideology: the paradox of 'a national tradition that absorbs outside influences without being changed by them', trailing 'a legacy of chauvinism, sexism and unexamined prejudice'.[39] This is an important qualification and, as we shall see, it presages some of the more experimental takes on that tradition by later artists who try to move the agenda on by sabotaging, or recirculating, the flow of the endless stream.

Irish music, O'Riada continues, utilizing a further series of naturalistic tropes, 'is essentially a cyclical form and is fundamentally more realistic than European form since it more truly corresponds to real life...Every day possesses the same basic characteristics...the same fundamental pattern...this is the idea that has lain at the root of all Irish traditional art, since pre-Christian times. It is represented in the carved stones of the great burial ground at New Grange, in *The Book of Kells*.'[40]

This discourse echoes the English folklorist Cecil Sharp who was instrumental in promoting a version of English folk authenticity. Like Sharp, O'Riada defined folk as the music of uneducated country people. Moreover 'meaningful' music could not take place within modern commercial structures, which were seen as a threat to Irish expression. And although O'Riada pioneered the marriage of high 'art' music with the 'music of the people' and formed an innovative orchestra to explore new arrangements and new combinations of instruments, he always had a traditional folk vision in mind. Maintaining the authenticity of Irish music led him to actively warn against the use of specific instruments: 'The use of piano is unfortunately prevalent. This is a scar, a blight on the face of Irish music and displays ignorance on the part of those who use or encourage it.' The céilí band is criticized for 'tending to imitate swing or jazz bands... first they added drums, then double-bass, then the final insult, saxophones, guitars and banjos'.[41] Finally, even O'Riada's acolytes, The Chieftains, were to be the butt of some trenchant criticism when he was less than effusive about their recorded output. 'I admire what they are doing but it has tremendous limitations', he told an RTÉ interviewer in 1970.[42]

So there were limits to the extent in which the music could be 'newly strung' and such a hard-line traditionalist attitude was to emerge again and again down the years with musicians who attempted to reconfigure the music – mildly so in early folk/traditional combinations like The Johnstons, Emmet Spiceland and Sweeney's Men but more forcefully in the musical explorations of Planxty, Horslips, The Bothy Band, The Pogues, Moving Hearts and even The Chieftains, who would go on to forge links with other forms of music in ways that O'Riada would have found incomprehensible.

The broader difficulty, then, is that traditionalism, while being invoked as natural, fixed and unchanging, also seemingly requires protection from outside forces – those same forces that were apparently so easily absorbed. The narrowness of O'Riada's definitional aperture, and the strictures of the traditionalists, creates contradictions: on the one hand, folk music is supposed to be spontaneous (yet boundaries have to be rigidly policed) while, on the other hand, the spontaneous incorporation of non-indigenous instruments (such as the piano) is deemed inauthentic. To confer authenticity, O'Riada has to isolate Irish music from its wider influences – to generate a selective tradition that pastes together elements that appear, at least in a contemporary context, to owe nothing to the world beyond the nation.

So, while he did not teach traditional musicians how to play in a more 'authentic' manner, he did select particular musicians as masters of the form (like Paddy Moloney). In one sense, then, authentic traditional music is what O'Riada decided it should be and this leads to a further paradox. He took 'organic' folk forms and transcribed them into notation. This was important both in order to study and to preserve them. However, in converting traditional music into written score, O'Riada was beginning the process of turning folk and tradition into western 'art' music. This was consolidated by bringing traditional musicians out of their 'authentic' locations and into the concert hall and organizing performance via the conventions of the chamber recital. In this way he had to engage in elaborate forms of rhetorical gymnastics to preserve the impression of purity and the myth of deep antiquarian origins. Richard Middleton surmises, in an insightful investigation of folk music and folk ideology:

> The politics of 'folk' centre...on the 'authenticity' of the music. Its value – particularly when set against other, less favoured kinds of music – is guaranteed by its provenance in a certain sort of culture with certain characteristic processes of cultural production. Thus the supposed purity of folk society...goes hand in hand with the 'authenticity' of the music...both are myths. Culturally they originate in the romantic critique of industrial society...The judgment of 'authenticity' is always directed at the practice of someone else. Either it removes this practice from its own mode of existence...or it scapegoats undesirable ('inauthentic') practices and casts them beyond the pale.[43]

The question of the authenticity of music has remained prominent in Ireland and the folk and traditional legacy was carried through to Irish rock ideology. Thus, for better or for worse, due to historical circumstance, traditionalism and Irish folk music were extremely influential on the formation of Irish rock. *Hot Press*, which includes regular reviews and features on folk culture, could write as late as 1993:

> To celebrate the music became an expression of identity, a statement of pride and freedom. Irish music, like the Irish language, is wild and passionate, celebratory and mournful...a distillation, as fine as the

finest poitin, of the spirit of the people... This, then, is the essence of
it... Despite everything that is wrong... Ireland remains a fine place
to live... the clean air, the wonderful landscape, the friendly people,
the drink, the conversation, the music and the craic... bureaucracy
hasn't taken over completely just yet... we are slaves neither to the
corporation nor to the State and... there is tremendous scope for freedom of expression despite the legacy of sixty-odd years of clerical
domination...[44]

Granted that this description was written before the impact was fully
felt of the booming 'Celtic Tiger' economy of the 1990s, with its
subsequent collapse in the economic crisis of 2009–10, nonetheless
the persistence of the vision is remarkable. It constructs Ireland as a
living folk festival and ignores the fact that developments in Ireland,
while particular, are in no sense unique. While Ireland is an island it
is certainly not isolated from all political and cultural influence as
has often been imagined, whereby cultural developments are seen as
the unique expression of the Irish people. Consequently it is difficult
to disconnect O'Riada and this type of discourse and the championing of folk from its status as a thinly veiled critique of modernity.
In this way, O'Riada's view that technology is unnatural and by
extension, un-Irish, was well suited to rock ideology. In the Irish
context, the question of authenticity in rock and the more general
concern about Irish traditional authenticity could on occasion neatly
coalesce, as they shared the same core values. Within folk and rock
discourse, technology is contrasted with, as well as seen as a threat
to, notions of an organic Irish community. Music's lifeblood was
seen to be in performance and in the investment of 'effort' and in the
values of collectivity and community. The linking of rock and tradition initially appeared in musical synthesis, bringing traditional
instrumentation to the rock idiom (as we shall discuss in relation to
Horslips). But, as we have noted, even The Chieftains as a band was
conceived as a recording band and down the years have experimented with 'industrialized' pop and country as well as other forms
of world indigenous music. Of course, these kinds of experiments
were likely to upset fundamentalists who regarded any involvement
with modern technology and mechanical reproduction as a dilution
of a unique form of expression (and of Irish identity and values).

However, developments in technology would play a part in shaping the form that 'authentic' Irish musics would take. Paradoxically,
in the sound of The Dubliners, or Christy Moore, while naturalized

folk instrumentation is employed, the vocal (often deemed the most natural and most 'Irish' of musical elements) is dependent on the techniques of 'close miking' associated with 'crooning'. Ironically, it is this use of the microphone that allows the voice, the accent, the intimacy and the phraseology to come to the foreground and to be heard clearly. Similarly, in the all-important live context, the use of amplification on the voice maintained this intimacy and the use of close miking was to become a central strand in the reproduction of Irish folk on record and a mark of its authenticity.

But O'Riada stood at the beginning of a tradition – one that would continue after his death – of maintaining a national musical lineage against the threat of industrialized Anglo-American culture, and while the definitional aperture would widen as the baton was passed to *Hot Press* in the late 1970s, the concern with musical authenticity was by no means redundant. As Middleton has argued, 'many attempts have been made to retain the traditional ideology of "authenticity", moving it across into new areas. Critics, fans and musicians have joined in these attempts to construct their own preferred music as a "pure" alternative to the "commercial" manipulations of the mainstream construed as a new "folk" genre.'[45]

In 1963, the forces that would coalesce to progress and define Irish rock culture were already in place. The modernization of the economy was beginning to bring the first signs of recovery and build a new mood of optimism that could sustain and support the emerging music industry and its attendant youth subcultures. The Beatles visited, The Royal Showband turned to Elvis and topped the Irish charts, and The Chieftains' first record was released so that its traditional airs and reels shared the musical soundscape in Ireland with Bowyer's rendition of Presley and The Beatles' rendition of black American music. The folk revival, drawing inspiration from Irish traditions and giving back to them a much-needed youthful profile, was already having an effect on Irish music making and listening. The simultaneous emerging of all these factors is not merely temporal or serendipitous. This melange of sounds and styles coming into and slowly emerging from Ireland was the beginning of a process that led to Ireland, despite its small size and relative insignificance in terms of the global marketplace, gaining a disproportionate importance to the international popular music story. And although often lauded for preserving and promoting a traditional form, The Chieftains in fact best illustrate the set of dichotomies that exists in relation to traditional music and folk but which underpins other popular music forms elsewhere: the contrast between *tradition* and *modernity*; between *authenticity* and *artifice*; between musical *purity* and musical *hybridity*; between *preservation* and *experimentation*.

As a counter to the singularity of traditionalism and as a response to the valorization of authenticity, the notion of hybridity and hybrid texts are often held up as examples of a healthy 'creolization'. While it is no doubt politically useful to invert the usual traditional-ist argument and assert that 'dilution' is a good thing, there is nonetheless a problem in uncritically celebrating hybridization as an end in itself. Nonetheless, hybridization may best describe the partic-ular array of cultural forces in play in Ireland in the 1960s. In order to become successful internationally and appeal to a domestic rock audience, Irish bands had to adopt elements of the dominant style of popular music making. This was not forced upon them by a simple process. Since the 1950s, local musicians, both the showbands and the beat groups, have learned to play from listening to records, borrowing poses, adopting looks and plundering other signifiers that are then blended with their own local context. Even traditional music became part of the process of hybridization and this is what makes the Irish case so interesting. As the story moved into the 1970s, the process of hybridization, operating with and against an ideology of authenticity, was to characterize Irish popular music and give it its own set of voices in the wider global noise.

NOTES

1. See http://www.rte.ie/laweb/ll/ll_t01d.html.
2. Daragh O'Halloran, *Green Beat: The Forgotten Era of Irish Rock* (Belfast: Brehon Press, 2006), p.19.
3. Michael Lynch and Damian Smyth, *The Beatles and Ireland* (Cork: Collins Press, 2008), pp.6–10.
4. Nuala O'Connor, *Bringing it all Back Home: The Influence of Irish Music* (London: BBC Books, 1991).
5. David McWilliams, 'March of the HiBrits', *Prospect*, 31 May 2007, http://www.prospectmagazine.co.uk/2007/06/marchofthehibrits/ (accessed 26 March 2010); Sean Campbell, *Irish Blood, English Heart: Second-Generation Irish Musicians in England* (Cork: Cork University Press, 2011).
6. O'Connor, *Bringing it all Back Home*, p.6.
7. Bill Graham and Caroline van Oosten de Boer, *U2: The Complete Guide to their Music* (London: Omnibus Press, 2004), pp.38–9.
8. Ritchie Yorke, *Van Morrison: Into the Music* (London: Charisma, 1975), pp.25–6.
9. Tony Clayton-Lea and Richie Taylor, *Irish Rock: Where it's come from, where it's at, where it's going* (Dublin: Gill & Macmillan, 1992), p.9.

10. Vincent Power, *Send 'Em Home Sweatin': The Showbands' Story* (Dublin: Kildanore Press, 1990), p.49.
11. Ibid., p.9.
12. Ibid., p.48.
13. Ibid., p.34.
14. Gerry Smyth, *Noisy Island: A Short History of Irish Popular Music* (Cork: Cork University Press, 2005), p.15.
15. Mark J. Prendergast, *The Isle of Noises: Rock and Roll's Roots in Ireland* (Dublin: O'Brien Press, 1987), p.11.
16. Niall Stokes, interview by Noel McLaughlin, 1995 (unpublished).
17. Ibid.
18. Van Morrison, 'The Great Deception', *Hard Nose the Highway* (Warner Bros, 1973).
19. Stokes, interview.
20. Prendergast, *Isle of Noises*, p.18.
21. Sean Campbell and Gerry Smyth, *Beautiful Day: Forty Years of Irish Rock* (Cork: Atrium Press, 2005), p.2.
22. Stokes, interview.
23. Ibid.
24. Bob Geldof, *Is That It?* (Harmondsworth: Penguin, 1986), p.69.
25. Lauren Onkey, *Blackness and Transatlantic Irish Identity: Celtic Soul Brothers* (New York and London: Routledge, 2010), p.5.
26. Geldof, *Is That It?*, p.69.
27. Joe Jackson, 'Interview with Brendan Bowyer', *Hot Press*, 19, 18 (September 1995).
28. Dick Hebdige, *Subculture: The Meaning of Style* (London: Methuen, 1979), p.13.
29. John Glatt, *The Chieftains: The Authorized Biography* (New York: St Martins Press, 1997), p.54.
30. Seán O'Riada, *Our Musical Heritage* (Portlaoise: Dolmen Press, 1982).
31. Douglas Hyde, 'The Necessity for De-Anglicising Ireland', in Douglas Hyde, *Language, Lore and Lyrics* (Dublin: Irish Academic Press, 1986), p.169. First published in 1892.
32. Glatt, *The Chieftains*, p.14.
33. Peter McNamee (ed.), *Traditional Music: Whose Music?* (Belfast: Institute Of Irish Studies, 1992), p.65.
34. Glatt, *The Chieftains*, p.14.
35. Bob Dylan, *Chronicles: Volume 1* (London: Simon & Schuster, 2004), p.83.
36. Mick Moloney, *Far from the Shamrock Shore* (Cork: Collins Press, 2002), p.3.
37. O'Riada, *Our Musical Heritage*, p.19.
38. Ibid., p.20.
39. Gerry Smyth, *Music in Irish Cultural History* (Dublin: Irish Academic Press, 2009), p.7.
40. O'Riada, *Our Musical Heritage*, p.22.
41. Ibid., p.73.
42. Glatt, *The Chieftains*, p.75.
43. Richard Middleton, 'The Real Thing? The Specter of Authenticity', in Richard Middleton, *Voicing The Popular: On the Subjects of Popular Music* (New York and London: Routledge, 2006), pp.199–246.
44. Chris Donovan, 'Hip to the Irish', *Hot Press*, 17, 17 (September 1993).
45. Richard Middleton, *Studying Popular Music* (Milton Keynes: Open University Press, 1990), p.140.

2

The Beat Groups: A Tale of Two Cities

They dug me in Ulster, but brother, when I got to the South, I was in dead trouble. Just before I went on one night, the manager came round and told me that he'd had complaints that my act was indecent. I told him that I didn't know what he meant by indecent. 'It's far too sexy – you'll have to stop that sort of thing,' he said. I tried to explain that when you sing rock, you've just got to rock, just got to move with the beat. (Billy Fury)[1]

It might be hard to appreciate today but in the 1960s Belfast was culturally a more confident and more exciting city than Dublin. This was partly because Northern Ireland shared in British post-war reconstruction and benefitted greatly from the setting up of the welfare state. As Jonathan Bardon points out, the expansion of higher education drew into the city a talented new generation of writers, dramatists and artists and by the mid-1960s Belfast had become 'one of the liveliest centres for the creative arts in these islands'.[2] Despite long-term industrial decline, Northern Ireland was still a more prosperous place with a more dynamic culture than the Republic whose economy was only slowly emerging from forty years of protectionism and isolation. Northern Ireland also benefitted from the new era of optimism that followed the ending of the IRA border campaign in 1962. In March 1963, the long Brookeborough regime at Stormont ended with the accession to power of the younger, more liberal and seemingly more dynamic Terence O'Neill. The start of North–South dialogue in the O'Neill–Lemass talks initiated in 1965 seemed to underscore the fact that a new era had dawned, much in line with the general optimistic mood elsewhere in the early 1960s.

Belfast, culturally, may have been a bit more 'rock 'n' roll' to begin with too. After a trouble-free appearance in Belfast, Billy Fury went south to Dublin. On 30 October 1959, the management of the Theatre Royal in Dublin stopped his show in mid-performance, finding his gyrations with the microphone too lascivious and too suggestive. (To be fair to Dublin, though, had they been on the ball, Belfast's sabbatarian Protestants would surely have been just as outraged as Dublin's Legion of Mary.)

Belfast had, of course, an underlying political instability that remained dormant but threatening. On 31 August 1964, The Rolling Stones appeared at the Ulster Hall and caused the same kind of frantic, hysterical reaction that The Beatles had the previous November. This enthusiastic response mirrored that of any other city in the Western world caught up in the youthful frenzy of the 'British invasion' and, as had been the case nine months earlier with the visit of The Beatles, the result was to fold Belfast into an international, increasingly global youth narrative. Nonetheless, the underlying problems remained and there were signs and forebodings of things to come. Just one month after The Stones' concert, rioting erupted around Divis Street in the Falls Road area when the Royal Ulster Constabulary (RUC) used axes to break into the election headquarters of the Republican Party and remove an Irish tricolour from display. Thus the new cultural agenda represented by the vibrant arts scene and the emerging youth subculture vied with the ancient quarrels for the allegiance of the young (and for space in the media). Generally, though, the era was characterized by the same mood of youthful optimism and progressive change that pertained all over the United Kingdom and Ireland at the time and it was in this mood that the beat scene emerged in Belfast.

When The Beatles visited Belfast in November 1963, the young Van Morrison was in Heidelberg, Germany, finishing off a long stint playing with The Monarchs Showband. By the following September, when The Stones visited Belfast, he was in London with Them recording the two singles that would give him immortality in terms of the pop charts and British rhythm and blues folklore. After a seemingly long period of stasis things were moving very quickly in the emerging rhythm and blues beat scene. In Germany, Morrison had begun to develop his singing and his predilection for rhythm and blues music and often fraternized with the black GIs stationed there who had access to the kind of music that was in his father's record collection, that he had grown up listening to. When he returned to Belfast at the end of 1963 the charts were already beginning to reflect the new era of British R&B groups and Morrison began to feel that it was time to move on from the showband scene that he had been part of for three years. All his biographers agree that the turning point for him was the brief stint in London at the beginning of 1964 when he saw various British R&B groups play in specialist clubs (he was especially impressed by The Downliners Sect who, unlike The Rolling Stones, The Yardbirds and The Pretty Things, were not destined to make it into the charts at the time). It seemed to him that he had once been ahead of the game but was now falling behind in the emerging new rock scene. 'I was doing what I was doing when the Rolling Stones were still in school', he observed later.[3]

His return to Belfast saw him join guitarist Billy Harrison's band The Gamblers, eventually taking up the option of playing in a newly announced R&B session to be held at the Maritime Hotel in central Belfast. The Gamblers became Them, a name suggested by the band's keyboardist Eric Wrixon, and if Morrison's oft-quoted comment that 'Them lived and died as a group on the stage of the Maritime'[4] seems today rather ungracious to their memory, it probably reflects well enough the fact that this was not *his* band in any meaningful way. In an early *NME* interview with the band in May 1965, Keith Altham refers to Billy Harrison as the band's leader and it is Harrison rather than Morrison who grumpily doesn't answer the questions. 'We're fed up with answering stupid questions', he complains bitterly. 'Three months ago we came across here and the same people are asking the same questions.'[5] Harrison here articulates the anathema that Them felt for the chores of being pop stars in the first flush of 1960s rock and pop, and expresses the same anti-commercial *authenticity* that motivated the emerging scene in Dublin, as remembered years afterwards by Bob Geldof and Niall Stokes. As a result, the band quickly gained a reputation for being surly, aggressive and uncommunicative, and their demeanour seemed to be a shared attitude rather than just the idiosyncrasy of their particularly shy lead singer.

If Harrison was the band's leader initially, it was Morrison who became its dominant creative force and his subsequent success as a solo artist rather eclipses Them's brief brush with fame and success. In some ways, this is a pity because Them at the time were important to Belfast, to Northern Ireland and to rock music in Ireland generally. As the first Irish rock band to make it on the bigger stage, Them were the inspiration for other aspiring bands and provided the template for ambitious bands to follow. The considerable chart success of their second and third singles – 'Baby Please Don't Go' and 'Here Comes the Night' – was greeted in Ireland with great acclaim and a deep sense of pride. There can be no doubt that the band's residency at the Maritime Hotel in Belfast forged the beginning of a proper rock music scene in Northern Ireland and their performances there as a live R&B band have become the stuff of legend. As Morrison told Ritchie Yorke (in an early, 'official' biography):

> the Maritime was like a stomping ground kind of thing. We ran the place, the whole show...when it came to making records, we were out of our depth. Because we were there in a studio, within another vibe. The way we did the numbers at the Maritime was more spontaneous, more energy, more everything because we were feeding off the crowd. And it was never really captured on tape...[6]

This is classic early rock authenticity, when even the act of recording is tainted with the dead hand of commercialism. For Morrison, the experience of playing live for three years in a showband had honed his skills as a performer and it is the performance aspects of Them that he prefers to remember.

Nonetheless, the only way most people could experience Them was through the records (just as the only way the young Morrison could experience black American rhythm and blues was through the records those legendary artists had made). And both by the standards of the time and with the benefit of historical hindsight, we can see that the single 'Baby Please Don't Go' b/w 'Gloria' was one of the great achievements of the British R&B scene of the time and, by extension, one of the most significant achievements of the beat era in Ireland. The sycophantic Ritchie Yorke defends Morrison's antipathy to Them's achievement by reference to the art/commerce divide. 'What some Them-boosters fail to grasp', he argues, 'is that for Morrison, the entire Them trip was little more than a very bitter subjection to the modus operandi of the music industry.'[7] Certainly, Van Morrison's lifelong antipathy to both the music industry and the music press emanated from this period when Them moved out of the Maritime womb and embraced the wider world of the British rock scene. As with Harrison, Morrison developed a very clear distaste for the way in which both the musical direction of the band and the management of their everyday touring life was organized outside of their direct control. He had a particular aversion to some of the chores associated with chart success – especially onerous for him was having to deal with the teen-centred music press with its 'star' banalities and having to mime the hits on *Top of the Pops*. But in terms of Them's chart success and its impact on the emerging scene back in Belfast and in Ireland more generally, this is all beside the point. Them and their success mattered for the Irish music fan, and the influence of the band, its enduring legacy, far exceeds the brevity of their fame and the indignities such fame visited on their lead singer at the time.

With somewhat mischievous hyperbole, Campbell and Smyth describe the B-side of the single, Van Morrison's 'Gloria', as '2 minutes and 36 seconds of primal garage rock that – more than transformations on the economic, political or religious fronts – announced the arrival of a new stage in modern Irish history'.[8] This is, of course, only a slight bit of hyperbole because this stomping blues rocker encapsulates perfectly the anticipation and the excitement of sex, that aspect of human nature most heavily discouraged and disapproved of by 'official' Ireland, in either its Catholic or Protestant forms. If sex and rock 'n' roll purred away quietly together under the radar in showband Ireland then they burst forth gloriously in full conjunction in this masterpiece of barely controlled hedonism. Within months, bands from the four corners of the rock 'n' roll world were practising their own versions of 'Gloria'.

More than that, though, for the Irish fan, especially in Belfast, the fact that Them's single was high in the pop charts and the band themselves were on television, participating at the centre of the pop world, was important. And there was more. The A-side of the single 'Baby Please Don't Go' was used as the signature tune for the most hip programme on British television at the time – 'Ready, Steady, Go' ('The Weekend Starts Here') made by ITV company Associated Rediffusion and shown live at six o'clock every Friday. Irish rock music had not only arrived but in one fell swoop it had become the hippest new sound in town and this is why, despite Morrison's own reservations, Them remain one of the most important bands in the history of Irish rock.

Smyth also alludes to the fact that this track came with 'one of the most instantly recognizable guitar figures in the entire popular musical canon' but a guitar part that has been the centre of controversy for decades. Who composed and played this signature riff – the band's leader and guitarist Billy Harrison or the jobbing session guitarist Jimmy Page who was contracted to play on the studio recording? In one sense it shouldn't matter – this riff has now sunk so deeply into rock music culture that whoever played it on the record is irrelevant to its historical significance. But, as Smyth argues, it matters to the *authenticity* of Them's legacy – 'Them *was* the guitar part from "Baby Please Don't Go"' and even if Page was to go on from jobbing session player to lead guitarist in Led Zeppelin and to become one of the great rock guitarists of the 1970s, Them's legacy and their credibility are severely diminished if Harrison did not play the riff. Smyth suggests that Page himself has claimed ownership of the riff while Harrison and keyboardist with the band, Eric Wrixen, dispute this.[9] Discussing the controversy in 2010, Page is adamant: 'I have always been clear about this, if only journalists had reported what I said accurately. I played on the record? Yes. I was the young gun for hire. But I didn't play *that* riff or write it. That is Billy Harrison's.'[10] Page concurs then that the record is essentially Them and not, as John Collis puts it, some 'Monkee-like studio confection'.[11] Them's R&B authenticity remains intact.

If their identity as a rhythm and blues band was never in doubt, their provenance was rather more problematic. In Britain, they promoted themselves and gained the reputation for being defiantly, aggressively 'other'. 'You're beginning to sound like an angry young Irishman', Keith Altham teased the surly Harrison in the 1965 interview. True to form, Harrison retorted, 'I'm not Irish! I'm an Ulsterman. Why does everyone insist on calling us Irish?'[12]

Johnny Rogan refers to this exchange in his biography of Morrison, provocatively entitled *No Surrender*, in which, sometimes tendentiously, he argues that Morrison's music, his demeanour and attitude are all the result of his Ulster Protestant heritage and that Harrison's 'sectarian' retort merely confirmed that Them were essentially 'a Prod band'.[13] For Morrison, however, it was not that simple. In the same interview with Altham, Morrison responds to Harrison's outburst about being called Irish with a conciliatory 'I don't see any harm in it.' In conversation with Happy Traum in 1970, six years after Them's Maritime stints, Morrison insisted that Them were a Belfast band first and foremost, 'but later on, when we had a couple of hit records, they started calling us a British group...then after that we became an English group! I don't know how in the world they mistook it for an English group, 'cause if they ever heard us talk, they'd know it wasn't. It was an Irish group!'[14] Them in the

United States were certainly seen as part of the first wave 'British invasion', a band that offered a diet of white rhythm and blues in the vein of The Animals and scored a minor US hit with Morrison's 'Mystic Eyes' in 1965.

But as Morrison's later interview confirms, Them were essentially a Belfast band and their influence on Irish rock was most keenly felt in the city's burgeoning rhythm and blues scene of the time. Their success at the Maritime led to a mushrooming of venues in and around the city that specialized in 'groups' as opposed to showbands and this live circuit slowly spread further afield (so, for example, Sunday evenings and some Saturday afternoons were reserved for groups in Derry's city centre ballroom, the Embassy). As the venues expanded a plethora of other local bands appeared to fill these, some playing top ten material as well as the rhythm and blues standards that had entered the charts at the time. Many of these groups were, in effect, cover bands; though defined as 'beat groups' rather than 'showbands', they largely adhered to a 'guitars, drums and keyboards' format and played the hits of the post-Beatles British groups like The Kinks, The Rolling Stones and The Small Faces or covered the standard R&B classics that all these groups also played. This was, as we shall see, most characteristic of the Dublin beat scene but the Belfast scene to begin with was dominated by the same kind of 'raw' white urban blues that was characteristic of the emerging beat scene in cities across the United Kingdom in the period 1964–66.

As Them headed off for London in 1964, their place at the Maritime was taken by the likes of The Aztecs, The Mad Lads and The Wheels (who later based themselves in Blackpool). Some of these bands appear on 1998's compilation album *Belfast Beat, Maritime Blues*, which captures the richness of the scene in the wake of Them's success. Particularly impressive is The Wheels' 'Bad Little Woman', a raw piece of (misogynistic) rhythm and blues driven to a frenzy by guitar, drums, harmonica and organ and Rod Demick's increasingly frantic vocal. While this compilation is studded with other good examples of the characteristic sounds of the time it is interesting that the songs and groups also indicate the way in which this scene would develop in the years ahead as the original raw sound of Them, The Mad Lads and The Wheels is filtered into a more gentle pop music. In the case of The Mad Lads, the single which they released under the Decca label as Moses K and The Prophets (the name change was imposed on them because their

4. 'A Belfast, Ulster, Irish or "British Invasion" Band?' – Them in
    1965 (Corbis)

original name clashed with an American band already signed to the
Stax label) was a pop tune, 'I Went Out With My Baby Tonight', that
mirrored the direction in which the label were also attempting to
push the recalcitrant Them. Tucked away on the compilation is a
track by Belfast band Luvin' Kind that interestingly was written by
(the not yet Sensational) Alex Harvey, an anti-nuclear bomb song in
the mode of Barry Maguire's 'Eve of Destruction' which indicated
that the authentic rhythm and blues scene was already extending in
other directions.

One way in which the authentic blues sound was maintained was
in the three-piece blues format pioneered in Britain by Cream and in
Ireland by Belfast's The Method and Rory Gallagher's Taste.
Although Taste hailed from Cork and played regularly in Dublin,
Gallagher centred their activities in Belfast and toured the wider
scene in Northern Ireland. When Taste began their rise to prominence in Britain, they were often taken to be a Belfast band.[15]
Gallagher himself never forgot the debt he owed to the Belfast audiences from his early Taste days and he continued to perform there
during the worst years of the Troubles in the 1970s. Colin Harper
sums it up aptly: 'Gallagher may have been "The First Irish Rock

Star" but he was a Belfast phenomenon.'[16] The vibrancy and excitement of the Belfast scene also produced the guitar talents of Eric Bell and Gary Moore, both of whom were to play prominent roles in the ascent of Thin Lizzy in the 1970s. If Morrison and Gallagher remain the two most celebrated artists nurtured from the Northern Ireland beat scene then guitarist Henry McCullough runs them close. And in many ways, McCullough's eclectic and varied early career in Ireland is an apt summation of the whole Irish music scene in the 1960s.

Born in Portstewart, Co. Derry, McCullough began his career, as so many Irish rock musicians had, playing guitar in showbands, first with The Skyrockets and later with Gene and The Gents, an apprenticeship, he noted sardonically much later, which stood him in good stead when he joined the 'showbandy' Paul McCartney in Wings.[17] In 1967, he joined Belfast band The People, which quickly established itself as one of the top bands in both the Belfast and Dublin scenes. The People moved to England and under the tutelage of Chas Chandler and with a name change to (the rather contrived) Eire Apparent they evolved into a psychedelic band, touring with Jimi Hendrix and Pink Floyd, the epitome of psychedelic 'cool' at the time. A drugs arrest in Toronto ended McCullough's stint with the band and back in Ireland he joined the folk rock band Sweeney's Men with Johnny Moynihan and Terry Woods who were later to play in various groups that marked the progress of Irish folk rock and electric traditional music throughout the 1970s. This might have seemed like a strange journey – from Hendrix to Irish folk – but in many ways it illustrates the characteristic pilgrimage of so many musicians and so much popular music in Ireland. The showband, beat group, pop music and folk/traditional scenes overlapped more than some accounts have acknowledged – as McCullough says of the time, 'folk musicians and the rock 'n' roll musicians had started coming to each other's gigs'.[18] McCullough's journey, in other words, from showband via beat group and electric folk to playing guitar in Joe Cocker's Grease Band at Woodstock in 1969 may have a hint of the epic about it but this variety of music making is more typical of 1960s Irish popular music than it might at first appear and, in this way, McCullough's musical career is quintessentially Irish.

The interplay of styles and audiences that such a varied career required was not always without its dangers and controversies. Outside of the beat club circuit, Them were often subjected to hostile abuse (penny throwing) by audiences angry with their surliness, alienated from a musical style they did not understand and resentful that they would not play more familiar chart music. These so-called 'penny riots' became news items towards the end of 1964 and in early 1965 just as Them began their rise in the British charts. A UTV interview with the band, from 5 January 1965 after just such a penny-throwing riot, is a study in collective surliness. Both Harrison and Morrison defend their R&B authenticity against more commercial pop music and against the commercial taste of many of the music-goers they have encountered doing the rounds of the wider circuit. Interestingly, the band pose, or were deliberately posed, in a record shop standing against a background wall on which a Jim Reeves album is prominently displayed. The band clearly wanted to signal the disparity of tastes that lay behind the hostility of some audiences but, just as surely, they were keen to highlight the changing of the musical guard in Ireland.

However, there was now a more amenable and welcoming club scene existing in and around Dublin too and their mean and moody R&B was readily accepted by the emerging Dublin beat audience. Following the publicity over their 'penny riot' gigs in Northern Ireland's 'sticks', the cosmopolitan atmosphere of the Dublin clubs was a welcome relief. The day after a riot in Cookstown, Them took the stage to great acclaim at the Stella in Mount Merrion, Co. Dublin (in the young Geldof's stomping ground) and helped to underpin the growth of the Dublin scene. For Daragh O'Halloran, there was a crucial difference in the type of music the Maritime bands offered from that normally available in the Dublin beat scene – the difference between the harder, less compromising sound of the urban blues from Belfast and a more pop sensibility in Dublin. Indeed, according to one of O'Halloran's witnesses,[19] the Northern bands, especially Them, The Mad Lads and The Wheels, kick-started the Dublin scene, though that may be to overstate the case.

If in Belfast, and Northern Ireland more generally, the beat scene was, to begin with, much stronger and more visible than in Dublin, the time scale involved is, with hindsight, fairly miniscule, merely a matter of weeks between Bluesville and The Greenbeats emerging in Dublin and Them first appearing in Belfast at the Maritime. And if Them are the seminal band in the North, Bluesville can lay claim to the mantle in the South and they even managed to achieve, before Them did, the nirvana of an American top ten hit when their single 'You Turn Me On' reached number eight in June 1965. This was a quirky, unlikely breakthrough record and even if the band's creative fountainhead was the English ex-Trinity College student, Ian

5. 'Imprisoned by the local scene?' – The Mad Lads

6.   'Forging Ireland's rock music scene' – the now demolished Maritime Hotel in Belfast

Whitcomb, and, typically, the song was received in the United States as part of the 'British invasion', nonetheless its achievement ranks with that of Them's success in the United Kingdom charts a few months earlier as a key moment in the emergence of Irish rock. In many ways it represented the more melodic pop sensibility of the southern bands, with the song's piano-driven riff and Whitcomb's falsetto delivery making for an unusual pop/R&B sound (like a lot of pop obscurities it can still be found today, lingering on the fringes of YouTube). And while Van Morrison's own American top ten hit 'Brown Eyed Girl' from 1967 has entered pop consciousness more completely than Ian Whitcomb's song, to Campbell and Smyth the record 'stands as evidence of a new phase in Irish popular-music-making, symbolizing the winds of change that by 1965 were already beginning to blow away fifty years of cultural cobwebs'.[20]

Bluesville pioneered the beat scene in Dublin but in the wake of The Beatles' 1963 visit, the number of bands that emerged, merged and consequently submerged is quite dizzying, as was the number of beat clubs which opened to cater for them. Prendergast has estimated that in the four years between 1964 and 1968 about a dozen clubs opened in Dublin itself but these complemented a circuit that included coastal clubs in both the northern and southern suburbs (the home of the young Geldof) as well as a middle-class beat circuit of tennis and rugby clubs around the city's wealthier suburbs. He also noted over twenty different beat groups (including the northern bands) that fed this circuit, though this was only a personal selection of what was at least twice that number.[21] As the Dublin scene grew, beat groups from all over Ireland, including, of course, those from the North, made their way to the city. By 1967, in other words, this was an extensive and lucrative circuit that was slowly taking over from Belfast as the centre of Irish rock and pop. The urban area covered included the wealthiest and most affluent suburbs as well as city centre dives, and the music being played had expanded beyond the raw R&B sounds of the Belfast bands. As writer Kevin Cully (a friend and contemporary of Geldof's) recalls, 'I was a member of the Caroline club (as in the pirate radio station) which was located where the old cinema in Glasthule used to be. For a while, this was a very "in" place. Favourite band was The Chosen Few who did a host of soul stuff. Granny's Intentions from Limerick were also a huge hit (lots of floral waistcoats and granny specs) and I recall they were a Small Faces type of band.'[22]

The standard analysis of this shift is that Belfast and the North were slowly sinking into communal breakdown as the Troubles began to ratchet up and that as a consequence the scene slowly died. Certainly, one of the results of the hardening of sectarian attitudes in the 1970s was the virtual collapse of nightlife (in Belfast, especially, where the sectarian killings were at their most intense) and this wasn't revived, as we shall see, until the emergence of punk in the late 1970s. But by 1968 – the year the Troubles finally grabbed world headlines – the moment of raw R&B that was characteristic of the Belfast scene was already over and popular music had moved on in directions that Dublin was better suited to accommodate. On one hand, the post *Sergeant Pepper* rise of psychedelic pop was important. Thus Dave Lewis's Belfast-based The Method metamorphosed from raw R&B to the psychedelic pop of Andwella's Dream, and McCullough's The People re-emerged as Hendrix-influenced Eire Apparent. Both of these bands had left Belfast behind musically before the city succumbed to sectarianism and communal violence. Dublin's more laid-back hippy culture and greater pop sensibility (captured in the hippy folk whimsy of Dr Strangely Strange who emerged in Dublin in 1967) suited such a musical direction better than Belfast's harder-edged urban blues tradition.

On the other hand, the marriage of folk and rock, encapsulated in Dylan's historic electric tour of 1965–66 and captured best by the emergence of The Byrds' folk rock hybrid also suited the more folk/traditional atmosphere to be found in Dublin and its environs. Dr Strangely Strange achieved a measure of fame (if hardly fortune) when the track 'Strangely Strange but Oddly Normal' from their first album *Kip of the Serenes* (1969) was included on the Island sampler *Nice Enough to Eat* (1969). They were, and still are, often likened to The Incredible String Band, England's quintessential hippy band of the time, both trading on pagan mysticism and faux-naif sentiments wrapped in the acoustic soundscape of folk music. Both of these eccentric and quirky bands grew out of the same broad culture of folk rock crossover and coexisted with a range of other hybrid bands in Britain and Ireland, such as Pentangle, Fairport Convention, Steeleye Span and Fotheringay. In Ireland, the merging of folk, traditional and rock music was pioneered and developed through the numerous collaborations that involved the exploratory talents of Paul Brady, Donal Lunny, Andy Irvine, Johnny Moynihan, Christy Moore and Gay and Terry Woods.

Paul Brady, like Henry McCullough, epitomized the porous nature of musical styles and genres of the time. He arrived in Dublin in 1965 to attend university but ended up being recruited as lead guitarist with the south County Dublin band The Rootz Group – 'We all thought he must be cool because he came from the North'[23] – before joining folk balladeers The Johnstons. They had already taken the folk ballad into the Irish charts when their version of Ewan McColl's 'The Travelling People' went to number one in Ireland in August 1966 and, with the addition of Brady and Mick Moloney, The Johnstons went on to enjoy substantial success in Ireland, introducing many of the songs and ballads that were to dominate the genre in the 1970s.

The two folk/rock crossover acts that best summed up the music scene in Dublin in the late 1960s were Emmet Spiceland and Sweeney's Men, both of which were to enjoy considerable chart success in Ireland and were to cement the place of folk and traditional musics within the culture of rock in Ireland. Emmet Spiceland, including a young Donal Lunny who was to be so influential in folk/traditional/rock hybrids in the 1970s and 1980s, certainly looked the part. Surviving footage of the band playing to the Croke Park audience at the 1968 All-Ireland hurling final shows a trio of trendy young lads in the mod style of the times singing an old emigration ballad in the close harmony style of California folk rock. Their first single, 'Mary From Dungloe', reached number one in the Irish charts in February 1968 and this close harmony style was to set the template for much of the Irish folk rock that was to follow.

Sweeney's Men have left the most lasting legacy from these early days, not least in that they brought together at various times the substantial and influential talents of Andy Irvine, Johnny Moynihan, Terry Woods and, as we have seen, Henry McCullough. The group explored and extended the ballad form and traditional music to the extent of introducing the Greek bouzouki (attributed to Moynihan) into the soundscape of Irish music where it now resides comfortably with the fiddle and the tin whistle. The group had two top ten hits in Ireland with their reworking of old Irish songs, 'Old Maid in the Garret' and 'The Waxies Dargle', but their first album, *Sweeney's Men* (1968), with its eclectic mix of American folk songs, Irish, Scottish and English ballads and traditional Irish music, best captures their adventurous probing of the musical interfaces of the period. (The album includes the celebrated sea shanty 'The Handsome Cabin Boy' which, depending on how the lyrics are interpreted, is a song about bi-sexuality and/or transgenderism and certainly introduced the earthy into Irish folk.)

If the emergence of rock music in the 1960s in Ireland had largely been the tale of two cities with differing music traditions, the 1970s would be the tale of such multiple hybrid experiments that attempted to blend the global sounds of rock with the folk and traditional sounds of home. In 1968 Belfast was immortalized forever in the release of Van Morrison's *Astral Weeks* and the city's pre-Troubles ambience continued to be an inspiration for much of Morrison's subsequent work. The musical energy it encapsulated in the period between 1964 and 1968 had, however, begun to dissipate and innovation, experiment and fusion had already headed south along with the best of the northern bands and musicians. Dublin itself, however, was only a staging post and most bands had to move on further afield if they were to achieve lasting success. Irish rock, like so much else in Irish culture, went into exile.

NOTES

1. Billy Fury, from the official website at http://www.billyfury.com/.
2. Jonathan Bardon, *Belfast: An Illustrated History* (Belfast: Blackstaff Press, 1983), p.256.
3. Ritchie Yorke, *Van Morrison: Into the Music* (London: Charisma, 1975), p.24.
4. Ibid., p.28.
5. Keith Altham, 'Them', *NME*, 14 May 1965.
6. Yorke, *Van Morrison*, p.29.
7. Ibid., p.36.
8. Sean Campbell and Gerry Smyth, *Beautiful Day: Forty Years of Irish Rock* (Cork: Atrium Press, 2005), p.10.
9. Gerry Smyth, *Noisy Island: A Short History of Irish Popular Music* (Cork: Cork University Press, 2005), pp.33–4.
10. Jimmy Page, in conversation with Noel McLaughlin, at the Westbourne, London W2, 16 July 2010.
11. John Collis, *Van Morrison: Inarticulate Speech of the Heart* (London: Little, Brown & Co., 1996), p.62.
12. Altham, 'Them'.
13. Johnny Rogan, *Van Morrison: No Surrender* (London: Vintage, 2005), pp.120–1.
14. Happy Traum, 'Van Morrison: In Conversation', *Rolling Stone*, 9 July 1970.
15. Daragh O'Halloran, *Green Beat: The Forgotten Era of Irish Rock* (Belfast: Brehon Press, 2006), p.124.
16. Colin Harper and Trevor Hodgett, *Irish Folk, Trad and Blues: A Secret History* (Cork: Collins Press, 2004), p.232.
17. Ibid., p.176.
18. Ibid., p.177.
19. O'Halloran, *Green Beat*, p.106.
20. Campbell and Smyth, *Beautiful Day*, p.15.
21. Mark J. Prendergast, *The Isle of Noises: Rock and Roll's Roots in Ireland* (Dublin: O'Brien Press, 1987), pp.14–15.
22. Kevin Cully, interview by Martin McLoone, November 2010 (unpublished).
23. Ibid.

3

Folk-Rock-Trad Hybrids

...we had absorbed Radio Luxembourg and we had also absorbed the traditional musics surrounding us. So we were living in overlapping cultural universes which didn't have any meeting point and we were trying to find some solid ground, somewhere in the overlap between these two cultural constructs. (Jim Lockhart)[1]

...*Ommadawn* includes a brass band from Hereford, the Irish uillean pipes of the Chieftains' Paddy Moloney, the African drums of Jabula, the voice of Clodagh Simonds [sic] ('just an Irish girl who sings and plays the piano'). (Steve Turner)[2]

...first The Church, then The Banks, now Fianna Fáil...we're nearly home and dry. (Christy Moore)[3]

Mike Oldfield's third solo album, *Ommadawn* (1975), is interesting from an Irish perspective. The name of the album itself is an anglicized version of the Gaelic word *amadán*, meaning 'idiot' or 'fool', and reflects the album's ambient 'Celtic' sound, especially in the second movement (side two on the original vinyl release). Part of this Celtic ambience comes from Paddy Moloney's uillean pipes and one of the most impressive passages on the album is his evocative pipe solo on side two. Moloney's presence on the record is an indication of how far he, and The Chieftains, had come by the mid-1970s in terms of peer esteem and global recognition. In an *NME* piece in March 1975, a few months before Oldfield's album was released, Fred Dellar puts this esteem into perspective: 'Jerry Garcia felt so strongly about the band that he had them play opposite The Dead at a San Francisco gig...though The Chieftains are still thought of as a cult band by the general music industry, the size of the cult is spreading at an enormous rate.'[4]

As we have seen, Moloney started out in the 1950s as a key player in the revival of traditional music, especially in Dublin, and he first came to prominence as part of Seán O'Riada's highly influential ensemble Ceoltóirí Cualann. He established The Chieftains in 1963 as a conscious attempt to take the music into a different (recorded) direction and he remained restless about the music's potential afterwards. By the mid-1970s, he was trying to explore this potential and to reconfigure traditional music by inserting it into an increasing range of diverse contexts (including his successful collaboration with Stanley Kubrick for the soundtrack of *Barry Lyndon*, 1975). His collaboration with Oldfield in 1975, in other words, was only one part of a journey that would lead him to a whole series of musical experiments encompassing styles and genres from across the globe – other Celtic influences from Brittany, Scotland, and Galicia (*Celtic Wedding*, 1985; *Over the Sea to Skye: The Celtic Connection*, 1990); a famous tour in China involving a collaboration with Chinese music and musicians (*The Chieftains in China*, 1986); collaborations with country music and various rock styles involving guest appearances with the cream of American, British and Irish rock, folk and country performers (among others, *The Bells of Dublin*, 1991; *Another Country*, 1992; *The Long Black Veil*, 1995; *Tears of Stone*, 1999; *Down the Old Plank Road: The Nashville Sessions*, 2002). Moloney even pioneered the idea of a traditional music 'concept' album, from *Bonaparte's Retreat* in 1976, celebrating the role that the Irish played in Napoleon's rise and fall, to the collaboration with Ry Cooder on 2010's Mexican influenced *San Patricio*, celebrating the San Patricio regiment of largely Irish soldiers which fought against the Americans in the war over Texas in 1836–38.

The significance of The Chieftains' career, under the restless urgings of Moloney, is that the traditional music they played and the contexts in which they played it, moved inexorably away from a purist authenticity to an eclectic cosmopolitanism without losing the distinctively Irish melodies and instrumentation that lay at the heart of the early recordings. The result, of course, was worldwide recognition and considerable commercial success and the patronage of the elite performers of global popular music. The Chieftains opened for Eric Clapton in London in 1976 and subsequently played with and performed for Paul McCartney, The Rolling Stones, The Grateful Dead, Van Morrison, Bruce Springsteen, Bob Dylan, Elvis Costello and Emmylou Harris among many others. The most celebrated of these collaborations was with Van Morrison on 1988's *Irish Heartbeat*, which gave a new lease of life to an artist whose stock at the time, in commercial if not critical terms, was low. Clinton Heylin compared the situation with a creatively becalmed and commercially ignored Bob Dylan at the same time. Dylan's album of largely cover versions *Down in the Groove* was to be his critical and commercial nadir while Heylin noted sardonically that for Morrison at the same time, 'his collection of Irish "folk" songs actually garnered his best reviews and sales in years'.[5] The coherence that Heylin noted in Morrison's cover versions was provided in large measure by The Chieftains.

Ommadawn's eclectic musical hybrid was to prove highly influential. Indeed in its meshing of the English, Irish and African rhythms, the album marks an early example of what later came to be called 'world music'. In this case the exotic African rhythms and the equally exotic Irish pipes are married to traditional English folk sounds to create a rich musical melange. (It has to be said, too, that the 'Celtic ambience' presaged by *Ommadawn* led to a distinctive genre best encapsulated in the music of Enya in which the Celtic sound slips into 'new age' ambience and creates, depending on one's predilection, atmospheric 'chill out' music or somnambulant 'musak'/'elevator music'.)

The reference to Clodagh Simonds in Steve Turner's original review of *Ommadawn* is also significant. The review mentions a telephone interview with Oldfield and the implication is that the quote ('just an Irish girl who sings and plays the piano') is from Oldfield himself. But is it merely explanatory, somewhat dismissive or knowingly ironic? From this distance it is difficult to decide. What is certain is that Clodagh Simonds was one of the creative inspirations behind what is probably Ireland's most celebrated and most revered cult band, Mellow Candle, whose one album, *Swaddling Songs*, had been released in 1972. The album fairly well sank without trace at the time but has since grown in esteem and in critical standing so that by 2005, Campbell and Smyth could call it 'a brilliant, beautiful collection' that has now achieved recognition as 'one of the most affecting and effective popular-musical documents of its era'.[6]

Swaddling Songs is, indeed a remarkable album, reflecting better than any other Irish record the prevailing folk rock ambience of the international hippy scene of the early 1970s. And yet it also reflects the musical heritage out of which it grew – Irish traditional music and balladry and especially the tradition of female singing often associated with both the sean-nós and lilting styles (this is especially so on the album's last track, 'Boulders on my Grave' which is a complex mix of instrumentation and 'mouth music'). Clodagh Simonds and her collaborator from schooldays, Alison Bools (later Williams and now O'Donnell), wrote most of the songs with their complicated melodies and labyrinthine structures and sang the elaborate and complex harmonies that sustain them.

For the most part, the songs are about the virtues of a simple rustic existence where one can commune with nature, possibly with God and most certainly with oneself. They reject the commercialism and consumerism of contemporary society in favour of a kind of pantheistic celebration (and fear) of nature. They reject contemporary urban culture in favour of the older wisdoms of the seas, mountains and fields (though surely there is something ambiguous in the refrain from 'Boulders on My Grave': 'I know the Dublin pavements/will be boulders on my grave'). The songs represent the counterculture norms of the time, in other words, so that the amalgam of rock, folk and Irish music creates its own quasi-medieval, quasi-mystical elemental landscape. In this regard, the nearest equivalent to Mellow Candle is the English folk rock band Trees, whose 1971 hippy masterpiece, *The Garden of Jane Delawney*, enjoys a similar cult status. There was, at the time, considerable interplay between British and Irish folk, traditional and rock musics. There was a shared interest in folk traditions generally but especially in folk songs that had been passed down through generations and back and forth across the Irish Sea. It is hardly surprising, therefore, that Trees recorded the Irish song 'She Moved through the Fair' for their *Jane Delawney* album or that some of the singing and sounds on *Swaddling Songs* resemble English folk rock acts of the era like Fairport Convention.

These musical borrowings and sharing were themselves influenced by the dominance of a folk rock tradition that emerged in the 1960s in the United States, following Dylan, The Byrds and The Band. Britain and Ireland also shared the fading but still potent hippy culture that such folk rock portended so that Mellow Candle existed among other things as a cultural expression of Ireland, of musical convergence with Britain and of the lingering aspirations of 'the Nation of Woodstock'. It is hardly surprising, then, that in the brief late-1980s' revival of such hippy music both Trees' 'The Garden of Jane Delawney' and Mellow Candle's 'Silver Song' were recorded by the band All About Eve, the era's main exponent of this revival.

The songs on *Swaddling Songs* are elliptical, obscure and

mystical, reflecting an imaginary abstraction rather than a concrete reality. The exception is the one track that directly addresses the Irish experience, Clodagh Simonds' powerfully ambiguous song about her strict Catholic upbringing, 'Reverend Sisters'. Alison O'Donnell briefly discussed the convent school that she and Clodagh Simonds attended, noting that far from being repressed by them, the nuns in fact gave the girls free rein to express themselves. 'They encouraged us and when we were sixteen they said, "Leave school, because you'll only want to do this – do it now." '[7] Clodagh Simonds's starkly affecting song suggests a more ambivalent response to the 'Reverend Sisters' as she remembers 'standing young and green before the wisdom/age and your black habits wrought' and there is a tangible feeling of dread when the young girl is invited to 'come into our office and I'll show you/come into our office and I'll tell you where to go'.

Mellow Candle and The Chieftains were not, of course, the only Irish bands involved in the cross-fertilization of musical genres that was typical of the late 1960s and the 1970s. The musical brilliance of Mellow Candle and their unique mix of mysticism, romantic aspirations and modernist discontents grew out of a cultural ferment in popular music that marked Ireland's emergence into the global world of rock and pop music. If their lyrics and sound reflect back to the hippy folk of Dr Strangely Strange, the wonderfully full acoustic sound, electric instrumentation and traditional ambiences of the songs reflect as well the spirit of adventure that marked the whole folk, rock and traditional fields of the early 1970s. *Swaddling Songs* was released in 1972, and in that same year, two other groundbreaking albums were released – Horslips' first album *Happy to Meet, Sorry to Part* and Christy Moore's second solo album *Prosperous* – both of which were to have a profound impact on Irish popular music.

'CELTIC ROCK': HORSLIPS

This was not merely a rocked-up version of a traditional tune, but a reinvention of the medium for a different version of history. It was as though we were being given a glimpse of what the radio might have sounded like if the past eight hundred years had happened differently. It was as though the underground stream of Irish music culture – the way it might have been – had suddenly erupted through the ground into the living rooms of early seventies Ireland. Horslips changed the history of Irish popular music, and possibly much more besides. (John Waters)[8]

John Waters's ecstatic memory of Horslips playing the track 'An Bratach Bán' on RTÉ reminds us just how important the band were to the generation of Irish teenagers coming of age in the decade after rock's first flourishing. If Waters is rather fanciful in his imagining of a pre-colonial (or, more accurately, a non-colonial) Irish culture, he is very precise about what exactly Horslips were doing in their mixing of Irish music with the look and sound of rock: 'It is impossible to convey today how deeply shocking this was to those of us who had been raised in an atmosphere of reverence for both Irish music and the Irish language.'[9] Significantly, Waters mentions that it was both the *sound* and the *image* of the band that caused the frisson he felt and at the beginnings of their careers, certainly, this was the 'double whammy' that Horslips dealt tradition. As we have seen, numerous bands and musicians earlier had begun to push at these traditions, mirroring in the cultural arena the spirit of adventure that characterized the times. Horslips took a particular road into musical hybridity and probably took it as far as it could go. In doing so, they created what was dubbed 'Celtic rock' and probably also set in motion a movement that would lead, through the 1980s and 1990s into the 'Celtic' branch of the world music phenomenon.

Horslips were formed in Dublin in 1972, the five members – Jim Lockhart, Eamon Carr, Charles O'Connor, Barry Devlin and Johnny Fean – constituting an unusually well-educated and articulate group of musicians with experience in business, marketing and promotion as well as in art and design and literature. Their sound was multi-instrumental, with traditional instruments – flute, bodhran, acoustic fiddle, pipes, mandolin, concertina – meeting with rock instrumentation – guitar, bass, drums, keyboards and vocals. Their debut album *Happy to Meet, Sorry to Part* (1972) was, in keeping with the progressive rock genre of the time, a rich tapestry of sounds – complex arrangements and symphonic textures allied to traditional airs and rhythms. Keyboard player and flautist Jim Lockhart, reflecting on the importance of Horslips and the context from which they emerged, notes:

When we were being pretentious we would say we were trying to forge a new rock and roll idiom. I remember talking to a guy in a band in the early '70s just before Horslips got started. He told me he had written a new song that went 'a nickel is a nickel and a dime is a dime...' I never failed to be overwhelmed by the complete oddness of that situation. A guy who is sitting in Dublin is singing about nickels and dimes! What is all that about? The point was avoiding writing about nickels and dimes and writing about things that had some kind of relevance to us...[10]

In one important sense, then, part of the pleasure in Horslips' music was hearing local place names and local sounds operating within a global rock format. The band challenged the easy and apparently unselfconscious adoption of Americanized references within the local context. However, Horslips did not refer to the mundane and everyday, the quotidian of ordinary life, but focused lyrically on the 'fantastic' – early Irish history, myth and legend. These themes reached their high point in two subsequent albums, *The Táin* (1973) and *The Book of Invasions: A Celtic Symphony* (1976), both generally regarded today as their best albums.

There are two important historical details of the Horslips approach that are worth stressing and which mark them out as true pioneers in the Ireland of the 1970s. The first was that the band brought their synthesis of traditional music, myth and progressive rock to the ballroom circuit throughout rural Ireland. This circuit, although past its mid-1960s heyday and already on the wane, nonetheless still dominated live music in Ireland and was still largely populated by the showbands providing cover versions of top ten hits and standard country and western fare. Lockhart summarized the Horslips strategy:

> We were the first 'non-showband' to go out and play in those venues. If we had an achievement it was that we did so much work in the ballrooms, the significance that we had was giving the kids something that wasn't an import. That in coming to see us, they weren't attempting to be second-hand English kids or second-hand American kids.[11]

There was, as well, a hard-nosed aspect to what the band were doing and this links to their second innovation. Rather than travel to London and try to break into the British market first – as so many Irish bands had done before them, with varying degrees of success – Horslips stayed in Ireland and nurtured their Irish market first. They set up their own record label as well so that all aspects of their strategy were controlled by the band themselves from their base at home.

They used their collective talents beyond music to design their record sleeves and their stage props and to publicize and market their image. For this strategy to become successful, Horslips needed to build up a following in the home market and hence the assault on the ballroom circuit. And from the security of their home base, the idea was to build the audience elsewhere. For Horslips, the strategy only half-worked but the same approach would be adopted in the next decade by U2, with spectacular results.

7.   'Modernizing Irish Tradition' – Horslips (photo: Ian Finlay)

Horslips may not have scaled the heights of international success but they did have a presence and an audience outside of Ireland. In fact, they elicited a range of responses from contrasting audiences and subgroupings that reflected the hybridity of their music. Thus they were able to play in the students' union at the Chelsea College of Art in London in the same year that they also played in the Borderland Ballroom at Muff, Co. Donegal, a few miles from Derry. These seemingly contradictory responses flowed from the meeting of various musical and visual forms. On the one hand they had 'druggy' connotations, as befits the complex structures, improvisation and other aspects of 'psychedelic coding',[12] and on the other hand they wedded these in a creative tension to the naturalistic and 'folkie' associations of traditional music.

As Middleton has pointed out:

> However arbitrary musical meanings and conventions are – rather than being 'natural', or determined by some human essence or by the needs of class expression – once particular musical elements are put together in particular ways, and acquire particular connotations, these can be hard to shift...it is not easy to disturb the connotations of folk song...as signifying 'community'; an organic social harmony.[13]

It is these intimations of an organic community, embedded in some ancient past and in the elemental presence of Nature, that lie behind the music of Dr Strangely Strange and most sublimely of Mellow Candle. When Bob Dylan withdrew from public scrutiny in 1966 he and The Band retired to rural Woodstock to re-engage with American folk traditions, and in many ways this set the template for the folk rock experiments that followed on both sides of the Atlantic. For much of the folk rock emanating from Britain at the same time, the reconfiguring of English traditional music required a retreat from the urban environment, the better to capture the ambience of such organic rural life, again located in the ancient past and conjured up in the old songs. In Ireland, of course, there was another discourse at work in the intimations of the organic community. As we have seen, in John Waters's use of the O'Riada metaphor of the underground stream, there was a strong sense of national identity to this community. It is hard to shift Irish national sentiment and aspiration or notions of the 'authentic' from the meanings which have accrued to traditional music in Ireland, no matter what kind of rock music idiom it has been inserted into and despite the best intentions of the band itself. When wedded to traditionalism in this way (with the added emphasis on the primitive timelessness of Celtic mythology) the rock music idiom runs the risk of being enlisted behind a very traditional notion of rural Irish identity (and O'Riada, as we have seen, reconfigured the music, the better to set it into the standard nationalist narrative of *Mise Éire*).

The irony is that the progressive rock of the late 1960s to early 1970s had countercultural and oppositional connotations linked to experimentation and the avant-garde, a very different set of accrued meanings to those of traditional music. Progressive rock, a heterogeneous mix of styles, emphasized individual virtuosity and personal expression, fetishized complex structures and diverse rhythms, and drew in elements from classical as well as folk music. One way of understanding Horslips, therefore, is that they were caught in a tension between a countercultural ideology of 'opposition' and the more mainstream cultural traditions of rural Ireland. In other words, they could be recruited into supporting traditional nationalist representations of Ireland and the Irish with an appeal to a rural romanticism and pre-industrial primitivism (and undoubtedly they were, both at home and abroad) but they were able to activate these within a 'hippie'-inflected version of the pastoral fantasy centred on alternative ways of living.

The historical judgement on progressive rock of the early to mid-1970s is now (and forever will be) delivered through the filter of punk rock, its great 'other' and it is hard now to appreciate the great critical and popular hold this kind of music had at the time. In discussing progressive rock, John Street argues: 'The music's complex structuring and barrage of sounds denied any opportunity for popular involvement. It was to be admired. In trying to transform popular music into electronic classical music, progressive music was, in fact, "regressive"; it sought to establish aesthetic criteria and patterns of consumption which were both elitist and traditionalist.'[14]

This, however, was patently not the case with Horslips and the popular involvement of the young John Waters was echoed throughout Ireland in the years of Horslips' ascendancy. They were a *dance* band, in the original definition of the word, and much of their music was built on the jigs, reels and rhythms of Irish dancing. Jim Lockhart regarded the incorporation of traditional elements as a way of making the music easier to dance to and accounts of the period reveal that Horslips encouraged popular involvement.[15] If there was a tension or contradiction in the music, then there was also the danger of this raising conflicting audience expectation. On one hand there were audiences composed of (largely middle-class) 'hippies', interested in the psychedelic aspects of the music and performance and who came along to watch, to listen and to be impressed. On the other hand, traditionalists were drawn to the jigs and reels (and frequently complained when the band did not play enough of these). Added to this, the Horslips hybrid certainly offended folk 'purists' who were not only angered by the apparent dilution of traditional form but also by the hedonistic and excessive elements that were now being attached to the folk and traditional modes.

The tension is also in the music itself. Some Horslips albums were poorly received at the time and the reputation of these has not measurably improved as the years have gone by. These are the albums in which Horslips attempted to emphasize their rock band, as opposed to folk/rock, credentials (*The Unfortunate Cup of Tea*, 1975; *Aliens*, 1977; *The Man Who Built America*, 1979; *Short Stories, Tall Tales*, 1980; and maybe even their third album, *Dancehall Sweethearts*, 1974). Their considerable reputation rests on their more traditional music hybrids: the first album, *Happy to Meet, Sorry to Part*, 1972, but especially *The Táin*, 1973; *Drive the Cold Winter Away*, 1976; and *The Book of Invasions: A Celtic Symphony*, 1976. The first album, which contained John Waters's history-shaking 'An Bratach Bán', was an eclectic mix of tunes and ideas that was, in retrospect, merely a statement of intent that was to be realized on later albums (though it contained 'Furniture' which was a big hit in Ireland and became a live favourite with Horslips' audiences).

With *The Táin* and *The Book of Invasions* the musical hybrid was at the service of a retelling of the ancient myths of Ireland so that the musical moods are created to enhance certain narrative moments in the story. *The Táin* is loosely based on the old Irish saga *Táin Bo Cuailgne (The Cattle Raid of Cooley)*, the centrepiece of the Ulster cycle of heroic tales and originally written down in the twelfth century. The songs and instrumental pieces on the album illustrate episodes from the saga and are linked to the key characters in the story – Maeve, the Queen of Connaught, Cuchulainn, the Ulster champion and Ferdia, his relative and hero of Maeve's army. The central spine of the album and the most characteristic Celtic rock elements are the tracks 'Maeve', 'Charolais', 'The March', 'You

Can't Fool the Beast' and 'Dearg Doom', the latter containing the most famous guitar lick in Irish rock. This song best illustrates the way in which Horslips worked. The guitar figure is taken from an old march 'Marcshlua Uí Néill' ('O'Neill's March') but is played on electric guitar with all the verve and thrust of heavy metal rock. The album, and indeed all of the band's early work, is peppered with traditional tunes – reels, jigs, laments, marches – but a rock rhythm section picks up and supports both the electric guitar/keyboards motif of the rock rendering and the more traditional versions played on fiddle, flute or uillean pipes.

'Dearg Doom' became the signature tune of the band and was their most popular and biggest hit. It later became something of a national treasure when it was incorporated into the official 1990 World Cup song for Ireland, 'Put 'em under Pressure', produced by U2's Larry Mullen. The song stayed at number one on the Irish charts for sixteen weeks and became synonymous with Ireland's successful campaign in Italia '90 when the team reached the quarter-finals, causing wild euphoria on the streets of Irish towns and cities. 'Dearg Doom' will forever be associated with those heady days and was the best demonstration of how Horslips, despite their concern with the tales of ancient Ireland, slowly but effectively insinuated themselves into the narrative of contemporary Ireland.

The critics and the Horslips audience were, however, unwilling to allow them to become just another rock band, so that having established the genre and mastered the interplay between the traditional and the contemporary they were not allowed to transcend this. Thus, despite the fact that it stated on the sleeve of the third album *Dancehall Sweethearts* (1974) that eight of the ten tracks had 'traditional airs concealed about their persons' the album was less well-received than either *The Táin* or *The Book of Invasions* because the traditional was, as it were, too far back in the mix. The last few albums which the band released had more or less dispensed with the traditional airs altogether as they pitched for a cleaner rock sound. Despite the fact that it could be argued that these albums are more politically and socially relevant than the early hybrids were (they deal with emigration, exile and the hardship of immigration in the United States from the Famine period onwards) they are largely dismissed in the story of Irish rock as unsuccessful pitches for easy-listening rock. This might suggest, as Street implies, that this forging of progressive rock with traditional elements ultimately has conservative implications. Within the musical hybrid, it was the traditional aspects that were taken to be the most significant and that were celebrated. The elements of progressiveness served to imbue traditionalism with a sense of a future – forward to the past, as it were. In the international arena, Irish rock, it could be argued, was being condemned to its Irishness, the old problem of adhering to colonialism's ethnic definitions (but also of maintaining and consolidating the intertwining of rock and national authenticities).

Horslips broke up in 1980, at the height of the punk explosion in Ireland. They were the first successful band to come out of Ireland trying to marry traditional music with the idioms of rock, and history has been kind to them. Thus, for Gerry Smyth, their achievement is precisely that they negotiated successfully the conservative conundrum. 'Out of such a cultural conundrum, Horslips managed to produce a body of brilliant music.'[16]

RAGGLE TAGGLE GYPSIES

Christy Moore released his second solo album, *Prosperous*, in 1972, the same year that Horslips launched their career and Mellow Candle released the incandescent folk rock of *Swaddling Songs*. If Mellow Candle's album had to wait nearly two decades before it found an audience, Moore and Horslips were immediately successful and Moore's album in particular proved to be one of the most influential albums of the period.

Although released as a Moore solo album, the backing musicians included Andy Irvine, Donal Lunny and uilleann piper Liam Óg O'Flynn, formidable talents in their own right. They joined with Moore later that year to form the band Planxty so that *Prosperous* is effectively the first Planxty album. It also marks a substantial advance for Moore, Lunny and Irvine on their own experiments either solo or with Emmet Spiceland and Sweeney's Men back in the 1960s. The *Prosperous* collection is more assured, more adventurous and more varied than the work of their predecessor bands, involving a range of sources from traditional Irish and Scottish balladry to contemporary songs by Bob Dylan, Woody Guthrie and Moore himself. The album has a strong political theme with songs about injustice, strikes and union struggles predominating but it is in its musical combinations that it marks a significant development for Irish folk song. As well as O'Flynn's uilleann pipes and tin whistle, the album also includes Irvine's mandolin and mouth organ and

Lunny on guitar and bouzouki. The intention of the album is made clear in the opening track in which Moore's version of the old Scottish/Irish ballad 'The Raggle Taggle Gypsy' is set to a new 'traditional' palette of uilleann pipes, mandolin, bouzouki, guitar and tin whistle before segueing into the old harp tune 'Tabhair Dom Do Lámh'/'Give Me Your Hand', a tune revived and popularized some years earlier by Seán O'Riada. The resulting combination neatly captured the twin discourses of Irish music, the traditional ballad and the ancient tunes, reconfiguring them into a new relationship – 'newly strung' for the new times.

'Raggle Taggle Gypsy' was redone to open the first Planxty album proper, also released to great acclaim in 1972. The musical palette on this album was enlarged and expanded and subsequent releases continued the process – as well as Moynihan and Lunny being responsible for introducing the Greek bouzouki, Planxty also introduced the synthesizer, the organ, the mandolin and even the hurdy-gurdy to traditional Irish music. What was happening here was significant. Planxty modernized the ballad tradition by giving the old tunes a contemporary makeover and linking them to the modern folk sound of the 1960s and 1970s. They then expanded on the usual acoustic guitar setting of the folk ballad by adding a traditional music palette. Although the sound remained largely acoustic, the whole approach to the music was 'very rock 'n' roll'. This was especially true in the way in which the band attacked the music, with the kind of verve and energy expected of rock performers.

When Lunny left Planxty in 1974 (to be replaced by Johnny Moynihan, the latter re-establishing his musical partnership with Irvine) he helped set up the equally influential Bothy Band with Matt Molloy on flute and tin whistle, Paddy Keenan on uilleann pipes, Tríona Ní Dhomhnaill on harpsichord, clavinet and vocals, her brother Micheál Ó Dhomhnaill on guitar and vocals and Tommy Peoples on fiddle. On their first album, released in 1975, the band rip through a medley of jigs and reels in the first two tracks, playing them with the speed and phrasing of a rock band before the tempo slows for Tríona Ní Dhomhnaill's slow ballad 'Do You Like Apples?' on track three. This was to be characteristic of The Bothy Band and even more so in live performance where they gave traditional music the pace and excitement of rock. The Bothy Band, in other words, stood up and rocked while The Chieftains, for all their musical probing and experiments, still sat and performed much as O'Riada had done a decade earlier. It was Irish traditional music with a contemporary rhythm section and a contemporary setting. Just as O'Riada earlier had doubts about the manner in which The Chieftains had reconfigured traditional music for the purposes of recording, so too did more purist commentators object to the direction in which Planxty and The Bothy Band were taking the music, especially in live performance with the increasing emphasis on accompaniment and a group dynamic.

Renowned fiddler Paddy Glackin, briefly a member of The Bothy Band when they were first established, argued the point in the 1970s: 'There's a better outlet for traditional music in solo performance. It's essentially a solo art. Groups are only incidental to traditional music.'[17] But as Lunny explained to a puzzled Bill Graham, 'An album of a solo piper is too intense, too demanding for the vast majority of people to sit down and listen to it. You relieve it by accompaniment. You add in various colours, and it also relates to contemporary music, because nearly all contemporary music is accompanied.'[18] Indeed it is this question of accompaniment and the group dynamic that unites the early work of The Johnstons and Sweeney's Men in the 1960s and Planxty and The Bothy Band in the 1970s. 'From a purist point of view,' Lunny continues, 'accompaniment of any kind is a dilution. It's water in the whiskey. And I realise that it's a contradiction to create and expand traditional music in purist terms, because traditional music, by definition, is music the way it was played two hundred years ago. Two hundred years ago, bouzoukis didn't exist.'[19]

However, the template established by Moore on *Prosperous* and pursued by him in his solo career and his careers in both Planxty and Moving Hearts also took the traditional and pushed it in a radical political direction, using the sounds and melodies of old Ireland to chart the injustices, hypocrisies and failings of the new Ireland (and the wider contemporary world). In this sense, Luke Gibbons's injunction that the traditional need not necessarily be conservative and reactionary is apposite.[20] Throughout the 1970s, 1980s and 1990s, Irish traditional music, folk music and balladry were at the cutting edge of change and experiment, 'newly strung' for progressive political and musical purposes. As Gerry Smyth has written of Moore: 'His extensive canon includes material on a variety of subjects sensitive to modern Ireland: emigration, immigration and racism, urban poverty and drugs, the itinerant community and vigilantism, industrial relations, landscape despoliation, religious hypocrisy, and political corruption.'[21]

The one area of this political agenda that caused trouble, though, was when the political turmoil in Northern Ireland was raised. Moore often expressed strong Republican sympathies in his songs, in interviews and through on-stage pronouncements. His political agenda in this regard was to link the situation in Ireland with wider political struggles and with the historical legacies of those who fought against the powerful for justice and basic rights. His songs and pronouncements about Ireland were, therefore, historicized and internationalized. In the end, though, it always came down to the question of whether or not he supported the IRA in the North. This particular controversy reached something of a crisis in 1981 when Moore and Lunny formed their most radical band so far, Moving Hearts, just as tensions in Northern Ireland had reached a critical point with the hunger strikes and the subsequent death of Bobby Sands.

The radicalism of the band was both musical and political. If Lunny's Bothy Band evinced a rock energy in its performance of traditional music, Moving Hearts was a rock band that used traditional elements to create a more challenging hybrid. As well as Moore and Lunny, the original band had Declan Sinnott on electric guitar, Keith Donald on alto sax (a major innovation for traditional music and unusual for mainstream rock), Eoghan O'Neill on electric bass, Brian Calnan on drums and, adding the traditional spine, relative newcomer Davy Spillane on uilleann pipes. The band had, therefore, a core rock sound of bass, guitar and drums around which traditional and jazz elements were woven in alternating fashion or in full-blooded combination. This musical adventurousness was matched by political radicalism and on the first album, released in 1981, there are songs about the nuclear threat, rack-renting landlords, political struggle in general and political struggle in Northern Ireland in particular. The musical and political credentials of the band were laid out unequivocally on the opening track, 'Hiroshima Nagasaki Russian Roulette'. Moore's self-penned anti-nuclear lyric is complemented in turn by acoustic strumming, lead guitar break, sax break and then an uilleann pipe break before the track climaxes with a full-on blast of musical interplay among all the instruments. The rhythm guitar sound is in a very American country music style and has a classic chorus pedal effect. The guitar plays some licks that copy the folk fiddle/pipe sound using some distortion which the sax repeats later on before the pipes and fiddle take on their usual role as the lead motif. All in all, it is quite an interesting mix of electric instruments and classic folk that begins the album in an arresting, and for some, a challenging manner.

For *Hot Press* critic Bill Graham, however, the musical explorations proved less of a problem than the band's stance on Northern Ireland. Graham objected in particular to the song 'No Time for Love' (that is, when there is a war to be fought there is no time for love, the reverse of the old hippy mantra). The lines that particularly irked Graham were 'The fish need the sea to survive/Just like your comrades need you/And the death squad can only get through to them/If first they can get through to you.' These sentiments, according to Graham, were filched from the Maoist revolutionary instruction manual suggesting that the people need to nourish and protect the gunmen just as the sea protects the fish (the same revolutionary metaphor, incidentally, that lay behind the name of the old hippy band, Country Joe and the Fish). In a tetchy interview with the band, Graham describes their political stance as naive and dangerous and throws down a challenge to them. 'If they intend to be "relevant"', he finishes off his piece, 'here's an issue from this week's papers – the Northern Ireland gay community, scourged by Paisley, O'Fiach [sic], the RUC, IRA, UDA and British Army, who had to go to the European Court of Human Rights for justice. Would Moving Hearts take songs supporting homosexuals to the halls?'[22]

The answer was, yes – probably. The band's second album, *Dark End of the Street* (1982), featured the eponymous song with its celebrated lyric about a socially unacceptable love affair being conducted in the shadows after dark. The song was originally read as adulterous but here the words are slightly reconfigured to also suggest a gay relationship. The cover of the album, showing two suspiciously male-looking silhouettes inhabiting the darkened shadows of a city street, only added to the impression that Moving Hearts had risen to Graham's challenge, making this one of the earliest (if indirect) references in Irish rock or popular music to the politics of the gay community.

The first two Moving Hearts' albums from 1981 and 1982 mark the culmination of the folk rock/trad experiments of the 1970s in terms of both the music and the politics. The musical palette suggested by the band was rock-based, as opposed to folk-based, and this was a tacit acknowledgement that by the dawn of the 1980s a new era in Irish rock had already begun. However in the space of just over ten years, folk and traditional music in Ireland, once seen as the preserve of and expression of a rural conservative Catholic ethos, had now been transformed into cutting-edge music inhabiting the dark spaces of urban culture and addressing its attendant class and gender politics.

These musical interchanges in the 1970s were dizzying and the results radical and adventurous. The thread that unites all of the experiments discussed here is that they start from the richness of the folk and traditional music cultures in Ireland and attempt to give them a contemporary relevance. But by the end of the 1970s, rock and popular music, in Ireland as elsewhere, was about to get a massive shake-up and the folk experiments were about to be shaken and stirred in an altogether more frenetic fashion. One result was the emergence in London of The Pogues, an extraordinary fusing of traditional music, balladry and punk.

TRADITIONAL PUNK: THE POGUES

Formed in King's Cross, London, in 1982, The Pogues began their career playing rebel songs in Irish pubs and busking on the streets of the predominately Irish enclave of Kilburn. Eamonn McCann has appropriately described The Pogues as 'Irish music viewed through the prism of a North London sensibility'[23] and, as Nuala O'Connor argues, the result was a belligerent interpretation and anarchic performance of traditional songs which served as an 'antidote to the stultification of folk music by purists'.[24] Elvis Costello famously and succinctly defined it: 'The Pogues saved folk from the folkies.'[25] Folk purism, certainly, was often intertwined with a narrow cultural nationalism and no doubt the music of The Pogues did, indeed, offend purists. There is, however, a suggestion in both O'Connor and Costello that somehow, through it all, The Pogues saved and reinforced tradition. However, it is precisely their very ambivalent relationship to tradition which makes them so interesting.

The Pogues used and abused blatant Irish stereotypes. In their music and performance, the nostalgic associations of Irish music were wrenched out of their context both by the irreverent way that folk forms were played (and played with) and in the lyrical associations that were attached to them. The Pogues parody and interrogate aspects of Irishness in complex and confusing ways and to see in them only a lack of positive stereotyping is to miss the point. What is interesting about them is the full range of characterization present – the drunken, sentimental, homesick, pathetic and nostalgic Irish in tandem with representations of an Ireland collapsing under the weight of tradition and economic peripherality.

The Pogues address the Irish emigrant through song narratives that offer an 'in-betweenness'. Within this there is a critique, through parody, of national stereotypes. They rant about the absurdity of nostalgia for Ireland and twist and bend sentimental ballads to re-articulate feelings of alienation in London or New York, capturing the pain and the hurt of the emigrant's experience as well as the exhilaration of escape. Although the boundary between parody and pastiche is not always clear, The Pogues introduce a debate within the Irish diaspora about the relationship between (the differently constructed) centre and periphery (and at the same time provide good rousing party music). The cover of their 1985 album, *Rum, Sodomy and The Lash*, based on French Romantic painter Gericault's *The Raft of the Medusa*, depicts the members of the band out at sea, 'in between worlds', looking for land. The tensions in The Pogues (between tradition and travesty, between insult and invocation, between critique and celebration) flows from their layered articulation of Irishness and offers an alternative to the narrow readings suggested either in their status as 'folk saviours' or in denigrating them as aberrations.[26]

The Pogues confirm that traditionalism does not (reductively) always equal conservatism. Coming in the 1980s, after the punk upheaval and after the years of careful folk experimentation, The Pogues were the last and very striking break with the narrow range of registers that had been associated with the music in the 1950s. The reconfiguring of Irish folk and tradition was, for the time being, completed.

Since the mid-1990s, The Corrs have been the most visible and commercially successful manifestation of this long tradition of hybridizing Irish folk and traditional modes with pop and rock conventions. However, The Corrs may be regarded as The Pogues' opposite. While the latter irreverently 'punked-up' traditional songs, The Corrs married traditional stylings to a more 'mainstream' pop aesthetic. This has led to the band being regarded as a traditional version of The Nolan Sisters or an Irish version of that fictional 1970s television pop family, The Partridge Family. The participant interviewees in John O'Flynn's *The Irishness of Irish Music* reveal some of the range of contradictory responses that The Corrs elicit. While many note the quality of the band's musicianship, nonetheless the use of 'light' pop appears to sit ill against the perceived 'weight' of Irish cultural traditions.[27] Thus, while the Corrs' fusion has found international success, it has not always been critically well received.

NOTES

1. Jim Lockhart, interview by Noel McLaughlin, 1995 (unpublished).
2. Steve Turner, 'Mike Oldfield', for *Rolling Stone*, 1975, unpublished, at http://www.rocksbackpages.com/article.html?ArticleID=2089&SearchText=mike+oldfield.
3. Christy Moore, http://www.christymoore.com/news/January—-February-2011-/.
4. Fred Dellar, 'The Chieftains: How to Record 4 Albums in 18 Years, and still sell out the Albert Hall', *NME*, 22 March 1975.
5. Clinton Heylin, *Dylan: Behind the Shades* (Harmondsworth: Penguin, 1991), p.417.
6. Sean Campbell and Gerry Smyth, *Beautiful Day: Forty Years of Irish Rock* (Cork: Atrium Press, 2005), p.41.
7. Colin Harper and Trevor Hodgett, *Irish Folk, Trad and Blues: A Secret History* (Cork: Collins Press, 2004), p.259.
8. John Waters, *Race of Angels: Ireland and the Genesis of U2* (Belfast: Blackstaff Press, 1994), p.97.
9. Ibid.
10. Lockhart, interview.
11. Ibid.
12. S. Whiteley, *The Space Between the Notes: Rock and the Counter-Culture* (London: Routledge, 1994).
13. Richard Middleton, *Studying Popular Music* (Milton Keynes: Open University Press, 1990), p.10.
14. John Street, *Rebel Rock: The Politics of Popular Music* (Oxford: Blackwell, 1986), p.101.
15. Lockhart, interview. See also accounts of the band's performances in Prendergast, *The Isle of Noises: Rock and Roll's Roots in Ireland* (Dublin: O'Brien Press, 1987), pp.79–86; and N. O'Connor, *Bringing it All Back Home* (London: BBC Books, 1991), pp.122–4.
16. Gerry Smyth, *Noisy Island: A Short History of Irish Popular Music* (Cork: Cork University Press, 2005), p.45.
17. Julian Vignoles, 'Going Against the Trends', *Hot Press*, 21 July 1977. http://www.hotpress.com/archive/425906.html (accessed 23 March 2010).
18. Bill Graham, 'Look What They've Done to Our Songs, Ma?', *Hot Press*, 4 August 1977. http://www.hotpress.com/archive/425870.html (accessed 23 March 2010).
19. Graham, 'Look what They've Done'.
20. Luke Gibbons, *Edmund Burke and Ireland* (Cambridge: Cambridge University Press, 2003).
21. Gerry Smyth, *Music in Irish Cultural History* (Dublin: Irish Academic Press, 2009), p.130.
22. Bill Graham, 'Irish Ways...Irish Laws: The Moving Hearts Interview', *Hot Press*, 24 October 1981. http://www.hotpress.com/archive/431544.html (accessed 23 March 2010).
23. O'Connor, *Bringing it all Back Home*, p.158.

24. Ibid., p.159.
25. Ibid.
26. For a fuller discussion of The Pogues and their cultural significance, see Sean Campbell, *Irish Blood, English Heart: Second-Generation Irish Musicians in England* (Cork: Cork University Press, 2011), pp.59–101.
27. John O'Flynn, *The Irishness of Irish Music* (Farnham: Ashgate, 2009), pp.140, 161–2.

4

Irish Rock Exiles

The important thing was just to get out, to escape to London... on the fastest boat possible. Dublin was bleak and stifling... A band gets a kind of tunnel vision – get out, get ahead – London was the fantasy escape. (Fachtna O'Ceallaigh)[1]

We lived in a van. The roof had a hole, so we had to park under a bridge. Any time we came across a gig we used to go down to the toilets in Leicester Square to change our gear and have a wash and brush up. (Henry McCullough)[2]

We had lost what we set out to do when we left Ireland. (Dave Lewis)[3]

One of the peculiarities of Irish culture is that while it maintains a strong national differentiation from Britain it also shares a large element of a common culture with its near neighbour. This is most evident in the fact that both are now (largely) English-speaking cultures so that the Irish enjoy British film and television; newspapers, magazines and journals; and literature and music, with as much ease and with as much relish as the British do. Irish supporters follow English (and Scottish) football teams with the same enthusiasm (and fanaticism) as the teams' local supporters do.

Britain and Ireland also share in large measure a common, if disputed, history. Ireland is, of course, a former colony of Britain, and Northern Ireland is still part of the United Kingdom so that one of the conundrums of the Irish experience is that it is both post-colonial and neo-colonial; national and regional; periphery and centre. As a result, Irish culture in general displays a complex set of some-times contradictory characteristics, and Irish artists work within, and against, such an intricate web of social, economic, political and cultural influences that their art raises dizzying questions about national identity. The case of Them is illuminating in this regard.

Coming from Belfast, they were Northern Irish (whatever that might mean) but were they also an Ulster band, as Billy Harrison suggested? An Irish band, as Van Morrison proposed? A northern band, as the Dublin audiences saw them? A Prod band as Johnny Rogan suggested or a British 'invasion' band, as the American view would have it? They were, of course, a rhythm and blues band but that only adds to the conundrum. Irish rock bands in the main play a brand of Anglo-American music and respond as much to influences from California and the American Deep South as they do to those from London, Liverpool, Dublin or Belfast. Irish rock music, in other words, inhabits that peculiar space that exists where the national and the global meet.

The problem in the 1960s and 1970s was that once a band reached a certain level of success in Ireland, the options were limited in regard to further progress. Despite the great strides that beat group culture had made in the 1960s, by the 1970s there were still too few venues, the infrastructure was still too primitive (especially for recording) and the media outlets, such as they were, were still too dominated by either the showbands or by folk/traditional music. The pattern that had been established by Them in 1964 – conquer the home market first and then move to London to record and build up a larger metropolitan following – was the only option open to ambitious Irish rock bands. There was a feeling as well that Ireland was rather peripheral to the great cultural upheavals that were part of the times – that as the rest of the world rocked, rolled and got high, Ireland was still half asleep watching it all on television. In the absence of radio and television programming at home which directly catered for the needs of the Irish rock and pop fan, British programmes such as *Ready Steady Go*, *Thank Your Lucky Stars* and *Top of the Pops* and, later, *The Old Grey Whistle Test* were required viewing for the rock fans of the 1960s and 1970s in Ireland. The British rock and pop scene next door, in other words, was the height of cool.

The result was that many of Ireland's best bands and most interesting musicians moved out, and if they succeeded they remained in exile, or if they failed they returned home to Ireland, often frustrated, demoralized and disillusioned. Another aspect of this pattern was that very often the bands that moved to England and signed to major labels were subject to the whims and machinations of the label management. The bands lost control of their own destiny, especially in the recording studio, just as Them had back in 1964–65. Them had succeeded but, if Billy Harrison and Van Morrison's version of events is to be believed, they did so despite being exploited, ripped off and cheated through dodgy contracts and musical opportunism. Morrison himself, of course, was to succeed in spectacular fashion as a solo artist when he moved to the United States and became Ireland's most celebrated musical exile. As the 1970s approached, however, there were as many casualties of the move to London as there were successes, leaving a lot of high-profile musical potential left unrealized.

The negative side of the London experience can be seen in the relative commercial failure of four of Ireland's best and most gifted bands. Granny's Intentions, Skid Row, The Method and The People all moved to London and looked set at one point to break through into the big time. However, they all eventually fell apart, wracked internally by the pressures (and poverty) that the pursuit of fame and fortune entailed and suffering from the kind of interference and industry machinations that Morrison has spent a lifetime railing against. What each band has done, though, is to leave behind at least one album that today confirms the quality they had at the time and tantalizes the contemporary audience with a sense of what might have been.

The two bands from Northern Ireland, The Method and The People, were to go through a name change as part of the move to London. The Method became Andwella's Dream (later Andwella), a name that reflected well enough the changing direction of the band from hard-nosed three-piece blues band to the kind of post-Hendrix psychedelic rock of the time. The name change also reflected the kind of songwriting now favoured by the band's main creative force, Dave Lewis. The ambience of the times is captured on the band's first album, *Love and Poetry* (1969), a kind of naive rustic innocence celebrated against acoustic guitar and bluesy electric solos (with intermittent bells and flutes giving it the requisite ethereal quality). The album's third track, 'Lost a Number, Found a King', is just such a melange – the bells and the flute conjuring up some mountain scene from Greek mythology with nymphs, satyrs and gods wallowing in the sun and then Lewis's surprisingly bluesy lyrics narrating a tale of an imagined Utopia of friends, peace and love. The sound on the album suggests Procol Harum, Traffic and 'White Album'-era Beatles with Cream or Hendrix guitar flourishes, an eclectic mix that locates the whole firmly in the summer of 1969. All the songs were written (and sung) by Lewis. These vary from acoustic soft rock to psychedelic workouts, with the occasional reminder of the band's harder Belfast roots in some of the singing, guitar and swirling keyboards (this is especially true on 'Cocaine' before the studio phasing and trippy sound effects take over). The album throughout exudes a quality of writing and performance that still seems remarkable today (O'Halloran suggests that it is possibly the best Irish rock album of the 1960s).[4] It shows its age, there is no doubt, with some of the excesses of the period sounding dated to the contemporary ear, but it is a strong collection that stands comparison with a lot of the more successful music of the time. The album did not sell, however, despite good reviews and it remains a cult curio (though apparently Lewis and his music really are big in Japan).[5]

If Dave Lewis was happy with the name change of his band, the same could not be said in regard to The People. This band, featuring originally the incomparable guitar playing of Henry McCullough, went to London as a tight R&B band in the Belfast mode but became the psychedelic Eire Apparent, the faintly ridiculous name imposed on them by the management of Chas Chandler and Mike Jeffery, the team behind the burgeoning career of Jimi Hendrix. Chandler adopted the band and, impressed by the fact that Hendrix himself rated McCullough's guitar playing, he arranged for them to go on tour in the United States and Canada with Hendrix and Pink Floyd. McCullough was asked to leave the band when he was arrested in Canada for possession of marijuana, an incident that he remembers with some bitterness as being 'sacked' by a cynical management. Drugs were undoubtedly a problem for many of the 1960s rock generation and high-profile drugs busts were common, but McCullough's take on the incident indicates another issue that dogged the bands at the time: 'I was shell-shocked getting the sack but I was the most rebellious in the band and they probably felt that if they got me out it might be easier to manipulate the rest.'[6] The issue here was money and it seemed that precious little of it was finding its way into the band's pockets. As McCullough remembered acerbically, 'I would wonder why we didn't have any money after a particular night after the gig being packed. "Don't worry, it will all go into your off-shore account, Henry." '[7]

Management manipulation went further than this, of course, and another recurring factor was the way in which the creative aspect of the group was moulded to fit a certain perception of chart success. All members of the band seemed dissatisfied with the choice of song chosen for the first single, 'Follow Me', as bass player Chris Stewart recalls: 'We weren't keen but Chas was the boss. We were an R&B/rock 'n' roll band, but the manager said this was the path we had to take.'[8] McCullough returned to Ireland, briefly joining Sweeney's Men before going on to Joe Cocker's Grease Band and Woodstock immortality. Eire Apparent, with Mike Cox replacing McCullough, stayed in the United States and continued to tour with Hendrix, eventually releasing an album, *Sunrise* (1969), on the small New York Buddah label with Hendrix producing and adding guitar textures to many of the tracks. This is another Irish psychedelic album very much of its time, its pop tunes psyched up with some studio effects and Hendrix's guitar. The lead track, 'Yes, I Need Someone', has long been a favourite on psychedelic compilation albums and the album itself, not least because of the Hendrix connection, has long been a cult favourite and an essential item for completists.

But again, despite the top-quality producer and guest guitar player, the album failed to launch the band into the big league (it sold reasonably well in the United States but did not do well enough to breach the charts). The combination of old-style pop – some of the songs are borderline 'bubblegum' – and psyched-up production makes for an uneven experience. There is an undoubted psychedelic classic in Cox's 'Mr Guy Fawkes' with its complex structure reminiscent of The Beatles' 'A Day in the Life'. A version of this track was recorded by New Zealand/Australian band The Dave Miller Set and was a big Australian hit in the late summer of 1969, providing one of the key sounds for Australian psychedelic pop.[9] The single 'Rock 'n' Roll Band' (included on the CD version of the album) is a pleasing mix of light pop and Hendrix guitar rock, but again it failed to breach the charts or to launch the band into the big time. Nonetheless, the album's overall tunefulness and the quality of the musicianship suggest that had the band been supported more by the management team after *Sunrise* was released, especially in Britain, things might have been different. It is also tempting to wonder what might have ensued if McCullough had also been supported at the time of his drugs bust and had been able to work with Hendrix during the writing and recording of the album.

The common denominator in the other two 'nearly' bands of the time, Skid Row from Dublin and Granny's Intentions from Limerick, is blues rock guitarist Gary Moore who had moved to Dublin from his native Belfast in 1969 at the age of 16. He joined Brush Shiels's Skid Row and quickly established himself as something of a guitar prodigy. Both bands had been around for a number of years by the time Moore arrived in Dublin. Granny's Intentions had started off playing soul music with a strong preference for Tamla Motown classics and relied on the considerable vocal talents of lead singer Johnny Duhan for impact. They quickly became a top attraction on the Dublin beat scene during 1966. In 1967, they moved to London and signed to the Deram label. They released a self-penned single, 'The Story of David', the same year, a song about a failed poet, its satisfyingly soulful narrative set against John Ryan's whirling organ and sung with earthy conviction by Duhan. The charts at the time, however, though full of all kinds of odd sounds and stories, were not awash with songs about failure, poetic or otherwise, and the single failed to chart in Britain. As a consequence, the record company took over creative control and the band's next two singles were written and moulded for them. 'Never an Everyday Thing' (1968) was a basic reworking of the Love Affair sound ('Everlasting Love' had been a big hit in Britain in January 1968) and while it failed again in Britain it was a big hit in Ireland where the band's popularity remained undiminished. The lack of chart success in Britain drained the band's confidence and by 1969 the core was reduced to vocalist Johnny Duhan, keyboard player John Ryan and guitarist Johnny Hockedy. To get an album recorded, Granny's Intentions hired (or borrowed) both Noel Bridgeman and Gary Moore from Skid Row and their one album, *Honest Injun*, was finally released in May 1970, four years after they had established themselves on the Dublin beat scene.

By this time, musical tastes had changed and the band's sound had moved on from the Tamla soul of 1966 to include also the more bluesy country rock of 1970. The album reflected these two influences. The centrepiece is the eight-minute sequence 'With Salty Eyes, Dirty Lies', two separate songs about the end of a relationship that are run together to showcase the band's versatility and the strength of the writing. The track begins in Tamla mode with Moore's guitar and a full brass section complementing Duhan's strong vocals, the whole reminiscent of other 'white' soul/jazz combinations of the time, like Blood, Sweat and Tears or early Chicago. At about three minutes in, the tempo changes and Duhan begins the second song, 'Dirty Lies', in full country rock mode with harmonica and guitar replacing the brass. Throughout, Moore's unmistakeable bluesy rock guitar holds the song together and provides tasteful lead licks to the country rock beat. It is an impressive sequence and complements well the other sounds across the album, including the more folksy tracks 'Fourthskin Blues' and 'Nutmeg, Bittersweet' with their Jethro Tull-like flute. *Honest Injun* is a strong debut album, a range of good original songs well played and sung with conviction by a vocalist with a good rock register. The album is eclectic, certainly, and this no doubt confused both the record company and the punters, but the standard of playing, writing and performing is excellent and the tasteful soloing from Moore is distinctive. The fact that the album failed to sell or to advance the band's appeal proba-bly reflects the fact that by this stage the musical landscape had become extremely complex. Despite the undoubted quality of writ-ing and performance the dominant sound on the album is that of a band falling between musical stools.

Skid Row, meanwhile, having ditched original singer Phil Lynott, now consisted of Brush Shiels, Noel Bridgeman and Gary Moore and they released their first album, *Skid* in October 1970, just five months after Granny's Intentions' *Honest Injun*. The album reached number thirty in the British charts before plummeting out to obscu-rity but this limited success suggests that the band, with such a charismatic guitar virtuoso in its ranks, should have had a long and successful future ahead. However, despite extensive gigging in Britain and the United States the band did not make it and the two Skid Row albums (*34 Hours* was released in 1971) stand as testa-ment to what might have been. In many ways, Skid Row's problem was that they were too experimental for the record-listening audi-ence, at one time sounding like a template for heavy metal and at other times, as with Granny's Intentions, sounding like an Irish response to American country rock. The single released from the *34 Hours* album was 'Night of the Warm Witch' which is a heavy rock number with echoes of Cream from the late 1960s. At four-and-a-half minutes the track is tight, with searing Gary Moore guitar breaks illuminating Brush Shiels's powerful vocals. The album, however, opens with a nine-minute version of the same song, this time dressed out in an experimental soundscape that includes wah-wah guitar screeches and long solos that reflect the band's (or Shiels's) predilection for jazzy improvisations. What is an almost classic rock song in its single version becomes an extended noodle on the album, a problem that Brush Shiels acknowledges himself:

> ...it had been getting so intricate that nobody knew *what* we were doing. That was the problem, and it was basically my fault. I'm very extreme: I'm either very intricate or I won't play at all.[10]

The other problem with the album was that the heavy rock/improvisational pieces sit strangely beside the more country rock songs. 'Lonesome Still' is classic country rock and it is brought home in a tight four minutes with Moore's mournful country guitar perfectly dovetailing Shiels's lugubrious country vocals. Better still is the album's third track, 'Mar', which manages to segue Shiels's soulful country vocal into a searing Moore guitar solo while holding on to the country feel. The track returns to the country lament by the end, having moved across the full range of the Skid Row sound of experimental heavy rock and country blues. The experimental side of Skid Row (and Brush Shiels) was more evident on 'Felicity', the last track on the first album, an eleven-minute extended improvisation of bass, guitar and drum that tasked the listener's patience. The album also contains Brush Shiels's bitter tirade against the showbands, 'Unco-op Showband Blues' (running at a mere six minutes), and in its extended guitar breaks, bass and drum solos and the interplay across all the instruments, the track launches an aural tirade against the pop and cover song ethos of the showbands. Following the sudden and unexpected death of Gary Moore (at age 58) in February 2011, a performance of Skid Row doing 'Unco-op Showband Blues' turned up on YouTube. What is obvious from this early footage is that the band also challenged the showband ethos in visual terms as well as in sound. Skid Row and Brush Shiels took no prisoners. And perhaps this is why, in the end, despite the quality of the playing and the performance, Skid Row failed to find, or sustain, an audience.

What Irish rock is left with, however, in the experience of these four undoubtedly gifted and creative rock bands is a tantalizing glimpse of what might have been. The bands themselves achieved a certain degree of success in live performance and, especially in the case of Eire Apparent and Skid Row, they played at the highest level with bands that were, or would go on to be, huge recording successes. But none of the four managed to take that final step into the big league and the albums they have left behind map out an alternative narrative of Irish rock music history.

Many of the gifted individuals involved in these bands – Dave Lewis from Andwella, Henry McCullough from Eire Apparent, Johnny Duhan from Granny's Intentions, and Gary Moore and Brush Shiels from Skid Row – went on to enjoy either major local success or a measure of international acclaim so that the potential evident in the albums was realized to some extent. But their potential as leading bands in the emergence of an Irish rock culture was unrealized and their failure to build on their local Irish success was to reinforce the sense of isolation that had always dominated the scene in Ireland. It would be some years still before that sense of isolation would be broken.

That sense of isolation, of marginalization, was reinforced by the fact that those major rock acts who left Ireland and *did* succeed were to remain in exile throughout the 1970s. Rory Gallagher and Taste emerged from provincial Ireland (Donegal via Cork) and forged their distinctive sound in the R&B and blues clubs of the main cities of Dublin and Belfast. Phil Lynott and Thin Lizzy emerged from the Dublin rock world itself, where in the late 1960s rock, folk and traditional music rubbed shoulders with poetry and drama. The differing experiences shaped the music of both and defined their relationship to rock authenticity.

RORY GALLAGHER AND TASTE

Rory Gallagher may be on the minds of many people this morning, following his premature death at 47 in a London hospital on Wednesday, but how many of them were thinking about him on Tuesday? (Joe Jackson)[11]

He had a lot of integrity and a complete devotion to making music that was authentic. (Niall Stokes)[12]

Joe Jackson's *Irish Times* tribute to Rory Gallagher emphasized what was undoubtedly one of the ironic aspects of his worldwide success. Despite the international acclaim and the huge album sales, Gallagher's adherence to a purist blues music meant that he had largely been forgotten by the general rock and pop audience by the time of his death on 14 June 1995. His dedication, in other words, to the kind of musical authenticity that Stokes refers to had seen him become a marginal figure to the continuing and evolving development of popular music and left him marooned on the fringes of public awareness. Gallagher and his band Taste were one of the groups that took over residency in the Maritime when Them and Morrison moved away and if he later left the Maritime himself to greater success, the Maritime ethos of uncompromising roots music never left him. From the beginning Taste were a three-piece, with fellow Cork musicians Eric Kitteringham on bass and Norman Damery on drums, a format similar to Cream, formed a few months earlier to great acclaim in Britain. Gallagher based his band in Belfast during 1966–67 and from here toured regularly around the clubs both north and south of the city (so that, for example, Taste turned up at least once a month in Derry's Embassy Ballroom at the Sunday night beat music sessions). During these years of hard gigging, Gallagher honed his virtuoso style and the band built up a large and singularly dedicated following (largely male, a factor that was also evident in the 1970s at the height of his international fame). For Gallagher, playing live to this audience was what defined his approach to the music. 'The clubs are the heartbeat of the music industry,' he told Keith Altham in 1971, just as his star as a solo artist was on the rise, 'they are where the groups are born and where they draw their soul from – right from the floorboards…If you want to get your head and your heart sorted out there is only one way – play to the people on the floor.'[13] This is the philosophy that was to determine the direction of Gallagher's successful solo career – live albums marking out the passage of his pilgrimage around the world's clubs and stadia.

Inevitably, having established themselves in Ireland, Taste moved to London in 1968. Gallagher had, in the meantime, changed things around, bringing in the line-up that would record the band's only two albums, with Richard McCracken on bass and John Wilson on drums. The band's reputation in Britain began to grow, the result of storming live performances in clubs such as The Marquee and a hectic schedule playing in the blues and R&B clubs the length and breadth of Britain. Taste's success in Britain is bounded by two performances in particular. On 26 October 1968 they were support band at Cream's farewell concert at the Royal Albert Hall, and the fact that they were to become Britain's pre-eminent rock blues trio on Cream's demise meant that Taste acquired the mantle of successors, much to the band's disadvantage (especially when they were dubbed 'lite-Cream'). Almost two years later, on 29 August they opened the main evening programme on the Friday of the Isle of Wight festival, their sturdy rock blues and extended guitar routines getting the now-legendary event off to a rousing start. Between these two events, the band released two albums, *Taste* in 1969 and *On the Boards* in 1970, the latter confirming the band's growing popularity by reaching the top twenty in the UK album chart.

Both albums highlight the strengths and weaknesses of Gallagher's commitment to the blues – his superb guitar playing as well as (at least for the record listener) the tedium of a relatively unchanging format. During Taste's slow but perceptible rise in the clubs of Ireland and then later in Britain, the Gallagher self-penned song 'Blister on the Moon' was a highlight of their live show, a rocky but melodic blues with crashing power chords, a driving guitar riff and pleasing changes of pace that play with and then satisfy the listener's expectations. As a single (which didn't chart) and the lead track on the album it comes across as a strong piece of rock blues but the recording doesn't capture the live performance – the sheer guitar 'blister' that the track's very name portended. Also, and this was often a problem with Gallagher, the lyrics in the recorded version stand out in a way that they didn't in the live show – as a record, the lyrics were foregrounded in the mix whereas live they were part of the overall aural texture. Gallagher's lyrics were never his strongest card and here – a rant against the establishment and its suppression of creativity and individualism – the lyrics merely sound weak against the glorious bluster of the music ('Everybody's saying what to do and what to think/And when to ask permission if you feel you want to blink').

The second track on the album, by contrast, is a bottleneck guitar version of Leadbelly's 'Leavin' Blues' which, as well as reinforcing the virtuoso quality of Gallagher's lead guitar, shows off the drums and bass to good effect. It may be a Leadbelly original but here it is given the white rock blues treatment, the folk blues electrified for the rock audience. The album amply demonstrates Gallagher's acoustic styling as well, especially on his original blues, 'Hail'. Indeed, throughout his career, Gallagher recorded and played live a whole range of acoustic songs and a compilation of these was posthumously released in 2003 as *Wheels Within Wheels*. The 'B' side of the first single, 'Born on the Wrong Side of Time', is another stately power rock song with interesting time and tempo changes (though, like 'Blister', with rather banal lyrics). This was a problem with much of Gallagher's songwriting – the sophistication and technical brilliance of his guitar playing was in stark contrast to the undistinguished and indistinguishable nature of many of the songs and the often obscure banality of their lyrics. Certainly, his writing improved from the rawness of the first Taste album and the second, *On the Boards*, was an altogether more sophisticated affair – more varied, more adventurous and more tuneful without losing the previous album's commitment to the blues. Gallagher attempts to broaden the blues palette, and the added sax and harmonica on some tracks provides a more satisfying range of aural textures than the hard grind of guitar blues on the first album. But this is mere tinkering within a rigid formula and for the rest of his career he was content to work within a style he mastered in the 1960s, a trio of electric guitar, bass and drums with the occasional embellishment of harmonica and other instruments.

He retained, in other words, the basic blues format of Taste even after he broke up the band, perhaps just ahead of it imploding: 'I remember playing the Isle of Wight Festival and we weren't talking to each other then. We took the ferry across, and we put on a reasonable show and got a great reaction, but musically it was all over between us.'[14] One might speculate that Gallagher's single-minded commitment to rock blues was becoming a problem for the others but by then he had established his template, a narrow one but one in which he excelled as a guitar virtuoso and this mattered more to him than making the concessions that might be required to achieve greater commercial success. His solo recording career began with the eponymously named 1971 album and although here there is an even greater variety of instrumentation – mandolin and piano as well as sax and harmonica – and a surer touch with melody and lyric, in the end it is essentially Rory with a three-piece band playing out the blues in the time-honoured manner.

8. 'A dogged commitment to live blues' – Rory Gallagher and Taste

Gallagher was prolific in these years and he followed up his second solo album, *Deuce* (1971), with *Live in Europe* (1972), the album that gave him his biggest hit and established his credentials as the era's finest blues guitarist. It also established his reputation as a live performer. Gallagher and his various bands were better as a live rather than as a recorded experience and much of what he tried to achieve on record was dictated by the desire to recreate on disc the spontaneity of the live event. As he observed early on: 'People like Blind Man Fuller...were musical entities unto themselves. Just one man in a chair playing guitar into one microphone and if you listen to those records they achieved feeling without all the present day recording techniques.'[15] Of course, no matter how ecstatic it has been, the live performance dissipates into the ether and becomes entombed eventually in the fading memories of the audience member. Like the tree falling silently in the forest, live music runs the risk of being rendered 'soundless' when the audience has gone and the live album at least remains as empirical evidence that it happened. The good thing about the prolific years of Gallagher's recording is that his incredible guitar playing has been preserved for posterity, both as live event and record, and as the years move on it is these records that will be remembered by history and not those coruscating live performances on which his reputation was built.

It has to be said as well that Gallagher was dismissive of the trappings of rock star success and wanted no part of the glamour superstardom of 1970s rock. He achieved a level of international celebrity during his 1970s heyday by adopting the persona of an 'everyman' blues guitarist – the blues for the blue-collar (male) audience and this is what suited him best: 'I want to be able to go to pubs, restaurants and places without feeling that I am a freak. I want to be able to go to the bar next to the gig and be able to talk to people. I can. I do. Once you get to a super-star status and your whole life swings out of control – normalcy gets lost.'[16] Rory Gallagher's integrity to what was seen as a more authentic kind of music won him praise and support from the blues cognoscenti but this was at the expense of a wider audience. Once the blues boom had passed and rock music had moved into and experimented across a range of disparate styles, Gallagher's appeal retreated back to a small minority of blues enthusiasts. He was, in the strict sense of the word, Ireland's first authentic rock star but, in the end, that very authenticity limited his appeal.

PHIL LYNOTT AND THIN LIZZY

Phil was the first proper Irish rock star. (Bob Geldof)[17]

Phil Lynott is now the most credible and accessible symbol of rock stardom that Britain possesses. (Chris Salewicz)[18]

Is the real clue to Phil Lynott's soul contained within his being a half-caste Celt with all the weirdness of the psyche that that implies? (Chris Salewicz)[19]

In an important and influential essay on rock music and sexuality, Simon Frith and Angela McRobbie refer to Thin Lizzy, and especially their bass player, singer and main songwriter Phil Lynott, as the embodiment of what they term 'cock rock':

> By cock rock we mean music making in which performance is an explicit, crude and often aggressive expression of male sexuality...The most popular exponents of this form currently are Thin Lizzy...Cock rock performers are aggressive, dominating, boastful and constantly seek to remind the audience of their prowess, their control.[20]

They use the album cover from the band's 1978 release, *Live and Dangerous*, to illustrate the point. The cover is a low angle 'crotch shot' of a bare-chested Lynott, his phallic bass guitar resting on his upper thigh as he (seemingly) groans in sexual ecstasy. As an illustration of their thesis on 'cock rock' there could have been no better image. The authors even refer to Lynott's notorious challenge to the audience heard on the album: 'Is there anybody here with any Irish in them? Is there any of the girls who would like a little more Irish in them?'[21] There can be no doubt that on the surface, Thin Lizzy were cock rock par excellence and at times Lynott seemed to deliberately go out of his way to push the image as far as he could (on tracks such as 'S&M' from 1979's *Black Rose* album and 'Killer on the Loose' and its execrable B-side 'Don't Play Around', the single released in 1980 at the height of the Yorkshire Ripper panic in Britain). But what Frith and McRobbie miss is that much of this was itself a pose, a point picked up at the same time by Peter Silverton, reviewing a concert in New York (with Gary Moore and Scott Gorham on twin lead guitar) in December 1978:

Although there's still all that macho bullshit deep down in there some-where, they treat it with something like affectionate parody. There's a moment at the end of 'Don't Believe A Word' when Phil, Scott and Gary hit that three men in a line and enacting every kid's fantasy of being a rock star that must be the perfect choreographed front line pose of all time.[22]

There was a lot more going on within the band and especially within Phil Lynott than merely posing, and the joke about 'a little bit of Irish' carries a depth of psychological significance. Frith and McRobbie do not mention it but Lynott was both Irish and black (his mother was from Dublin and his father from Guyana) and he was 'illegitimate', a significant factor in the staunchly Catholic Dublin that Lynott grew up in during the 1950s and 1960s. He was, literally, a 'black bastard' in white Ireland and this was a significant factor in his strongly autobiographical songwriting. The B-side to Thin Lizzy's first big hit, 'Whiskey in the Jar', is a song that remains relatively unknown in the Lizzy repertoire, called 'Black Boys on the Corner'. This is a typical early Lizzy song – an emotional narrative wrapped in a heavy rock sound underpinned with Eric Bell's virtu-oso guitar. 'I'm a little black boy', Lynott sings, 'and I don't know my proper place...I'm a little black boy, I just play my bass.' The song is not, however, one of withdrawal and self-pity – Lynott is proud to challenge anyone who objects to 'his head in its place'. The challenge is thrown outward to the audience and to the critics: 'I'm a little black boy, recognize my face.' A lot of Lynott's brashness stems from this challenge and a lot of his music replays his auto-biography as myth.

Lynott remained intensely proud of his Irish identity as well. Indeed, part of his approach to music and to his own creativity was governed by the fact that he was, by and large, the only black face in Ireland at the time which gave him the considerable advantage (and disadvantage) of always standing out in a crowd. When you are doubly 'othered' at home, like this, it is not surprising that a lot of the songs you write tend to glorify being 'one of the gang'. 'The boys are back in town' indeed, for the boy who grew up never quite being at home in his own town. There is an element here also of Lynott over-compensating for the fact that there is 'only a little bit of Irish' in him. 'My cause is more the half-caste cause', he told one inter-viewer at the time[23] and the Irish part of the equation resonates throughout his music in the words, the sentiments and the guitar

styling of a lot of Thin Lizzy's trademark dual lead guitars. Early
Thin Lizzy songs are replete with references to Irish mythology and
especially the heroes and warriors of ancient Irish folklore ('Eire'
from the eponymous first album in 1971 and 'Warriors' and
'Emerald' from their breakthrough album *Jailbreak* in 1976).

Lynott responded to his unusual parentage in song as well. His
father played no part in his upbringing and his mother sent him back
to Dublin from Manchester at age 4 to be raised by his grandpar-
ents. Clearly, there were oedipal anxieties at play in Lynott's
songwriting and the compulsion to work these through stemmed
from the late 1960s when he befriended the amalgam of folk musicians, hippies and poets that made up much of the Dublin Bohemian
scene. As a member of Brush Shiels's Skid Row (as singer) and with
his own band, Orphanage, he had dabbled in poetry. He had played
with folk hippy band Dr Strangely Strange and had been part of the
scene that developed around Tara Telephone, a kind of beat poet and
performance artist troupe that included future Horslips drummer
Eamon Carr. In the early Lizzy recordings, the poetry, the folk influences and the autobiographical dimension of Lynott's songwriting
are much in evidence. On one quite extraordinary track on the first
album, 'Diddy Levine', Lynott articulates the troubled and puzzled
voice of the half-caste: 'Inheritance, you see, runs through every
family/Who is to say what is to be is any better/Over and over it
goes, goodness and badness winds blow.' The song itself is one of the
oddest in the Lynott oeuvre – a bizarre tale of a restless mother,
unable to settle down to one relationship so that her daughter grows
up without a stable father figure in her life. This restlessness, it
seems, is passed on to the daughter.

The nearest Lynott gets to writing a proper Irish ballad is
'Philomena' on *Nightlife* (1974), the first album to feature the twin
lead guitars of Scott Gorham and Brian Robertson. The song is a
paean to his real mother, Philomena, but it seems to hark back to
Diddy Levine as a reminder of his own complicated parentage and
nurturing. The missing father is another feature of Lynott's complicated Oedipal universe so that, again on the first album, on 'The
Return of the Farmer's Son', a track that contains a blistering guitar
solo from Eric Bell, he sings: 'And I've been down, so down/Don't
you know, don't you know/I'll always love my father/I love him so.'
This is heavy rock with a vulnerable actor at its centre. In fact,
Lynott here inhabits some of the same Oedipal territory that John
Lennon did on many of his autobiographical songs and if Lynott

seems less of a troubled artist than Lennon, these anxieties, nonetheless, form a subtext to his life and to his macho bravado performance.

The career of Thin Lizzy, as many critics have argued, falls into two distinct phases, the early period as a trio with Brian Downey on drums and Eric Bell on guitar, with Gary Moore doing short-term shifts as Bell's replacement, and the second, more commercially successful period when Lynott and Downey were joined by Gorham and Robertson to create their signature twin guitar sound. In their later manifestation as Britain's biggest hard rock act the band rarely returned to the songs that they recorded on their first three albums. But these albums – the more recognizably Irish albums – are remarkably adventurous and experimental, full of oddities and surprises populated with melodic and challenging songs and complex time changes and pacing. Lynott wrote from a deeply personal set of concerns with a humorous and knowing awareness of the cartoon mythology at the centre of popular culture. The rocker, the boys who do the jailbreak and the boys who are back in town, just like boys who are posing out front, are all part of this cartoon performance universe. The earlier songs were more or less abandoned as Thin Lizzy's popularity grew and the first three albums, as a consequence, have come to seem less vital in the overall work. Graeme Thomson's judgement is typical: 'The early albums...have their moments but they're somewhat convoluted and self-consciously arty with their spoken poems and meandering melodies.'[24] This might be to underestimate them, however, because in Lynott's work the sensibility and sentiments – and sometimes the sentimentality – of these early songs remained a constant factor throughout his work. Lynott moved on to create a distinctive sound but it was more than, and deeper than, merely macho 'cock rock'. The anxious romantic of the earlier period is still the narrator of the 'gang rock' of their heyday and the romantic narrator of one of the band's biggest hits, 'Dancing in the Moonlight', is the same anxious kid who worried about his strange parentage.

In January 2011 an exhibition on Phil Lynott's life and work opened in Dublin to mark the twenty-fifth anniversary of his death from drugs-related illness on January 4 1986 at the young age of 36. His life in the gang and his life as a rocker finally killed him, so at least one part of his act – tragically – was not a pose. Since his death, Lynott's reputation has grown and Thin Lizzy's achievement is now secure. What is remarkable is that in his hometown of Dublin he remains an incredibly popular rock icon who commands genuine

9. 'My cause is more the half-caste cause' – Phil Lynott and Thin
   Lizzy (Corbis)

affection and respect. The statue erected to his memory in Harry
Street, just off Grafton Street, is a place of pilgrimage for Lizzy fans
both local and from abroad, and has become a tourist attraction in
its own right. Lynott himself had always retained a great love for
Dublin. In the track of the same name released originally as an EP in
1971 he sang: 'How can I leave the town that brings me down/That
has no jobs/Is blessed by God/And makes me cry/Dublin.' This is a
consummate summary of the love/hate relationship that the exile
often feels for home and in a few brisk lines he summarizes the social
deprivation and religious stranglehold that so angered Bob Geldof.
Like so many other aspiring rock stars, Lynott had to leave Dublin
to achieve success. He became one of rock's biggest stars in Britain
and Europe and like Rory Gallagher he died in exile in London from
the bodily abuse that the rock star life sometimes entails. Like
Gallagher, Thin Lizzy's success was built on charisma, talent and
hard work. During the years of their slow rise to the top, they
worked at a ferocious pace. The band's first guitarist, Eric Bell,
became the first victim of the Lizzy lifestyle when he collapsed on
stage in 1973. Brian Robertson suffered in 1978 and finally it caught
up with Lynott himself in 1986.

Four years before his death, in 1982 an open-air concert was held at Punchestown Racecourse in Co. Kildare, just outside Dublin. The concert was to mark the fifth birthday of *Hot Press* magazine and to raise some essential funds for the then-ailing paper. Phil Lynott showed up on stage unexpectedly with headline act Rory Gallagher, Paul Brady and some members of a young U2 helping out. It was an enjoyable and good-natured jam of Irish rock talents. In retrospect, it was something of a passing of the baton – the two biggest Irish rock stars of the 1970s handing over to the young pretenders who would dominate the 1980s and 1990s. Lynott and Gallagher had helped put Irish rock on the map internationally and to do so they had to leave Ireland. The young pretenders from Punchestown would try another route to international success based on the need to stay at home and provide a *placed* and *centred* identity for a global assault.

VAN MORRISON: ROOTEDNESS AND TRANSCENDENCE

Whatever the premium, Morrison was prepared to pay it just to get the hell out of Belfast...It would take a major hit record to get him away from this hopeless island for good. (Clinton Heylin)[25]

The other thing that nearly everyone accepts about Van Morrison is that he is one of the most accomplished musical artists of our time, the one figure who not only ranks alongside Bob Dylan as a songwriter of transcendent capacity, but also stands comparison with Smokey Robinson and Sam Cooke as a vocalist. (Jon Wilde)[26]

...the saddest old dinosaur in the park. (Barney Hoskyns)[27]

Ireland's greatest rock exile of the 1970s was, of course, Van Morrison. Even for the internationally successful Rory Gallagher and Phil Lynott, Morrison was the towering presence they had to emulate, an artist who straddled Irish rock music like a colossus and who would not be shifted from his pre-eminent position until well into the 1980s. As his achievements mounted in the global rock world of the 1970s, his presence outside the country merely emphasized the sense of isolation that prevailed for rock music at home. He was too long in exile, as he himself put it.

After the break-up of Them and his disillusionment with the rock industry in London, Morrison had gone to the United States in the spring of 1967 and a few months later had achieved the remarkable feat of having an American top ten hit with 'Brown Eyed Girl', a song that went on to soundtrack a generation's memories of summer and young love. After forty years, this is one of the most played records on American radio and pops up in countless movies to signal (albeit sentimentally) both a certain historical period and a certain stage in the adolescent cycle (the joys, hopes and sexual promise of young love). For Morrison himself, though, this was a 'throwaway' song. 'I've got about 300 songs that are better than that', he told a bemused interviewer in 2010,[28] so cementing his own curmudgeonly reputation and, as with Them, downplaying his commercial pop achievements while denigrating the affectionate role his songs play in the collective memory bank of his audience. This is rather unfortunate because for Morrison's generation – the one he addresses so eloquently on 1973's *Hard Nose the Highway* – his music, in its throwaway pop mode and in its complex syntheses on the albums, has been a soundtrack for their life journey.

Hard Nose the Highway was his sixth album for Warner Bros and at the time of its release it elicited only a lukewarm response from the critics, many of whom found it rather a let-down after the quality of the previous five albums. As Charlie Gillett put it: 'Despite the lack of lyric inspiration and of melodic focus, the record is attractive to listen to ... But Van Morrison has set high standards for himself, and *Hard Nose* doesn't meet them.'[29] Condemned, in other words by both strong and faint praise.

Wayne Robins noted: 'Aside from being non-committal and insubstantial, there's virtually no rock 'n' roll on this album at all. That's tragic, considering that Van has proven ... that he is one of the most valuable composers and performers of real human rock 'n' roll that we have.' Robins also criticizes the lyrics on the album – the words are not up to Morrison's usual high poetic standard, he argues, quoting lines from 'Warm Love' and 'Snow in San Anselmo' to make his point.[30] It is a moot point, of course, whether Morrison would ever see himself as a 'rock 'n' roller', human or not, but both critics' comments about Morrison's words are extremely interesting. It is always problematic to lay song lyrics out on a bare page, or to quote them out of context, but in the case of Van Morrison's words this is a particularly vexed issue.

One routinely gets the sense in Morrison's work that words are not up to the task of conveying the necessary emotion; that words fail to *represent* adequately – a proverbial case of blunt tools for an intricate job. Thus, in Morrison's work, words are often deployed as much for how they *sound* – their textural and timbral qualities – as they are for the images they evoke or for what they may mean in an overarching narrative, hence the growling and moaning that have been a recurring authorial feature. Indeed, repetition of key words and phrases outside of the chorus (where, of course, repetition is routine) is a feature of the singer's solo work. A good example of this is the way in which he repeats the images of 'I saw you walking down by Ladbroke Grove this morning', the 'brand new boy' and 'rides as white as snow' in 'Slim Slow Slider', the closing track on *Astral Weeks* (1968), or the coda of 'Listen to the Lion' on *St Dominic's Preview* (1972): 'And we sail and we sail and we sail and we sail ...'

Morrison has referred to this fascination with repetition many times in interview. It is especially linked to his love of blues singers such as Huddy Ledbetter and John Lee Hooker and their ability, in his words, 'to sing the same thing over and over again without you getting sick of it'. Part of what is significant in Morrison is the combination of *plaisir* and *jouissance*: the use of words for *what* they mean (and the poetic images they conjure), and the way in which the lyrical/semantic register shifts into the voice as *sound*: as an instrument, as timbre, where words, as it were, escape what is said. Hence the infamous growling and roaring on 'Listen to the Lion' or the bending and morphing of 'Geronimo' through repetition in 'Fair Play', the opening track on *Veedon Fleece* (1974) where the voice is less a voice than a muted trumpet. Indeed Morrison vocally employs an extensive range of non-verbal, non-lyrical inflections: snarls, grunts, growls as well as scatting, spitting, low moans and tender falsetto.

In Morrison's work, the everyday takes on transcendent and majestic qualities: the eroticism of the rain and the images of 'the water' in 'And it Stoned Me' from *Moondance* (1970); and sometimes Morrison plays with the inverse: the high cultural as banal, the world of fame and celebrity as a curse. In *Hard Nose* the words are sometimes banal because the moment is banal in itself. Like the Romantic poets he much admires, Morrison finds moments of transcendence in this banality – without the ordinariness to contrast it, how can the transcendent be recognized? One of the lines that Robins objects to from 'Warm Love' – 'Look at the ivy on the old clinging wall/Look at the flowers and the green grass so tall' – works as a song lyric, not as poetry on the page, and it is the song itself which becomes the transcendent moment. Snow falling on San Anselmo is pretty ordinary as well (even if it hasn't happened in over thirty years) until Morrison's soulful singing and the soaring Bach choir render it quite extraordinary.

What is most surprising in some of the negative criticisms is the accusation that the album lacks theme, focus, perspective or gravitas. This is the album on which Morrison addresses his generation, the 'wild children' or war babies (or 'Baby Boomers' as American sociologists called them). He namechecks some of the popular cultural icons that influenced this generation (Rod Steiger, Marlon Brando, James Dean, Tennessee Williams) but really it is Morrison and his music which is the real soundtrack of their lives. The album contains the first great song of disillusionment written of and for this generation – 'The Great Deception' – which pours scorn on the revolutionary promise of the earlier years, encapsulated in so much of the music of the era. The whole dream has fallen apart in hypocrisy, greed and duplicity. It is an amusing game to try to guess who Morrison has in mind when he lambasts 'the plastic revolutionaries' but what he implies is that these are just as much a part of the war-children generation as the great icons were. For Morrison, of course, this was his way of purging the deep sense of injustice (and resentment) he felt over the way in which the music industry had treated him in his earlier career. This was to become (almost tediously) a lifelong gripe with Morrison but what elevates it here is the way in which it is linked to a generational sense of betrayal and disillusion. We have all been betrayed, he says, and this sense of collective protest, one of the 'war children's' defining characteristics, is always a much more attractive proposition than a personal grudge.

Morrison, nonetheless, retained a deep suspicion of the music industry and its emphasis on style, fame and celebrity. If he stands over Irish rock and popular music as its most critically revered artist, he has remained remarkably suspicious of 'image' and the world of fashion and style. For most of his career Morrison has preferred the look of unstudied ordinariness, sharing a dress sense more in common with poets such as Seamus Heaney, Ted Hughes and Philip Larkin than the icons of rock culture. This emanated from the early days of Them, when the band collectively dressed down rather than up, the ordinariness of the dress merely emphasizing the authenticity of the music. When Morrison did dabble in 'style' or 'fashion' culture these have been relatively fraught affairs: the unfortunate blue, high-buttoned cape glimpsed on the *Tupelo Honey* shoot

(1971); his red velvet suit on *The Last Waltz* (Scorsese, 1976); the Zorro/Iberian poet look, complete with cape, on the rear cover of *A Sense of Wonder* (1985); and his appropriation of the blues/soul brothers iconography of *Days Like This* (1995). Of course, through-out the 1980s he sported a 'comb-over', the most maligned hairstyle in popular culture, the butt of jokes and one associated with ageing footballers (Bobby Charlton was a famous exponent) and the middle-aged male establishment. It is perhaps to his credit that Morrison, more than any other artist of his generation, has lived out the idea that music can be separated from 'image' and that image culture, in the words of Will Straw, offers 'effects to be feared' for the rock listener, especially that of making style more important than the music itself.[31] Certainly Morrison wasn't gifted a rock star physique and his short, dumpy stature may well have been a factor in his general resentment of stardom and celebrity. Nonetheless, his lack of 'style-literacy' and his general grumpiness with the music industry's obsession with style and celebrity is ultimately a result of his desire to foreground his music.

By the time he had made *Hard Nose*, Morrison had given his generation one of the era's most distinguished run of albums and established himself right at the pinnacle of contemporary rock music. What is also remarkable about this body of work was that it was grounded in Ireland, and especially in Belfast, and yet it spoke to a generation across the world, linked by the kind of Anglo-American popular music that nourished Morrison in Belfast and which he then enriched from his base in the United States. He remained, as he maintained in relation to Them, an Irish artist.

In August 1969, Belfast erupted into the kind of rioting and sectarian violence that was to define its international media profile for the next three decades. This effectively killed off the music scene in the city and had the result of closing down the city centre. A decade later, rock music would be the catalyst in the cultural rebirth of the city, but shortly after the violence began, and largely unno-ticed by all but a few dedicated fans, rock music provided one of the city's most eloquent and emotional tributes. In September 1969, Morrison released what he regards as his first proper solo album, *Astral Weeks* (it had been released in the US the previous year). Today, *Astral Weeks* is considered to be one of the great achieve-ments of twentieth-century popular music and in various polls over the years it has been voted one of the top five best albums of the rock and pop era. It is an album about childhood memories and the journey through adolescence to adulthood. It is a cycle of songs about romantic love and the capacity of human beings to experience something of the mysticism and the sublime central to so many different religions. It is, finally, a cycle of songs about Belfast and remains one of the most evocative portraits of Belfast produced in any art form.

In its carefully layered references to the city as it was before the outbreak of violence there are textures of a recognizably 'ordinary' working-class lifestyle. This is the key to understanding the music of Van Morrison over the last forty years or so and to assessing its importance in the cultural context of Northern Ireland. For at its heart lies a paradox. He, more than any other Irish (or British) rock musician, has maintained a strong sense of his roots while at the same time exploring – and extending considerably – the international rock idiom. His art is an art of the periphery, soaking up the influences from the outside, adapting them to its own designs and then offering them back to the outside in a wholly unique form. A powerful and recurring symbol of this process of cultural interchange in his music has been the role that radio has played in his own musical development.

In the track 'Caravan', from his second album *Moondance* (1970), he invokes it for the first time – 'Turn it up, turn it up/Little bit higher/Radio' – but returns to the theme many times throughout his work (on songs like 'The Days Before Rock 'n' Roll' from the 1990 album *Enlightenment* and 'Hyndford Street' from 1991's *Hymns to the Silence*). A peripheral culture's relationship to the influences emanating from the outside (symbolized, in this instance, by the radio) is an extremely complex and contradictory one. On one hand, the radio can represent a threat to the integrity of indigenous culture, the possibility that the local will be overwhelmed by the culture of the centre, pouring down the airwaves from the outside. It is assumed in this case that the indigenous culture has a quality and a relevance worth preserving – the 'rootedness' from which a sense of identity grows. On the other hand, however, this local culture can also appear insular and stifling to such an extent that the cultural influences from the outside are to be welcomed as positively liberating and life-enhancing (as was the case with American cinema in Catholic Ireland up until the 1960s). In his work of the early 1990s, especially in *Enlightenment* (1990) and *Hymns to the Silence* (1991), Morrison has given the world some unforgettable images of listening in to the exotic sounds of American jazz, gospel and blues music – as if this were some secret ceremony beyond acceptable behaviour. These are, of course, cherished memories of his childhood roots but they are also moments of transcendence – memories of imaginative escape from these very same roots.

This contradiction is central to Van Morrison's music. *Astral Weeks* remains his most complete celebration of his Belfast roots, a collection of songs – of emotion recollected in tranquillity, as Wordsworth described it – which evokes a place that is real and yet is also a place of the imagination. Throughout his work he continually returns to the Belfast of his youth for inspiration – Protestant East Belfast where the Sunday 'six-bell chimes' – but, as often as not, he does so to recall those moments of transcendence that lifted him out of that very environment in the first place. Referring to his 'baby boomer' song, 'Wild Children', Morrison explained: 'I think that where that song is coming from is growing up in another country and getting our releases through figures from America, like the American anti-heroes.'[32] And yet, when this imaginative transcendence became physical exile following the success of his band Them in the mid-1960s and the long sojourn in the United States from 1967 onwards, the pain of being distanced from his roots provides continuing inspiration from *Astral Weeks* on (and is explored again in his 1993 album, *Too Long In Exile*, among many others).

The song that perhaps best sums up the paradox between rootedness and transcendence is his reworking of the traditional Christian hymn, 'See Me Through Part II (Just a Closer Walk With You)' from *Hymns to the Silence*. Against a gospel rendition of the hymn, Morrison remembers again the days before rock 'n' roll and incants a list of influences that are rooted to his Belfast upbringing and, at the same time, have transported him out of this. In doing so, he paints an evocative picture of a Protestant Sunday in Belfast, which is nostalgic, spiritual and full of warmth, and yet from which he seeks to escape through the un-Godly (and very un-Protestant) practice of 'tuning in of stations in Europe on the wireless'. The object of his Sunday worship would not have appealed to traditional Sunday-school values either – 'Jazz and blues and folk, poetry and jazz' or 'Hank Williams, Louis Armstrong, Sidney Bechet' (and elsewhere on the album Morrison acknowledges the influence of Jellyroll Morton, Big Bill Broonzy, Mez Mezro, Jack Kerouac, Sonny Boy Williamson and Ray Charles). All the Morrisonian themes of ambiguity, contradiction and paradox are here – belonging and yet trying to escape; the competing pleasures of the spirit and the flesh; the relationship between the local and the foreign, between the inside world and the outside, between Ulster and America, between the private and the public persona. Most importantly, this track conjures up the almost illicit thrill and excitement of 'the Devil's music'.

Another musical path which Morrison's explorations have taken is, of course, through Irish traditional music with a concomitant interest in notions of Irish and Celtic identity. These interests first emerged in 1974's *Veedon Fleece*, re-emerged with vigour in the recordings of the early 1980s and reached their high point in the collaboration with The Chieftains on 1988's *Irish Heartbeat*. The nature of Morrison's Irishness is interesting and complex and is articulated well in the music. *Veedon Fleece*, like *Hard Nose the Highway* before it, is a Morrison album rescued by critical hindsight. It was not favourably reviewed at the time and the songs from the album are the most unrepresented in the artist's live sets.[33] In fact, *Veedon Fleece*, despite its lukewarm reception, has become one of the most critically lauded of the artist's albums, with both Johnny Rogan and Greil Marcus going so far as to claim that it would not have been a great loss if Morrison had never recorded again after this point.[34]

Moreover, in the incredibly fertile first six years of Morrison's solo career – marked by seven studio albums – *Veedon Fleece* stands out as the most conspicuously 'Irish' in tone and register, notwithstanding the lyrical content of *Astral Weeks*. Morrison had returned to Ireland in 1974 for the first time in seven years, travelling to Killarney, Arklow and 'the west' (places that are explicitly referenced in the lyrics). Most of the songs on *Veedon Fleece* were written during or shortly after this visit, suggesting that the visit itself was an excuse to re-engage with his muse. As Campbell and Smyth have pointed out, the green-tinged cover artwork of Morrison being flanked by two Irish wolfhounds on the rolling lawns of Sutton House near Dublin gives a clue to the contents.[35] There are, as well, many lyrical references to Irish places, Irish idioms, ('fair play to ya' and 'tit for tat') as well as 'Irish' institutions, such as the Sisters of Mercy. The album is also populated by Irish artists and characters: Oscar Wilde and Linden Arden.

The eponymous fleece sounds mythical, invoking Jason's golden fleece from Greek mythology. Morrison's fleece, too, suggests the pre-modern, and similarly functions as a magic talisman, or Holy

Grail, to be fought for and discovered somewhere in 'the west'. In one sense, *Veedon Fleece* seems to dovetail with the work of Horslips, invoking a pastoral Ireland as a place of legend, full of spiritual treasures and answers to be discovered.

Yet there is no such fleece in mythology, Irish or otherwise. It is a construction, an invention, as Morrison has widely acknowledged: 'I just made it up.' This was to be a recurring tension in Morrison's work: the complexity of the mental landscapes offered in its musical/lyrical forms; and the artist's apparent resistance to interpretation of his work, most evident in the banal and curt answers he has offered when questioned. This is a significant tension that studs Morrison's entire oeuvre: his respect for critical ideas – for the canon of literature, poetry and philosophy – and his simultaneous distrust of – even outright antagonism towards – ideas, critical debate and interpretation in respect of his own work.

The 'Veedon Fleece' is a powerful invented motif and functions a little like the wizard in *The Wizard of Oz* (directed by Victor Fleming, 1939): a sought-after supernatural being/object that turns out to be a construction, something all too pathetically human. The 'Veedon Fleece' is, of course, conjured up on the album's fifth track, 'You pull no punches but you don't push the river', one of Morrison's most critically lauded songs, and a complex whirling, undulating, fever of a performance. The song is often read as an odyssey – both literal and figurative – into the mythical west of Ireland where philosophical, existential and spiritual truths can be discovered, as evidenced in lines such as 'getting down to the west...down to the real soul people' (a line that, as Sean Campbell reveals, was hugely influential on the young Kevin Rowland of Dexy's Midnight Runners[36]). This is supported in the references to the metaphysical, to gestalt theory, existentialism and a litany of poets and philosophers – most notably William Blake and the Eternals – that suggest a concern with enlightenment, of being at one in space and time. This incantation of poets and philosophers is most apparent in the opening track, 'Fair Play' (Thoreau, Edgar Allan Poe, Oscar Wilde), and marks the introduction of a device that would surface throughout Morrison's work, most notably in *Common One*'s 'Summertime in England': the tendency to explicitly reference canonical figures. However, in the latter album, these references work as more-or-less straightforward homage and, as such, it is easy to see how they irked Morrison's critics with the singer foregrounding, by association, his place in an elite literary heritage

('James Joyce . . . wrote stream-of-consciousness books' and the like).

The use of conspicuous referencing is, however, markedly different in *Veedon Fleece* and 'You pull no punches but you don't push the river'. The song's protagonist is addressing his words, including the litany of philosophers, to an anonymous other, presumably a lover (either former or present). Thus: 'We were contemplating Baba, William Blake and The Eternals/Standing with The Sisters of Mercy . . . looking for the Veedon Fleece'. The straightforward reading – the song as powerful poetic endorsement of mystical poetry and mystical Ireland – is undercut by the terse, staccato and even bitter delivery, the frustration that permeates the finger-pointing assertion: 'you pull no punches but ya don't push the river'. While on the one hand the song may be heard within the terms of rock romanticism ('learn to just *be*') and the countercultural cliché of the time ('don't push the river, it flows by itself'), the song offsets this. The subtext seems to be: you don't hold back, you might win the argument . . . but so what, it doesn't change much. Therefore, while the poets and philosophers constitute a shared mental landscape for the protagonist and his partner, as discussion points for their (pastoral Irish) journey, it is by no means clear that it is a journey towards oneness or enlightenment, or to questions answered. Nor is it a straightforward reinforcement of the canonical. Lauren Onkey has drawn attention to the surreal aspects of Morrison's lyric and its eclectic imagery: of William Blake fronting The Eternals (imagined in this case as the doo-wop group) with The Sisters of Mercy as a group of 'female backup singers'.[37] It is a bizarre historically, geographically and generically dispersed confection – a hybrid Irish *Sergeant Pepper's* cover of sorts. Even though the imaginary landscape of *Veedon Fleece* marks the first explicit and sustained return to Ireland after *Astral Weeks*, as an album it weaves in and out of the richly invoked ideal of the west of Ireland as a land of poets, artists and pastoral beauty and a concomitant undercutting of the trope, subjecting the very things it sets up to sarcasm, critique and extension.

The sense of frustration is further heightened in the use of instrumentation. While the song's powerful build-up has been widely noted, it is not a straightforward upward drive towards ecstatic release. In fact, the tension among the double-time bass, the undulating strings, piano and violin and Morrison's abrupt changes in register and pitch gives the impression of the song working against itself, tearing itself asunder (with Morrison tersely barking out 'The river is not, the river is not' over and over). To deploy a well-worn sexual analogy: 'You pull no punches' can be read as a struggle to climax or as an unsatisfactory release. Thus the tension between rootedness and transcendence becomes increasingly intertwined with suspicion, scepticism and unease. Hence the 'looking for the Veedon Fleece' takes on an ironic undertow. The song is therefore more of a tension-ridden experience than is often allowed for.

On *Irish Heartbeat*, recorded fourteen years later, Morrison embraces another version of Irishness, a collaboration with The Chieftains, now well into their long journey to internationalize Irish traditional music. Morrison gets to share, though not actually to sing, a song in the Irish language and The Chieftains get to play the Orange marching song 'The Sash' on the tin whistle. This collaboration was Morrison's most commercially successful recording for some time and certainly his most accessible. The possible political implications of this meeting of two traditions was much commented on at the time of the album's release but one needs to be a little cautious about reading too many metaphorical meanings into such a collaboration. While there is no doubt that the album remains an interesting example of cultural pluralism (Protestant Belfast meets Nationalist Ireland; one of the most distinctive voices in rock music meets the unmistakable rhythms of Irish traditional music, setting up interesting tensions both musical and cultural), this caution is warranted.

Morrison said at the time of *Veedon Fleece* that it was 'just a bunch of songs'[38] and it is probably advisable to view the whole of *Irish Heartbeat* in the same light. It was a process of musical interchange, rather than evidence of Morrison having discovered 'his essential Irishness'. Throughout his career, Morrison invokes too many cultural influences to warrant raising The Chieftains collaboration above all others or to suppose that his sense of cultural identity is synonymous with a traditional Irish nationalist conception. The geography of his mental landscape is too complex and too idiosyncratic for this, taking in contemporary myths like Woodstock or California and the 'ancient roads' that lead to Caledonia, Avalon, Albion and the England of the Romantic poets. Just as, over the years, he has continually acknowledged the influences of a whole gallery of popular American musicians, so too he has addressed a pantheon of literary figures, including Walt Whitman, Tennessee Williams, James Joyce, Yeats and Samuel Beckett, as well as the Romantic poets of literary England. Against all these invocations

10. 'Rootedness and Transcendence' – Van Morrison in performance (Corbis)

and influences, The Chieftains' traditional Irish music must stand in line.

Indeed, *Too Long in Exile* from 1993 is probably a more representative collection of songs – to mark his return to Ireland, an 'end-of-an-era' retrospective of his own biography and the influences on his music. The key tracks here are two duets with blues legend John Lee Hooker: a reworking of Morrison's 'garage band' classic from the days of Them, 'Gloria', and a new song of regret and reaffirmation, 'Wasted Years'. Elsewhere on the album, Morrison does versions of R&B classics and jazz standards, and the overall musical style is a blues-inflected jazz, the source of his musical hybridity. And in the end, it is the music that really matters, more so than the literary figures, the mysticism, the esoteric speculation, pastoral invocations of a primordial Garden of Eden and the sometimes incongruous incantations – a sentiment with which Morrison himself would no doubt agree. As he has said on many occasions, he is a working musician doing a job. Thus it is the tensions and balances in the music, rather than the speculations in the words of the songs, which mark out his unique take on the question of cultural identity.

In the sequence of albums released in the 1980s, beginning with *Beautiful Vision* in 1982, the sense of a 'dweller on the threshold' or an 'in-between' traveller – in the real world and in the imagination – allows for a unique synthesis of musical influences: American black music (including gospel, blues, jazz and an early form of white-adapted rap), Irish traditional music and song, English balladry, a touch of Scotland and a good dose of Belfast Protestant hymn-singing. The resulting hybrid has taken all these musical influences into new and surprising territories, creating in the process a body of work which lies at the pinnacle of rock music's achievements. Not everyone agrees. Barney Hoskyns infamously labelled the later Morrison 'the saddest old dinosaur in the park' and Greil Marcus bemoaned the 'endless stream of dull and tired albums through the 1980s and '90s, carrying titles like warning labels'.[39]

THE BELFAST SONGS

Morrison had learnt many of the songs he recorded with The Chieftains from listening to his mother and other ballad singers in his formative years in Belfast. The city is a constant reference point with Morrison, hardly a surprise in such an autobiographical artist. *Astral Weeks* contains two great songs in particular about Belfast, 'Madame George' and 'Cyprus Avenue', both of which offered a vision of the city very different in style and tone to the image that was to dominate the media throughout the years of violence and conflict. In many ways, his invocation of the city provided a thirty-year-long alternative to the dominant media image – a parallel Belfast of the imagination, insulated and isolated from the grim and gruesome realities of the Troubles. Morrison has, of course, received criticism over the years precisely because of this but this criticism seems a harsh judgement on a Belfast artist who achieved an international reputation through writing about, rather than ignoring, his native city. Morrison's Belfast has a greater artistic and social integrity than that of any of the 'parachute' songwriters over the years who dropped in hoping for some street credibility or who dabbled with the city's problems out of a sense of political duty.

Morrison, of course, did not totally ignore the impact of the Troubles. On 1972's *St Dominic's Preview*, the title track is inspired by his own dilemma – how the increasingly successful and famous Belfast singer can come to terms with the spiralling cycle of violence in his own hometown. Morrison paints the dilemma beautifully and with commendable honesty. He reads about the violence and the prayers for peace that are offered up by well-meaning people in church and realizes that his life of wine receptions and record company publicity rounds is now a long way removed emotionally and geographically from the realities of his hometown. Typically, he sees Belfast's problems, and his own, as essentially stemming from self-absorption and a lack of communication. For an artist so determinedly apolitical as Morrison has been, his lyrics here conjure up a strangely familiar political landscape: 'All the orange boxes are scattered/Against the Safeway's supermarket in the rain/And everybody feels so determined/Not to feel anyone else's pain.' There is, for the singer, a lack of graciousness, understanding and communication and he rails against 'all the chains, badges, flags and emblems' that block such communication.

Morrison's Belfast is not usually invoked so politically. His vision is essentially that of a Romantic poet, a man of the eighteenth or nineteenth century living and reliving his romantic experiences through an essentially twentieth-century art form. While he certainly escaped from the 'chains, badges, flags and emblems' of his Belfast upbringing, he never escaped the city in which these continue to hold such political sway. And that is the nature of Morrison's dilemma. He had to get out of Belfast to grow as an artist and a songwriter but he is continually drawn back to his hometown for inspiration and emotional sustenance. He is caught between staying and escape, between belonging and exile, between rootedness and transcendence. This is the Belfast that emerges again and again in his work and which is so magnificently conjured up for the first time in 'Cyprus Avenue' and 'Madame George'. As the real city was blown apart by political violence, Morrison's city remained the pre-Troubles city of his childhood – sometimes a place of simplicity and banality, and at other times the site of extreme emotional euphoria and mystical experience.

In both these songs, Cyprus Avenue acts as the catalyst for his memories and his emotions. 'I'm caught one more time up on Cyprus Avenue', he sings on 'Cyprus Avenue' itself. 'I'm conquered in a car seat/Not a thing that I can do.' On 'Madame George', he echoes the sentiment. 'Down on Cyprus Avenue/With a child-like vision leaping into view'. This street is in a middle-class area near his home in East Belfast and, because of Morrison's music, it has become as famous throughout the world today as either the Falls Road or the Shankill Road, bringing very different connotations of Belfast to the global audience. Morrison's memories of Cyprus Avenue are adolescent reminiscences of a time when the young romantic in him was caught between childhood and the adult world, between the world of flesh and the mystical world of the sublime. The sheer ordinariness of the street – its tree-lined vista, the schoolgirls rhyming songs on their way home, the leaves falling in autumn – is conjured up. However, this ordinariness then sparks a meditation on love and an evocation of the transcendent power of nature, the ability of a few trees and falling leaves, or the snatch of a rhyme, to lift the young Morrison out of the back streets and onto a higher level. In this way, Cyprus Avenue and its environs is to Morrison what the Lake District was to Wordsworth, or Sligo to W.B. Yeats. It is his inspiration, his muse and the vehicle that elevates him to a higher state of consciousness. He loves the ordinary but relishes the way in which he is lifted up to the extraordinary. He loves the banal but also craves intimations of the mystical. Morrison's Belfast is a mixture of both.

As he has grown older, Morrison's invocation of the ordinariness of Belfast life has become more pronounced. However, even in the heightened romanticism of the songs on *Astral Weeks*, he re-enacts the banality of life in Belfast in the 1950s and 1960s: 'The kids out on the streets collecting bottle-tops/Going for the cigarettes and matches in the shop'. Ordinary details of daily life in Belfast are recalled – 'Now you know you gotta go/On a train from Dublin up to Sandy Row/Throwing pennies at the bridges down below/In the rain, hail sleet and snow.' This reference to the practice of dropping pennies into the River Boyne as the Belfast train travelled through Drogheda is typical of the local detail that peppers his memories of Belfast. In the process of remembering, 'Madame George' (or 'Madame Joy' as he seems to sing) becomes a metaphor for Belfast itself, both the ordinary mundane life experienced on the streets and those moments of heightened experiences that were so much a part of his childhood in these streets. The area around Cyprus Avenue and his home in Hyndford Street remained a source of inspiration, and over the years he has recreated the details of his own upbringing with great clarity – his years at school in Orangefield; the river and railway tracks that intersect his area; the fishing and rambling trips he undertook for relaxation; the everyday culture of the 1950s, including barmbracks, snowballs and pastie suppers; the simple joy of working as a window cleaner; and the view of the Castlereagh Hills that provided him with the desire for escape.

In many ways, this is the ultimate irony of Morrison's Belfast: he is rooted to its culture and yet he is driven by the desire to escape it. This escape is sometimes a spiritual moment of transcendence, like those he describes in 'Cyprus Avenue' and 'Madame George'. Often his escape is imaginative, inspired by the music he hears on the radio – the great array of jazz, blues and country singers who vied with the Protestant six-bells to dominate the soundscape of his childhood Sundays. Finally, of course, his escape was physical and most of his music was conceived and recorded in exile, becoming in time a high point in the international flow of rock music.

There is now one final irony about Van Morrison's relationship to Belfast. As the peace settles in Northern Ireland and old enmities seemingly disappear under compromise and accommodations, the city is being rebuilt, re-imagined and re-imaged in film and television. As part of the booming tourist industry, Belfast has also begun to exploit its famous past denizens – both footballer George Best and C.S. Lewis, the author of the Narnia books, are now firmly established as 'selling points'. Even the city's past tragedies – the *Titanic* notably, but also the recent Troubles – are being recycled for tourism. The parts of the city that were namechecked in the songs of

Van Morrison – and especially Cyprus Avenue – are now also firmly on the tourist trail. Van Morrison may be a dinosaur to some, an exile and an international 'dweller on the threshold' to others, but he is now a well-established part of Belfast's new theme-park culture.

EXILES LIVE

There is an interesting coda to the story of Irish rock exiles in the 1970s. Between them, Van Morrison, Rory Gallagher and Thin Lizzy produced three of the best and most influential live albums of the era and did much to establish the credentials of the live album as a significant artistic statement. We have already noted the importance of Rory Gallagher's *Live in Europe* (1972) to the success of his solo career and its achievement in bringing the immediacy of his live performance to the recorded medium. The album was a significant milestone in the development of live recording of rock music. Granted, it was neither the first nor the only early success in the process – The Rolling Stones had released the distinctly underwhelming *Got Live If You Want It* (in the USA only) as far back as 1966, and in 1970 both they and The Who had significant successes with *Get Yer Ya-Ya's Out!* and *Live at Leeds* respectively. But Gallagher's *Live in Europe* successfully integrated the live sound of the performance on stage with the crowd reaction, capturing both the musicianship of the guitarist in his prime and his singular rapport with the audience.

The most celebrated live album of the era, however, and the most influential in terms of historical legacy, was Morrison's *It's Too Late to Stop Now* (1974), described by the normally sober Clinton Heylin as 'incandescent'[40] and by Peter Mills as 'the first recording...to stand alone as an integral work of art, and a document of a truly distinctive live experience'. In doing this, Mills contends, Morrison effectively invented a new art form.[41] The album was recorded during Morrison's Caledonia Soul Orchestra tour of 1973 and was drawn from three shows at the Troubadour in LA, the Santa Monica Civic Auditorium and, most significantly, the Rainbow in London's Finsbury Park. The last was significant in terms of British broadcasting development since this was the first time the BBC broadcast a rock show in 'simultaneous broadcast' – on the radio in stereo and on television. This allowed the listener to experience 'stereo television' and was a significant breakthrough technologically for rock music on television, which until then had suffered greatly from the tinny reproduction that TV sound normally offered.

The album has stood the test of time and is continually cited as one of the greatest live albums of all time. Morrison's refusal to allow for overdubs to correct 'mistakes' kept 'Moondance' off the album and has given the whole project the stamp of approval as an 'authentic' live experience. The same cannot be said of Thin Lizzy's 1978 album, *Live and Dangerous*. Although again the album's reputation as one of the great live albums is secure, its status as 'authentic' is in dispute in a way that neither Morrison's or Gallagher's efforts are. The question here is that of overdubs, and it seems likely that the live sound on the album was considerably enhanced in the studio. Indeed the album's producer, Tony Visconti, comparing *Live and Dangerous* to the over-dub-free live album he had just completed for David Bowie, claimed:

> If you want to know about the Thin Lizzy live album, that was almost totally the reverse, because we erased everything except the drums on *Live And Dangerous*. The voices were done again, so were the guitars, and even the audience was done again in a very devious way. One of the songs, 'Southbound' wasn't even recorded in front of an audience – it was recorded at a sound check, and I added a tape loop of an audience just sort of screaming in the background. That was a totally manufactured live sound.[42]

Manufactured or not, the album was hugely successful at the time, lifting Thin Lizzy into superstardom. Even Visconti has relented to some extent, adding that despite the trickery he engaged in, the album is 'very real' representing 'electrifying moments before an audience and fabulous second chances to get it right in the studio'.[43] The live experience captured on the album became the soundtrack of the summer of 1978 and, as we have noted, the album cover featuring the phallic Phil Lynott became the epitome of 'cock rock'.

It is difficult, however, to make any great national claims about the fact that three of the key live albums of the 1970s came from Irish rock acts in exile. It is interesting and noteworthy but perhaps it was also just coincidence. However, the success of the stars in exile, in such high-profile and innovative ways, reinforced the paucity of the rock scene in Ireland itself and it was inevitable that Irish rock music at home would have to respond to this success and to this paucity.

NOTES

1. Fachtna O'Ceallaigh, interview by Noel McLaughlin, 2011 (unpublished).
2. Colin Harper and Trevor Hodgett, *Irish Folk, Trad and Blues: A Secret History* (Cork: Collins Press, 2004), p.188.
3. Daragh O'Halloran, *Green Beat: The Forgotten Era of Irish Rock* (Belfast: Brehon Press, 2006), p.133.
4. Ibid., p.132.
5. See Dave Lewis's own webpage at http://www.elpianista.com/aboutDaveLewis.html.
6. Harper and Hodgett, *Irish Folk, Trad and Blues*, p.177.
7. O'Halloran, *Green Beat*, p.182.
8. Harper and Hodgett, *Irish Folk, Trad and Blues*, p.189.
9. For a full history of the Dave Miller Set and some sense of the cultural importance in Australia of their version of 'Mr Guy Fawkes', see http://www.milesago.com/Artists/dms.html.
10. Harper and Hodgett, *Irish Folk, Trad and Blues*, p.208.
11. Joe Jackson, 'Lest We Forget', *Irish Times*, 16 June 1995, 'Arts', p.16.
12. Quoted in Brian Boyd, 'Blues Guitarist dies in London', *Irish Times*, 15 June 1995.
13. Keith Altham, 'Rory Gallagher: Fresh Taste for Rory', *Record Mirror*, 8 May 1971.
14. Quoted on one of the many websites now devoted to the 1970 Festival: http://www.ukrockfestivals.com/iow70-info.html.
15. Keith Altham, 'Rory Gallagher: Full Blooded Gallagher', *NME*, 13 October 1973.
16. Altham, 'Rory Gallagher: Fresh Taste'.
17. Graeme Thomson, 'Vagabond of the Western World', *Uncut*, February 2011, p.62.
18. Chris Salewicz, 'Thin Lizzy: A Peep into the Soul of Phil Lynott', *NME*, 10 September 1977.
19. Ibid.
20. Simon Frith and Angela McRobbie, 'Rock and Sexuality', *Screen Education*, 29, (Winter 1978/79), pp.3–19.
21. Ibid., p.13.
22. Peter Silverton, 'Thin Lizzy: Joints', *Sounds*, 16 December 1978.
23. Salewicz, 'Thin Lizzy'.
24. Thomson, 'Vagabond'.
25. Clinton Heylin, *Can You Feel the Silence? Van Morrison: A New Biography* (Harmondsworth: Penguin, 2002), p.149.
26. Jon Wilde, 'Into the Mystic', *Uncut*, 98, 164 (July 2005), p.49.
27. Barney Hoskyns, 'Van the Sham', *Mojo*, 1 (November 1993), p.91.
28. '10 questions for Van Morrison', *Time Magazine* video, *YouTube* (2009), http://www.youtube.com/watch?v=QVHbUPNcTiU (accessed 26 March 2011).
29. Charlie Gillett, 'Hard Nose the Highway', *Let it Rock*, September 1973.
30. Wayne Robins, 'Review of the Album', *Zoo World*, 11 (January 1973).
31. Will Straw, 'Popular Music and Postmodernism in the 1980s', in Simon Frith, Andrew Goodwin and Lawrence Grossberg (eds), *Sound and Vision: The Music Video Reader* (London: Routledge, 1991), pp.3–4.
32. Ritchie Yorke, *Van Morrison: Into the Music* (London: Charisma, 1975), p.105.
33. Heylin, *Can You Feel the Silence?*, p.287.

34. Johnny Rogan, *Van Morrison: No Surrender* (London: Vintage, 2005); Greil Marcus, *Listening to Van Morrison* (London: Faber & Faber, 2010).
35. Sean Campbell and Gerry Smyth, *Beautiful Day: Forty Years of Irish Rock* (Cork: Atrium Press, 2005), p.48.
36. Kevin Rowland, in Sean Campbell, *Irish Blood, English Heart: Second-Generation Irish Musicians in England* (Cork: Cork University Press, 2011), p.34.
37. Lauren Onkey, 'Ray Charles on Hyndford Street: Van Morrison's Caledonian Soul', in Diane Negra (ed.), *The Irish in Us: Irishness, Performativity and Popular Culture* (London and Durham: Duke University Press, 2006), p.194.
38. Heylin, *Can You Feel the Silence?*, p.281.
39. Hoskyns, 'Van the Sham'; Marcus, *Listening to Van Morrison*, p.9.
40. Heylin, *Can You Feel the Silence?* p.287.
41. Peter Mills, *Hymns to the Silence: Inside the Words and Music of Van Morrison* (London: Continuum, 2010), p.210.
42. Stuart Grundy and John Tobler, 'Tony Visconti Talks', in Stuart Grundy and John Tobler, *The Record Producers* (BBC Books, 1982), http://www.rocksbackpages.com/article.html?ArticleID=5417&SearchText=thin+lizzy (accessed 24 March 2011).
43. Tony Visconti homepage: http://www.tonyvisconti.com/artists/thinlizzy/live.htm#c, (accessed 24 March 2011).

5

Waking Up the Banana Republic

If Oxfam were to adopt the same strategy towards rock starvation as they do towards the plight of the world's hungry, then one of the first mercy flights would be to Ireland. No exaggeration. The state of rock there is really that bad. (Harry Doherty)[1]

If pop music is going to be used to destroy our established institutions, then it ought to be destroyed first. (Marcus Lipton)[2]

I'd never been hot to trot for Irish people, much less Irish rock bands...I had always harboured some vague notion that The Boomtown Rats were some bandwagoneering, year-too-late bunch of scumbags. (Sandy Robertson)[3]

By the mid-1970s, the situation for rock music in Ireland, as Harry Doherty describes it in his *Melody Maker* article, was grim and made even worse by the fall-out from the continuing violence in Northern Ireland (and especially from the murders of members of The Miami Showband, ambushed and shot by Loyalist gunmen on 31 July 1975). The result of all the adverse publicity was that few of rock's main headline acts were willing to travel to Ireland, North or South, and live music was an impoverished affair. Doherty details, as well, the sad state of Irish indigenous rock, with a handful of bands trailing around a truncated rock circuit, eking out a living on the edges of a still-strong showband scene and the burgeoning folk and traditional circuit. It was this Ireland and this rock scene that Bob Geldof returned to in 1975 after some years working the roads in England, teaching English in Seville and then starting a career as a rock journalist with the *Georgia Straight* in Vancouver. 'I was returning to a parochialism and a morality so stifling it literally manifested itself in me as an inability to breathe. I was returning to a place where ambition and talent were denigrated.'[4]

Geldof had earlier noted while working for the *Georgia Straight* that global rock music had itself descended into similar state of stifled creativity. 'The music had changed: no longer adventurous, it was self-indulgent or narcissistic or engaged in embarrassing pastiche.'[5] Indeed, the international band that features prominently in Doherty's article as a 'no-show' in Ireland was Sutherland Brothers and Quiver, suggesting that Geldof may well have had a point.

In early 1976, the state of rock music everywhere looked (and sounded) glum. The excitement of the 1960s and the experiments of the early 1970s seemed to have given way to either pretentious bombast or somnambulistic country-rock. Harry Doherty may have been talking about the specific case of rock in Ireland but he was writing at a time, as history and hindsight confirm, just before the storm of punk rock blew away much of this pretension and bombast. Like the persistent sound that is only noticed when it stops, the lethargy and complacency of mainstream rock only became obvious after it had been blown away in the storm. The punk storm clouds had been gathering mainly in London during 1976 and they burst with the infamous Bill Grundy TV interview with The Sex Pistols on 1 December of that year. The following year – the year of punk in the UK – punk was to wake up the music industry from its complacent doze and, in the process, it attempted to create something of a year zero for the 'boring old farts' of the established bands.

There were rumblings in Ireland, too, and even to notice the malaise, as Harry Doherty and Geldof had done, was to will into being the solution. In Ireland there were a number of factors that coalesced to waken up the still-dozing culture. In many ways, 1977 was also a key turning point for music in Ireland. There was a change of government and even if, in Ireland as elsewhere, a change of government meant little to youth subcultures, nonetheless it signalled the end of a particularly unpopular coalition government led by a Taoiseach, in the guise of Liam Cosgrave, who was so conservative and so Catholic that he voted against his own government's bill to enact a mild liberalization of contraceptive laws. More pertinently for rock music, this year saw arguably the most important development in popular music culture with the founding of *Hot Press*, the country's first dedicated rock paper. This was to prove an important factor in the post-punk Ireland of the 1980s when it became both the main conduit for Irish rock culture and also a key

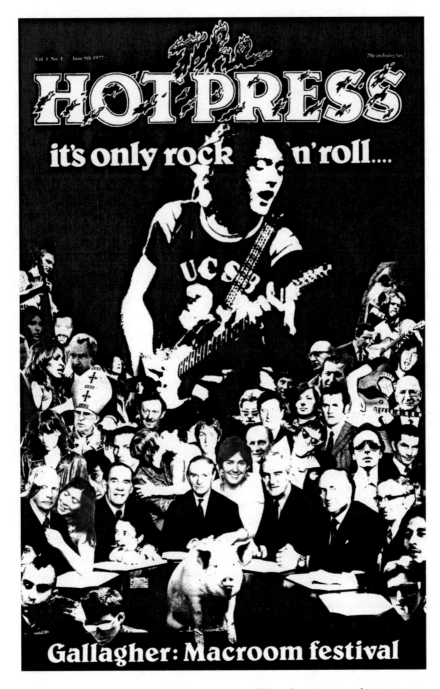

11. Rory Gallagher adorns the cover of the first issue of *Hot Press*

site for general political and cultural analysis. 1977 was also the year in which The Boomtown Rats broke through in both Ireland and the UK and the results were profound.

Geldof had assembled The Boomtown Rats in the autumn of 1975 and by the summer of 1976 they had become Dublin's most popular live act. The lack of a rock infrastructure was a problem – as Geldof noted: 'There was nothing in Ireland. No studios, no pop paper, no gigs, no nothing. We were trying to create a pop sensibility in 1975 and 1976 that could make these things thrive.'[6] As part of this process, he had organized the so-called 'Falling Asunder' tour with two other Dublin bands in an attempt to open up an alternative gig circuit outside Dublin that was different to the ballrooms of the showbands. Later on, Geldof would declare war on the Ireland of Liam Cosgrave, eliciting the condemnation of both Church and State, and part of his importance as a home-grown pop star was the fact that he was articulate in his anger and indiscriminate in the hypocrisies that he railed against. But The Rats were also an assault on the pretentiousness of mainstream rock music with a return to an R&B aesthetic and at the end of the tour they brought that to London, in the time-honoured fashion, to get to the next level of success. Two aspects of the move to London were to haunt the band as far as the British music press was concerned. First of all they had signed a contract before they left Dublin and thus, according to the more militant punk ethos, they had 'sold out' to the music industry already. Secondly, Geldof, waving his own red rag at the punk bull, declared the band's aim to be nothing more grandiose than 'to get rich, get famous and get laid'.

It is hardly surprising then that when The Rats arrived in London at the height of post-Grundy punk fury they almost immediately fell foul of the music press, especially the two papers most committed to the emerging punk ethos, *NME* and *Sounds*. It is one of the astounding ironies of The Boomtown Rats that they were reviled in England, not by the establishment, as were The Sex Pistols, but by the music critics and music press (and other punk bands) that otherwise might have been sympathetic to the band's assault on complacency. In Ireland, the establishment was queuing up to condemn Geldof as the devil incarnate and for this reason the legacy of The Boomtown Rats looks completely different when viewed from either a British or an Irish perspective.

An early example of the hostility to the band was Pete Silverton's review of their first gig at London's 51 Club in May 1977: 'they've

been watching the new wave. Very attentively. And decked themselves out in the correct London '77 handmedown threads.' He also
makes a disparaging reference to the band's 'Feelgoods/Rods rivvum
'n' blues axis'.[7] In his highly acclaimed study of punk rock and The
Sex Pistols, Jon Savage mentions 'the Irish R&B group The
Boomtown Rats' with just a slight air of knowing dismissal.[8] The
question of the band's music is a first bone of contention and the
accusation is that The Rats were 'merely' a 'back-to-basics' R&B
band who wandered into the wrong musical revolution, a pub rock
band thrust into the spotlight by accident. Geldof's own take on this
is interesting: 'We could not help being around the same age as the
people in the other bands, or that the fashions and styles of our time
made us appear to be in the same camp as them. All we had in
common was the conviction that something new needed to happen
in music.'[9]

To that extent, the critics were right but in some sense the musical disagreements were because the band could play well and did
write their own songs in a literate and musically adept manner (a
point that has been lost over the years). They also, quickly, became
successful so that Geldof's personal fame agenda had been realized
within a year of the band arriving in London. All of this, as Geldof
implies, was used to attack The Rats and in this he has a right to feel
aggrieved. The Rats played a form of R&B but played it fast and
furious with a sound, consisting of guitar, keyboards, and occasional
sax, that was richer than the punk three-chord thrash. The songs
utilized imaginative melodic time changes and hooks and had either
a strong narrative line or a deeply ironic point of view. Their first hit
– 'Looking after No 1' – is a case in point but The Rats' style – and
the characteristic Geldof stance – is perhaps best seen in what was
their eighth consecutive hit single (including two number ones),
'Someone's Looking at You', which reached number four in the
British charts in January 1980. It is a song about paranoia, but
whose paranoia – mine or yours, the establishment's or the music
press's? 'They saw me there in the square', Geldof sings, 'when I was
shooting my mouth off/About saving some fish/Now could that be
construed as some radical's views or some liberals' wish?' As it
turned out it would not be through saving the whale that Geldof
would find his politics in the mid-1980s but through the rather more
challenging need to save lives and feed the hungry. By then the punk
wars were an irrelevance and Geldof's own life was radically redi-
rected. The Rats did not push the boat out as far as radical musical

innovation was concerned. But for a while they dominated the British charts with a slew of exciting, literate and musically clever singles that brought a degree of energy back to the charts and they did not deserve the amount of negative press they generated at the time.

However, the politics of punk is interesting and in this Geldof may have been guilty of wilful blindness. Again it is a matter of the difference between Ireland and Britain, the similarities of the common culture sometimes disguising the profound nature of the different polities. Geldof was involved in the Irish politics of the time and was intensely political, even writing one of the most cutting political invectives of the period in 'Banana Republic', a number three hit in both Britain and Ireland. Geldof's main political target was the stifling conservatism of Catholic Ireland and he knew well how to elicit the apoplectic wrath of Church and State with civic leaders and chairmen of the Gaelic Athletic Association (GAA) branches vying with one another to condemn this loudmouth yob. But he was less sure about the British context as it then was. Undoubtedly there was a lot of music press posing and a lot of band posturing but the politics of late 1970s Britain were nonetheless real for all that.

One might compare two important media events to see both the contrasting political context and the way in which the music inter-acted with this. Geldof went on Ireland's 'Late Late Show' in January 1978 and stirred up a major media storm when he criticized 'the banana republic' as 'riddled with prejudice, stymied by the dead hand of conservatism, tainted by the false martyrdom of nationalism, in the thrall of medieval-minded clerics, despoiled by the greed of property speculators, betrayed by the mendacity of corrupt politicians, it suppurated in a sea of self-pity and hypocrisy'.[10] The analysis was spot on (and many of these accusations could have been applied just as well to the Ireland that collapsed under huge debts in 2009/10). The media storm that this raised in Ireland made Geldof public enemy number one for the Irish establishment, and The Rats subse-quently found it difficult to play in their own country. The media storm and subsequent difficulties in performing are reminiscent of the Bill Grundy storm that followed his TV interview with The Sex Pistols just a year earlier but this was not the media interview in Britain that most parallels Geldof's political intervention in Ireland.

A much more politically important interview was Tommy Vance's discussion with Johnny Rotten on his Capital Radio show on 16 July 1977. Rotten chose the records that Vance played (and this turned out to be an adventurous and eclectic mix) but the real political impact was when Vance discussed politics. Vance asked Rotten about The Pistols' manager, Malcolm McLaren: 'Someone once said to me he's a fascist.' Rotten retorted: 'That's absolute rubbish. He couldn't be. He's a Jew for a start. No, rubbish! Nobody should be a fascist.'[11] The combination of Rotten's musical tastes, involving reggae and soul music, and his unequivocal condemnation of fascism was a real moment of change within the British punk scene. The politics of the time were very different to the situation in Ireland that Geldof was familiar with. As the Labour government drifted towards its demise the far right was on the rise, given impetus by the high rate of inflation, rising unemployment and falling expectations. The streets in large working-class areas, especially where there was a strong ethnic mix, were becoming more violent. Within the social fragmentation that resulted there was a struggle over the political soul of the punk movement. The National Front went out of its way to recruit the disaffected youth of the punk (and skinhead) subculture and its own paper *Bulldog* attempted to enlist punk songs and icons to the fascist cause. There was a deep-seated and casual racism in British culture at the time and the Irish were not exempt from this, as some of the comments about Geldof and The Rats confirm. Both Rock Against Racism and the Anti-Nazi League were organizations set up to deal with the rising tide of right-wing politics.

The Rats arrived from Ireland into this political maelstrom and they were not at ease with the fractious nature of the fallout. Ironically, the British-Irish John Lydon was, and his mesmerizing performance on the Tommy Vance show was a major turning point. Geldof called the *NME* and *Sounds* 'the Stalinist press' and maybe some of the opponents of fascism were indeed Stalinist (although Trotskyite was far more likely). However, this was not (yet) his fight so he reacted only to the superficial style and stance issues. Perhaps he was clever enough to realize that he had no right, nor the detailed knowledge, to intervene on this topic (anymore than The Clash had on the topic of Northern Ireland). His deliberate goading of the press, so appropriate to the conservatism of Ireland, was out of place in the hothouse atmosphere created by the class and ethnic politics of late-1970s London. The result is that looking back over thirty years later, The Boomtown Rats' legacy is very different. Despite their long run of chart success, The Rats have been almost forgotten in Britain, bar 'I Don't Like Mondays'; their attack on Irish conservatism has been overlooked and they are remembered only as an unfashionable 'catch-up' punk band. Geldof's high profile is for altogether other reasons. But they remain an important, vital and politically charged memory for a whole generation of Irish people whose frustrations they voiced so eloquently and so belligerently – divided by a common culture, indeed.

12. 'Waking Up the Banana Republic' – The Boomtown Rats (Corbis)

The Boomtown Rats were the most successful of the 'new wave' bands that resurrected rock music in Ireland and stirred things up generally but of course they were not the only such band to do so. Also from Dublin were The Radiators from Space who followed The Rats to London and made two excellent albums but failed to achieve the same success. Maybe part of the problem here was the narrow vision that punk had acquired, though even the so-called political press could be guilty of casual racism as far as the Irish were concerned. One review of The Radiators in *Sounds* began: 'Irish punks? Will it start "One, tree, faw, two"?'[12] The Radiators were probably the best of the plethora of bands that emerged in the wake of The Rats, and their two albums *TV Tube Heart* (1977) and especially *Ghostown* (1979) were well received at the time. As to their relative failure, guitarist Phil Chevron, later to join The Pogues to great success and acclaim, makes an argument similar to that of Geldof:

> The mistake The Radiators made was aligning themselves with a movement they had bugger all to do with. Interestingly enough, a lot of our second album, *Ghostown*, was written before the first album, and *Ghostown* is a very unpunky album. But it got shelved. Everything was moving so fast in those days. If we'd been asked, 'Do you really want to be involved in this phenomenon because you have the right co-ordinates and the same general sort of attitude,' we'd have said no. But that's not the way it happened. At the time I was just pleased to get a record out and if this was the way to do it, fair enough, up to a point. In retrospect, I think it was a mistake, a huge mistake... Suddenly we were part of this thing, punk rock. To be fair, it did become obvious to us that we were not part of it. We didn't wear spiky hair, we didn't have safety pins through our noses. We were aware that we had something different to offer which, alluding back to Horslips, was that we were an Irish rock band. That's something we expressed on *Ghostown*, but by that stage it was too late.[13]

The band that really shook things up, stylistically as well as musically, was The Virgin Prunes, emerging from the throes of punk and scandalizing Ireland in an altogether different way from The Boomtown Rats.

THE VIRGIN PRUNES

> I have been with Rough Trade from the beginning. I had lived through the counter-culture and through punk and consequently thought I was unshockable. Then The Virgin Prunes came to London...(Nigel House)[14]

> But then, what is Ireland? It's a very easygoing place. The Waterboys make more sense in Ireland, because people like their pint, their bit of blow and a bit of a vibe. They don't want to be hearing Prunes' songs. The Prunes looked to Europe – I still do – while about 90 per cent of Irish people look to the USA. Then they get romantic and bring in the fiddle. (Gavin Friday)[15]

The legacy of The Virgin Prunes, the 'imagined community' of Lypton Village and the band's aggressive assault on Irish society in the late 1970s to mid 1980s has been comprehensively narrated and explored in both journalistic and academic accounts of Irish rock.[16] All authors appear to concur that the collective successfully shocked conservative Ireland in the late 1970s and early 1980s, attacking, among other institutions, the Catholic Church, the GAA, the ideology of the family, the persistence of heteronormative and patriarchal structures in the Irish body politic and the country's residual philistinism, many of the same areas identified by Geldof in his 'Late Late Show' diatribe. As John Waters put it: 'The Prunes were an angry bunch and here you find sideswipes at... the favourite Aunt Sallies of the time.'[17] All of these 'Aunt Sallies' have been duly noted to the point that The Virgin Prunes' 'heroic' assault on conservative Ireland has become, unfortunately, something of a cliché. In one sense, the band has been burdened with having to do too much, for standing in for a range of performative absences in Irish rock and popular music that were commonplace in neighbouring Britain. In this context, bands deploying the same sonic repertoire as The Virgin Prunes – discordant structures, wailing vocals, angular post-punk guitar and tribal drumming – were fairly common (Psychic TV, Coil, Siouxsie and The Banshees, The Cure and others).

Equally unfortunate is the manner in which The Virgin Prunes' oeuvre has been subsumed under 'Goth', that enduring genre/subculture with its fascination with death, the macabre, the horror genre, Edgar Allan Poe, and so forth (so that 'Pagan Lovesong' has become something of an enduring Goth club anthem). If Goth, for Simon Reynolds, is fixated on a gothic past, nostalgic in impulse (and hence retrogressive) and marked by an inability to explore the culturally or politically specific, it is easy to see why The Virgin Prunes would distance themselves from the movement. The band, in the context of Ireland especially, offered a very particular, and targeted, kind of politics.

The Virgin Prunes' achievement is in 'making strange' Irish society and doing this via the possibilities of immediate post-punk. Gavin Friday has recounted on several occasions the boat ride he took over to England to buy post-punk records. Indeed the musical, iconographic and ideological aspects of the movement were to be an important aspect of the band's 'rhetoric of shock'. This reputation was consolidated early on when they supported The Clash in Dun Laoghaire in 1978, when Gavin Friday's trousers split at the crotch revealing his genitals. The audience also became increasingly angry on discovering that the blonde, long-haired and heavily made-up

13. 'Perverting and subverting Irish rock' – The Virgin Prunes (Corbis)

Guggi was not female as they had initially assumed (an aspect revealed during the set by some figure-hugging clothing around the crotch). Indeed, such was the extremity of their performance in this support-slot that The Clash dropped them from the tour for their 'lewd behaviour'. It would be a mistake to claim that The Prunes were a simple clone of developments elsewhere, and while ideas of the time clearly informed their work, the consensus seems to be that the band were more extreme, especially in performance and iconography, than many of their English counterparts (successfully shocking the more recalcitrant centre), as well as something of a lone voice in their immediate milieu.

The Prunes also owed something to pop trends and 1970s' glam rock in particular (a form that has been largely absent from Irish performance styles). In other words, performativity – of putting on the show of gender construction, challenging sex and gender norms and fixed gender binaries – was to be of more importance in conservative Ireland/Northern Ireland than across the water where a range of performative stars occupied the musical landscape of the early 1980s (but in both cases the performative was ahead of its absorption into academic discourse).

Nonetheless The Virgin Prunes faced the same problems of the modernist avant-garde that they are frequently likened to (and heavily borrowed from) and had to face the impasse of shock tactics much like their forebears: in short, where do you do the rhetoric of shock, when shock itself becomes expected? This is a factor that Friday is extremely aware of: the 'clichés come in – you pull out the old pig's head and the dress'.[18]

One thing we have little knowledge about is just how many Bowie boys and girls existed in the Ireland of the time, and whether The Virgin Prunes were like the Dadaists in the sense of staging a heroic confrontation between artist and audience, or, in part at least, catering to those post-punk avant-gardists present, who were already formed. In this sense the story as written offers The Virgin Prunes as unique, as isolated avant-garde pioneers at some distance ahead of their default conservative audience. The history as told provides little sense of how much of their audience were identifying in a similar fashion and investing in this aspect of post-punk elsewhere. The impressive and powerful legacy of The Virgin Prunes (after all, the band with Friday only made two albums proper) has also had the unfortunate tendency of marginalizing Friday's (arguably more interesting) solo work.

The other sustained attack on the conservative musical values of the time came from the North. If punk in the South seemed well insulated from and marginal to the punk agenda of London, the continuing violence and political instability in the North seemed a much more appropriate environment for the punk ethos.

NORTHERN PUNK

According to journalist John Bradbury, the 1977 concert by The Clash was the main catalyst for kick-starting the Belfast punk rock scene.[19] In fact, the concert was cancelled (the excuse given was a problem with insurance) and attempts to restage it at other venues the same evening were thwarted by the police and other civic authorities. The disappointed Belfast punks who turned up for the gig in a sense found each other. The evening ended in a riot and the Royal Ulster Constabulary found themselves battling a different kind of 'white riot' to the ones they were used to. On that night, in other words, the individual punks of Belfast coalesced into 'a scene' and many of the bands that would emerge in the next few months could trace their genesis back to these events. That The Clash were the catalyst in the birth of punk music in Northern Ireland is not surprising, given the overtly political nature of many of Strummer's pronouncements back in 1976–78. In December 1976, for example, as The Clash set out as support band on the much-troubled Sex Pistols' 'Anarchy' tour of that month, he defined the band's political principles in very unambiguous terms: 'I think people ought to know that we're anti-fascist, we're anti-violence, we're anti-racist and we're procreative. We're against ignorance.'[20] This combination of radical politics and multicultural solidarity was particularly attractive in the sectarian political culture of Northern Ireland, especially for the emerging punk sensibility. Joe Strummer and The Clash came to represent an ideal that was in marked contrast to the dominant political modes of late-1970s Belfast – be these the establishment politics of the parent generation or the violent and blatantly sectarian politics of the paramilitaries. On the night of the failed Clash gig, Caroline Coon found many examples of a daring new sensibility in the air. One punk waiting outside the Ulster Hall that night told her: 'We all mix and we get on together. Everybody's bored with the fighting. Only a minority are fighting. It's music we want to hear – not religion.' And another, faced with the fact that the gig had been cancelled, complained bitterly: 'Whether you're a Protestant or Catholic here, you get it if you're a punk.'[21]

Andy Medhurst, commenting on a contemporary tendency to be nostalgic about the heady days of punk, has written:

> A central thread in punk's semiotic and ideological repertoires was its scorched earth, year-zero attitude to tradition and the past...whereas nostalgia often springs from an attempt to seek consolation and security in times gone by. Getting nostalgic about punk is worse than a contradiction in terms; it's a betrayal, trading in punk's forensic nihilism for a rose-coloured cosiness.[22]

As Medhurst acknowledges, though, the situation is more complex than this. On one hand there is a music consideration. It remains difficult today to fit the raw, angry sound of first-generation punk rock into the contemporary mainstream and especially into the musical soundscape of easy-listening radio and golden oldie retrospectives; by the same token, it is difficult to reconcile the anarchic, do-it-yourself values of 1977 with the current generation of formulaic, designer punks. This gives old-school punk a continuing resonance beyond the sentimental. More importantly, punk music was itself part of a broader and deeper movement of dissatisfaction with the political and cultural establishment and this is one reason why the contemporary radical sensibility is inclined to look back at punk music and its attendant culture with something akin to longing.

In another way, however, Medhurst considerably overplays punk's radical impulses. His is the punk of the metropolitan centre rather than of the provinces and the situation for punk (and for punks) was very different outside of its art/pop epicentre on the King's Road. Paul Cobley has noted the dilemma for the provincial punks, denied the protective environment of London's cosmopolitanism. Punk, he argues, was a considerable affront to a host of deep-rooted values, including class, masculinity, 'decent' behaviour, locality and tradition:

> That punk had to negotiate a set of pre-existing national attitudes is well-known; but...the fact that these attitudes were even more formidably entrenched outside the main urban centres meant that being a provincial punk represented a considerable leap of faith. The social context of the provinces therefore made the punk 'phenomenon' a much different proposition from that which has been so slavishly rehearsed in written accounts.[23]

Cobley was talking about his experiences of being a punk in Wigan but his point is all the more pertinent for Belfast. In some ways, late-1970s Belfast and punk were made for one another. If there was an element of 'the abject' about punk – gobbing, vomiting – there was no more abject place in the Western world than Northern Ireland, specifically Belfast, in 1977. The deep-rooted traditions that Belfast punks had to negotiate were not only those that punks nationally had to contend with but also included the IRA (Irish Republican Army), the UDA (Ulster Defence Association), the INLA (Irish National Liberation Army), the UVF (Ulster Volunteer Force), an armed RUC (Royal Ulster Constabulary) and an unreliable UDR (Ulster Defence Regiment). Johnny Rotten had only to namecheck them in his music to gain some street credibility but Belfast punks had to deal with them every day. In Northern Ireland, punk nostalgia is not just about fond remembrance of a golden time in the past (though there is undoubtedly an element of this). Rather, punk nostalgia is about 'what might have been' – a nostalgia, in other words, for a sense of a better future and a nostalgia that is given added political poignancy by the nature of sectarian politics in contemporary Northern Ireland, even after a decade of relative peace. What is being remembered and what is being longed for is the opportunity that punk music once offered of an imagining beyond the sectarian politics of Northern Ireland's older generation, as articulated to Caroline Coon back in 1977. In this regard, punk was not just a revolt into style. It was also a revolt into a new politics.

If the punk explosion in Britain was a revolt against the complacent certainties of the parental generation (the one that most fully enjoyed the consumer boom of the 1960s), in Northern Ireland it was a rebellion against the complacent certainties of a sectarian political culture that had delivered nothing but social disharmony and communal breakdown. And therein lies the irony: the original British punks, epitomized by Johnny Rotten's sneer, may have spat their venom at the hippies but punk in Northern Ireland offered a confrontational style that in the end seemed to endorse the old hippie dream of peace, love and understanding. Punk music in Northern Ireland, in other words, was an original 'community relations council', emerging from the bleakness to offer hope when despair and negativity was the more usual response. This reading of punk is not just a contemporary reappraisal of events, tinged with well-meaning but naive sentimentality. John T. Davis's celebrated film on northern punk, *Shellshock Rock* (1979), was made in the eye of the storm itself and is the original progenitor of the thesis.

SHELLSHOCK ROCK – POLITICS

In its own low-key, almost subterranean way, John T. Davis's film has been a remarkably influential cultural document. Perhaps it is not so surprising, then, that the film should have caused the controversy that it did at 1979's Cork Film Festival. Originally chosen and scheduled for a screening on the second-last day of the festival, the film was mysteriously dropped during the festival week itself. The only explanation that Davis was given at the time was that the film was withdrawn because it was 'technically not up to standard'. The idiocy of the Cork festival decision was confirmed later in the year when the film won a silver award at the International Film and Television festival in New York.[24]

Davis felt at the time that the film was banned for political reasons but, if this is so, it was for the same complacent, conservative politics that attempted to deny The Boomtown Rats a gig in Dublin the following year. The film does indeed have a particular political message but it is more likely that it was banned for moral and aesthetic reasons. There is a certain racy vernacular in the songs and in the comments made to camera (also there is one incidence of 'mooning') and this was always going to annoy a conservative and complacent middle-class jury. The film's energetic style – rapid editing cut to capture the breakneck speed of the music; a moving, hand-held camera caught in the swirl of youthful energy – was equally challenging. In its own way, *Shellshock Rock* showed up the huge gap that by then existed between the southern cultural establishment and the culture of the streets. Looking back at the whole controversy now, especially through the prism of the post-Celtic Tiger economy, it seems like an incident from another planet and not just another time. With hindsight, we can see that it brought into focus a deeper set of contradictions that ran through a southern Irish society on the cusp of significant social and cultural change – another attack on the old guard, this time from the industrial North.

By this stage, punk music in Northern Ireland had already begun to break out into a wider audience. Belfast band Stiff Little Fingers' first two singles, 'Suspect Device' and especially 'Alternative Ulster' (both 1978), attracted wide attention, and Derry band The Undertones' 'Teenage Kicks' reached number thirty-one in the British charts and got the band onto 'Top of the Pops' for the first time. *Shellshock Rock* explores the breadth and depth of the punk scene, especially in Belfast and Derry, and captures on film a number of bands who were destined not to make it (including Rudi, whose single 'Big Time' was the first to be recorded on Terri Hooley's Good Vibrations, one of the main conduits for the northern bands). In many ways, Rudi – the band that didn't make it – are presented in the film as the heroes of Belfast's punk and, in contrast to Stiff Little Fingers, represent a sense of authenticity and anti-commercialism that was central to the punk ethos overall. This brings to mind Jon Savage's analysis of punk's central paradox: 'Built into Punk from the beginning was not only a tendency to self-destruction but also a short shelf life. Despite what many of the groups professed, the movement enshrined failure: to succeed in conventional terms meant you had failed on your own terms; to fail meant you had succeeded.'[25] The utopian moment of punk, in other words, the moment when the young working-class people of Northern Ireland crossed the sectarian divide in the name of a shared new imagining, resides with the bands like Rudi, The Outcasts, Protex and The Idiots – who did not make it – almost as much as it does with those who did. In *Shellshock Rock*, Davis intercuts a number of live performances of these bands (including Stiff Little Fingers and The Undertones performing their two most famous songs) with interviews of the punk musicians and their supporters. Through the live music and the interviews a picture emerges of this new space – mental as well as physical, musical as well as social, economic as well as political – that has been opened up in an otherwise claustrophobic world.

The film opens to the ethereal, heavily echoed sound of The Idiots singing the chorus from the film's title track: 'For I am so afraid ... For I am so afraid ...' (a refrain that is repeated later in the film and gives an eerily appropriate sound for the tracking shots of Belfast's darkened streets that occur throughout). This refrain is heard over very rough footage of a punk rock gig, shot in a grainy, smoky blue and strobe-lit to achieve a disorienting and maybe even alienating combination of sound and image. The film then cuts to the first interviews, three young punks who begin to put some substance to the slightly other-worldly feel of the opening sequence. They articulate what is the political message of the film and five points in particular emerge.

First, like punk elsewhere, indeed like all post-war youth subcultures, the Belfast punks articulate a general anti-establishment philosophy – a rebellion against conformity in general and against their parents in particular. Second, however, it is the sectarian nature of their parents' culture that is seen to be the main problem, the designation by society of religious labels and the consequent division of young people into opposing religious camps. The third point emerges logically from this rejection: punk music and the punk scene in general is all about giving an identity to the young that would allow them to come together with a shared set of cultural beliefs and tastes that are beyond religious and political norms. This is the key political message of the punks and it underpins the whole film. It is emphasized later in the film when, in voice-over, a young punk notes that after 2,000 deaths nothing has been achieved: 'Who wants a united Ireland? Who wants to be in the United Kingdom or anything?'

The fourth point that emerges from the interviews is a reminder of the old Maritime days and what had been lost in the interim. The space that was created for this new coming together was Belfast city centre itself, at this time abandoned and deserted at night by everyone else except the security forces. The darkened and empty city centre provided a meeting place where the overwhelmingly working-class punks could get together outside the sectarian pressures of their home housing estates. The venues for live music were seedy pubs – the Harp Bar and the Pound – and the meeting place was Terri Hooley's record store on Great Victoria Street. The final point that emerges from the interviews is perhaps the most utopian. The punks in Belfast are anxious to differentiate themselves from the London punk scene of two years earlier. This is dismissed as a passing phase, a fashion and a mere empty style that lacked the social and political edge of its Belfast counterpart. The English punk scene was essentially a negative style while punk in Northern Ireland was a positive social and cultural force. It was, according to the punks themselves, destined to last because it was engaged in a process of establishing an alternative to both the parent culture and the culture of dissent that was represented by Republican and loyalist paramilitaries. It did not last, of course. The dirty protests and the Republican hunger strikes of 1980–81 raised the sense of the abject beyond that of a mere subcultural style. The political temperature was raised and as the music and the styles elsewhere transmuted from new wave to New Romantic, from punk to post-punk, the punk scene in Belfast collapsed back into sectarianism. This 'dissent from dissent' is important, nonetheless, for understanding the nature of the punk moment in Northern Ireland and for understanding the kind of nostalgia that it can generate even thirty years later.

SHELLSHOCK ROCK – THE MUSIC

If the interviews and voice-overs in Davis's film carry the political narrative of the film, then the music provides the central focus. Appropriately, Davis cuts from the first set of interviews to footage of Stiff Little Fingers performing 'Alternative Ulster' live at the New University of Ulster. The sequence has all the energy and excitement that we associate with the live punk scene, shot in close-up and edited rapidly to match the band's breakneck delivery. 'Alternative Ulster' was Northern Ireland's first punk hit in the UK and has come to symbolize the attempt to forge an alternative politics by the province's severely bored, annoyed and disaffected youth. The film cuts from the live performance to an interview with the band in the dressing room after the show. Lead singer and guitarist Jake Burns talks about the threats the band has faced and the political danger that is inherent in championing an alternative cultural space beyond the clutches of both the political mainstream and the political opposition represented by Republicanism and loyalism. Again, the message is clear: it is easy to be oppositional and alternative in cosmopolitan Britain but more difficult in Ulster where one's kneecaps (or even one's life) are at risk. Burns articulates a viewpoint that valorizes his band as heroes and pioneers, pushing a message of hope and a new beginning against formidable paramilitary odds.

Objectively, of course, this is true and it is the one characteristic of the punk scene in Northern Ireland that was not replicated anywhere else in Britain or Ireland. It requires no great courage in cosmopolitan London to wear a tee shirt showing the face of the Queen defaced by a pin; it is quite another matter to do so in loyalist Belfast. Equally, it requires an act of substantial bravery in the Republican areas of the city to reject the platitudes of the parental culture when these are invested with so much martyrdom, patriotic sacrifice and oppositional rhetoric, and carry a substantial physical threat about collaborating with the enemy.

However, in some of the other interviews in the film, *Shellshock Rock* suggests that there was less than universal approval of Stiff Little Fingers' approach to the situation in Northern Ireland amongst the punks themselves. To some extent, this was the result of 'local knowledge'. The band had been well known in the city as a heavy metal covers band until a visiting English journalist, Gordon Ogilvie, turned them into a punk band and helped to write the kind of songs that he knew would go down well in Britain. The band's first two singles, 'Suspect Device' and 'Alternative Ulster', and their first album, *Inflammable Material* (1979), left no doubt as to their subject matter. However, the feeling persisted at the time that this was a 'Johnny-come-lately' band that exploited the situation in Northern Ireland for commercial gain and spoke more to the disaffected British audience than it did to, or for, the Northern Ireland punks.

If Stiff Little Fingers preached about an alternative Ulster, then The Undertones lived the alternative and wrote about it by ignoring the political situation completely. In *Shellshock Rock*, the band performs the hit single 'Teenage Kicks' live, and the contrast here with The Fingers could hardly be greater. The Undertones played a form of power-pop driven by a superb twin-guitar 'wall of sound' in support of singer Feargal Sharkey's choirboy warble and the melodic wit of John O'Neill's lyrics. The sound and the performance is every bit as frantic and as energetic as the Fingers' raw agitprop but the content is very different (the film later features The Undertones playing 'Here Comes the Summer'). The Undertones made a particular point about their subject matter. The opening track on the their second album *Hypnotised* (1980) is a song called 'More Songs about Chocolates and Girls'. This makes an ironic nod towards the title of Talking Heads' 1978 second album, *More Songs about Buildings and Food* (itself a quirky, ironic comment on the po-faced seriousness of the times). However, it is primarily a statement of intent and it is hard not to see in the title and in the band's whole stance an implied criticism of Stiff Little Fingers (and perhaps even of The Clash, with whom they toured in the US in 1979).

Jon Savage noted the contrast between the two bands – Stiff Little Fingers' 'Belfast social realism' as opposed to The Undertones' 'incandescent pop/Punk flash'. More problematically, he describes The Undertones as the 'missing link between the 13th Floor Elevators, the Stooges, and Irish traditional music', a remark which exudes more than a trace of Irish essentialism. But the musical and lyrical contrast between Northern Ireland's two most 'successful' punk bands is clear enough. Savage quotes a 1990 comment by Undertones singer Feargal Sharkey that reinforces the point: 'People used to ask early on why we didn't write songs about the troubles: we were doing our best to escape from it.'[26]

It is ironic that more than twenty-five years later some of the band members seem to have regrets about their decidedly apolitical or anti-political stance of the time. When The Undertones broke up

14. 'Incandescent pop/Punk flash' – The Undertones (photo: Larry Doherty, courtesy of The Undertones)

the O'Neill brothers were to assuage any residual guilt they felt about the band's lack of politics by forming the much more politically charged That Petrol Emotion in 1985.[27] However, as *Shellshock Rock* shows, in 1978–79, The Undertones captured the mood of the times and the aspirations of the punks better than most other bands through their aggressive concerns with adolescence and sex. In a way, 'Teenage Kicks', by being about the ordinary, was an extremely political statement in the highly charged, extraordinary atmosphere of Northern Ireland at the time. In Northern Ireland's briefly flourishing punk scene, the aggression of the music and the anti-establishment culture of punk in general was utilized to express an ironic political position. For Northern Irish punks, the establishment then meant their slightly older siblings as well as their parents. Their opposition was to the status quo as well as to those aggressive and violent opponents of the status quo who had reduced daily life to the abject. Punk was a third space beyond the fixed binaries of these opposing forces; it gave a sense that, *pace* Rotten, there could be a future, if not in England's dreaming, then certainly in Northern Ireland's re-imagining.

NOTES

1. Harry Doherty, *Melody Maker*, 15 May 1976.
2. Labour MP Marcus Lipton, quoted in Jon Savage, *England's Dreaming: Sex Pistols and Punk Rock* (London: Faber & Faber, 1991), p.365.
3. Sandy Robertson, 'Boomtown Rats: Do you sincerely want to be rich?', *Sounds*, 17 December 1977.
4. Bob Geldof, *Is That It?* (Harmondsworth: Penguin, 1985), p.119.
5. Ibid., p.116.
6. Ibid., p.138.
7. Peter Silverton, 'Boomtown Rats: Club 51, London', *Sounds*, 28 May 1977. To be fair to Silverton, he did come around in later articles on the band.
8. Savage, *England's Dreaming*, p.383.
9. Geldof, *Is That It?*, p.152.
10. Ibid., p.156.
11. See the transcripts of the interview at http://www.fodderstompf.com/ARCHIVES/REVIEWS2/capital77.html.
12. Alan Lewis, review of 'Television Screen', *Sounds*, 7 May 1977, quoted in Roger Sabin, 'I Won't Let that Dago By: Rethinking Punk and Racism', in Roger Sabin (ed.), *Punk Rock: So What? The Cultural Legacy of Punk* (London: Routledge, 1999), pp.199–218.
13. Eamonn McCann, 'Down All the Days', *Hot Press*, 24 May 1988.
14. Nigel House, Manager, Rough Trade Records, London, interview by Noel McLaughlin, 2010 (unpublished).
15. Tony Clayton-Lea and Richie Taylor, *Irish Rock: Where it's come from, where it's at, where it's going* (Dublin: Gill & Macmillan, 1992), pp.65–6.
16. Mark J. Prendergast, *The Isle of Noises: Rock and Roll's Roots in Ireland* (Dublin: O'Brien Press, 1987), pp.212–19; Clayton-Lea and Taylor, *Irish Rock*, pp.61–7; Gerry Smyth, *Space and the Irish Cultural Imagination* (Basingstoke: Palgrave, 2001); Gerry Smyth, *Noisy Island: A Short History of Irish Popular Music* (Cork: Cork University Press, 2005), pp.54–5, 85–6; John Waters, *Race of Angels: Ireland and the Genesis of U2* (Belfast: Blackstaff Press, 1994), pp.35–45, 60–5.
17. Waters, *Race of Angels*, p.38.
18. Clayton-Lea and Taylor, *Irish Rock*, p.65.
19. John Bradbury, 'Big Time, you ain't no friend of mine', *Causeway*, 4, 1 (Spring 1997), pp.40–5.
20. John Tobler, 'Star Quote: Joe Strummer', *NME Rock 'n' Roll Years* (London: BCA, 1992), p.295.
21. Caroline Coon, 'The Clash in Belfast', *Sounds*, 29 October 1977.
22. Andy Medhurst, 'What did I get? Punk, Memory and Autobiography', in Sabin (ed.), *Punk Rock: So What?*, pp.219–31.
23. Paul Cobley, 'Leave the Capitol', in Sabin, *Punk Rock: So What?*, pp.170–85.
24. 'Punk Film Lifts Silver Award', *Spectator*, 24 November 1979.
25. Jon Savage, *England's Dreaming: Sex Pistols and Punk Rock* (London: Faber & Faber, 1991), p.140.
26. Ibid., pp.596–7.
27. That Petrol Emotion were also musically adventurous and their early and distinctive indie–dance cross-over was well ahead of the 'Madchester' scene.

PART 2

U2

6

U2: Irishness and Identity

Being Irish is very important to U2. It is the most important thing to them and the most important thing about them. (John Waters)[1]

What are you currently grooving to?
It's just whatever gets stuck on the stereo, mate. Loads of rap and hip-hop and dance, I don't buy records. There's a record by someone called Little Eejit that I like. But I don't know who the fuck he is or where he came from. (Shaun Ryder)[2]

It was a cold day on Wednesday, 18 January 2009, two days before the inauguration of America's forty-fourth president, when U2 took to the stage in front of Washington's Lincoln Memorial. The band was in the US capital to play at a party to commemorate the historic inauguration of the first African-American president. In a bill that included Bruce Springsteen, Usher and Beyoncé, U2 played a short set that included the Barack Obama favourite 'City of Blinding Lights' (*How to Dismantle an Atomic Bomb*, 2004) as well as their earlier anthem 'Pride: in the Name of Love' (*The Unforgettable Fire*, 1984), a song deemed particularly fitting for the moment, as the event was also promoted as a celebration of the legacy of Dr Martin Luther King. In the context of the line-up on the day, it is tempting to read U2 as representatives of Ireland and Irish-America, just as Springsteen could be regarded as the representative of the blue-collar white working class, and Beyoncé and Usher as African-America's delegates. As such, the concert sought to represent one cluster of the United States' main ethnic groupings. The event was yet another prominent chapter in the intertwined histories, part of the 'intimate connectedness', of Ireland and America; or to echo Hazel Carby, another high-profile symptom of the cross-cultural traffic of the Irish-American Atlantic.[3] Perhaps even more significantly, though, it opened up questions about the musical and political relationship between Ireland and Black America. In celebrating this historic and progressive political turn, U2's affirmative, anthemic and uplifting sound appeared a fitting soundtrack to the upward drives of American political narratives – whatever the problem 'you (too) can do something about it'. U2 were clearly on the side of progressive liberal forces and few would dispute the enthusiasm for the band's performance, evident in the rapturous response of the sizeable African-American audience on that day. The year, if not the day, was significant for another reason: it marked the anniversary of a thirty-year recording career for the band, one encompassing twelve studio albums and several globe-straddling sell-out tours.

Since the release of 1987's *The Joshua Tree*, U2 have been (arguably) the biggest rock band in the world. No band, it seems, are loved and loathed in equal measure; attracting open hostility – especially towards lead singer Bono – and apparent slavish devotion. Indeed, many U2 fans are caricatured as adoring their idols without being very much interested in other music (as a brief perusal of the many internet fan sites reveals). U2, in other words, veer between being regarded as the most fascinating rock band of recent years, keeping rock's romantic flame alive and capable of the form's oft-noted ability to transport its listeners to a utopian 'somewhere else'; and condemned as representative of all that is banal in contemporary rock. In this latter view the band is criticized for lacking a certain 'edge', whether this is defined as hedonistic abandon or a perceived failure to inhabit the types of 'outlaw' masculinity that have long been regarded as a core rock 'n' roll virtue. Whichever way, U2 stands out in the current climate: an international rock band that has retained its original line-up for over thirty years and, unlike The Rolling Stones, hasn't fallen into the role of a 'greatest hits machine' tacitly acknowledging that their best work may be securely in the past.[4]

As befits U2's status as a global phenomenon, the story of the band has been told many times by a variety of commentators with different agendas, and thus offers little in the way of surprises. The U2 history has been well picked over. A cursory glimpse at the music press would do nothing to dispel such a view – *Rolling Stone* and *Q*, for example, have run regular centre-page feature articles on the band as well as retrospectives of past albums and tours. The last two decades in particular have also witnessed the growth of a substantial secondary publishing industry, comprising various U2 'readers', biographies of both band and lead singer, picture-book histories and academic and semi-academic accounts.[5] While this secondary material provides a useful resource, much of it borders on hagiography. In addition to an extensive recording and gigging career, this considerable discourse on U2, and its sheer volume alone, creates difficulties for critical exploration. The problem is further exacerbated because in popular music the 'text', for study purposes, is not as easily identified as in other cultural forms. If one is hoping to explore the U2 'text', what precisely, is one referring to: what aspect of text, what media, which period? However, if the U2 story is well picked over in popular Anglo-American media, the band's Irishness is an unfleshed-out 'other' (particularly in academic writing).[6]

At times, it seems that U2 themselves are everywhere: at Barack Obama's inauguration, opening 2005's Live 8 in London's Hyde Park with Paul McCartney, Bono's audiences with the Pope and other world leaders, and even a surprise appearance via video link at the 2009 Tory Party conference. The 2009 tie-in with the BBC prompted accusations that the United Kingdom's national broadcaster had morphed into the 'Bono Broadcasting Corporation' – a slogan taken up right across the British press – given the virtual round-the-clock coverage accompanying the release of their 2009 studio album, *No Line on the Horizon*.[7] In the United States, a week of appearances on the BBC was matched with a five-night consecutive run on the primetime 'Late Show with David Letterman'.[8] U2 are not simply everywhere, their presence is frequently read as an *imposing* one, a symptom of global cultural colonization and an icon of popular musical imperialism.

Despite the group's ubiquity and their dominant presence *within* popular media, the academy – popular music studies, media and cultural studies – has been fairly silent on the subject of U2 and Irish rock and pop. In fact, from the perspective of the music industry, *No Line on the Horizon* became something of a test case for the fate of the mega-band in general and the long-term future of the album format in the age of the digital download and peer-to-peer file-sharing systems.

Given this prominent presence, the relative absence of U2 in academic popular music studies is quite striking, especially compared to the wealth of material exploring English rock's 'golden age' and the sheer volume of work exploring the legacy of The Beatles, The Rolling Stones, The Who, Led Zeppelin and more recently the swathe of work on punk and Britpop.[9] One could argue that nostalgia in popular music studies has been going on for a long time, echoing the more widespread 'retro-mania' in popular music culture at large.[10] While much of this work has been invaluable – one need only think of the way in which the English rock canon has been deconstructed, its nationalistic register critiqued and subjected to scrutiny from a variety of theoretical perspectives – the net effect has been, somewhat ironically, to remake Britain and English rock's centrality to debates about popular music culture.[11] This of course leaves other 'peripheral' music scenes marginalized, much in the same way that British cultural studies has been unable to shake off the 'British' of its title, despite the theoretical claims that run in the opposite direction (anti-nationalist, anti-imperialist, post-colonial, anti-essentialist, transnational, multicultural, the critique of Anglo-centrism and so forth). One has a situation analogous to the ideological ambivalence of the 'tension-ridden text' in film studies: the narrative argues one direction, the visual style another. Or, in this context, the Anglo-American is reinstated via critique. Academic writing about Britpop has oddly shared a formal similarity to its object of critique, oscillating between a suspicion of the nationalistic thrust of its 'Little-Englandisms' and a valorization of its central tropes, such as the focus on the minutiae of English life and institutions (The Kinks, David Bowie, The Smiths, Blur, The Libertines, The Streets, and many others).

Is this exclusion on aesthetic grounds: are U2 just not as good or important as The Beatles or The Stones? Or is the reasoning socio-historical: is the moment of U2's emergence not as important a period politically as the radical ferment of the 1960s, with its narratives of sexual liberation, the counterculture and endless images of Swinging London? Or maybe, to look at the band through a widely deployed term that revels in its own mystification, U2 are simply not 'cool'? To invoke Simon Frith's appropriation of Frank Kogan's distinction between the discourse of the classroom and the discourse of the hallway, are U2 something of a 'popular music studies joke' outside of the seminar room?[12] Brian Eno, renowned musician, artist and producer, and someone marinated in the discourse of cool, has claimed:

> Cool, the definitive eighties compliment, sums up just about every-thing that U2 isn't. The band is positive where cool is cynical, involved where it is detached, open where it is evasive. When you think about it, in fact, cool isn't a notion that you'd often want to apply to the Irish, a people who easily and brilliantly satirize, elaborate and haggle

and generally make short stories very long but who rarely exhibit the appetite for cultivated disdain – deliberate non-involvement – for which the English pride themselves.[13]

Unlike Eno, the academy has been reluctant to explore U2's Irish provenance. U2 are quite simply a big, even bland, rock band in the Anglo-American mould and Irishness is registered as a simple and relatively uncontroversial fact of origin – a mere backdrop to the group's emergence. Even in positive critiques, the tendency is to ignore, or at best to make cursory reference to context, and argue that U2 are just a great rock band that would have shot to international prominence whatever the circumstances. Indeed, the issue of genre and style has been much more prominent in these discussions than the question of national identity, let alone how national 'locatedness' may shape the former. In this vein U2 is mapped to the so-called rock revival of the mid-1980s or explained as 'conscience' or 'caring' rock.[14] And it is worth noting here that rarely, if ever, has a revival been judged to be as good as that which it is reviving.

Martin Cloonan has argued for the national's importance in the face of its relative neglect in much popular music studies writing where the focus has been on the local/sub-national and/or the global. He notes that Irishness is routinely mentioned in music press writing on U2 just as the Welsh identity of the Manic Street Preachers is similarly signposted. Despite theoretical claims that the band are best regarded as a regional inflection of a transnational style, Cloonan argues that 'somehow it seems to matter to the writers and readers of these articles that those artists come from particular nations or Nation-States' and that 'following on from this are claims that these artists can tell us something about the countries from which they come'.[15] And clearly the band's Irishness is not just academic, or only of interest to 'home' fans or reducible to local/national pride, but is of great importance to its international fans, as evidenced in the hoards of 'U2 tourists' who have made the 'pilgrimage' to Dublin (with the most devoted leaving their mark on the already graffiti-smattered walls surrounding Windmill Lane Studios). However, while Cloonan offers this useful and timely corrective, he also reproduces the silence and does not explore how U2 signifies Irishness, nor considers what kind of Irishness is articulated by the band.

Perhaps most worryingly, despite the predominance of theoretical anti-essentialism in the academy, when Irishness has been considered

beyond a simple fact of origin there has been a tendency to reproduce some of the dominant, if more benign, representations of the
Irish prevalent in popular media and in the British and American
music press. Thus U2's sincerity, 'Irish spirit', passion, heart,
unworldliness and ethereality and so on are duly noted. For example, Lynn Ramert, in an otherwise informative discussion of Bono in
the early 1990s, somewhat problematically notes the singer's 'innate
awareness of Irish culture'[16] and his 'Irish wit'.[17] These discourses are
not mere reportage, they don't just possess a descriptive, 'after-the-
fact' role, but are themselves what Michel Foucault referred to as
'regimes of knowledge' that create interpretive frames: shaping what
is and is not Irish, what can and cannot be said about particular
peoples and their music, and therefore what Irish music can and
cannot be.[18]

The reason for pointing out U2's absence in popular music studies is to lay the ground for an analysis of the band that will hopefully
inform the discipline. Of central importance here is how Ireland and
Irishness is constructed in and by music and performance as well as
in discourse about music. This is not to suggest that only Irish
cultural studies will have answers to Irish popular musical questions.
There is now a large body of academic Irish writing exploring the
post-colonial, but, with the possible exception of John Waters[19] and
Lauren Onkey,[20] it has been reluctant to consider U2 (and indeed
Irish rock and pop more broadly) in these terms – an ironic position,
given that the island is highly visible and audible through the band's
music.[21]

However, it is a simple fact that the band and its ubiquitous lead
singer have dominated, and continue to dominate, international
perceptions of Ireland and the Irish in musical and in celebrity terms.
As Smyth has argued, U2 are, 'as far as most people are concerned,
the sound of Irish rock – the reality...with which alternative realities are obliged to contend'.[22] U2 are the only globe-straddling rock
band that are not straightforwardly Anglo-American. Throughout
their thirty-plus-year career the band members have had their
primary residences in Ireland and continue to write and record the
majority of their music there. U2, in other words, have brought to
an end the exile narrative in Irish popular music, where artists such
as Van Morrison and Rory Gallagher and bands such as The
Boomtown Rats and Thin Lizzy had to leave Ireland to find success:
hence the importance of so-called 'homecoming' U2 concerts, starting with 1983's conclusion to the *War* tour, 'A Day at the Races',

right through to the Slane Castle concerts of 2001, which were significantly released on DVD as *U2 Go Home* (Hamish Hamilton, 2003). In other words, U2 helped to consolidate the *centring* and *placing* of Irish rock *in* Ireland.

This ushers in the other side of the argument that, perhaps more problematically, conceives of U2 as uniquely Irish. Within Irish popular music discourse the status of U2's ethnicity has been a given, although broadly and schematically two positions have emerged. In the first the band is regarded as the embodiment of a modernizing, liberalizing and increasingly secular Ireland, of an Ireland, for good or for ill, rejecting its 'traditional' past. In the context of the highly monocultural Dublin of the late 1970s, the young band was read in the pages of Ireland's rock magazine *Hot Press* and in Eamon Dunphy's controversial biography, *Unforgettable Fire: The Story of U2*[23] as emblematic of a progressive and multicultural Irishness. Famously, guitarist the Edge (Dave Evans) was born in England to Welsh Presbyterian parents; Adam Clayton was born in England to English parents; Bono, the product of a 'mixed' marriage (Protestant mother and Catholic father, though brought up Protestant), was born in Dublin; only drummer Larry Mullen is representative of the majority or 'orthodox' Irish identity (i.e. born in Ireland of two Catholic parents). Much has also been made of all four band members' education at Mount Temple Comprehensive in Dublin, Ireland's first non-denominational secondary school. In fact, accounts of their early years reveal suspicion, even enmity, towards both band and management on the Dublin scene. One faction, calling themselves The Black Catholics, was particularly hostile towards the group and their perceived Englishness/Britishness and the favouritism their ethnic status apparently bestowed.[24] Indeed, U2 in certain sections of the Dublin scene at the turn of the 1970s into the 1980s were regarded as British as much as Irish and, as such, were seen (in somewhat conspiratorial terms) as able to court favour with the anglicized 'Dublin 4' media. In this sense, but to a lesser degree perhaps, the band embodied an island-Irish version of the types of 'in-between' struggles of second-generation Irish bands in Britain as described and analysed by Sean Campbell.[25]

The second position conversely sees the band not as modern and progressive but as being connected, perhaps subliminally, to more long-standing Irish cultural and musical *traditions*. This perspective rejects narrow nativistic definitions of Irishness, but moves authentic Irishness onto the (post)modern. Once again, the favoured metaphor here, deployed most prominently by writer John Waters[26] is the 'underground river' of essential Irishness, very much like Seán O'Riada's use of the same metaphor. U2 are thus conceived of as pre-colonial, racial Irishness preserved, as it were, in rock. And, of course, 'good' rock, with its emphasis on authenticity, whether libidinal, sexual, racial or otherwise, and the primitive, is precisely valued for facilitating a raw 'essence' of identity to emerge. The interpretative dialectic is, therefore, that in U2 rock has obliterated essential Irishness, a sign that colonization is complete and Anglo-American dominance secured; or that in U2 rock has become the vehicle for tapping into and preserving a deep-lying essential Irishness.

U2, in other words, are a conundrum. What other global rock band can be read both as the sound of pre-colonial racial authenticity *and* of global imposition? In this respect, U2 are both centre *and* periphery, simultaneously the colonizer and the colonized, the authentic and the inauthentic. Inauthentic, that is, when contrasted to folk and traditional music in Ireland which is regarded as that which is most Irish (i.e. *heard* as Irish); and authentic, in that they are a band furthering rock authenticity, and keeping Irishness alive (somewhere) in the midst of its conventions, textures, chord structures and performance modes. The Irish-based writing on U2 has been of critical importance and has had an edge over writing in Britain and the United States by obstinately focusing on the band's ethnicity. *Hot Press* and Bill Graham, for instance, have considered the national context of their emergence, and have explored their post-colonial provenance, despite the risk of essentialism that may accompany such an endeavour.

This echoes the important work of Sean Campbell and his study of the Irish popular music diaspora in England. Campbell has drawn attention to two issues of critical importance. Firstly, how the British music press has consistently 'othered' Irish rock and pop musicians, often in fairly stereotypical, hackneyed and even downright racist terms. And second, how the *NME*, *Q* and others have ignored the Irish aspect of second-generation 'British' and 'English' rock artists and bands, 'focusing on the musicians' English nationality at the expense of their Irish ethnicity'.[27] As Nabeel Zuberi has forcefully put it, Irishness is, at best, 'something to be noted but then obscured in a narrative of British national identity that for obvious reasons finds the question of Ireland's relationship to Britishness too troubling'.[28] This list of artists, perhaps ironically, includes some who are regarded as quintessentially English, such as Morrissey and The

Smiths (where seven of the eight parents are Irish) and Noel and Liam Gallagher of Oasis (ironically, the band most linked to a 'laddish' English nationalism), but also Johnny Rotten/Lydon of The Sex Pistols and Public Image Limited, Elvis Costello, and Kevin Rowland of Dexy's Midnight Runners. The exception here is, of course, Shane MacGowan and The Pogues, who are less problematically regarded as Irish (with the justification presumably residing in the band's overt performance of ethnicity). As John O'Flynn has argued, in the most complete ethnographic survey of responses to Irish music to date, 'for many people, the social fact that a particular musical product or practice is Irish means little unless the same music actually *sounds* Irish'. [29] One can imagine how problematic it would be if the ethnicity of second-generation Afro-Caribbean musicians was ignored by the British music press, or not heard or registered as 'black'. The Irish, it appears, are too alike for difference to matter, except in the most banal or stereotypical terms: traditional and ethnic folk music, talking, drinking and fighting. If not these, where exactly is the Irish in Irish popular music? Irish rock, therefore, exists in a liminal zone between having its difference, its national specificity, overlooked on the one hand, and being condemned to a narrowly defined Irishness on the other. Thus, the Irish, in Richard Dyer's terms, are not black enough, yet not securely white,[30] or as Homi Bhabha has put it in relation to the Anglo-American centre, 'almost the same but not white'.[31] U2 are locked in a tension between carrying and displacing the burden of representation.

If U2 are the most recognized signifier of Irishness in modern history, Bono is undoubtedly the most famous Irish citizen globally. In recent years the most prominent aspect of the singer's star-text has been his widely reported role as political campaigner/agitator for organizations committed to African and 'third-world' issues, such as Jubilee 2000's 'Drop the Debt', and more recently with his own organization DATA (Debt, AIDS, Trade, Africa) and the ONE campaign. The singer has won numerous awards for his work in this role and has even been nominated for the Nobel Peace Prize on three occasions. Predictably enough, this increasingly conspicuous role in global politics has ushered in a certain amount of criticism from both inside and outside rock culture and from across the political spectrum, most vocally perhaps from Paul Theroux in *The New York Times*, who has pointed to – among other things – the unelected aspect of such campaigning.[32] It is not the concern here to address the complex ethical and political dilemmas of global celebrity's somewhat rocky relationship to debt management; rather, to explore the implications of this area for debates about music, Irishness and identity. These criticisms were at some point about the 'right' of rock stars to meddle in politics proper, and the argument that appearing to 'do good' is a cynical 'cashing-in', a way for the star, and by association the band, to reinforce its popularity through the acquisition of what might be termed 'conscience capital'. These well-worn arguments centre, to a degree, on the issue of sincerity – a subsection of the more endemic discourse of rock authenticity and a focus on authorial intention – and on whether Bono is, or is not, *for real* – thus setting in motion a circuit of claim and counterclaim.

More intelligent criticisms have suggested that whether sincere or not, Bono's campaigning has always been safely inside the dominant neoliberal consensus and in no sense has the singer offered a radical critique of existing geopolitics. Nor has band or singer been associated with the revival of anti-capitalist activism or with figures such as Slavoj Žižek and organizations such as Attac. What can be reported with some certainty is that, with regard to the workings of the band, accounts of the production and touring of their 2004 album, *How to Dismantle an Atomic Bomb*, have noted the singer's regular absenteeism in support of such causes and the tensions this created within the U2 organization. This signposts the considerable risks involved in such strategizing and the fact that, with regard to political work of this sort, U2 does not, as it were, sing with one voice, with drummer Larry Mullen particularly critical of the problematic politics of the singer's association with George W. Bush.[33] Of course, the argument against conscience rock conceivably works in the reverse direction: that Bono, and by extension the band, is taking a risk, given the critical flak that such campaigning has attracted (especially since 1985's Live Aid). Moreover, after the experimentation and apparent hedonism that marked the band's work in the 1990s, the return to more of a traditional U2 sound and performing style (marked by the release of *All That You Can't Leave Behind* in October 2000), together with Bono's campaigning, was regarded as the group revealing its true colours, and retreating to the 'caring' rock that marked its assent to global stardom during the 1980s. In some senses, the volte-face was seen as undoing the 'good work' of the *Achtung Baby*/*Zoo TV* era, when the band had subverted the stereotype of the four over-earnest young men. It is hard to imagine Bono as his hedonistic alter ego, the Fly, offering a thesis about the asymmetrical power of transnational capital and its effect on the so-called third world (especially after many politically incorrect utterances such as wanting 'to put the spastic back in rock 'n' roll'). Whichever way, the return, and even extension, of this 'conscience Bono' does raise interesting questions about rock, stardom and national identity that have been frequently overlooked in writing that has broached the topic. Brian Eno summed up the governing perspective of the star's campaigning thus:

> Bono commits the crime of rising above your station. To the British, it's the worst thing you can do. Bono is hated for doing something unbecoming for a pop star – meddling in things that apparently have nothing to do with him. He has a huge ego, no doubt. On the other hand, he has a huge brain and a huge heart. He's just a big kind of person. That's not easy for some to deal with. In most places in the world they don't mind him. Here, they think he must be conning them.[34]

This passage is interesting not least for raising the issue of national identity and for highlighting how both band and singer are perceived in Britain. U2's, and particularly Bono's, relationship to Britain and British/English music fans has always been a strained and contradictory one. As an example of this, the band headlined on the Friday night of 2011's Glastonbury Festival for the first time (U2 had been due to play the previous year before emergency surgery on Bono's back resulted in cancellation). However, the coverage of the lead-up to the band's appearance (and non-appearance) at the Festival was interesting. Organizer Michael Eavis's evident enthusiasm, encapsulated in the phrase 'the biggest band in the world is about to play the best festival in the world', certainly did not silence detractors. Topping the bill at the world's most famous rock gathering, predictably enough, ushered in a great deal of critical invective. Some suggested that the band did not belong at a festival that is just about clinging on to radical late-1960s countercultural politics, or that U2, a band that, while undoubtedly popular, is divisive in UK audience terms. Either the band is regarded as too political in the sense that campaigning is not 'cool', or it fails to embody the easy hedonism required by a summer festival crowd (indeed, perhaps U2 share with Jay-Z in being regarded as 'un-Glastonbury').

 Bono's Irishness, however, has allowed him to adopt the mantle of rock activist and campaigner in this area of global politics, because his national identity draws upon Ireland's status as 'Britain's first and oldest colony'[35] and the 'prototype for all others'.[36] It would be difficult, one could surmise, for a prominent English rock star to take up such a role, perhaps in large part due to the residue of Empire and England's former position as pre-eminent colonial power. English rock stars such as Sting and Peter Gabriel have, of course, been involved in similar politics but, arguably, their degree of access to relevant political circles or the scale of receptiveness in many quarters of the world has been qualitatively different. It is easier to countenance prominent English rock stars acting as representatives of class politics, or anti-racist issues, than engaging explicitly in the vortex of global power relations in the wake of Empire. Irishness, it seems, functions as a complex form of political currency.

Where the national dimension has been more explicitly explored across the world's press is in the 2009 scandal about the band's tax evasion and its offshore accounts in the Netherlands. Of course, this raises interesting questions about what it means for a band to *come from* a nation, or its benefit to that nation in monetary terms. As other commentators such as O'Flynn,[37] Smyth[38] and Rob Strachan and Marion Leonard[39] have observed, even prior to the tax evasion scandal, little revenue earned by the band went directly into the Irish economy, despite many altruistic gestures. From a political-economic perspective, then, U2 are best understood as a transnational phenomenon: global recording artists, signed to a multinational conglomerate, hailing from and residing in a small, post-colonial nation with offshore monies that largely bypass its by now fragile, post-Celtic Tiger economy. This may explain the highly ambivalent attitude to the band in Ireland. Homecoming concerts, of the type referred to earlier, may have been the focus of celebration in the past with 'home' fans' national pride co-mingling with more specifically musical pleasures. However, the series of concerts in Dublin's Croke Park in the summer of 2009 were met with protests and blockades by local residents at the disruption caused to the road infrastructure around the venue (as well as much debate in the Irish press about the ethics of the band's offshore monies).

The problem with this type of approach is that it does not tell us very much about how U2, musically and in performance, may signify Irishness globally – that is, 'articulate' Irishness, as opposed to merely reflecting aspects of a pre-given sense of Irishness. After all, the band are perhaps the most successful Irish export in any field in history. Accepting, then, that it is difficult to sever U2 from their

Irishness, what type of identity does the band articulate? How might this be best approached? The group certainly do not 'sound' Irish in the widely accepted sense, in that recognizably 'ethnic' signifiers are largely conspicuous by their absence, with 'traditional' instrumentation only appearing on a fraction of the band's extensive back catalogue; most notably Vinnie Kilduff's Uilleann pipes on 'Tomorrow' (*October*, 1981) and Steve Wickham's fiddle on 'Sunday, Bloody Sunday' (*War*, 1983). Even a broad analysis of the band's lyrics would reveal little in the way of specific references to Dublin or Ireland (the exceptions here are 'Sunday, Bloody Sunday' – the only song title to explicitly refer to Ireland – and 'An Cat Dubh' (The Black Cat), the only album track to use the Irish language as a title and/or a lyric). The band's lyrics do not refer to Irish institutions and/or cultural practices in a way that has been common in British rock and popular music from the Kinks onwards. In fact, songs taken to be *about* Dublin, such as 'Bad' and 'Running to Stand Still', offer no particular or grounded references to place. The latter track, with its line 'I see seven towers, but I only see one way out', is taken to refer to the (now demolished) seven tower blocks of the Ballymun estate on the northernmost fringe of Dublin's north side.[40] A socio-historical interpretation would be interesting here as well, given that the estate, with its seven towers – each of which was named after the individual leaders of the 1916 Rising – was Ireland's first high-rise housing development and one synonymous with the city's heroin problems in the 1980s. However, even here, there is a degree of abstraction and it is in no sense necessary to decode the reference to enjoy the song as a musical/semantic experience, as the openness of the image and its poetic latitude invites a range of readings, whether biblical, mythical, or author-anchored.[41] This 'universal' address evidently works in tandem with the band's hyper-inclusive name, their 'one-world' politics and global ambitions, and raises the related question of whether cultural and historically specific references may act as a barrier to global acceptance.

Moreover, it would have been difficult for any Irish band to invoke the type of urban mythology common in British/English rock and pop, with its uneasy mix of poetic detail/celebration and barbed critique. British rock and pop was able to draw upon, invoke and extend a long tradition of introspection which existed across a range of cultural forms, from Victorian Music Hall to Philip Larkin's poetry; from the writings of the Angry Young Men to the films of

Mike Leigh and Terence Davis. By contrast, Irish urban and suburban life is relatively unelaborated and certainly did not possess this extensive range of a priori myths, tropes and archetypes that could be reworked and woven into popular musical expression; and this perhaps explains why the type of overt references to Dublin and Ireland offered in the punk of The Radiators' second album, *Ghostown* (1979), failed to find a larger audience. U2 have not, lyrically at least, explicitly textualized the cultural details of Irish life in the way that The Kinks, Blur, The Smiths and The Fall have fashioned versions of Englishness. The band's articulation of, and to, Irishness has clearly worked in a different way, as we shall see when we come to consider U2 in performance.

Bono is interesting particularly in the way he circumvents the two dominant traditions of Irish performer, as identified by Gerry Smyth: 'Paddy Mad' and 'Paddy Sad'.[42] This is not to suggest, however, that Bono escapes well-worn Irish stereotypes entirely. While drinking and fighting are evidently not a conspicuous part of the Bono star-text, the singer's propensity for free-form conversation, highly subjective philosophizing and revelling in the texture of words and ideas is well known. As Bob Dylan put it, 'spending time with Bono was like eating dinner on a train – feels like you're moving, going somewhere'.[43] Simply put, most of the world is aware that Bono likes to talk. Alas, the term 'garrulous, autodidact Paddy with a political conscience' has yet to be coined in the repertoire of Irish stereotypes, even though the island's two most famous citizens over the past two-and-a-half decades – Bono and Bob Geldof – have, perhaps, made the role their own. In fact, U2, even early on, were largely non-drinkers (with the oft-noted exception of Adam Clayton), regarding the world of pubs and alcohol as markers of mediocrity (something they shared with Bob Geldof). This distance from the drinking culture had a twofold aspect: first, pubs, from a subcultural perspective, were uncool, and thus part of the majority experience; second, the world of the Dublin/Irish pub was a national cliché and hence to be avoided (in much the same way that The Pogues had to sweep alcoholic beverages out of way in photo-shoots, so as to avoid furthering retrogressive images of Irish drinking).[44]

As well as sidestepping the drinking stereotype, Bono and the band – in their early days especially – also contradicted the widely circulating perception in England of the Irish as stupid. Clearly this had some significance. In the late 1970s and throughout the 1980s these old colonial stereotypes were more than a mere residue. In one sense, U2 helped to obliterate negative images such as these. Moreover, this period was also one where the association of the Irish with irrationality and violence was especially potent, with a sustained IRA mainland bombing campaign in the wake of the Maze Prison Hunger Strikes. For good or for ill the band avoided associations with Irish Republicanism in both its organized and 'physical force' manifestations. This, of course, led to some criticism and resentment in certain quarters at home, with the band regarded as failing to deal with the persistence of age-old colonial issues and the unresolved question of the North.[45]

However, the band were to become important in articulating, and in becoming the focus of, a new, confident and intelligent Irish identity, one at some distance from prevailing archetypes. Indeed the band, in these early years especially, were a vital force in offering ways of being Irish that were at some distance from these types of inferiority. Of course, the English music press – *NME*, *Melody Maker* and *Sounds* – for obvious reasons has preferred to focus on Bono and to stress, or construct, the messianic aspects of his persona (the preaching Bono) rather than historicize and contextualize the identity he has articulated. The Bono persona clearly takes on a different hue when looked at from the Irish perspective and he occupies an interesting place within the history of Irish identities broadly, one that has sought to counter, explicitly or implicitly, colonial stereotypes. And this is where Ireland's rock magazine, *Hot Press*, has been especially important, as it has offered a powerful parallel discourse about band and singer that has frequently acted as a counterweight to these powerful and recurrent negative images.

If U2, musically and in performance, are 'uncool' in the Eno sense, we can certainly say that the band is not 'hot' in the way that the blues, New Orleans funk or various Latin musics have been described. 'Hot', 'smoking' and 'cookin' are terms frequently associated with, and discursively constructed as, 'warm-blooded' music that in some ways oozes sexuality, passion, fire and so forth. Certainly, prior to the early 1990s, U2 were not associated with sex, 'sexiness', or sexuality in any primary sense.[46] Rather, U2 have been associated with the majestic, the celestial and the spiritual. As Simon Reynolds and Joy Press have argued, U2's music in the 1980s sublimated sexuality, 'inviting a lofty gaze upwards, but paralysing you from the waist down', with the emphasis drawn to Bono's plaintive vocals and the Edge's chiming guitar over what the authors describe as the 'inert rhythm section'.[47] Therefore, U2 could best be described as 'warm', even 'lukewarm', and perhaps ironically for a band read as the harbinger of a multicultural and modernizing Ireland, their music in the early years seems to embody the spirit of Ireland's first president, Eamonn de Valera, and his famous maxim in the days immediately after independence, that Ireland should 'set a good, chaste and moral example to the rest of the world'. Or, from an international perspective, U2 is the band that sought to save rock 'n' roll from sex and drugs.

The exception with regard to the critical silence about U2 in popular music studies has been the attention given to the band's radical reinvention in the *Achtung Baby/Zoo TV* period of 1991–94, which has produced two dedicated articles/book chapters in popular music studies in the late noughties,[48] as well as attention in media and cultural studies more broadly. This is, of course, to be welcomed, but in one sense the emphasis on this aspect of the band's career has been somewhat predictable, given the vogue for theoretical postmodernism and/or theorizing the postmodern in the mid-1980s and the 1990s. The *Zoo TV* period thus offered an easy 'fit' between the overt discourses of mediation offered by the band and the critical concerns of the time. With hindsight, one can question the usefulness of postmodern approaches as, firstly, they appear to neatly dovetail with advertorial writing on the band, and secondly, and perhaps ironically for a critical endeavour that proclaimed the death of the author, affirmed U2's apparent authorial sophistication. Indeed, the governing critical perspective was to celebrate the band's apparent reinvention and debate the significance in authorial terms. In another sense, *Zoo TV* became a popular musical performance equivalent to a Brian De Palma film where the pleasure was centred on counting the intertexts and revelling in the playful inauthenticity of it all. It also gave ample opportunity to explore the wearing of masks, role-playing and debating other performative strategies (as well as reading *Zoo TV* via the writings of Baudrillard, Lyotard *et al*). Simon Frith has argued against this type of postmodern theorization, and while he notes the truth of some of its claims, he moves onto critique its 'wilful ignorance of history'. Videos, he writes, 'are analysed as if pop stars didn't perform before the camera was there to record them'.[49] In a similar vein, what was frequently missing from the discussion of *Zoo TV* was consideration of music, and the bodies performing it, leaving the concert as a form of postmodern silent cinema.

15. 'Saving rock 'n' roll from sex and drugs' – Bono and U2 in performance (Corbis)

Again, and perhaps most importantly, even critical work that engaged with music and performance in discussing this apparent postmodern U2 was reluctant to explore its connection to discourses of Irishness. Part of the argument here is that *post-colonial* criticism, attuned to the specificities of popular music culture, is a more suitable method through which to approach this significant moment in the band's career than is postmodernism.

Therefore, before proceeding further with considering how U2 has constructed a sense of Irishness in popular musical terms, it is necessary to explore briefly the context of the band's emergence. Here particular emphasis will be placed on the Dublin 'scene' in the late 1970s/early 1980s, beginning with analysis of *Hot Press* reportage of their early career.

NOTES

1.   John Waters, interview by Noel McLaughlin, 1995 (unpublished).
2.   Shaun Ryder, 'Still Hanging In!', *Mojo*, 187 (June 2009) p.9.

3. Hazel Carby, 'What is this Black in Irish Popular Culture?', *European Journal of Cultural Studies*, 4, 3 (2001) pp.325–49.
4. U2, despite their distinctive sound, have experimented throughout their career and can boast an impressive list of collaborations: Johnny Cash, Clannad, Emmylou Harris, Mick Jagger, Jay-Z, B.B. King, Sinéad O'Connor, Luciano Pavarotti, Lou Reed and Frank Sinatra amongst others.
5. This would be a prohibitively long list. See, for example, Hank Bordowitz (ed.), *The U2 Reader: A Quarter Century of Commentary, Criticism and Reviews* (Milwaukee, WI: Hal Leonard, 2003); Eamon Dunphy, *Unforgettable Fire: The Story of U2* (London: Penguin, 1987); Bill Flanagan, *U2: At the End of the World* (London: Bantam, 1995); Bill Graham, *U2 – The Early Years: Another Time, Another Place* (London: Mandarin, 1989); Bill Graham and Caroline van Oosten de Boer, *U2: The Complete Guide to their Music* (London: Omnibus Press, 2004); Neil McCormick, *U2 By U2* (London: Harper, 2006); Niall Stokes, *U2 – Into the Heart: The Stories Behind Every Song* (London: Sevenoaks, 2006); Mick Wall, *Bono: In the Name of Love* (London: Andre Deutsch, 2005); John Waters, *Race of Angels: Ireland and the Genesis of U2* (Belfast: Blackstaff Press, 1994).
6. See Visjna Cogan, *U2: An Irish Phenomenon* (Cork: Collins Press, 2006); Lauren Onkey, *Blackness and Transatlantic Irish Identity: Celtic Soul Brothers* (New York and London: Routledge, 2010); and Waters, *Race of Angels*. These are the only academic single-authored monographs to deal explicitly, and at length, with U2's Irishness.
7. Paul Connolly and Liz Hazelton, ' "From Bono Broadcasting Corp" to five-night-run on *David Letterman*: How U2 pulled off the biggest publicity coup in music history', *Daily Mail*, 9 March 2009; Neil McCormick, 'U2 live at the (Bono Broadcasting Corporation) Radio Theatre', *Daily Telegraph*, 27 February 2009; and Miranda Sawyer, 'The Bono Broadcasting Corporation', *The Observer*, 1 March 2009.
8. The BBC coverage was a week-long affair and included appearances on 'Zane Lowe' (23 February), 'Front Row' (24 February), 'Live Lounge' and the 'surprise' gig on the roof of Broadcasting House (both on Friday 27 February) and 'Listener's Questions', as well as 'U2@The Culture Show' (24 February) and two appearances on 'Friday Night with Jonathan Ross' (27 February and 17 July 2009).
9. Even Gerry Smyth's *Noisy Island: A Short History of Irish Popular Music* (Cork: Cork University Press, 2005) skims past U2 relatively quickly.
10. For a more detailed discussion of nostalgia in popular music culture and the presence of the past in the present, see Simon Reynolds, *Retromania: Pop Culture's Addiction To Its Own Past* (London: Faber, 2011).
11. Martin Cloonan, 'State of the Nation: "Englishness", Pop and Politics in the Mid-1990s', *Popular Music and Society*, 21, 2 (1997), pp.47–71.
12. Simon Frith, *Performing Rites: On the Value of Popular Music* (Oxford: Oxford University Press, 1996), pp.12–13.
13. Brian Eno, 'Bringing Up Baby', in *Rolling Stone* Editors, *U2: The Rolling Stone Files* (New York: Hyperion, 1994), p.165.
14. See, for example, Simon Reynolds and Joy Press, *The Sex Revolts: Gender, Rebellion, and Rock 'n' Roll* (London: Serpent's Tail, 1995); and Steve Redhead, *The End of the Century Party: Youth and Pop towards 2000* (Manchester: Manchester University Press, 1990). These two monographs understand U2 within the rock revival as 'conscience' or 'caring' rock and there is little engagement with national identity and/or ethnicity.
15. Martin Cloonan, 'Pop and the Nation-State: Towards a Theorisation', *Popular*

Music, 18, 2 (1999), p.202.

16. Lynn Ramert, 'A Century Apart: The Personality Performances of Oscar Wilde in the 1890s and U2's Bono in the 1990s', *Popular Music and Society*, 32, 4 (2009), p.449.

17. Ibid., p.447.

18. Michel Foucault, *The Archaeology of Knowledge* (New York/London: Routledge, 2002).

19. Waters, *Race of Angels*.

20. Lauren Onkey, 'Ray Charles on Hyndford Street: Van Morrison's Caledonian Soul', in Diane Negra (ed.), *The Irish in Us: Irishness, Performativity and Popular Culture* (London and Durham: Duke University Press, 2006), pp.161–95; and Onkey, *Blackness and Transatlantic Irish Identity*.

21. Gerry Smyth, *Music in Irish Cultural History* (Dublin: Irish Academic Press, 2009), pp.1–14. Significantly, Smyth argues that Waters's *Race of Angels* is 'compromised by a fast-and-loose attitude towards highly sensitive critical and cultural theories' (p.6).

22. Ibid., p.85.

23. Dunphy, *Unforgettable Fire*.

24. Waters, *Race of Angels*, p.44; Ian Wilson, interview by Noel McLaughlin, 1995 (unpublished).

25. Sean Campbell, *Irish Blood, English Heart: Second-Generation Irish Musicians in England* (Cork: Cork University Press, 2011).

26. Waters, *Race of Angels*, pp.35–7.

27. Sean Campbell, 'Ethnicity and Cultural Criticism: Evocations and Elisions of Irishness in the British Music Press', *Celtic Cultural Studies: An Interdisciplinary Online Journal*, 2007 http://www.Celtic-Cultural-Studies.com/Papers/01/Campbell-01.html.

28. Nabeel Zuberi, *Sounds English: Transnational Popular Music* (Chicago, IL: University of Illinois Press, 2001), p.67.

29. John O'Flynn, *The Irishness of Irish Music* (Farnham: Ashgate, 2009), p.99.

30. Richard Dyer, 'White', in Richard Dyer, *The Matter of Images: Essays on Representation* (London: Routledge, 1993), pp.141–3.

31. Homi Bhabha, 'Of Mimicry and Man: The Ambivalence of Colonial Discourse', *October*, 28 (1984), p.128.

32. Paul Theroux, 'The Rock Star's Burden', *New York Times*, 19 December 2005.

33. McCormick, *U2 By U2*, pp.428–9.

34. Paul Morley, 'On Gospel, Abba and the Death of the Record: An Audience with Brian Eno', *The Observer*, Review, 17 January 2010.

35. Anne McClintock, *Imperial Leather: Race, Gender and Sexuality in the Colonial Conquest* (New York: Routledge, 1995), p.52.

36. Ella Shohat and Robert Stam, *Unthinking Eurocentrism: Multiculturalism and the Media* (London and New York: Routledge, 1994), p.85.

37. O'Flynn, *Irishness of Irish Music*. The tax evasion issue came to the fore at 2011's Glastonbury Festival appearance and, alongside the band's polarization of UK audiences, was the subject of much press reportage. As a symptom of this anti-U2 sentiment, the activist group Art Uncut planned to stage a protest at U2's apparent non-payment of taxes to the Irish exchequer during the band's set (it was, controversially, stifled by heavy-handed tactics by security staff). The tax issue does, however, raise a number of ironies. Many of the bands who played at the festival (and their management) may be guilty of similar tax arrangements, but U2 appeared to be singled out as the lone culprits. This may be as much to do with a desire to expose Bono as a hypocrite (as the band's tax regime clearly is at odds with the singer's stance on world poverty and debt

relief) as it is to raise broader political issues. It is, of course, ironic that political commitment of any sort results in being singled out for blame in what is
surely a more widespread problem. One could surmise that it would be every
bit as politically expedient to highlight bands and artists for tax evasion that
are much less politically active than Bono and U2 (it appears, once again, that
hypocrisy is a greater crime than tax evasion). Significantly, nearly three
decades earlier, the *Exile on Main Street*-era Rolling Stones were able to
construct themselves as outlaws and heroes for escaping the taxman and
decamping to the south of France. This appears to confirm Eno's observation
that Bono's greatest crime is doing 'something unbecoming for a rock star'.

38. Smyth, *Noisy Island*.
39. Rob Strachan and Marion Leonard, 'A Musical Nation: Protection,
    Investment and Branding in the Irish Music Industry', *Irish Studies Review*, 12,
    1 (April 2004), p.42.
40. Stokes, *Into the Heart*, p.69; Graham and van Oosten de Boer, *U2*, p.33.
    Alongside 'Bad' and 'Wire' (*Unforgettable Fire*, 1984), 'Running to Stand Still'
    is one of the 'heroin songs' that studded the band's oeuvre in the 1980s. Social
    and political issues such as the city's heroin problems were, however, explored
    in a 'universal' fashion and references to place, or socio-political specifics are
    largely absent.
41. See Theodore Gracyk, 'To Find a Song that I Can Sing: What Philosophy of
    Language Can Tell Us about Popular Success', in Mark A. Wrathall (ed.), *U2
    and Philosophy: How to Dismantle an Atomic Band* (Chicago, IL: Open
    Court, 2006), pp.163–76. Gracyk challenges the types of author-grounded
    readings of the band's songs offered by Niall Stokes, claiming that the notional
    listener does not need to know that 'I Will Follow' is 'about' Bono's mother,
    or that 'Stuck in a Moment' is 'about' the suicide of Michael Hutchence, to
    enjoy the songs.
42. Smyth, *Music in Irish Cultural History*, pp.51–64.
43. Bob Dylan, *Chronicles, Volume 1* (London: Simon & Schuster, 2004), p.174.
44. Campbell, *Irish Blood*, p.98.
45. In the context of Thatcher's Britain and the IRA bombing campaign in the UK,
    Irish ethnicity was not yet a desirable commodity, except perhaps to swathes
    of the British left for whom Irishness was associated with oppression, anti-
    Imperialist rebellion, ethnic difference, folk authenticity and a vaguely spiritual
    (even pre-modern) disposition. For a more thorough exploration of these
    issues, see Campbell, *Irish Blood*, pp.35–6.
46. In fact the Van Morrison-inspired 'Promenade' from 1984's *The Unforgettable
    Fire* may mark an early foray into sexualized imagery.
47. Reynolds and Press, *Sex Revolts*, pp.82–3.
48. See Ramert, 'Century Apart'; Susan Fast, 'Music, Context and Meaning in
    U2', in Walter Everett (ed.), *Expression in Rock-Pop Music: Critical and
    Analytical Essays*, 2nd ed. (New York: Routledge, 2008), pp.175–97.
49. Frith, *Performing Rites*, p.224.

_____

7

U2: Discourse and Performance

Aren't U2 in Ireland valued above anything else as 'our boys made good'?
The problem with that kind of thinking is it doesn't tell you very much about what sort of boys are making what sort of good. (Bill Graham)[1]

U2 came from nowhere, they had no consciousness of what had gone before them; no band they wanted to ape, no sound, ethnic or contemporary, inspired the formation of U2. (Eamon Dunphy)[2]

U2 emerged from the aftermath of punk, especially the move-ment's 'back-to-basics', 'do-it-yourself' ethos.[3] The energies released by punk represented a certain 'clearing-of-the-decks', real-ized in a whole series of immediate post-punk reinventions of rock sound, some explicitly anti-rock or non-rock in approach. As Smyth has noted, in common with punk elsewhere, Dublin witnessed some-thing of an explosion in elemental guitar-based music with a host of bands absorbing the influential sounds and styles of The Sex Pistols and The Clash,[4] with the latter band's appearance at Trinity College, on the *Get Out of Control* tour, on 1 October 1977 frequently taken as a landmark moment in the birth of a modern, urban Irish music scene (and a suitably impressed young Paul Hewson was in the audi-ence). Punk, as Barbara Bradby described it, represented 'a sort of musical glasnost' in late 1970s Ireland. 'For the first time', she writes, 'rock music and national identity were not mutually exclu-sive',[5] even if this is not strictly true, as the case of Horslips attests.

In Ireland punk could not only be regarded as a riposte to the middle-class-dominated 'complexities' of progressive rock and the apparent 'banalities' of 'mainstream pop' (as in Britain and the United States), but also something of a rebuttal to the residual pres-ence of folk and traditional musics and the enduring (yet waning) appeal of the showband. In this sense, the embrace of punk could be construed as part of a longer popular musical history where any semblance of cultural and political 'progressiveness' was, in Frith's words, 'likely to reject the sounds of local nationalism (whether historical or tribal or folk sounds) in favour of the sounds of inter-national "corruption"',[6] although, as will become apparent, the Irish case adds some interesting perversions to this local/global dialectic.

This emergent Dublin 'scene' of the late 1970s possessed little in the way of a rock music infrastructure of recording studios, rehearsal rooms and dedicated venues. As we have seen, the found-ing of *Hot Press* in 1977 and the establishment RTÉ's pop station, Radio 2, in 1979, were two of the most significant factors in boost-ing and developing an Irish rock culture. *Hot Press* has remained for over thirty years a left-liberal music and cultural magazine, and is something of an unusual hybrid of the Britain's 'inkies' (*Melody Maker*, *NME* and *Sounds*) and *Rolling Stone*. It became an impor-tant cultural force in both challenging residual socio-political conservatism and in opening up and constructing a local rock culture that was largely ignored in the mainstream press such as *The Irish Times*. While *Hot Press* clearly grew out of the energy of punk, it was, perhaps somewhat ironically, staffed by a generation of writ-ers who 'came on stream' musically amidst the cultural ferment of the late 1960s. As with the United Kingdom, the core journalists were mainly drawn from university backgrounds, chiefly University College Dublin and Trinity College Dublin. Most central were brothers Niall and Dermot Stokes, the magazine's founders (with Niall the long-serving editor), and their friend Bill Graham, the writer who would, up until his death in 1996, be regarded as Ireland's pre-eminent rock journalist and U2's most influential domestic interpreter. Graham is credited with introducing the young band to their long-standing manager, his friend and fellow Trinity student Paul McGuinness.[7] As Dave Laing has observed of the British context, this college background gave these writers access not just to socially useful connections, but also to academic discourse, especially the tools of literary and cultural criticism, as well as a variety of politicized interpretive strategies.[8] Therefore, like its British counterparts, *Hot Press* was marked by a seriousness of approach, but one allied to a strong (yet 'progressive') nationalist imperative, manifest in the desire to actively construct a canon of Irish rock artists and to give scope to the social and political context within which the music was produced and circulated. The magazine was also concerned to counter the lack of English music press interest in Ireland and Dublin and 'de-homogenize' the island's popular music, and to 'fan out' and give texture to the various regional scenes of Cork, Galway, Limerick, the North and so forth (though despite this noble enterprise, *Hot Press* would face accusations of being Dublin-centric on many occasions).

Not unlike the scene it was reporting, the magazine was something of a late developer compared to its counterparts on either side of the Atlantic and was thus able to model itself on these now relatively long-established traditions of rock writing. It was then able to selectively draw upon the writing styles, tone of address, and thematic preoccupations established by a range of auteur rock writers such as Lester Bangs, Barney Hoskyns, Nick Kent and Charles Shaar Murray.[9]

In this sense the magazine was a sometimes uneasy hybrid of libertarian 1960s countercultural politics and the more snarling polemical thrust of punk writing. However, it differed in two vital respects from its transatlantic cousins. First, the magazine enjoyed a virtual monopoly of coverage of the island's developing music scene (a music press extension of the nation's highly centralized infrastructure), and second, as Ireland is a small nation and hence a relatively insignificant popular musical market, the magazine had a higher degree of autonomy from the centralized music industry at large and was under less pressure to follow the industry-led agenda of reportage. These two factors were to prove important, firstly in the degree to which it was able to report the initially unsigned U2, and secondly in the extent of its influence nationally.

Another issue of importance arises here. Despite punk's role in energizing the Dublin scene, *Hot Press*, editorially at least, was not a great lover of Dublin punk, with Niall Stokes finding many of the bands derivative of developments across the Irish Sea. The significant exception here is the commercially unsuccessful second Radiators album, 1979's *Ghostown*, which was lauded for its Irish-specific style and themes, its references to James Joyce and other canonical literary figures.[10] In fact, punk in Northern Ireland was regarded much more positively by the magazine, presumably for its strong regionally and nationally specific elements, evidenced in the accents of The Undertones, the idiosyncratic agit-pop of Rudi and the Northern bands' distinctive take on punk elsewhere. Also, as Dave Laing has pointed out, despite the aesthetic and political gains of punk, punk was still punk *rock* and as such conformed to many of the masculinist aspects of rock more generally.[11] While punk in the United Kingdom was marked by a high percentage of strong iconographically and performatively distinct women, regrettably the same could not be said for punk in the Irish context. The only significant female punk band was The Boy Scoutz, fronted by Catherine Owens (who later designed stage sets for U2).

Hot Press, then, played a pivotal role in constructing a coherent discourse of Irish rock, giving texture and nuance to an Irish rock 'scene', and, most importantly perhaps, in constructing a canon of Irish rock artists. What became a central editorial strand was an ongoing process of (re)appraisal of U2, a band the magazine could, with some legitimacy, claim to have discovered (although Graham somewhat self-deprecatingly claimed that U2 were very adept at getting the right people to discover them).[12] Indeed, a superficial symptom of the band's predominant place in the magazine can be glimpsed in the annual readers' polls for best artist, album and so forth (beginning in February 1979 with runner-up position for 'most promising' new act), and consistently featuring in either top positions or near the top ever since. More importantly, *Hot Press* provided the band with substantial coverage before a major record deal was forthcoming. U2 did not sign with Island until 19 March 1980, releasing their first international single, the Martin Hannett-produced '11 O'Clock Tick Tock', on the label in late May. In the interim between forming and playing locally and the beginning of their recording career, *Hot Press* narrated the band's emergence, drawing attention to their specific qualities: in short, providing the notional listener/reader with cues of what to look and listen for. The scale of the reportage for an unsigned band was considerable. The first mention of U2 in *Hot Press* occurred on 30 March 1978 and the first feature – 'Yep! It's U2' by Bill Graham – appeared on 28 April of the same year.[13] Graham profiled the band again, less than a year later, in March 1979, with editor Niall Stokes providing the band with its first cover/feature interview – 'Boys in Control' – later that year in October.[14] These and other articles by Declan Lynch[15] and Peter Owens[16] were to play a pivotal role in giving U2 a 'leg-up', as it were, to international visibility. In this sense, the magazine didn't merely *document* a scene and neutrally *report* U2. Rather, the magazine effectively canonized the young band early in its career. This discourse had a reciprocal effect, shaping the texture of the scene it was otherwise reporting.

As we have seen, the Republic didn't have a success story grown on native soil (the important exception being Horslips). In fact Belfast and the North was to be more successful initially in terms of 'growing' bands from the local infrastructure than their larger south-ern neighbour, which the case of Northern Irish punk and especially Terri Hooley's Good Vibrations ably demonstrated. In this sense, *Hot Press* was keen to promote and assist a non-derivative and 'home-grown' Irish rock act on the road to international visibility. When looked at from the perspective of the local industry at the time, part of the success of U2 is a paradigm case of the skilful manipulation of the emergent national popular musical infrastruc-ture. The band's success is evidently not reducible to this but it would have been unfeasible without it.

Hot Press's open support, primarily through Bill Graham's writ-ing, was followed by the extraordinary three-way alliance offered for their debut single by the magazine in conjunction with RTÉ, Radio 2's 'The Dave Fanning Show' and CBS Ireland. U2 had signed an earlier Ireland-only record deal with Jackie Hayden at CBS, presumably in frustration at not securing an international deal. This sense of frustration was similarly shared by key personnel in the Irish popular music media.[17] As Neil McCormick has reflected of the time, 'U2 were, quite simply, far and away the best band in Dublin – maybe not the best musicians – but they had something distinct, a power. If anyone deserved to get signed it was them.'[18] This resulted in the release of the band's first single, the three-track 'U23', initially offered as a hand-numbered limited edition 12 inch (and the island's first), which was immediately followed by the conventional 7-inch format. This first release was accompanied by a week of appearances on 'The Dave Fanning Show'. Listeners were invited to choose which of the EP's three tracks would be the A-side (with 'Out of Control' becoming the debut single). To coincide with the release and complete the synergy, *Hot Press* ran its first cover/feature interview with the band. What is significant, however, for our purposes is the paradigm case of strategic nationalism it represents. U2 and Ireland's popular musical fates intertwined, in a sense, and this was a blatant attempt to use national media resources to maximize the band (and the nation's) opportunity for international recognition. As Ian Wilson, producer at the time of 'The Dave Fanning Show' put it: 'I'm unapologetic. We didn't do it before; we did it once, then. And we'll never do it again.'[19]

Hot Press acted as both legislators and interpreters and hence mediated between band and audience, binding them together into a 'knowing' rock 'community'. Utilizing the familiar rock journalistic trope of 'insidership', its discourse was authorized, and thus authenticated, by its closeness (literal and institutional) to the band. This allowed writers, primarily Bill Graham, to claim a unique insight into what U2 *really* thought and felt. While this may be a feature of the music press in general, there are some local specifics to consider, as the *insider* discourse had some important variations in the Irish context. This reportage may be described as patronage and paternalism (or maternalism), with U2's fate often explicitly articulated to the 'health' or success of the nation: a specific type of expressive musical barometer of the national zeitgeist. There is nothing unusual in this. The British music press has always offered a similar intertwining of rock success and celebratory nationalism, evident, for example, in *NME*'s reporting of Oasis in the early to mid-1990s. Ironically, though, *Hot Press* has frequently pointed a critical finger at this kind of nationalistic sentiment in the British music press.

Moreover, *Hot Press* was involved in producing discourse that foregrounded U2's difference from their British contemporaries. These 'strategies of differentiation'[20] routinely involved comparison to absent/present 'others', with English pop and rock the predominant bête noire. The magazine also championed U2 in its construction of an informal 'battle of the bands' with their post-punk contemporaries in the United Kingdom, and especially in the race to conquer the all-important US market.[21]

The reader was invited here to care about the young U2's *fate*. This early discourse tended to construct the group as emerging from a 'blank slate',[22] a proverbial empty page to be written on, insisting that in terms of musical influences they were not significantly indebted to anyone. So, while musically U2 clearly emerged from punk, deploying the drum kit and 'driving bass' associated with the movement[23] and the clean 'broken glass'[24] guitar sound of post-punk (especially Public Image Limited, Tom Verlaine of Television and Andy Gill of Gang of Four), the magazine was keen to construct and reinforce the band's distance from both punk and post-punk movements elsewhere.[25] While originality is a common enough marker of value and authenticity within rock discourse, in the Irish context the surrounding metaphors allude to the arrival of U2 as if by 'virgin birth', within a discourse about 'spirituality'. Indeed, frequent recurring attributes bestowed upon the young U2 were their 'innocence', 'conviction', 'spirit', 'passion' and qualities such as 'hardworking'. Sonic influences were, in a sense, downplayed and 'attitude', approach and informing 'spirit' were 'talked up'. Indeed, what was missing in punk and post-punk elsewhere, from the perspective of Irish rock writing, was affirmation, grace, redemption; in short a certain *positivity*. This aspect has been neglected in critical discussions of the band, as clearly these signified qualities – enterprise, ambition, a commitment to work – were largely absent from the narrow repertoire of stereotypes assigned to Ireland and the Irish. In addition to this, it was also difficult to map punk and post-punk's urban aesthetic – what, as a shorthand, Bill Graham calls 'The Clash's tower-block imagery' – to a low-rise, and patently less urbanized, island-Irish experience.[26] In this sense, what could have been image/identity weaknesses – the majority of the band's 'born again' Christian beliefs, the lack of an explicitly urban milieu, the 'warm' and affirmative aspect of their post-punk sound, as well as Dublin's relative invisibility in rock history – were turned into strengths and foregrounded in *Hot Press* (with the notable exclusion of explicitly religious references). This was post-punk re-imagined and re-articulated for, and in, a post-colonial Irish context. Early U2 album covers, videos and publicity photographs are a useful indicator of this. After flirting briefly with urban and vaguely modern(ist) imagery – especially evident in photographer Hugo McGuinness's early pictures of the band – U2's imagery shifted to the rural iconographies, desolate landscapes and 'serious' high-contrast black-and-white photography with which the band became associated in the 1980s. These 'qualities' were to become core aspects of an emergent Irish rock scene that could be promoted as aesthetically and attitudinally distinctive internationally. However, as we shall see, even positive critical appraisals of the band have implications and are ideologically interesting.

In the first major feature interview with U2 in *Hot Press*, Bill Graham claimed, in a manner difficult to imagine in British rock journalism:

> U2 are unmarked by sin, exuberant because they retain innocence. Rock has so many lurking demons, in both its temptations and its traps that a band find themselves inexorably impelled towards the devil's party (who, of course has the best songs!). U2's determination and dedication could be a necessary shield; it also could bar them from the Faustian forces that generate rock's dreams as much as its nightmares.[27]

From the outset, the young band was offered as a metonym for the nation and imagined as residing at a distance from Anglo-American rock culture and particularly its British variants, the better to construct a specifically Irish version of modernity. This 'other' world and its value system were also significantly being announced as both a danger and a threat to the innocence and spirituality we noted earlier as the young U2's positives. While on tour with U2 during their first 'assault' on Britain, Graham confessed to the national rock reader: 'You get so scared and exhilarated, worried and enthralled and then so protective of the U2 *child*. You know he's well past the walking stage, you know he's restless and impatient to cavort and provoke' (italics added).[28] Graham's 'band-child'-as-provocateur became explicitly linked to a desire to achieve international visibility and the creation of an Irish rock success story. The military metaphors, such as the 'assault' on Britain, are combined with the image of a mother (Bill Graham, *Hot Press*, the reader, the nation) worried about her offspring (U2). This parental theme was, of course, accompanied and consolidated through the cover art of the first U2 album, *Boy* (1980), and the (at the time) controversial image of a bare-chested, blond-haired, pre-adolescent boy, and the lyrical preoccupation with adolescence and rites of passage. The virgin birth/genesis imagery is retained in subsequent features and reviews. Reflecting on the band's achievement, Graham announced, as if to the world, in a highly idiosyncratic fashion:

> By their genes, by their early essential bloodings, ye shall know a band. U2 were born into a scene that was a blank slate, and they had the bravado and instinctive insight to scrawl their own signature on the board. They found their own fulfilment by recognising that they weren't tied by rigid expectations of what rock should or shouldn't be. Beginning in a backwater, U2 would redefine Ireland's often-incoherent aspirations.[29]

This is quite extraordinary rhetoric. There is an implied linking of the blood of belonging to the blood of Ireland, the sense of a virgin birth and cleansed souls, a belief in instinct over intellectual reason and all of this wrapped up in a slightly sonorous biblical prose. There is even, against the magazine's avowedly left-liberal stance, a tinge of the fascist about this blood and belonging rhetoric (though this merely reflects the ultimate destination of such essentialist national sentiments, rather than the politics of the writer). Also, while the national musical infrastructure may have been something of a blank slate, it would be a mistake to elide this with Ireland's place in the broader popular musical world. Clearly young Irish people – as elsewhere – were buying music, forming bands, playing live and investing in, and arguing over, particular musical styles. Once again, despite a lack of infrastructural opportunity, it is doubtful whether Ireland was very different from anywhere else, or more or less impoverished, in popular music terms, than Bradford or Barnsley (but probably more linguistically advantaged than, say, Frankfurt). Before we explore this argument in more detail it is worth noting that, significantly, these interpretations of U2's 'arrival' cut against the other major trope used in ascribing importance to U2 in the Irish context – that of 'roots' and a rootedness in Irish experience. But what sort of rootedness is being invoked and how is it imagined? The construction of an Irish rock 'community' or 'Irish sound' and 'Irish meaning', is, in part, established by (usually favourable) comparison to British popular music culture, with U2 at the top of the national hierarchy, as emblematic of what is good about Ireland and Irish rock. Thus, in this discourse, the primary problem with British popular music culture is its lack of roots. As John Waters puts it:

> British music has always lacked a certain something – depth, maybe, and certainly soul. There are exceptions, of course, like John Lennon, who drew his inspiration directly from source (and had an Irish grandfather stashed away in his ancestral cupboard . . .). British music has always suffered from a style-obsessed superficiality which came to see youth as a tangential phenomenon, a heady cocktail of fashion, youth and – at most – a merely social change.[30]

So, initially, U2 were validated on the basis that they emerged from a rock culture that had no roots, one unfettered by tradition, as the proverbial pre-Oedipal 'innocent' child prior to entering into language and culture; yet on the other hand, it is suggested that U2 have had a greater musical resource to draw upon than their British counterparts, an underlying, informing ethereal and instinctive impulse – Seán O'Riada and John Waters's underground river. Therefore, U2, it is now being inferred, were part of a popular music-making tradition that stretches back hundreds of years. What is being articulated here is the desire to conceive of Irish rock as a 'genuine' folk music. Graham and Waters were thus attempting to unify pre-industrial and industrial forms of music making, and what is supposed to provide continuity is the discourse of 'race', nationality and *tradition*. What Britain therefore lacks – that Ireland possesses – is not just an unbroken 'tradition' but also its endurance. This is evidence of an attempt to import the supposed essential purity of Irish folk music into Irish rock, with rock validated as having maintained the informing impulse of traditional music making, and in doing so Ireland is again taken to have 'leapfrogged' over modernity, escaped industrial alienation and remained unsullied.

In the ongoing construction of an Irish rock culture as 'other' to British (primarily English) pop, a number of binaries are therefore established: commitment versus opportunism; authenticity versus fabrication; celebration versus criticism; roots versus transience; depth versus superficiality; community versus consumerism; creativity versus restriction; and tradition versus modernity.

Discursively, therefore, Irish rock has been dominated by an intertwining of rock and national/racial authenticity. Like all authenticities, they cast their object as perpetually beyond analysis, as always one step ahead of containment.[31] More concretely, this authenticity was set against a notion of the 'Great Other' as British rock and pop. This other was defined in very specific terms, especially in the post-punk period when U2 emerged. It is defined by *Hot Press* as the pop-inflected, self-consciously 'artistic', playful and ultimately 'plastic' sides of the post-punk movement in Britain. This 'plastic pop' (a little like the later 'plastic paddy') sensibility was a critical negative and conspicuous by its absence in Irish rock production. As Bill Graham has argued in interview, 'on the issue of authenticity: I always feel that the British could have done with more, and we could have done with less'.[32] What has been most glaringly absent has been the self-conscious experimental pop/rock synonymous with the British post-punk period, although one can only come to this conclusion by downplaying, or even ignoring, the achievements of bands such as DC Nein and The Fountainhead and burdening The Virgin Prunes with 'flying the flag' for experimental post-punk. (We shall discuss this aspect in more detail later in relation to Perfect Crime and Gregory Gray).

AN ORGANIC IRELAND?

Irish rock has, therefore, been framed within broader expectations of Ireland and the Irish. This we have called the *organic paradigm*.

This explains the predominance of various folk/rock hybrids, the emphasis on naturalist imagery, or what Susan Fast has termed 'rural authenticity',[33] and styles of dress that fit into the wandering bard, traveller, and gypsy wanderer archetypes. In part this limited range of music, image and performance styles, and a concomitant emphasis on the primitivist, is informed by a nationalist imperative and is, therefore, counter-imperialist, born of a desire to resist the perceived 'inauthenticity' of the centre (and it has been noted that it is frequently England and British rock and pop that has been read as the ultimate index of an imperializing presence in musical terms, and not the United States). A particular target at the time of U2's emergence was the New Romantic and New Pop movements (subsections of the broader post-punk church), which were regarded, crudely, as the musical corollary of Thatcher's Britain: superficial, materialist, aspirational, all surface and no depth, glorifying conspicuous consumption and so forth. In a reflective article written in 1993, Graham articulates the position (and note the shift from British to 'English'):

> The Brits did rock as a pose... Britpop has always been opportunist. English pop has always worked through fabrication; not by witness and celebration of anything else besides shared consumption and membership of a temporary style faction. Sometime along the way comes the reckoning: you can't continue to play style games with shrinking assets. After all, The New Romantics emerged out of Thatcher's eighties' recession. Who'd emulate Spandau Ballet and Duran Duran? Sixties' Brits could embarrassingly plunder the blues exactly because there was no black community at home to reproach them.[34]

This is, of course, not to suggest that synth-based experimental music didn't exist in Ireland but to note its virtual invisibility in the Irish rock canon.[35] Ireland, therefore, leapfrogged post-punk *pop* – moving from punk *rock* to the 1980s rock revival – and thus missed the joyful creativity described by Simon Reynolds in *Rip It Up and Start Again* – and post-punk's explosion of genres, the rewriting of rock and pop norms, the deconstruction of the traditional four-piece band, the 'gender-bending' and futurism, the search for a musical and performative language outside of the blues evident in the embrace of art school experimentation.[36] Even John Lydon by the end of The Sex Pistols was expressing his irritation at the Chuck Berry riffs that underpinned punk.[37]

However, despite what Bill Graham and *Hot Press* contend, it is patently obvious that U2 (just as we have seen earlier with The Virgin Prunes) were influenced by and indebted to post-punk elsewhere. In U2's sound it is possible to hear the sonic registers of early Siouxsie and The Banshees, Television, Joy Division and Public Image Limited. Nonetheless, U2's accommodation to the styles of the burgeoning rock revival, best encapsulated in *Under a Blood Red Sky*, gave credence and substance to the *Hot Press* definition of a suitably Irish rock.

'UNDER A THUNDER-CLOUD AND RAIN': U2 IN PERFORMANCE

U2 performed at the Red Rocks arena, outside Denver, Colorado, on 5 June 1983 as part of the promotional tour for their third studio album, *War* (1983). The performance was released in November of that year on video as *Under a Blood Red Sky* and a number of the tracks formed the basis of a live mini-album bearing the same name and artwork. This televised concert was the performance that most emphatically marked the band's international emergence and built upon, and even extended, the success of *War* – the album entered the UK charts at number one (displacing Michael Jackson's *Thriller*) – and was extremely important in helping to win over the all-important US market. The 1985 Live Aid performance in front of a Wembley crowd of 72,000 people and a potential television audience of 1.5 billion further capitalized on this success.[38] The big-budget Hollywood production of the concert film *Rattle and Hum* in 1988 updated U2's on-screen live image. It is somewhat ironic then, that, firstly, in terms of (Irish) rock ideology, U2's international prominence was at least partially attributable to the 'modern' media of the time – television and film; and secondly, that both *Under a Blood Red Sky* and *Rattle and Hum*, the productions over which the band had control, largely sidestepped Irish locations for the United States.[39]

The Red Rocks concert was filmed and part-financed by Tyne Tees Television in the north-east of England and broadcast in the United Kingdom on Channel 4's now-defunct rock programme 'The Tube' as a twenty-minute 'Special' on July 1983. As had been noted by Dunphy,[40] the Red Rocks concert was a considerable financial risk for the U2 organization, with most of its available monies being devoted to the event. It was also an acknowledgement of the importance of television in furthering the group's international career. In this respect, the collaboration with 'The Tube' is especially significant. The programme team and the U2 organization formed, in the words of 'The Tube' and *Under a Blood Red Sky* producer Malcolm Gerrie, 'a close bond', with them becoming 'virtually the house band',[41] playing live a number of times on the show. Moreover, the producer described how the programme's personnel were impressed by the 'warmth, savvy and intelligence' of both band and management.[42] The band, reciprocally, enjoyed playing on the programme, as it was unusual in that it was broadcast live with a studio audience to play to, and thus felt more akin to a gig. It was, therefore, far removed from the miming to studio playback that was customary on other UK major television outlets of the time, such as BBC's main prime-time music programme, 'Top of the Pops', or the audience-less live studio sessions for terrestrial television's other 'serious' rock programme, 'The Old Grey Whistle Test'. Perhaps most importantly, Gerrie recalled how both band and 'The Tube' team shared the same hunger to break down what they perceived as the 'metro-centric cartels' that shaped rock and popular music culture in the United Kingdom and by extension Ireland. In other words, based in Newcastle in the north east of England, 'The Tube' team greatly identified and empathized with the band's peripheral position in Dublin and its deliberate circumvention of London.[43]

The concert is also historically significant because more than any other single event it pushed U2 onto the mainstream televisual outlets for music in the United States, such as Showtime and Viacom, allowing the group to stand alongside the established artists and 'mega-bands' such as Bob Dylan, Bruce Springsteen and The Rolling Stones. Furthermore, Music Television (MTV), now well established in the United States, had begun transmission in Europe (as MTV Europe) and the version of 'Sunday, Bloody Sunday' from the concert was to receive heavy rotation on the channel.

Television's ability to convey a sense of immediacy and intimacy for rock audiences has been well documented[44] and *Under a Blood Red Sky* was to satisfy in this regard, giving audiences close proximity to the group. Simon Frith has argued that rock music on television and video is best understood as a type of 'idealised live performance',[45] emphasizing the kinetic qualities of performance through rhythmic editing and the recurring use of close-ups foregrounding facial expressions and the specific qualities of the moving bodies in question. In this context, the particular kind of 'idealised live performance' at Red Rocks and the correspondence between the musical and the visual tell us much about U2 mythology and the construction of ideologies of Irishness.

Both the televised live performance and its video/DVD counterpart open with Clannad's 'Theme from Harry's Game' (*Magical Ring*, 1983), a minimalist piece with ethereal Celtic connotations. The track acted as a form of 'musical establishing shot', invoking the image of a misty (feminine) pastoralism – the mythical west of Ireland and Ireland as mother. In fact, the Clannad track concisely drew upon the two main discourses of representation of Ireland and the Irish: the romantic/pastoral and images of violence and 'the troubles' in Northern Ireland,[46] consolidated through its use as the title music to the ITV/Yorkshire Television mini-series and 'Troubles drama' of the same name (Lawrence Gordon Clark 1982). These twin discourses, already present in the representational arena, were attached to the U2 performance. In fact, the Clannad track straddles the traditional and the modern, deploying synthesizers and samplers to convey a sense of the ancient and the 'Celtic'. While the track mobilizes a sense of a vague, Celtic pre-history, it uses modern studio and production techniques to consolidate this (the synthetic in the service of the 'organic', as it were). It thus opens up a hinterland between the 'traditional' and the 'modern' which U2's performance will fill.

Visually, the televised concert, video and 2009 DVD reissue all open with a brief aerial sequence shot from a helicopter that moves over Denver's high-rise central business district and continues away from the city to the mist-soaked mountainous stone slabs near the Red Rocks area. This establishing shot affirms the ethereality of the soundtrack. What is being established is a move away from one set of associations perhaps deemed unfavourable – modernity, the urban, artificial, secular, corporate, soulless; to the preferred – mystical, spiritual, pre-modern, timeless, sacred, rural, 'Celtic'. This pastoral discourse is continued in a further sequence of aerial shots (in the same direction) moving towards the concert arena, a large amphitheatre of imposing rock formations, high in the Colorado Mountains. The 'red' rock formations that give the arena its name surround the venue on every side, making for a particularly impressive stage backdrop, situated at the bottom of the valley formed by the terrain. The rocks at the rear of the stage were illuminated in a high-contrast style. These 'earthy' red textures were continued in the minimalist stage setting, emphasizing nature and focusing attention on the primacy of performance as befits rock stage shows. The only other conspicuous use of colour in the stage design was the red carpet bedecking the stage floor (and the cover of the *War* album emblazoning the backdrop at the rear of the stage behind the drums). This and the 'red rocks' formed a neat fit with the *War* iconography: the red of spilled blood and the line from 'New Year's Day', 'under a blood red sky', that gave the video and mini-album releases their name.

The Clannad track also offered an aural *celticization* of the American landscape. The connotations of the ancient, the timeless, the seductive and vague ethereality of the Celtic mingled with the similar connotations of the landscape (after all, this is a area reputed to be a sacred meeting place for Native American tribes, particularly when debating what do about the presence of white European invaders).[47] However, what was offered here was a very particular version of the Irish-America relationship – one that has echoes of John Ford's Monument Valley – and it is difficult to imagine The Rolling Stones or Oasis or indeed any English rock band slotting into, or exploiting, such a mise en scène in the manner that unfolded.

Prior to the event, Colorado experienced a series of violent thunderstorms and heavy rain, reputedly the worst weather in the area for a century.[48] These climatic conditions nearly resulted in cancellation. U2 were introduced from the stage – 'all the way from Dublin, Ireland...' – foregrounding place and identity from the outset and consolidating the link between U2, Irishness, the Celtic imagery and the introductory soundscape/landscape connection. Once the band appeared on stage the event follows the largely standardized formal conventions of the televised rock concert, constructing and foregrounding Bono as star, and counterposing images of him with shots of rapturous fans, intercut with aerial wide-angle shots emphasizing the spectacle, the scale of the crowd and the majesty of the surroundings. Here there was a degree of direct manipulation: through the use of wide-angle lenses and selective camera positioning, the viewer is given the impression that the band are performing in front of an arena-sized crowd (15,000 people plus). It looked as if U2 had 'arrived', despite the fact that this was the beginning of the band's 'international' career. In fact, the venue capacity was around 9,500, but only 6,000 tickets were sold and, presumably because of the weather, only around 4,400 were estimated to have turned up.[49] In other words, to film a half-full venue and make it look like a sizeable crowd required a high degree of direct manipulation.

The weather created a melodramatic ambience far in excess of what would have been normally possible given U2's economic position at the time. As Gerrie recalled, 'even the mega-budgets of Hollywood cinema, represented by directors such as Spielberg, would have found it difficult, if not impossible, to manufacture the atmosphere captured on *Under a Blood Red Sky*'.[50] The entire Red Rocks arena was drenched in heavy mist in a way that was similar to dry ice that is frequently used in rock performance to create an ethereal effect. However, the *lack* of manufacture added to the authenticity. This aspect was fully capitalized on. Once darkness fell, the individual band members were bathed in a romantic halo, with steam rising off the soaked skin of Bono's face and body and streaming from his breath. Together with the low-angle shooting, this fortuitous construction of the celestial was heightened with Bono framed from below against the dark sky. To mark the performance of 'Sunday, Bloody Sunday', large propane fire torches were lit at strategic points along the upper surface of the amphitheatre illuminating both band and surrounding rock formations. Thus a cluster of tropes about nature – rain/storm/fire/earth/steam – were yoked together, building a primitivist vocabulary of sorts and constructing the Red Rocks arena as a pre-modern pilgrimage site with U2 as spiritual guides, in an arena where the earthy and the metaphysical, the natural and spiritual, were being carefully forged into one. This helped to underscore the sense of the event being 'more than a concert' and emphasized its 'ritualistic' aspect. Indeed, it is somewhat ironic that it would be hard to think of an Irish location, stadium, venue or amphitheatre that could have offered such an 'authentic' invocation of ethereal 'Irishness' (nor a national context where Irish ethereality could be put to such use and so enthusiastically received).

The manner in which the event was shot is similarly important. *Under a Blood Red Sky* owes a great deal to television documentary techniques with the use of hand-held cameras, the camera often being 'surprised' by the action. In this vein, the camera becomes a performer, jostling for position. It was certainly not the controlled 'blocked-out' mise en scène of later U2 audio-visual releases where multiple camera placements are factored into the stage design. As director Gavin Taylor[51] has revealed, the camera operators on 'The Tube' shot directly into the lights, an approach widely used in the obstinately urban style of punk (as in, say, The Sex Pistols' 'Anarchy in the UK' promo). This, as Taylor puts it, 'went against technical etiquette' and was certainly not a style deployed in large-scale music events for US television and as such led to some controversy.[52] This was not a mere flouting of the rules. Together with the documentary techniques this conveyed a sense of realism. So while it was a big-budget event, it was one with clear connotations of 'rawness', drawing upon the 'rough-and-ready' technical aspects of punk and immediate post-punk. Indeed, the band's iconography owed something to punk and to The Clash in particular, echoing the militaristic themes – particularly U2's avowed 'aggressive pacifism' – but eschewing an urban milieu in favour of the very specific pastoral qualities just described.

'Sunday, Bloody Sunday' also drew intertextually on Northern Irish punk and Stiff Little Fingers (SLF) in particular, deploying the dampened staccato riffs and martial rhythms that had become a musical index of the barricades, of metal bars rattling across corrugated iron and other 'Troubles' imagery such as dustbin-lids hammered on the ground. During the performance of the song, Bono marches across the stage with a white flag, planting it amongst the front row. Politically, the white flag in combination with the other areas of the iconography was to construct the Red Rocks amphitheatre as a type of international Celtic 'neutral zone'. Its use in 'Sunday, Bloody Sunday', though, may be more than a general emblem of peace. It can be read in an Irish-specific sense, as it invokes the white handkerchief waved by Father Daly on Bloody Sunday in Derry 1972, the event to which the song directly refers. The visual iconography echoes the 'meaning' of the song itself and its dalliance between the universal and particular. The song has been widely criticized for its 'this is not a rebel song' politics and hence 'universalizing' a specific event (the most officially documented single military atrocity in history) into a generalized anti-violence anthem. This argument has been made most forcefully in articles by Barbara Bradby and Brian Torode[53] and Bill Rolston,[54] who accuse the band of political 'quietism'. Despite the force of the critique, the weakness in both articles is the exclusive focus on lyrics and lyrical meaning and a concomitant neglect of not just the music, but the relationship of the words to the musical setting (as well as the very different contexts in which the song has been performed in the band's lengthy career). It could be argued that the song's very title, and the aggressive, mournful chant of its eponymous chorus constantly drags the listener back to the specific event so that, however generalized the address, the song invokes the memory of that very specific atrocity. (In fact, Bono's lyric-less lament at the song's opening is vaguely redolent of keening, that traditional Irish form of mourning, giving the track a further layer of specificity.) Moreover, the military snare pattern and 'the Troubles' sonics musically invoke the menacing presence of the British war machine, loyalist marching bands and the Unionist regime and thus works against the non-specific anti-war message. Attention to musical style and performance would suggest that the track is a more tension-ridden experience than has been allowed for (and, whatever the interpretation, the track was clearly controversial and, significantly, did not even penetrate the top thirty of the UK singles chart).

The old tube video cameras that were used to capture the concert reacted to the lights and the atmospheric conditions. This created streaks or 'burns' on the image, and worm-like trails caused by condensation. The result was a lo-fi, eerie luminosity, as if the technology itself was breaking down in the face of the climatic conditions, the 'raw' force of the weather intruding on the aesthetic. This lo-fi yet strangely Turner-esque ambience perfectly captured and added to the melodramatic performance of the band. The dominant TV broadcast aesthetic was also of great significance with its connotations of the live event and its immediacy. The sense that the cameras were capturing a 'live' event was palpable and in no way resembled the slick and controlled manner of later U2 filmed performances such as *Rattle and Hum* and *Zoomerang* (directed by David Mallet, 1994). In these, the filming and the presence of cameras are factored into the very stage design (particularly evident in the U2 360° tour of 2009–10 where housings for the cameras were pre-designed into the claw structure of the stage).

'The Tube' was influential in other ways. Both producer Malcolm Gerrie[55] and director Gavin Taylor[56] have noted how 'boring' the stage area at Red Rocks was, despite the impressive amphitheatre around it. 'The Tube' team sought to get around the problem by replicating the stage design from an appearance of U2 on the programme earlier that year (18 March 1983). This required building the stage upwards, in order to give the audience a better view of the band; and, perhaps more importantly, building the stage outwards by creating a gangway for Bono to move out into the audience (something the team had learnt from their intimate knowledge of the singer's performing style). Significantly, in terms of U2's performing history, the band has been extending gangways into the audience since 1983. At Red Rocks, this extended platform also allowed Bono to be framed surrounded by fans and also permitted the singer to be framed by the hand-held cameras against the dramatic sculpted sandstone (allowing the location to become more than a mere background). It could, in fact, be argued that *Under a Blood Red Sky* succeeded in its filmic treatment of live performance in a way that the much bigger budget *Rattle and Hum* failed, as the latter film didn't make use of this extended gangway facility (and is, therefore, strangely audience-less).

The aesthetics and experience of 'The Tube' was crucial, then, to the eventual shape and design of the Red Rocks concert and it is in this way, remembering back to the role that RTÉ and 'The Dave Fanning Show' played in breaking U2 originally and forward to the BBC's coverage of the Live Aid concert in 1985, that we can say with some conviction that public service broadcasting and particularly regional broadcasting, was central to the success of U2.

The impact of the weather on the Red Rocks concert also involved the live audience (and by extension, the watching video audience) in a semi-religious pilgrimage narrative where the difficulties that the audience had in even getting to the concert were mirrored in the difficulties that the band and crew had in mounting the event in the first place. The concert, then, is offered almost as a triumph of hope and determination over adversity, a quasi-religious celebration of the power of positive thinking. Even the high altitude was a test of endurance and Bono had to use oxygen tanks to get through the show.[57]

These aspects were, in turn, consolidated by another recurring rock trope – that of *performance-as-work*, and being seen to invest 'serious' effort, visible in the close-ups of straining faces and sweat. Even Bono's exhaustion between songs, such as the pauses for rest in both the middle eight and at the end of 'Sunday, Bloody Sunday', became a significant part of the performance. These indices of effort serve to signify passion, commitment and dedication to rock's cause – markers of the band *giving* their all to the audience. As Barbara Bradby has asked, 'hard work plus spirituality – dare we call it the Protestant work ethic'?[58]

This carefully constructed combination of the 'hardworking', the pagan and the 'ethereal' is carried through in Edge's sound and performance. The guitar is heavily reverberated and bathed in echo/delay. The emphasis is on texture brought about by long sustained single notes and pitch bending, suggesting wide open (natural) spaces. As the guitarist has put it in conversation with Neil McCormick:

> We didn't like major chords because they sounded too happy, and minor chords sounded too down, so we stripped things back to absolute fundamentals, with fifths and root notes, no frills whatsoever. The third became our enemy...if you leave out the third note, the key becomes more ambiguous and much more open to different melodies. I came up with chord voicings where there was no third; basically you play the root with a fifth and the octave of the root, with maybe some intervals in there. It worked quite well because it kept the canvas really open.[59]

The timbre is, therefore, stylistically distinct from many of his 'mainstream' American and English rock counterparts (with the possible and significant exception of Charlie Burchill in early-1980s Simple Minds, who in some ways shares the Edge's 'warming-up' of the clean, 'broken glass' guitar sound of post-punk we alluded to earlier). The recurrent use of bottleneck and harmonic 'chimes' further this sense of broad expanses of landscape. This first performance mode is counterposed with the second mode – a more conventional rhythm guitar, where he switches from the former 'timbral' mode to choppy, militaristic rhythms and angular riffs. Therefore two 'languages' with different associations are employed – on the one hand, ethereality, on the other, 'rawness' (which works in tandem with the visual style).

The different areas of the performance we have been discussing meet forcefully and are expressed most strongly in Bono's vocal signature. The singer's 'big voice' – with its distinct vocal timbre – is marked by a strong presence in its upper range: the voice's oft-remarked ability to cut through the air. His voice, moreover, is marked by a constant climbing, in the straining to reach higher registers. In one sense, the voice signifies passion and commitment and neatly dovetails with the band's affirmative liberal ideology – 'whatever the problem you can do something about it'.[60] The authority of the big voice is, in turn, consolidated by the singer's powerful performing style, his confidence in commanding the stage (and in the crowd diving and speaker-stack climbing that studded the band's early period). Bono's performance signifies dissolution in the music's power, and oscillates between the 'crafted' – performing expertly for crowd and camera – and expressing abandonment (of not 'looking cool', and making the bodily shapes the music requires).

The lyrical themes, the recurring references to earth elements – sky, sea, rain, storms, clouds, lightning, electricity (in 'Seconds',

'Electric Co.', 'New Year's Day', 'October', '11 O'Clock Tick Tock') – throughout the set, and the frequent references to 'oneness' ('Sunday, Bloody Sunday'), 'unity' ('New Year's Day'), 'spirit', going 'higher' ('Gloria') and breaking down walls and barriers ('I Threw a Brick through a Window') support the other areas of the aesthetic just described. While the musical/performance syntax is clearly not traditional, it does not work against the Celtic connotations of traditional music. This allows the style to be easily subsumed into the Celtic 'aura' set up elsewhere in the performance overall: the modern is *celticized* and the Celtic is modernized.

The Red Rocks concert performance and video established U2 as a potentially stadium-filling guitar rock band. It also established their credentials internationally as an *Irish* rock band. In this way Red Rocks performed admirably the function of vindicating the *Hot Press* construction of U2's Irish rock authenticity.

NOTES

1. Bill Graham, interview by Noel McLaughlin, 1995 (unpublished).
2. Eamon Dunphy, *Unforgettable Fire: The Story of U2* (London: Penguin, 1987), p.228.
3. Dick Hebdige, *Subculture: The Meaning of Style* (London: Methuen, 1979), p.112.
4. Gerry Smyth, *Noisy Island: A Short History of Irish Popular Music* (Cork: Cork University Press, 2005), p.51–2.
5. Barbara Bradby, 'God's Gift to the Suburbs? A Review of *Unforgettable Fire: The Story of U2* by Eamon Dunphy', *Popular Music*, 8, 1 (1989), p.110. Indeed, Bono has described The Clash at Trinity College as 'his greatest gig ever': 'Can't remember the set list, can't remember much about the music...I just know that everything changed that night, and I'm sure it was not just for me...It wasn't so much a musical event. It was more like the Red Army had arrived...to force feed a new cultural revolution, punk rock'. '25 of the Greatest Gigs Ever', *The Observer* (21 January 2007).
6. Simon Frith, 'Critical Response', in Deanna Campbell Robinson, Elizabeth Buck and Marlene Cuthbert, *Music at the Margins: Popular Music and Global Cultural Diversity* (London: Sage, 1991), p.287.
7. Bradby, 'God's Gift'; Dunphy, *Unforgettable Fire*; Bill Graham, *U2 – The Early Years: Another Time, Another Place* (London: Mandarin, 1989).
8. Dave Laing, *One Chord Wonders: Power and Meaning in Punk Rock* (Milton Keynes: Open University Press, 1985), pp.106–7.
9. Jason Toynbee, 'Policing Bohemia, Pinning Up Grunge: The Music Press and Generic Change in British Rock and Pop', *Popular Music*, 12, 3 (1993), pp.289–300.
10. Niall Stokes, interview by Noel McLaughlin, 1995 (unpublished).
11. Laing, *One Chord Wonders*.
12. Graham, *Early Years*, p.10.

13. Bill Graham, 'Yep! It's U2', *Hot Press*, 1, 23 (28 April 1978).
14. Niall Stokes, 'Boys in Control', *Hot Press*, 2, 9 (26 October 1979).
15. Declan Lynch, 'U2 Treats U', *Hot Press*, 2, 6 (31 August 1979).
16. Peter Owens, 'Close to the Edge', *Hot Press*, 4, 2 (20 June 1980).
17. Dunphy, *Unforgettable Fire*, pp.161–2; Jackie Hayden, 'Stories of Boys', *Hot Press*, 9, 13 (20 June 1985); Jackie Hayden, interview by Noel McLaughlin, 1995 (unpublished); Ian Wilson, interview by Noel McLaughlin, 1995 (unpublished).
18. Neil McCormick, interview by Noel McLaughlin, 2010 (unpublished).
19. Wilson, interview.
20. David Bordwell, 'Art Cinema Narration', in David Bordwell, *Narration in the Fiction Film* (Madison, WI: University of Wisconsin Press, 1985).
21. Bill Graham, 'U2 Versus the US', *Hot Press*, 5, 8 (1981); Bill Graham, 'The People's Choice: U2 Hit No. 1 in Britain', *Hot Press*, 7, 5 (1983); Graham, *Early Years*.
22. Graham, *Early Years*, p.8.
23. Allan F. Moore, 'Looking for the Kingdom Come: Questioning Spirituality in U2', *Popular Musicology Online*, 2002 http://www.popular-musicology-online.com/issues/01/moore.html.
24. Simon Reynolds, *Rip It Up And Start Again: Post-Punk 1978–1984* (London: Faber, 2005), p.12. Reynolds quotes PiL guitarist Keith Levene on the post-punk guitar sound: 'It's so clean, so tingly, like a cold shower' and the author claims 'you can hear U2's The Edge in its radiant surge' (p.12).
25. John Waters, *Race of Angels: Ireland and the Genesis of U2* (Belfast: Blackstaff Press, 1994), p.46; Bradby, 'God's Gift', p.109.
26. Graham, *Early Years*, p.16.
27. Bill Graham, 'U2 Could Be a Headline', *Hot Press*, 2, 19 (8 March 1979).
28. Bill Graham, 'The Battle of Britain', *Hot Press*, 4, 4 (19 July 1980).
29. Graham, *Early Years*, p.8.
30. Waters, *Race of Angels*, p.48.
31. Richard Middleton, 'The Real Thing: The Specter of Authenticity', in Middleton, *Voicing the Popular*, pp.199–246; Allan F. Moore, 'Authenticity as Authentication', *Popular Music*, 21, 2 (2002), pp.209–23.
32. Graham, interview.
33. Susan Fast, 'Music, Context and Meaning in U2', in Walter Everett (ed.) *Expression in Rock-Pop Music: Critical and Analytical Essays*, 2nd ed. (New York: Routledge, 2008), p.178.
34. Bill Graham, 'Has Pop Eaten Itself?', *Hot Press*, 17, 4 (February 1993).
35. The prominent exception here is synth-group The Fountainhead, a 'delayed' version of a form common in British popular music in the early 1980s.
36. Reynolds, *Rip It Up*.
37. Ibid., p.xix.
38. Dunphy, *Unforgettable Fire*, pp.1–5; Matt McGee, *U2: A Diary* (London: Omnibus Press, 2008), pp.88–9.
39. For a more in-depth discussion of music, place and identity in *Rattle and Hum*, see Noel McLaughlin, 'Rattling Out Of Control: A Comparison of U2 and Joy Division on Film', *Film, Fashion and Consumption*, 1, 1 (2012), pp.99–118.
40. Dunphy, *Unforgettable Fire*, pp.278–80.
41. Malcolm Gerrie, interview by Noel McLaughlin, 2009 (unpublished).
42. Ibid.
43. Ibid.
44. Andrew Goodwin, *Dancing in the Distraction Factory: Music Television and Popular Culture* (London: Routledge, 1993); Simon Frith, *Performing Rites:*

      On the Value of Popular Music (Oxford: Oxford University Press, 1996).

45. Frith, *Performing Rites*, p.225.
46. John Hill, 'Images of Violence', in Kevin Rockett, John Hill and Luke Gibbons, *Cinema and Ireland* (London: Routledge), pp.147–93.
47 Gerrie, interview.
48. Dunphy, *Unforgettable Fire*, p.279.
49. Gerrie, interview.
50. Ibid.
51. Gavin Taylor, 'Director's Commentary', *Under a Blood Red Sky* (2009, DVD Extras).
52. Ibid.
53. Barbara Bradby and Brian Torode, 'To Whom Do U2 Appeal?', *Crane Bag*, 8, 1 (1985), pp.73–8.
54. Bill Rolston, ' "This is Not a Rebel Song": The Irish Conflict and Popular Music', *Race and Class*, 42, 3 (2001), pp.56–7. In simple terms the song was regarded with suspicion, even enmity, by many Unionists and Republicans: the former for seemingly pointing the finger at the political corruption of the Unionist regime, and the latter for sidestepping colonial oppression.
55. Gerrie, interview.
56. Taylor, 'Director's Commentary'.
57. Gerrie, interview.
58. Bradby, 'God's Gift', p.60.
59. Neil McCormick, *U2 By U2* (London: Harper, 2006), p.103.
60. The sheer size of the 'straining' voice and its powerful upper register have given rise to the allegation that everything he sings is given epic proportions.

8

U2 after 'U2'

You can see why my mum and dad could never live in Ireland... It's all like a postcard scene. It never moves. It's a void. How can you have a sense of belonging to something that never changes? No future, literally. (John Lydon)[1]

The experience of living in contemporary Ireland is that of living in an in-between world, in-between cultures and identities, an experience of liminality... of what one might call the coexistence of both discourses of tradition and modernity in Ireland. (Carmen Kuhling and Kieran Keohane)[2]

You didn't like me when I was me, so I found somebody new. (Bono)[3]

During the Obama inaugural concert Bono interjected his performance of 'Pride' with the comment that Martin Luther King's dream was 'not just an American dream' but 'also an Irish dream, a European dream, an African dream, an Israeli dream'. And, after a pause of realization, 'and also a Palestinian dream'.[4] Apart from this one moment of hesitation, there was little critical 'noise' thrown up by the Obama concert. Nonetheless, U2's relationship to African-American culture has not always been so straightforward. *Rattle and Hum*, despite impressive sales, attracted popular critical dismissal. As Niall Stokes complained, the album was 'hammered in the press', in large part due to its perceived hijacking of African-American music and its plundering of the blues in particular (leaving it vying with 1997's *Pop* as the group's critical nadir). This is ironic as the album, from Bono's perspective, sprang from a desire to achieve the opposite, to respond musically to accusations that the band attracted a predominantly WASP audience (a criticism that apparently 'really stung' the singer) and to reach out to potential African-American fans.[5] In addition to this, the band had been criticized for their apparent lack of knowledge and respect for musical 'tradition', their

naivety about (Irish) rock's 'roots', an observation that emerged
from such authoritative luminaries of the folk authenticity paradigm
as Bob Dylan, as well as Keith Richards and Mick Jagger from The
Rolling Stones, and consequently carried considerable critical
weight.[6] *Rattle and Hum* could thus be regarded as a problematic
and flawed attempt by the band to 'un-whiten' its sound and to
intertwine the two authenticities of blackness and Irishness. This had
considerable political consequences. As Lauren Onkey has argued,
'declarations of black identity by the Irish or Irish-Americans usually
depend on essentialized notions of both blackness and Irishness; the
point of making the alliance is to suggest that both groups share
access to an authentic identity distinct from a dominant culture'.[7]

Indeed, the turn of the 1980s into the 1990s offered up a series of
such intertwined yet strained and essentialized 'necessary connections' between black and Irish. The other most prominent example
was found in Alan Parker's 1991 hit film *The Commitments*, based
on Roddy Doyle's original novel, with its famous epithet: 'Don't you
know the Irish are the blacks of Europe, so repeat after me I'm black
and I'm proud.' Much less discussed but just as relevant here,
however, is the famous comedic section of the film where the young
soul-obsessed impresario, Jimmy Rabbitte, invites auditions from
all-comers for his authentic soul band. He ends up actually and
symbolically slamming the door shut on a range of musical styles
and related subcultures deemed inauthentic. Thus (once again)
English pop subcultures – post-punk, synth-pop and performative
androgyny (pastiches that clearly invoke figures such as Marc
Almond, Boy George, Morrissey and Siouxsie Sioux) – act as the
negative 'other' to the positive authenticity of black-Irish soul and
they all bear the butt of the 'joke'. In fact, the film offers more
evidence of this position with lines such as 'art school wankers' and
musicians 'dicking around with synths' in order to hammer its point
home. Significantly, Irish traditional music and Dylan-esque folk
pastiche are treated much more sympathetically in the audition
sequence, as they are more in keeping with the film's ideological
project. It would have been a risky strategy to have subjected traditional musics to this satirical impulse (although it is important to
stress that Doyle's source novel, in contrast to the film version, is
more wry and ironic in its treatment of the Irish as the blacks of
Europe).

Onkey goes on to argue that in *Rattle and Hum* (as in *The
Commitments*), 'blackness is evoked to access primal expression of

authentic emotion, to legitimize the Irish as Celtic soul brothers. This forges a purportedly unproblematic link with African-Americans: the Irish have been oppressed, and therefore soul and rhythm and blues are appropriate vehicles for Irish musicians.'[8] After raising the attendant problem of primitivism, Onkey goes on to claim that 'the Irish can use African-Americans as a tool to become authentically Irish, to get in touch with their authentic suffering, or their precolonial ethnic authenticity; but the definition of Irishness that emerges is as retrograde and limiting as depicting blacks as noble savages'.[9] While this is unquestionably the case, *Rattle and Hum* is perhaps more complex than is often acknowledged, and for two reasons. First, the album (and film) may be regarded not as a work of singular blues-derived authenticity but as a musical hybrid of U2's distinctive post-punk sound. This itself draws on a myriad of influences from Television to Joy Division which exists in uneasy synthesis with the roots-searching, blues-based rock countercultural canon: Hendrix, B.B. King and Dylan.[10] Second, the album and film do not just appropriate the blues – surely a homology that dogs The Rolling Stones, Eric Clapton and others – but they deploy a broader repertoire of influences including The Beatles, Billie Holiday and Elvis Presley. If the album can be justifiably critiqued it is for its apparent hubris. In terms of the musical traditions invoked, the blues has to stand in line with the others involved. In many respects what jars about the album is the sound of a post-punk band, born of a moment when the roots narrative and blues template were wilfully abandoned, now attempting to attach themselves to what, for them, must be a form of 'prosthetic memory'[11] – the legacy of the folk blues world. This possibly helps explain why the covers of Dylan/Hendrix's 'All Along the Watchtower' and The Beatles' 'Helter Skelter' fail to convince and have never been regarded fondly, even by many fans. By analogy, it's as if The Sex Pistols did a U-turn to embrace the music of The Rolling Stones and brings to mind the line from *Achtung Baby*'s 'Trying to Throw Your Arms Around the World': 'how far you gonna go, before you lose your way back home'. The blues 'moment', as it were, had passed when an earlier generation of Anglo-American white rock groups in the 1960s appropriated its register, leaving U2, in the late 1980s, looking pious and 'out of touch'. Indeed, despite the fact that U2's novel synthesis of blues, country and post-punk was achieved through original composition, it is somewhat ironic that *Rattle and Hum* was critically lambasted while *The Commitments'* showband-style pastiche of soul music was generally well received.

Critically, it was not, therefore, the album's flawed attempt at authenticity that was the problem; rather, it was its hybridity that made it fit uncomfortably into the authenticity paradigm. This was most glaringly apparent on 'Silver and Gold' when, on concluding a rant about the injustices of apartheid, Bono extolled the Edge to 'play the blues' with the guitarist obliging by doing anything but, and resorting to his trademark echoed, and decidedly post-punk, ethereal sonic swirl. As Smyth has argued, 'U2 was one of the most interesting rock bands of the 1980s in terms of its regard for texture and the spatial connotations afforded by specific manipulations of sound.'[12] This sense of musical space was very different to the blues and, even at the height of the band's fascination with Americana, this register was maintained to greater or lesser degrees depending on the track in question. While 'Love Rescue Me', 'Van Diemen's Land', 'Angel of Harlem' and 'When Love Comes to Town' may have been informed by, and largely conformed to, clearly defined musical traditions (with 'Hawkmoon 269' even echoing the allitera-tion of Dylan's 'It's Alright Ma, I'm only Bleeding'), 'God Part 2' and the bridge of 'All I Want Is You' drew from a different well, with the former track frequently taken as a precursor for the *Achtung Baby* sound. For Simon Reynolds, U2's sound has consistently retained a post-punk, 'non-rock' concern with timbre and texture, most evident in the use of guitar, which further complicates any simple narrative of wholesale appropriation of the blues.[13] Moreover, U2's sound on *Rattle and Hum* was at some distance from the 'bump and grind' and libidinal racial authenticity appropriated most famously by The Rolling Stones. The U2 fascination with African America was more to do with furthering their brand of 'caring rock', draw-ing on a mix of African-American political struggles (most notably the civil rights movement) and a respect for musical traditions, than with reproducing any racialized sexual essentialism. In this sense, as Reynolds and Press have argued, sexuality in U2 was sublimated into 'lofty', spiritual or political concerns.[14]

U2's success in the 1980s was to generate a sense of musical and cultural possibility in Ireland. This success further consolidated the idea of the Irish as an inherently musical 'race' and fostered the idea that creative labour in rock and popular music could be a route to advancement, economic or otherwise. Therefore, *Rattle and Hum*, in keeping with the rest of the band's output throughout the decade, was to leave a lasting aesthetic template in Ireland that influenced musical styles, performance modes and song structures (and one that involved a degree of standardization, cutting sharply against the avowedly 'wild' and organic notions of Irish musical creativity). And for ideological reasons – the maintenance of the intertwined discourses of rock and Irish authenticity – the band was to help the rock revival of the mid-to-late 1980s survive longer in Ireland than in neighbouring Britain. With its emphasis on authenticity, seriousness and self-expression, it was 'rock' in its folk mode that had been central to Irish popular music and rock that had become intimately connected to national cultural identity in this period. Indeed, prior to 1990 Dublin was known internationally as a 'rock city', with live music a ubiquitous presence, and dominated by a *rock-as-folk* ideology (A House, The Black Velvet Band, Cactus World News, Cry Before Dawn, Hothouse Flowers, In Tua Nua, Les Enfants, Light a Big Fire, Something Happens and many others, the majority of whom never signed a record deal or became widely known). In fact, Dublin as the 'city of a thousand bands'[15] may have been a gross underestimation. (Despite the relative homogeneity of the Irish rock sound, U2, it is important to point out, had their 'internal others', bands that ploughed a different aesthetic and political furrow, such as Cork's Microdisney, and bands that were anti-U2 or even parodied U2, like The Joshua Trio.[16])

In the early 1980s U2 were, therefore, regarded as the elemental, organic and sincere antidote to the artificial 'other' of British/English 'Thatcherite' new pop (although several ironies are overlooked in this crude correspondence of musical meaning, politics and nationhood). As we have seen, Ireland was marked by the relative absence of synth-based post-punk bands in The Human League, Depeche Mode or Soft Cell vein, further locking Irish rock in the organic paradigm, with *rock-as-folk* suggesting both a pure, unbroken tradition and a notion of unified expressive community. In the decade's latter half, Bono fittingly became a rock star in the pre-electric Bob Dylan mould and U2 became a band that were increasingly regarded as a vessel taken to express, or read as emblematic of, national concerns. Indeed, the U2 sound of the 1980s may be regarded as caught in a dialectic between post-punk and the more roots-based sonics of the rock revival, with the latter dominating the former as the decade progressed.

Many of the bands to follow the template went further with this roots-based folk-rock authenticity, particularly Hothouse Flowers and The Waterboys (a band comprised of Scottish and Irish musicians). Hothouse Flowers, for instance, could boast a history as street buskers (as The Incomparable Benzini Brothers) and, unlike U2, were located in an Irish-speaking milieu and offered a sound that owed more to Dylan, early Van Morrison and Irish traditional music and instrumentation. Their debut album, *People*, released on U2's Mother Records, went to number one in the Irish charts. It is, however, somewhat ironic that Hothouse Flowers' international commercial visibility was, in large part, due to their appearance on the 1988 Eurovision Song Contest as the interval act. Hence, the world's most famous 'cheesy' popular music contest showcased authentic 'raggle-taggle' Irish rock. This musical style and its related 'gypsy wander' and pastoral iconographies became so popular in Ireland, and so associated with authentic Irishness, that it penetrated the world of Irish alcohol advertising.[17] Despite the popularity of the raggle-taggle style in Ireland and its increased association with 'authentic' Irishness internationally in the late 1980s, U2's post-punk aspects clearly set them apart from the movement and it became clear as the decade petered out that the out-and-out roots search had limitations in terms of innovating within the form and was also something of a representational and musical cul-de-sac.

AN INORGANIC, 'CHEMICAL' IRELAND?

The emergence of dance music, acid house and the much-mythologized 'second summer of love' of 1988–89 in Britain were to change patterns of production, pleasure and textuality in Irish popular music culture. In fact, dance culture was to be as influential a catalyst for U2 to ponder their legacy as the backlash against *Rattle and Hum*. By the late 1980s, British rock and pop music had absorbed aspects of dance music's sonic, rhythmic and iconographic features, visible in a number of significant rock/pop/dance hybrids, such as Primal Scream, The Happy Mondays, The Soup Dragons, 808 State and many others. Here, a rock/pop performance mode and conventionalized song structure was frequently retained, but married with dance grooves gleaned from selected areas of house, techno, dub and hip hop. The 'Mad-chester' scene, as described by Jon Savage, was perhaps the most celebrated of this fusion of rock and dance.[18] The combination of aspects of contemporary 'underground' dance grooves with rock 'swagger', psychedelic and/or pop 'style' was in marked contrast to the optimistic, anthemic rock, liberal sincerity and expressive authenticity associated with U2 up to this period. Indeed, U2 would have been construed as either 'the enemy', figures of ridicule, or simply irrelevant to many of dance culture's 'tribes'. As these rock/dance styles filtered into Ireland, changes of fashion led to 'the city of a thousand bands' myth no longer dominating Dublin and, like many other European capitals, Dublin was recast as a dance city with a vibrant scene covering the spectrum of drum and bass, house, techno and break-beat (a scene we will be exploring in more detail in a later chapter). This radically altered musico-cultural context – with blissed-out, chemically enhanced euphoria at its centre – generated a challenge to U2's legacy, their sonic hegemony and artistic relevance.

It also presented difficulties for the ongoing discourse of Irish rock and in particular for U2's main narrators and interpreters. *Hot Press* initially struggled to make sense of the emerging dance culture, uncertain as to whether it was worthy of detailed coverage, perhaps expecting dance music to be a transient phenomenon. They were also wary of dance culture's perceived nihilistic hedonism and apparent conservatism. When dance began to be covered, perhaps included due to rock's ongoing fetish for 'youth', the magazine struggled to find a mode of reportage, giving rise to certain difficulties in analysis and interpretation. Dance genres were generally marked by an absence of performer-as-star, conventionalized lyric-based song structures, and by an ideology that was non-rock and, indeed, frequently and explicitly anti-rock. It was as late as the summer of 1994 before *Hot Press* added a specialist section devoted to reviewing dance events and recordings. The somewhat awkwardly titled 'Rave On' began as a small column, becoming the 'Digital Beat' pages a year later, signalling the realization that perhaps dance culture was not reducible to the tabloid term 'rave'. Indeed, only in Ireland could a column devoted to modern dance music appropriate and pun upon a Buddy Holly or Van Morrison song title ('Rave On', 1958 and 'Rave On John Donne' from 1983's *Inarticulate Speech of the Heart*). Significantly, these pages were added much later than in their UK counterparts; the *NME* covered dance culture as early as 1989. This was an indicator of how much slower *Hot Press* was to throw off the legacy of the 1980's rock revival and the folk-rock ideology that had been a cornerstone of musical production, interpretation and evaluation in the Irish context (although this is not entirely surprising given the core writers' socio-musical location, products of the mid-to-late 1960s).

The aesthetics of dance music and the structure of dance culture, its apparent anonymity and absence of visible performance modes also meant problems for the articulation of (and to) Irish identity/identities. As we have argued, rock was frequently articulated to the national (and the national to rock) and a group or a star's 'characteristics' could become bearers of national identity (irrespective of the tensions involved). The aesthetics and ideology of rock could be forged in a fashion that corresponded to national imaginings. Dance music, by contrast, created problems for evaluation centred on performance. It was difficult to imagine musicians 'performing' merely from records and to apply to them value markers, such as 'expression', 'soul', lyrical meaning and performative 'originality'. Moreover, dance music tended to articulate very different images of place – cyber space, the dance floor, the urban (often the inner city): 'placeless', futuristic, technological and metropolitan images that did not neatly fit into broader Irish cultural imaginings, and indeed the Irish rock lexicon. If, as Smyth puts it, rock had 'solved' the problems thrown up by the showband, rock had now to deal with the problems thrown up by dance culture.[19] It was therefore difficult for *Hot Press* to find continuity with the national rock tradition, as its concern had been, in part, to construct a canon of Irish rock artists.

By contrast, emerging Irish dance producers appeared to actively 'play down' their Irishness, frequently taken to be a distinct cultural and aesthetic disadvantage in that it tended to anchor music and style to a restricted, even disabling, set of cultural signifiers. The aesthetic vocabulary of 'Irishness' was now bordering on cliché in that it signified certain rock and folk modes and an imaginary that was largely Bohemian and pastoral in focus. At the turn of the decade, the dominant signifiers of Irishness internationally had moved from cool to 'uncool' (although the significant exception here is the synthesis of dance genres with 'the Celtic' that is often a conspicuous feature in world dance fusions and 'New Age' styles). While *Hot Press* steadily increased dance coverage, a higher proportion of rock writing was increasingly devoted to nostalgia and Irish rock's 'golden age', comprising of reprints of classic interviews and retrospective features on significant moments in the narrative of Irish rock (such as 'classic' Van Morrison interviews and Horslips' first tour of the United States). Like its counterparts in the United Kingdom, *Hot Press* was now increasingly using the past tense.

Making sense of this tension between a new emerging, 'placeless' urban dance culture and Irish rock's recourse to nostalgia was to create problems for U2. This allowed the band to take a risk and break out of the organic paradigm to embrace an altogether more radical form of musical and cultural hybridity. Significantly, on the seventh studio album, 1991's *Achtung Baby*, U2 appeared to be listening to their own sounds with greater self-consciousness. The band exchanged much of their folk-rock/pastoral post-punk aesthetic for a sound and iconography that was more markedly urban, pop and playful, executing a campaign of 'semiological guerrilla warfare'[20] against themselves (and with it the dominant signifiers of Irishness that they had a pivotal role in articulating). Reynolds and Press provide a sense of the prevailing mood:

> On 1991's *Achtung Baby* U2 demolished their persona, their distinctive sound, and their reputation as chaste and pompously pious. They went out of their way to absorb ideas from underground rock, defacing their sound with industrial clangour and funking up the previously inert rhythm section. Their *Zoo TV* tour attempted to replicate the chaos of media overload; in one fell swoop, U2 went from pre-modern missionaries to late C20th postmodernists. Videos were doused in sleaze; Bono changed his image from the rugged pioneer/Inca mountain guide look circa *The Joshua Tree*, to a wasted, pallid leather-clad, chain smoking rock reptile sporting sun glasses after dark... U2 reinvented themselves with a fervour that rivalled the chameleonic metamorphoses of Bowie or Siouxsie Sioux.[21]

FROM THE DESERT TO DECADENCE

In *U2: At the End of the World*, his detailed account of the *Achtung Baby/Zooropa* period, Bill Flanagan describes many attempts on the part of the band to incorporate the sounds and rhythms of 'Madchester'.[22] During recording, a central tension appeared to be whether to remain faithful to their former epic rock sound and 'natural' iconographies, or to embrace the rock-dance synthesis. U2 had, of course, been accused of ripping off Manchester bands before, as evidenced by the pronouncements of the late Tony Wilson of Factory Records[23] and Peter Hook of New Order[24] and their somewhat caustic accusation that U2 had mimicked the post-punk sound of Joy Division and taken it onto the global stage (a somewhat ironic position given that, unlike Dublin, Manchester is one of the most mythologized and heavily promoted popular musical cities/regions). However, Simon Reynolds, perhaps the most authoritative analyst of post-punk and hardly a straightforward supporter of the band, has argued that U2, while a definitive post-punk band, differed in vital respects from the peers they allegedly pilfered from. Significantly for Reynolds:

> U2 go against much of the grain of the original post-punk sound, although there was a mystical strain in post-punk too – it was there in Joy Division, which is spiritual music, about existence and the human condition... But with Joy Division it is a religion of the void, whereas with U2 there is faith, grace and redemption. And there wasn't much of that going around in post-punk![25]

Reynolds goes on to note how U2's ambition, their openness to America, clearly set the band apart from Joy Division (and from other groups of the period). Indeed the two divergent positions of their respective lead singers symbolized each band's attitudes to global success, as well as their attitudes to the United States. While Bono openly embraced the United States, Ian Curtis – like many British icons of the period – was sceptical about stateside success (and perhaps symbolically committed suicide just prior to Joy Division's first tour there). In contrast to this antipathy towards the United States, Bono's position is encapsulated in his declaration of February 1981 to *Rolling Stone* journalist, James Henke: 'It is my ambition to travel to America and give it what it wants and needs.'[26] Similarly, *Achtung Baby*, like the early post-punk U2 of *Boy*, is no mere 'Madchester' or indie dance derivative with only the conspicuously postmodern anthem, 'Even Better than the Real Thing', conforming to Primal Scream's swagger.[27]

   In fact, it was the novel and challenging hybridity and the range of influences on the album, as well as how it straddled the dialectic between confirmation/affirmation and challenge, between past and present U2, that made it interesting. Brian Eno, who produced *Achtung Baby*, his third U2 album, argued that when the material succeeded, 'a hybrid' emerged: 'there is a synergy of feelings and nuances that nobody ever foresaw. If that happens, it's news. There's a lot of that kind of news on this record... To find a single adjective for any song proves difficult: it's an album of musical oxymorons, of feelings that shouldn't exist together but that are somehow credible.'[28]

Any borrowing, then, from the so-called dance underground not only intermingled with the previous U2 sound but also with European 'art rock', specifically the so-called 'Kraut-rock' associated with Can, Kraftwerk, DAF and Neu! It was also influenced by Bowie and Eno's trio of Berlin albums of the 1970s that were, in turn, heavily influenced by Kraut-rock. Many of these groups had recorded in Hansa Studios in Berlin, home of auteur producer Conny Plank, which was renowned as a centre in the production of electronic and 'industrial' sounds. Significantly, the first section of the production of *Achtung Baby* was recorded here, an aspect of the album that was foregrounded in the rock press. In accounts of the period, a host of contemporary bands – such as Nitzer Ebb and My Bloody Valentine – are also namechecked as influences, bands at some distance from the organic paradigm of Irishness. U2 were now articulating a place in Europe, much as their early post-punk contemporaries had done in the late 1970s and early 1980s, and it was immediate post-unification Berlin and the former East Germany, not Manchester, Ireland or the United States, that was to dominate the album's mood and the band's iconography. Indeed the tensions and contradictions of identity and ethnicity were foregrounded, with difference itself actively explored rather than glossed over by the one-world address of yore.

The Berlin of the period suggested uneasy coexistence, with a myriad of unresolved national and ethnic tensions in wake of Soviet Communism's collapse, as opposed to an idealized, multicultural 'melting pot' implicitly yearned for in past material. The title, which yoked together the American rock counterculture and urban Germany in a camp and playful fashion, signposted the new aesthetic and broke with the tradition of sombre and naturalistic album names (and one could imagine a louche Keith Richards using the album title to greet friends in a Berlin nightclub). Indeed, the title economically signposted the type of hybridization offered and spatially evoked U2's geographical base in Ireland. In Smyth's words, the band exploited 'the island's location between the two main centres of western cultural history: the United States and Europe'.[29] In this way the title succinctly evoked the complex trajectories of musical space, style and genre involved, or as Smyth goes on to argue, 'the band exploited Ireland's traditional imaginative location – marginal from Europe, residual to America – to produce deeply compelling engagements with both those large cultural entities',[30] even though here the 'balance' is pulled strongly in the direction of a highly selective 'European' aesthetic.[31]

In a sense, U2 could be described as going on a different kind of 'roots' quest, a journey into the origins of their post-punk sound. Thus, to simply argue (as has been commonplace) that *Rattle and Hum* is 'authentic' (albeit flawed) and *Achtung Baby* postmodern, and hence 'inauthentic', is clearly inaccurate and problematic. As we have argued, the former album is as much driven by reference, inter-textuality and pastiche – postmodernism in the service of authenticity, as it were – as its more superficially 'postmodern' successor. Allan F. Moore has usefully argued that much of popular music culture incorporates pastiche, referentiality and homage.[32] Therefore, when discussing this period of the band's output, the crit-ical terms of postmodernism appear largely unhelpful.

Most importantly, *Achtung Baby* was a more *conspicuous* stylis-tic hybrid (a hybridity that is registered in interpretation and as a pleasure) than any previous U2 album and was taken to represent an aesthetic and sonic departure from previous releases. The band were going out of their way to sound 'experimental', emphasizing unusual 'dirty' timbres and grainy textures, encapsulated in Bono's famous description of the album as 'the sound of four men chop-ping down the Joshua Tree'.[33] The sense conveyed was disjointed and uneasy, musical 'space' giving way to sonic density with synthe-sizer sounds re-routed through amplifiers and effects pedals to forge a 'bespoke' soundscape. The all-important opening track, 'Zoo Station', was most representative of the 'new' musical aesthetic with a higher proportion of synthesized sound than on previous albums, and industrial drums and sequenced pulses to the front of the mix. Taken together, these rewrote, to shocking effect, prior expectations of the U2 sound, establishing them within the pantheon of rock's European avant-garde experimentalists. Not only did 'Zoo Station' sound industrial, it also conveyed a different sense of 'space' and movement, musically invoking the urban and train travel and, in particular, of a train bursting from darkened tunnels into the light (especially as the verse gives way to the chorus).[34] This stylistic ensemble – European iconography, indus-trial noise, dance rhythms, indie-rock 'swagger', together with the past U2 legacy – was perhaps an attempt to appeal to a broader constituency of listeners, and was perhaps a reaction to the increased fragmentation of the rock audience into discrete yet over-lapping taste-clusters and dispersed age-groupings. As such it offered a challenge to existing fans as the album expressed elements of incoherence, as opposed to passion and 'spirit'. As Richard

Middleton has argued, 'once established, particular musico-techno-logical crystallizations can take on definite connotational or ideological references; and these can be hard to shift. Because of its history in rock music, the electric guitar itself signifies "passion" and "sexuality", almost inescapably. Similarly, synthesizers, because of particular usages, have acquired connotations of "modernity", the "future", "space-exploration", "rational control".'[35] Eno has described 'Zoo Station's' disruptive hybridity as 'industrially jovial'.[36] After the subversion and potential disorientation of the song's opening, the introduction of the Edge's signature 'chiming' guitar offered a sense of melody and the familiar U2 and acted as a form of anchorage and reassurance. Bono's voice was given different treatment on this track and the first single release, and seventh track, 'The Fly'. Normally centre-stage and to the forefront of the mix, it was here uncharacteristically recessed, occasionally obscured and treated with distortion effects or over-lapped with itself. On the chorus of the latter track the singer duetted with himself in a fractured call-and-response manner: the first, a newly deployed falsetto (his so-called 'fat lady' voice), was redolent of 1960's black soul music; the second, was a contrasting deep and close-miked, distorted growl – both of which were not immediately recognizable as the star. This 'fat-lady' voice was arguably Bono's most performative moment and (s)he was to resurface more prominently on the Euro-disco-influenced 'Lemon' from 1993's follow-up album *Zooropa*. It was certainly unusual for a U2 track to have this type of voice, let alone to have it emerging from such a hard and aggressive industrial backing track (or a black American 'female' soul voice ushering forth from 'European' industrial grooves). If the voice, 'words being spoken or sung in human tones', is a sign of 'personality', as Frith has argued,[37] then together the two unfamiliar voices offered here could be regarded as the musical expression of a split personality – an articulation of Oscar Wilde's 'Victorian cliché of the divided self'[38] – and a move away from the 'grounded' Bono of before. Susan Fast, in perhaps the most complete musicological analysis of any track from *Achtung Baby*, has argued that Bono's 'utilisation of a lower range than previously' may be read as the sound of a more mature man and that this 'maturity' helped reinforce the sense of irony and cynicism that pervades the album.[39]

This sense of dislocation and the unfamiliar was echoed in the cover art, which abandoned the 'serious' black-and-white rock realist photography of both *The Joshua Tree* and *Rattle and Hum*, and the recurring use of expansive pastoral locations, for a colourful collage of images of European decadence and urban claustrophobia: a naked Adam Clayton, Bono wearing make-up and the band driving around Berlin in graffiti-smattered Trabants. What is superficially apparent is the rejection of the former rock 'n' roll 'roots' narrative and its accompanying concern with a specific version of rock authenticity in favour of a more pluralistic, even ambiguous, aesthetic – one that had connotations of a future of fragmentation/dislocation, industry and the (post)modern as opposed to the pre-modern discourse of 'authenticity', 'roots' and unity.

The 'big' universalist address, characteristic of past output, was more subdued, and a much more ambiguous and shifting use of the pronouns 'I', 'you' and 'we' was in evidence (as well as Bono singing the rock cliché, 'baby', for the first time on record). *Achtung Baby* lyrically was more intimate – the emphasis on relationships, the tensions and ambiguities of sexuality, and an avoidance of 'widescreen' political 'issues', such as apartheid in South Africa or political upheaval in El Salvador, for which the band had been criticized in the past. Righteousness, it appeared, had been replaced by doubt and contradiction. Also, broadly speaking, the lyrics moved away from naturalized imagery and the elements – the constant references to 'earth, desert, sky, sea, rain, sleet, snow, fire' and so forth – were replaced by a repertoire of urban and sexualized images. Indeed, the album was praised for its traditional 'rock' virtues: lyrical complexity, emotional maturity, insight and 'relevance'. Bono still frequently reverted to his 'big voice', making ample use of his trademark 'uplifting' high register. However, the new associations of the music often served to offset the prior affirmative drives. This was particularly evident in the album's sixth track, 'So Cruel'. The song is essentially a ballad, based around a sparse down-tempo hip hop (or trip hop) rhythm, but it does not conform to expectations of the band or the ballad form. While Bono's voice attempts to climb skyward, instead of offering emotional uplift and catharsis – the musical equivalent of 'climax-oriented narrative'[40] – the song builds uneasily, struggling to climax. In many ways, 'So Cruel' could be regarded as the sound of guilty, or unsatisfactory, orgasm (rather than the ecstatic release, the upward drive of before) and the song shudders to a halt, offering no tidy resolution. The words corresponded to the sonic mood: 'I'm only hanging on/To watch you go down/My love', and, 'I disappeared in you/You disappeared from me/I gave you everything you ever wanted/It wasn't what you wanted.' As the song builds uneasily, the imagery becomes darker: 'You don't know if it's fear or desire/ Danger the drug that takes you higher/Head of heaven, fingers in the mire.'

This type of sexualized imagery, its mix of the biblical and the profane, was maintained throughout the album: 'Surrounding me/ Going down on me/Spilling over the brim' (from 'Until the End of the World') and 'You can swallow and you can spit/You can throw it up or choke on it' ('Acrobat'), signalled a move away from the righteous, lofty abstractions of the past. On the single, 'One', the prior emphasis on unity, togetherness – on 'being as one' – was subjected to bittersweet contradiction (albeit in a moving fashion). In short, Bono had abandoned his pedestal in favour of 'crawling around on [his] hands and knees' ('The Fly'). In fact, the blues and country explored on *Rattle and Hum* was to play an important if critically under-explored role in this more experimental incarnation, jarring against the European, electronic and postmodern elements. Ironically, if taking the words in isolation, *Achtung Baby* is a much more convincing blues-country album than its more 'roots'-based predecessor, evident in the recurring motifs of earthly temptation, failed redemption and partial healing (which further problematizes any simple narrative of wholesale transformation from the authentic to the postmodern). This novel hybrid of modernized blues-country narratives, electronica and experimental 'European' rock was maintained and heightened at the lyrical level.

However, sitting uneasily alongside this 'authored' mode of 'sincerity' and 'depth' was a more straightforward postmodern appropriation of aphorisms, slogans and clichés (such as 'a liar won't believe anyone else'), drawn from the work of New York conceptual artists Barbara Kruger and Jenny Holzer (as well as inspired by William Burroughs's 'cut-ups', just as Bowie had been nearly two decades earlier).[41] Therefore, *Achtung Baby* not only worked against, and in tension with, U2's past work, but it was internally contradictory. It was precisely the musical and associated visual contradictions between past and present U2, between vocal style, lyrical meaning and musical aesthetic, 'American' and 'European', authentic and inauthentic, the 'complex' and the 'throwaway', coherence and uncertainty, that made the album disruptive and engaging. Moreover, one of the other ways that *Achtung Baby* fanned its address out further was in the appeal to dance subcultures through the practice of including remixes by 'underground' producers (even if these tended towards the populist end of the underground spectrum, such as Paul Oakenfold and Apollo 440). This served to attract the dance music press – *Mixmag*, the now defunct *Muzik* and *Wax* – which could not have been targeted previously, as well as drawing on the 'subcultural capital' of dance music 'credibility'.[42]

Any radicalism evident on the album was, however, to become much more apparent in the band's new iconography and performance, and this is one of the most interesting aspects of the hybrid pop 'text' (or paramusicality), the possibilities for setting up tensions among its various levels. The promotional video for the single release, 'The Fly' (1991), the first public glimpse of the band's new sound and iconography offered a mise en scène that reinforced this sense of estrangement: a sexualized as opposed to chaste Bono – premiering his Fly character – in shiny black PVC, located in a grainy and murky, low-key, neon-lit urban netherworld surrounded by banks of television screens (redolent of Bowie in *The Man Who Fell To Earth*, directed by Nicolas Roeg, 1976). This was in marked contrast to the consistent stream of pastoral locations that dominated video releases hitherto.[43] In fact, the band was to capitalize on this, maintaining a pre-tour media silence in order to maximize the potential shock of their new iconography and live performance image (against the more open and orthodox publicity campaigns of preceding albums and tours).

THE MEDIA ZOO: OR, FROM BALLYKISSANGEL TO BLADE RUNNER

U2 toured *Achtung Baby* as *Zoo TV* in 1992 in the United States (and as *Zooropa* in Europe). The title is derived from the opening track, 'Zoo Station', which in turn references Zoo Bahnhof in Berlin: the station at the centre of the Uli Edel's cult 'heroin chic' film, *Christiane F/Die Kinder vom Bahnhof Zoo* (*We Children from Bahnhof Zoo*) of 1981 which featured David Bowie as the 'thin white duke' in concert performing 'Station to Station'. It also referred to the 'mobile TV station', or 'media zoo', at the centre of the live event. This enabled live satellite link-up and the capacity to record received images for playback on a series of giant, individually controlled video screens or 'vidiwalls' suspended above the stage and smaller video cubes that peppered the stage floor. Specially commissioned film treatments were also incorporated. *Zoo TV* was being announced as something new in the much-maligned stadium rock genre, using these onstage screens in an active and playful manner, to incorporate images from television – often from the hosting national context, to establish critical positions on television and on rock culture itself. The concert was filmed from a number of angles, in much the same way as an orthodox rock concert is filmed for video or television release, except that these images were assigned 'live' to the various screens and cubes, allowing the band and particularly Bono to interact with the on-screen images. This permitted the physical (and symbolic) insertion of rock star performance into the televisual frame – literally a fly inside a television screen (most evident in the introduction of Bono's high-kicking Fly and his excessive rock poses in front of screen static at the concert's opening). Throughout the concert, images of the star were 'vision mixed' with the commissioned material, animations and other film treatments, as well as other images apparently 'grabbed' from satellite both recorded and 'live'.

Zoo TV was thus both an extension of live performance possibilities and an integration of pop video visuals brought to the live arena. It also represented a similar approach to pop visuals as the mixing desk and multitrack recorder have been to pop sound – that is, a dub or cut 'n' paste sensibility brought to images, with each vidiwall and cube analogous to the individual tracks of tape on multitrack and so on. This allowed visual discourses to be bricolaged and brought into juxtaposition with one another much in the same way that sounds are made to correspond (or jar) on multitrack. As Frith has noted, 'the "creative" use of the mixing desk'[44] has been a central feature of rock and pop history, and a similar ethos was brought over to vision mixing, and the mixing of sound and image, allowing contradictory discourses to be brought into exciting correspondences with one another. Historically, one aspect of the concert was the appropriation of a series of popular music performance strategies relatively common during the post-punk period and associated with 'electronic' and/or experimental bands such as Cabaret Voltaire, Psychic TV, Soft Cell and the early Human League (amongst others), who in their different ways used banks of televisions, video screens and slide projections. What marked this work out from the use of visuals in pre-punk rock was the modernist imperative, the desire to explore self-consciously mediation itself as opposed to creating a psychedelic backdrop. *Zoo TV* was the first time these strategies were taken and expanded into a stadium context.

This point is supported by Allan F. Moore who has argued that the use of vidiwalls in *Zoo TV* was not simply a way of getting around the stadium problematic and to generate a sense of intimacy in a large space (as had been the case in stadium concerts in the 1980s). Rather, the screens were deployed to create a sense of critical distance.[45] However, in rock and pop concerts, the visual level cannot work independently of the soundtrack and, as with the pop video, the different visuals were 'cut' rhythmically in time to reinforce the dynamics and tempo of the songs. The musical and visual then could be brought into obtuse correspondences, playing on the meeting of different associations anchored within the 'onstage' rock performance.

BRINGING UP BABY AND BLOWING UP BUSH: HIP HOPPING
THE APOCALYPSE!

The stage-set resembled a *Blade Runner*-style cityscape, with its suspended vidiwalls and Trabants, scaffolding towers and smokestacks. The neon *Zoo TV* logo at the uppermost point of the stage consolidated the science-fiction aspect offering a pastiche and critique of corporate identities and branded merchandizing. This set was offered as both a spectacle to marvel at, with its intricate network of different sized screens, varied sight lines and stage-levels, but also had dystopian connotations – a future where 'image' swamps 'meaning' (though there is nothing futuristic about this position, as it is an ideology that has been commensurate with rock culture for quite some time).

The concert opened in suitably dramatic fashion with the then president, George Bush Senior, appearing on the screens, accompanied by a hip hop drum loop. In a direct address to the audience, characteristic of newsreaders and television authority figures, Bush rapped the chorus of Queen's 'We Will Rock You' repeatedly in sync to the rhythm. This juxtaposition of Bush and hip hop was an interesting stylistic tension, the agitprop possibilities of bricolage, the divergent associations of the musical and visual being used for political purposes. It was also funny. Bush was being made to rap – a musical form with primarily African-American associations – and the televisual authority address was undermined by being turned into 'pop' spectacle (and also because Bush was a prominent supporter of the conservative Parent's Music Resource Centre, or

PMRC, which was explicitly anti-rap). It thus offered a number of interpretations. It can be read within the terms of reference of rock romanticism, where the incorporation of the president into the opening sequence of the concert is 'bizarre' and 'very rock and roll'. However, an aspect of 'double-coding' is that Bush was quoting a well-known Queen song, and that, more significantly, the 'rock' of 'we will rock you', is frequently read in rock culture as a synonym for 'fuck', adding a critical subtext to the opening address ('we will, we will fuck you') and a barbed critique of the Republican administration's first Gulf War policy, with Bush rapping the subtext, 'I instructed our military commanders to totally rock (fuck) Baghdad.' Decoding the latter references of course raises the issue of the audience's cultural capital, but examples such as this one do not appear to operate off a simple 'either/or' binary of parody *or* pastiche, critique *or* homage, as all areas can be argued for.

Significantly, the Rhodes Island-based 'guerrilla' video production collective, Emergency Broadcast Network (EBN), was responsible for the Bush rapping clip and their 'underground' connotations have been appropriated by U2 in this context (with EBN reciprocally reaching a much wider audience). One thing was certain, however: U2 were decentring themselves by incorporating such work while simultaneously extending their performance lexicon and revitalizing the stadium rock format.

These images of the president were intercut with atomic explosions in time with the accented bass drum, establishing a musical/visual juxtaposition that invited the audience to dance in time to apocalyptic explosions (a visualization, perhaps, of the line from 1983's *War* album and the track 'Seconds' – 'where they dance the atomic bomb' – suggesting a continuity with selective aspects of the band's earlier work). Here, rock culture and its utopian thrust were subject to critique in the formal combination of the cerebral and the hedonistic, the rhythmic and the visual and their conventionalized associations. The PMRC-endorsing Bush was being made to rap, and hip hop's 'black underground' urban credentials were attached to the U2 authorial text in a novel and adventurous fashion (just as the EBN text had been similarly appropriated).

However, amidst all the irony, referentiality and play, the band were evidently taking a clear political stand in literally detonating Bush's image while at the same time openly supporting Democrat presidential candidate Bill Clinton (with Bono's tired lothario, Mr McPhisto, even 'joking' in the conclusion *Zooropa* concerts that U2 had given the world Bill Clinton). Overall, then, *Zoo TV* was something of a Wagnerian *Gesamtkunstwerk*, or total artwork, inviting the audience to look and listen across its various discourses – part play, part homage, part critique – and was very different to the spartan stage-shows of the past, especially the Celtic mistiness of the Red Rocks concert almost a decade earlier.

Bono's adoption of the Fly was a significant shift and departure from the authenticity of his earlier persona. It marked the period when the singer began to sport large wrap-around sunglasses which have remained a signature of his identity and a permanent fixture ever since. They were also the primary sign that he had changed: the most visible index of a 'new' Bono. Smyth has fittingly described the character as 'louche' and 'slightly camp…a figure further from the various heroic, "grounded" Bono personae of the 1980s [it] is hard to imagine',[46] and certainly the role-playing of the period – *Zooropa*'s Mr McPhisto and *Zoo TV*'s Mirrorball Man – was, for many, a thankful respite from the lead singer's liberal crusading. What was less clear was how to read these images, as they seemed complex and ambiguous. As Andrew Goodwin has pointed out in his discussion of stars playing characters, any postmodern 'role-playing' is anchored by the knowledge, that it is, of course, still the star.[47] While the creation of the Fly did indeed serve to reinforce and promote Bono as star, it had different implications from the former persona. The Fly was a self-critique of the former Bono persona, as well as a parody/homage of other rock stars, such as Elvis in the '68 *Special*, Jim Morrison of the Doors, the stars of 'Glam rock' or Lou Reed circa *Transformer* (1972). It also invoked a popular cultural black leather-clad lineage stretching back to Marlon Brando in *The Wild One* (directed by Laslo Benedek, 1953).

POST-IMPERIAL LEATHER, POST-COLONIAL PVC

What was especially significant was not any role-playing per se, as chameleonic reinvention has been a staple part of the iconography of many rock and pop stars, most famously David Bowie, Madonna and Kylie Minogue, but the force of the reinvention in this context. Bono had offered up a fairly consistent star-text from the band's inception to 1991. What the Fly offered was an abrupt volte-face of over a decade of rock star authenticity, particularly the rural authenticity, casual muscularity and the pre-Fordist iconography of the rural dispossessed of the two preceding albums. In this sense, reinvention was in no way a routine expectation, which meant that any iconographic alteration was all the more potentially subversive, particularly to long-term fans. Whereas for a famous chameleon such as Bowie transformation arguably is expected and located firmly in the inauthenticity paradigm, Bono's reinvention constituted a wholesale paradigm shift, a move from the organic to the synthetic, from authenticity to artifice, fair-trade clothing to industrial PVC, long lank natural hair to dye and hairspray, the 'natural' to the conspicuously manufactured. It was also a move from commitment and 'caring' to uncertainty and ambiguity, or from a 'trustworthy experience' to one that offered a sense of 'menace'. In short, transformation is much more difficult if the basis of your persona is sincerity and authenticity.[48]

There was, however, a note of fatalism and futility in the Fly. Firstly it drew on the literal, an insect pest 'living on shit', actively feeding off human waste, but also one impossible to get rid of. Second, it also invoked the more metaphorical idea of 'fly-on-the-wall' (as in documentary), with connotations of omniscience and tied in with the song lyric from the track, 'The Fly' ('A man will beg/A man will crawl/On the sheer face of love/Like a fly on a wall'). Therefore, while the character of the Fly might be 'all-seeing', having the vantage point to observe from odd angles and from a distance, it has little power to effect change, apart from being able to make an ineffectual 'bite', alluding to both the insect's, and the pop star's, brief lifespan (a move from 'U can do it 2', to 'U2 can be squashed'). The character may have been inspired by David Cronenberg's *The Fly* (1986), drawing upon that film's connotations of abjection, monstrous hybridization and failed metamorphosis. Therefore, the icon and its meaning was a critical engagement in performance terms with issues of pop celebrity, rock stereotypes, stardom, and expectations about rock, politics and power. To a limited extent the conventions of rock stardom and what they are taken to represent were debunked. However, while this adopted alter ego was parodying existing rock tropes and performance conventions through an exaggerated and bombastic re-articulation of these, he was *still* a rock star, playing a rock star in a rock concert. This had a dual function. First, it attached U2 to a 'great' rock past, and simultaneously cross-promoted that past (with nostalgic consequences); second, it also problematized, through parody and critique, the rock 'n' roll nostalgia it otherwise set up. So, once again, the terms of critical reference of postmodernism, whether it is parody, pastiche or homage, seem strangely unhelpful, merely setting up circular arguments.

Again, this is not especially significant in an Anglo-American metropolitan context as a range of 'performative' stars populate the pop/rock landscape, but it is certainly of some import in relation to discourses of Irishness. The dandy, the gender-bender, the chameleon and the leather-clad rock star have all been largely absent from the Irish popular music lexicon (the notable exceptions are of course the late leather-clad Phil Lynott, or the gender play of Gavin Friday and Guggi of the Virgin Prunes). Indeed, what is significant for a national music culture framed within the residue of authenticity, of traditional music and a rock-as-folk ideology is that swinging to rock-as-art in such a fashion and appropriating that which was regarded as, in some senses, 'un-Irish' was a radical gesture. But it is important to explore the specific way in which this occurred.

As the Fly, Bono was able to perform the explicitly (hetero)sexual and authentic male rock star as a necessary masquerade,[49] overtly sexualizing the apparently 'sexless' paradigm of Irish rock stars. It can be read as an appropriation of the kind of 'cultivated disdain' associated with the English and English rock stars invoked by Eno earlier: a move from a known and 'caring' Bono to an altogether more ambivalent star-text. The Fly was thus caught between ironic parody, where the wearing of the mask was made explicit, and skilfully inhabiting the role. In this respect, a further connotation of 'fly' comes into play, as the character appositely invokes the adjective 'fly' in black American slang meaning 'cool' (as in, say, Curtis Mayfield's 1972 funk classic 'Super Fly'). Perhaps more importantly in this context, however, 'fly' can also refer to someone attempting to be cool but failing (often spectacularly). Hence the alter ego can be described as oscillating between the 'fairly ridiculous'[50] on the one hand, and as conventionally seductive on the other (or suitably performing the cliché of being caught between the sublime and the ridiculous). As Fast has noted, Bono as the Fly was voted the 'sexiest male artist' in a *Rolling Stone* readers' poll of 1993, a sign that irony and play was not top of every fan's interpretative hierarchy.[51] In interview about the period, Bono appears to have it both ways. First, the Fly was openly intertextual: 'the rock star I put together for myself was an identikit. I had Elvis Presley's leather jacket, Jim Morrison's leather pants, Lou Reed's fly shades, Jerry Lee Lewis's boots, Gene Vincent's limp', and we could add Elvis's hair.[52] Second,

16. 'An inorganic Ireland? Post-imperial Leather' – Bono as the Fly (Corbis)

Bono claimed that 'we weren't parodying...these were other sides of myself'.[53]

Therefore, not only did Bono subvert his prior 'authentic' persona and with it the dominant discourses of performing Irish masculinity, but, as Ramert has usefully observed, the singer had little material or discursive support in the popular music iconographies circulating at the time. This was an era dominated by grunge and hip hop styles in the United States and various popular music fashions in the UK, such as ethnic tribal, sports casuals and 'indie baggy'; clothing styles that support hetero-normative positions, leaving the Fly's excesses as something of an isolated reference point. If, for example, the English rock band Suede in the same period had to, as it were, 'dress down' to subvert sedimented expectations of camp, queer or self-consciously performative strategies in order to re-energize them,[54] Bono and U2, in order to do the same things to their star-text, and to the dominant performing Irish identities they had helped consolidate, had to 'dress up' (even though it was a dressing up without explicit attachment to discourses of gender play). However, clothing, in short, became a vital means for breaking out of (pop) colonial expectations of Irish rock authenticity.

Also, the previous 'sincere' and 'worthy' Bono persona looked radically out of step when contrasted with the stars of the rock-dance synthesis, such as Shaun Ryder of The Happy Mondays, who in their very particular ways tapped into the 'every lad' zeitgeist of the period. Bono's earnest rural 'pioneer', in a sense, looked quaint when contrasted to figures such as the habitually hedonistic Ryder who represented the drug-fuelled boredom born of the enforced urban leisure of Thatcher's Britain. In short, Ryder was a proletarian performer, who alongside his equally famous and chemically-enhanced (and non-musician) friend and band mate Bez was easy for many to identify with, in that they offered hedonistic respite in the face of social adversity. Bono's reinvention as the Fly, in other words, was also a way of responding to the rise of figures such as these.

The urbane and sexualized leather-clad rock star has been on the margins of Irish rock and pop experience. But the style of black 'leather' employed here was incredibly significant (though an aspect overlooked in critical writing on this period of the band's oeuvre). Bono is not wearing orthodox black leather of the type sported by Jim Morrison, Elvis or Brando, but rather a type of mottled, grainy or textured PVC, with the jacket in the so-called 'rocker' style (which Elvis did sport on the *'68 Special*). This material offers a visually interesting and tactile surface in its combination of matt and shiny textures. Alongside the 'fly' shades, this fabric, with its odd light refracting qualities, invites the audience to look and to explore its quality. At a rudimentary level, it enables Bono to 'literalize' the insect fly – bug-eyed and a mix of matt and shiny surfaces – but also, as in much post-punk as described by Reynolds,[55] to open up and reinforce a 'meta-critique' of rock stardom and celebrity. This certainly invites interpretation beyond those raised by the much-discussed figure of the dandy.[56] Clearly, the dandy is of great import to debates about the unmasking of conventionalized masculinities. But merely labelling and exploring Bono's Fly in such a way fails to register the icon's popular musical provenance, neglecting other important contexts, and does not consider the ways in which he signifies differently from other famous pop 'dandies', from Jagger to Bowie.

But black leather – and invoking a black and leather-clad lineage – is also a gamble. To reference and to revive a great 'outlaw', masculine and sexualized rock past is to invite failure; to risk, in a sense, 'falling flat on one's face' in aspiring to join such celebrated and highly mythologized, company. This was particularly risky for Bono, as he has never secured his position as one of rock's great outlaw performers. Not only is the 'great' leather-clad rock star safely quarantined in the past, his best moments over and never to be successfully repeated, but black leather has become something of a cliché, drawing in connotations that are unwelcome in early-1990s male-dominated rock culture – the idea that leather is 'cheesy', 'naff', even comical. Significantly, black leather is also symbolically ambivalent. It has not just been the iconography of 'outlaw' hetero-masculinity from bikers to punk, but it also 'belongs' as much to the disco group Village People and the metropolitan gay underground, most visible in the cinema of Kenneth Anger and the postcards of Tom of Finland. It is also the garb of provincial and out-of-step macho. Some of these aspects have been played with in the 'tongue-in-cheek referencing' of 'mainstream' popular culture, most famously perhaps in *Terminator 2: Judgment Day* (directed by James Cameron, 1991) where Arnold Schwarzenegger in the epony-mous role self-consciously acquires the biker uniform (to go to war with a shape-shifting 'cop'), dredging up the meanings just described.

However, one fact surprisingly overlooked in discussions of *Zoo TV* was the precision required in the choice of 'leather'. For exam-ple, if Bono as the Fly had dressed in a classic double-fly bike jacket of the type worn by Schwarzenegger, Sid Vicious or The Clash, it would have risked toppling the entire technological multimedia extravaganza, overshadowing the screens, and ushering in some of the powerful connotations just described. After all, and the contem-porary U2 is no doubt aware of this, there is only so much audience interest that can be sustained by long shots emphasizing the specta-cle, the sheer scale of a stadium concert. Ultimately, however innovative the concert, it must eventually conform to popular music's long-established televisual conventions, and here the music, and the clothed bodies performing it, is arguably of the utmost importance.[57]

Whichever way, parody or pastiche, the performative and chameleonic role-play only accounts for part of the story. For exam-ple, at the end of the second song in *Zoo TV* – 'The Fly' – Bono mimics, or ventriloquizes, Elvis Presley successfully. This is not just an empty reference, nor parody or pastiche. Elvis, the icon who most embodies poor white America's appropriation of the blues, is fetishized visually by the excessive manner of the performance and the shrink-wrapped plasticity of Bono's costume (the idea of the star as 'untouched' commodity, delivered 'fresh' for the consumer) and destabilized by the onstage setting.

When compared to its Anglo-American counterparts, Irish rock has been distinctly anti-fashion in outlook and Irish rock stars have rarely, if ever, been regarded as fashion-leaders, nor have they attracted the attention of the fashion press (especially in the 1980s). 'Raggle-taggle' and hobo archetypes, or the iconographies of the rural dispossessed, have predominated. As befits Irish folk-rock discourses of authenticity, labels – designer or otherwise – have been largely absent. Bono in the mid-1980s even bequeathed what was perhaps the most famous mullet (a hairstyle marked by a short top and sides and a very long back) to rock and pop history, a style often stereotypically associated with 'red-neck' car mechanics – and 1980s footballers – and one at a great distance from the style cultures of the metropolitan centre.

Thus, Ramert notes that when Bono appeared on the front cover of *Vogue* in December 1992 alongside supermodel Christy Turlington, he was first male to do so in three decades and only the second to ever do so.[58] Despite the overt critique of commodity culture, the singer – as the Fly – escaped the magazine's customary practice of detailing the fashions worn by its cover stars. While Turlington's hair, clothing and make-up were all listed, the Fly's 'inauthentic' apparel was kept carefully under wraps. This preserved rock star dress as beyond the 'feminine', as 'outside' of fashion and commodity culture. In short, it maintained one of the central tenets of rock authenticity. It seems that the U2 organization has been keen to protect the make and model of both clothing and sunglasses (something that seems to frustrate many U2 fans across the web).

It is significant, though, that the Fly iconography remained intact only for the first third of the concert. In the same way that *Achtung Baby* straddled the conventional and the disruptive, the sincere and the ironic, *Zoo TV*, despite its popular modernist devices, retained many aspects of a folk address and ideology. Just in case the audience became too alienated midway through, Bono abandoned the Fly persona and the band regrouped to the smaller B-stage to play in the round, in a more stripped-down, 'unplugged-style' set (and hence 'unmasking the mask', as it were). This more orthodox 'good ol' sweaty singalong' of past and present hits returned the audience to the pleasures of the familiar, keeping long-term fans 'connected' and satisfied.

Zoo TV was, therefore, highly ambivalent and in no sense a straightforward critique of image culture. Rather, the critique of spectacle served the spectacle of the rock concert; the critique of television, similarly, depended on the appropriation of television and televisual strategies to revitalize the stadium concert format. Nonetheless, the specific tensions established here between music and performance, between, 'old' and 'new' U2, along with the synthesis of the 'traditional' ('authenticity', affirmative uplift, emotional 'sincerity', passion, spirit) and the modernist (distance, self-reflexivity, critique, parody) were clearly of critical importance, especially to discourses of Irishness and Irish popular music. *Zoo TV*, then, was a paradigm case of Bakhtinian polyvocality; of an Irishness opened up to, and articulating, competing, contradictory and overlapping cultural discourses (or, in pop historical terms, a marker of how much the 'gimmick' and the 'happening' of the show-band and beat eras had developed).

'A SORT OF HOMECOMING'?

Zoo TV was critically hailed as a new phenomenon right across the music press. It even reintroduced the group to the 'serious' arts pages of the 'quality' papers: a vindication of just how much *Achtung Baby* and *Zoo TV* did constitute a radical rupture with U2's past and the dominant discourse of Irish rock. However, *Hot Press*, which had been instrumental in building up the original U2 image, was less convinced by this new departure. While the magazine emphasized the concert as spectacle, as 'bizarre' and 'carnivalesque', and how 'crazy' it all was, it clearly missed the 'old U2' and frequently criticized the concert as lacking in the folk-inflected 'real' rock values of 'intimacy' and 'passion'. For example, Helena Mulkearns wrote in an early review:

> The *Zoo TV* stadium tour has become a huge, terrible rock 'n' roll *beast*, a high tech cyber creature which has long ago overshadowed the four human beings...What happens if a band gains the whole world and loses its soul?
> ...never have (U2) been so *distanced*, so *controlled*, so *inaccessible*...don't expect any *emotional spontaneity*...it seems something has been lost along the way, that human dimension that comes with feeling first and foremost, that there are four guys up on stage, play-

ing their hearts out. It's that old stadium trap – and the trouble is that the technological extravaganza amplifies rather than defeats it.[59] [Italics in the original.]

Zoo TV appears to have precipitated a crisis in reading, value and judgment for the journalists at *Hot Press*. Bill Graham reviewed the *Zoo TV/Zooropa* concerts several times, consistently noting his unease at the spectacle. Initially he appeared to defer judgment on the performance and elected to extend U2's place in the ongoing master national narrative. As he had done at the beginning of the band's career on their first tour outside of Ireland, Graham relied on metaphors of conquest, re-invoking the 'war' of the stadium bands, utilizing the trope of insidership, sweeping away any 'noise' generated by *Zoo TV* and engaging in a whole set of military and sporting metaphors to display how the Irish were winning the 'battle of media sales' – 'round one to U2' and so on. When he finally proceeded to discuss the concert itself, Ireland's most revered rock critic was evidently worried about the lack of core rock (or is it folk?) values: 'so much for any notion of authenticity...U2 are killing naturalism.'[60] However, most revealing is Graham's review of the 'homecoming' *Zoo TV* Ireland concerts:

> What is *Zoo TV*? Perhaps the final white heat supernova, death of stadium rock spectacle...? Or a strangely flexible and inclusive validation of a new and only partially formed Irish identity...? Or a unique effort to take the avant-garde to all those who never attend an art gallery installation...? At times *Zoo TV* does become less interactive, a far more reliably scheduled affair than any Irish Rail timetable.[61]

After this set of questions, he goes on to offer judgement:

> U2 do really look as if they're going to be snowed under...the audience seems to be gorging themselves on the hail of imagery and their own collective idea of U2 – which may not necessarily be that of the four small figures on stage who almost seem to be surrendering to all the million contradictory images of themselves. It's almost Kraftwerkian. U2, you momentarily think, could put four robots or impersonators on stage and watch 'themselves' from the sound-desk. Is the spectacle so overloaded and saturated as to be ultimately devoid of meaning? Are we watching faith being sucked into the black hole of nihilism?[62]

'Kraftwerkian', of course, could be regarded as a compliment. It is not as if Graham or *Hot Press*, at this juncture, thought badly of band or album; this would be to overturn fifteen years of critical writing on U2. However, what was significant about *Zoo TV* was that it subverted existing expectations of the band, favouring alienation, uncertainty and confusion above coherence and (national) celebration. The magazine had a difficulty both in finding traditional rock values and in claiming the usual rhetorical ownership of U2. It had to work hard to find an area where the traditional discourse was applicable, where the readership could be reassured: 'if you only knew them...[and] make no mistake about it, in person and in private, the members of U2 are very human. They may be shrewd and careful about their money and their merchandising, but they are also very likable.'[63] This was also a sign that any formal radicalism could be eclipsed by the powerful discourses of musical and national authenticity. However, the final word on this rupture of the horizontal togetherness of the nation must go to John Waters:

> I remember in the summer of 1987, walking back towards O'Connell Street in Dublin after seeing U2 perform in Croke Park. Having conquered the world, the band had just played to their home-town audience...The U2 fans were everywhere...There was an openness about the fans that ran into one. It was tribalism, but a benign tribalism, a moment of sheer joy and release, a little death in another's arms. I felt as though I could talk to anyone and we would know what to say about anything. We would recognise one another. There was a sense for that moment of being in the Ireland we had grown up expecting to inhabit.
>
> Six years later, I went to see *Zoo TV* at the RDS in Dublin. There was nothing of that feeling there. There was a band and there was an audience...There was no sense of unity to be felt in the crowd.[64]

As with dance culture, *Hot Press* and Waters found it hard to articulate U2 to the same discourses of the national in musical and performance terms, as these had shifted beyond the former folk-roots narrative and outside of the identity frame associated with imaginings of Ireland and the expectations of Irish rock. This was the first time that an existing set of ideological accretions were thrown out and replaced with an alternative set of associations (and to such a wide audience). It had the side effect of challenging and replacing existing representations of Ireland and the Irish internationally. This is not to suggest that *Achtung Baby* or *Zoo TV* are reducible to overturning sedimented representations and national stereotypes, merely to argue that this was a vital consequence of their aesthetic. In one vital sense, the U2 of *Achtung Baby* allowed the musical styles symbolically 'shut out' in the audition sequence in *The Commitments* back in through the front door and acknowledged the modern, and indeed *modernist*, music making and performance that had been consistently marginalized in the Irish popular musical canon. The album and its accompanying *Zoo TV* tour remain one of the most disruptive assaults on the paradigm of Irish sounds and images of the 1990s.

However, the U2 that performed for Barack Obama in 2009 appear to have retreated back into the anthemic sincerity of their earlier incarnation, a position they have maintained since regrouping in the aftermath of the relative commercial and critical failure of *Pop* and *PopMart* (1997). The period of *Zoo TV* remains a surprising and exciting challenge to the intertwined authenticities of rock and Irishness. The sunglasses that Bono continues to wear today function a little like Clementis's hat in the opening page of Milan Kundera's *The Book of Laughter and Forgetting*. Clementis flanked his comrade Gottwald on the balcony of the Winter Palace in Prague in 1948 on the day that modern Czechoslovakia was formed. As it was a cold day, Clementis took off his hat and put it on his colleague's head. It became a famous photograph that Czech citizens of the period all knew. Some years later, Clementis was found guilty of treason and 'disappeared', airbrushed out of history and that famous photograph. All that remained of him, Kundera poignantly reminds the reader, is the hat placed on Gottwald's head.[65] Thus the 'radical' Bono of *Zoo TV*, with his wilful subversion, in audio-visual terms, of the organic paradigm of Irishness, is retained as a lipstick trace, a cue to a significant moment when centre and periphery, the colonizer and the colonized were thrown into temporary confusion. But the powerful and interesting use of clothing in the performance setting of *Zoo TV* displays that the critical post-colonial, its disruptive hybridity, is not just articulated in literature, in the writing of Joyce, Toni Morrison or Hanif Kureshi, but can be articulated in fashion and performance, by a black plastic/leather jacket, trousers and wraparound sunglasses, which work alongside, and against, other areas of the hybrid pop 'text' to unsettle the expectations of Irishness and Irish rock both at home and in the broader Anglo-American, and European, firmament.

This appropriation of post-punk strategies is therefore significant, not as mere authorial reinvention, but as an act of 'revenge' against how U2, and Irish rock and pop more generally, has been formed by the centre. In a sense, *Achtung Baby/Zoo TV* is U2 reclaiming aspects of the post-punk moment within which they grew up and to which they are heavily indebted, but which they have had to downplay in order to meet expectations of Irish rock in Anglo-American discourse and at home. As Bono has put it, 'the sound of getting out of the ghetto is very different to the sound of getting into one. It's a very different sound, whether the ghetto is an intellectual one or the place where you grew up.'[66] What better way to do this than offer an ambivalent, shrink-wrapped, and thus commodified, cyber Elvis/Jim Morrison, fronting a Kraut-rock-indebted industrial ensemble playing in front of banks of television screens to an audience, many of whom were there to enjoy the reassuring pleasures of authentic rock and organic Irishness. If the underground river of essential Irishness was still flowing, *Zoo TV* both acknowledged and contributed to its healthy pollution.

NARRATING THE NATION: THE END OF 'OUR BOYS MADE GOOD'?

The shift from *Rattle and Hum* to *Achtung Baby* we have been exploring has been largely understood in authorial terms in popular discourse, usually with recourse to Bono's oft-quoted pronouncement on 30 December 1989, during the Dublin concerts of the *Lovetown* tour, that the band had to 'go away...and dream it up again'. These stylistic changes, we have argued, have therefore been grounded in this tendentiousness. While this is clearly mappable to the band's subsequent 'reinvention', the authorial interpretation conceals as much as it reveals. The 1990s marked a hiatus in the discourse of U2, as it were, 'narrating the nation'; or expressing, in Bill Graham's words, 'Ireland's often incoherent aspirations'.[67] Indeed, the 1990s brought to an end the linking of U2 to an explicitly national narrative and the idea of the band as a complex barometer of national success. If anything marked this shift in aesthetic and textual terms, it was *Zoo TV* which interrupted this trope of the band as a 'national beacon'.

However, *Zoo TV* was as much about Irish issues as *Rattle and Hum* was concerned with Irish-American issues. Just as Campbell argues that Dexy's Midnight Runners' Kevin Rowland 'found it easier to engage with Irish issues dressed as a yuppie or a docker in a brass-led ensemble than when clothed as a Celtic gyspy',[68] Bono and U2 in the *Zoo TV* period similarly were able to explore (and indeed even pre-empt) the increased internationalization of Irish culture in the early 1990s and the problems of media conglomerate control and the persistence of pastoral authenticity and nostalgia in the Irish body politic. In relation to discourses of Irishness, *Zoo TV* appears to fit Marshall McLuhan's famous dictum that 'the medium is the message'. While there will always be complaints that U2's 'mobile TV station' could have been deployed to greater critical effect than was apparent, this is to overlook the fact that it was a commercially-driven rock concert and, as such, there were limitations placed on just how radical any counter-positions offered could be. From this perspective it is perhaps surprising that such a large space was created for sloga-neering and critique. Moreover, *Zoo TV*, in many ways, reflected contemporary Ireland's reality: the nation's place as the most cabled country in western Europe at the time, with many of its citizens employed in web media, virtual technologies and financial services and, thus, an economy firmly caught in the tramlines of transnational capitalism (and one vulnerable to the complex vicissitudes of such an elaborated, technologically-driven and ultimately volatile system, as the close of the noughties attests).

In fact, by the turn of the next decade U2 had become a residual and commonplace part of the national fabric, marking a shift from their early years as a complex aspirational phenomenon to something of an accepted institution, from indicator of the state of the nation to commonplace part of the national fabric. This was marked in a number of ways. The same youthful optimism and channelling of hope evident among audiences at homecoming concerts, as the Waters quotation indicates, were much less in evidence throughout the 1990s. In large part, this was because the domestic U2 audience had aged with the band, bringing to an end the types of scenes typical throughout the previous decade where the stadium floor became a giant trampoline in the collective euphoria. One of the most striking examples of this was captured in the 'World in Action Special'[69] filmed on *The Joshua Tree* tour 'homecoming' concerts in Croke Park. During the opening song, 'Where the Streets Have No Name', the camera picks out clumps of youthful faces locked in a type of enforced collective pogoing, punching the air in unison to the track's polyrhythmic uplift. One needs to be wary, of course, of reading the emotions registered in those faces, but the sense of total involvement in the performance, of immersion in the power of the music, is palpable. Moreover, even a cursory glimpse at the audience at these homecoming occasions would have revealed an abundance of 'Bono-clones', sporting the different hairstyles, hats and clothes of the respective albums and tours. The run of 1990s' albums and tours – *Achtung Baby*, *Zoo TV*, *Zooropa*, *Pop* and *PopMart* – marked a different national audience/band relationship. Firstly, the iconographies of the band were much less heavily mimicked. This is not to suggest that the intimate identificatory solidarity of fan/star mimicry was entirely absent, merely to note its relative scarcity throughout the decade. As we have seen, *Zoo TV*, aesthetically and iconographically, was to render these types of identifications more problematic. However, one could argue that these changes – the conspicuous role-play, the elaborate dressing up – would create difficulties for the 30-something (and older) audiences (with many, as it were, wearing the clothes on the inside). U2 in the decade gradually moved away from being a tribal phenomenon, either in terms of 'youth' or nation. Second, and just as significantly, the early part of the 1990s also witnessed the gradual demise in bands emulating the U2 template and there was little overt mimicking of the contemporary U2 sound, 'attitude' or style as the decade hit its midpoint. In short, these aspects of the band's overwhelming influence in the 1980s were, to a degree, over. Even as late as January 1993, Barry McIlheney could claim that Northern avant-metal band Therapy? were 'alone among Irish outfits in sounding as if they haven't been listening to the U2 back catalogue'.[70] Certainly, by 1995 such claims would have lost their purchase. In fact, and perhaps ironically, it would be a later generation of British and American bands (Coldplay, The Kings of Leon and *The Bends*-era Radiohead amongst others) that would adopt aspects of U2's anthemic sound. U2 were to become influential to many so-called 'post-rock' bands outside of Ireland who sought to revitalize guitar and song-based rock in the wake of dance culture's demise.

POST-MILLENNIAL U2: GET ON YOUR (RE)BOOTS

2000's *All That You Can't Leave Behind* marked a return to the pre-*Achtung Baby* sound with a consequent downplaying of the experimentation of the band's work in the previous decade. As an album it was less sonically dense and in many regards was a more conventional rock album: guitar-driven, anthemic and spacious. However, in a manner akin to the 'lipstick trace' of *Zoo TV*-era experimentation maintained by Bono's sunglasses, *All That You Can't Leave Behind*, despite its apparent conservatism, carried a residue of the more conspicuously experimental work of the 1990s. Indeed, as Fast has persuasively argued, *All That...*, while anthemic in a way that is redolent of the first three albums, is marked by a compositional and lyrical sophistication when contrasted to this earlier work.[71] Therefore, while 'Beautiful Day' and 'Walk On', two of the singles from the album, clearly conform to the soaring uplift of 'New Year's Day' (*War*,1983) or 'Rejoice' (*October*, 1981), the guitar timbres are more varied and lyrical allusions more complex. In many ways, then, aspects of the sonic complexity announced by *Achtung Baby* were carried into this later work, making it more than a mere retreat into the past. However, unlike *Achtung Baby* the albums of the first half of the noughties offered little in the way of references, veiled or otherwise, to sex, sexuality or sexual identity, nor did they convey the same degree of anguish, uncertainty and doubt that marked the 1991 album. Thus, while 'Stuck in a Moment' and 'Kite' (and 'Sometimes You Can't Make It On Your Own' from 2004's *How to Dismantle an Atomic Bomb*) display in their different ways the influence of classic soul songs (such as 'Stand by Me'), they are harnessed to the distinctive U2 signature sound, most apparent in the Edge's spacious, chiming guitar and Bono's 'big voice'. And while keyboard and synthesizer sounds were featured, they were largely in a supporting role to 'traditional' core rock instrumentation, to provide textures and atmosphere.

This more conventional, if self-consciously 'crafted', U2 sound was supported in the band's iconography and performance. The *Elevation* tour was a partial return to the more spartan stage-sets of the early years, when contrasted with the elaborate spectacles of the 1990s. Despite the sophisticated lighting and sound systems befitting a band of their economic stature, the *Elevation* tour's only innovation as such was the heart-shaped 'circular' walkway into the audience floor. Cutting sharply against the visual display of *Zoo TV* and *PopMart*, the tour made use of only four relatively modest video screens, which focused on each band member and included virtually no animations or other visual treatments. In fact, the band began each concert date playing the single from which the tour took its name, with the arena house lights turned on and the stage lights of the show muted. The interpretation invited is clear: the band was emphasizing its 'honesty', playing 'naked' under the unflattering illumination of the auditorium lights. This was a strategy – a non-verbal means of conveying that it is 'the music that matters most' – rendered all the more potent by the stark contrast offered by the previous two tours. This 'back-to-basics' approach played by modification and contrast on their previous work (and Bono was back to being who he claimed to be).

In many respects *All That You Can't Leave Behind* developed the lyrical themes of *Boy*. If the first album invited, for *Hot Press* and others, a reading in national allegorical terms, with both 'the boy', Bono, and the band read as emblematic of the nation, then the 2000 album locked onto the problems of midlife crises of different sorts (with 'figure out my mid-life crisis' forming part of the lyric to 'New York'). Indeed the title/cover offered a cue to the lyrical themes within and to the problems endemic in advanced economically affluent neoliberal societies, especially the pressures connected to consumption, acquisition and the status-identity nexus borne of the former. Significantly, of course, *All That You Can't Leave Behind* could be regarded as the band's 'Celtic Tiger' album. If the 1980s albums articulated the varied and complex narratives of Ireland's (and U2's) journey from economic, cultural and popular musical periphery to the centre, the millennial album was concerned with the problems of economic success, of what might be lost in the journey to affluent cosmopolitanism. The cover crystallized and reinforced these themes. The band is framed against the grey concrete modernism (the paradigm 'international style') of Charles de Gaulle Airport in Northern Paris. They are alone in the grey space. Not only is it a graphically strong and simple image (and an – albeit urbanized – return to the 'simpler', more 'elemental' black-and-white photography of the 1980s album sleeves), it evidently draws upon the airport and the airport lounge as a metaphor for late-capitalist modernity and the complex socio-political geographies these institutions/spaces suggest. On the one hand, the space suggests cosmopolitanism, of geographically and ethnically dispersed peoples meeting in what is technically international territory. On the other, there is an irony here, in that such a potentially 'ideal' melting pot of peoples, of 'diversity under one roof', are simply waiting to travel or waiting to collect their 'baggage' (which ties in neatly with the album's title). Thus global connectedness is figured as banal, as a liminal zone of sorts, but one populated with

17. 'Playing naked under the house lights' – U2 live in Bercy (Corbis)

multinational businesses where people share – or are confined within – a transient (and relatively standardized) space. The 'Beautiful Day' video takes the airport – as a type of 'no-person's land' – as its mise en scène, thus consolidating the cover aesthetic and reinforcing the themes (at one point the band members are even put through the baggage check). The airport location was to be prescient in other ways, as it prefigured the importance that airports and air security were going to occupy in the aftermath of 9/11 and pre-empted star-vehicle Hollywood films set in such locations, such as *The Terminal* (directed by Steven Spielberg, 2004), starring Tom Hanks, and *Up in the Air* (directed by Jason Reitman, 2009) with George Clooney.

However, this album, though undoubtedly successful in restoring U2's commercial and critical fortunes after *Pop* and *PopMart*, offered little in the way of the overt challenge, musically or performatively, of the whole *Zoo* period. U2 hadn't just jettisoned its 'irony shield', but had resorted to a much less tension-ridden experience, one less focused on animating contradictions, whether ideological or aesthetic, than the early 1990s work.

In this sense *Pop* and *PopMart* formed a bridge between the 'rein-vented' U2 of *Achtung Baby/Zoo TV* and this more orthodox incarnation. Despite maintaining the overt interest in the postmod-ern, manifest in the *Zoo TV* era, there is a sense that the vogue for the postmodern, both academically and in popular culture, had waned, leaving the fetish for referentiality and spectacle looking tired. Indeed, Simon Reynolds has argued that the band in the early 1990s was just about able to explore and deploy the postmodern as the cultural vogue for its particular cluster of theoretical/aesthetic discourses was on the critical turn.[72] Moreover, if *Zoo TV*, as we have argued, sat in the hinterland of the popular modernist and the criti-cal postmodern/post-colonial, and deployed various kinds of distantiation strategy, *PopMart* by contrast appeared rather blank, devoid of *Zoo TV*'s conspicuous and disruptive hybridity – its satiri-cal impulse and ambivalence – and hence comparatively uncritical. Jameson's contested distinction between parody and pastiche certainly appears to be helpful in this regard (or, to coin a blunt ana-logy, *PopMart* is U2's Brian De Palma film to *Zoo TV*'s Godard). Indeed, any apparent critical impulse appears rather crude, such as the appropriation of one half of the McDonald's 'M' for the stage's central arch and the related and clumsy agitprop anti-consumerist messages. Furthermore, the 'blank' incorporation of Pop Art imagery from Andy Warhol to Roy Lichtenstein invited the more conservative pleasures of reference and spectacle than the previous two tours. In fact, pastiche also suffused the music. For an album heralded in marketing discourse as the band's most overt embrace of dance culture, and one where the production and composition techniques of that culture were foregrounded in press reportage, it is perhaps ironic that only 'Mofo' and the first single 'Discotheque' could be construed as resembling up-tempo dance genres. Conversely, if any aspect of 'dance' permeated the album it is the down-tempo genre of 'trip hop' (for 'headz' as opposed to body and feet), which is audible in tracks such as 'If You Wear That Velvet Dress', 'Miami' and 'Do You Feel Loved'. *Pop* is, in many respects, a relatively conventional album, one that seeks to keep long-term fans satisfied (hence the anthemic 'Gone', The Beatles/Oasis pastiche of the second single release, 'Staring at the Sun'). In fact pastiche was to become most pronounced on 'Do You Feel Loved' which is based on the guitar-motif and rhythm of the track 'Alien Groove Sensation' from Naked Funk's 1996 album *Valium* (on *Pop* producer Howie B's Pussyfoot label). While Naked Funk are thanked on the sleeve 'for inspiration', the single 'Discotheque' appears to be greatly indebted to Pop Will Eat Itself's 'Menofearthereaper' (*Dos Dedos Mis Amigos*, 1994). Moreover, the embrace of dance is ambivalent and while in the 'Discotheque' video the band appear as 1970s' disco group Village People it is unclear whether this is parody, reference or homage. While the lyrics to the single appear to be conversant with modern dance culture and specific drug references (such as 'love doves' on 'lovey, dovey stuff'), and despite the 'fun' aspect of the band dressed as Village People, the track swings perilously close to the well-worn rock anti-dance sentiments and easy anti-disco mockery. The apparent 'superficialities' of club culture – 'You know you're chewing bubblegum/You know what that is, but you still want some' – construct a position of easy superiority to club culture, appropriating the clichéd chewing-gum metaphor to suggest its association with banal pleasures, its ostensible appeal to the body and not the mind. Rock culture has frequently attacked dance musics of various sorts for being lacking in the cerebral and hence poverty-stricken in affect (and in this sense U2 are perhaps not terribly different to the conservative anti-disco movement in the United States in the late 1970s).

In this context, *No Line on the Horizon* is much more of a synthesis of U2's back catalogue than *All That You Can't Leave Behind*: from the Kraut-rock-inspired title track with its wall of fuzzed guitars, across to the 'classic' U2 of 'Magnificent', to Bono's more pronounced use of writing and singing in the role of different characters – such as the unhinged protagonist of 'Breathe' (with lines such as, 'running down the road like loose electricity as the band in my head is playing a striptease') and the cynical and world-weary foreign correspondent of 'Cedars of Lebanon'. The album also represents a partial return to the embrace of contradiction evident in *Achtung Baby* period. As the band remain a feature of global celebrity and less articulated to Ireland and Irishness, the biggest tension appears to be a familiar one for them and the handful of global rock bands of their commercial stature: how far they can push the experimental aspects of their music without losing swathes of their audience. In fact, the band's often overlooked 1995 collaboration with Brian Eno – Passenger's *Original Soundtracks One* – marks their most sustained, and in places imaginative, engagement with dance culture and experimental electronica. On this album (and on the soundtrack to Wenders's *Million Dollar Hotel*) the members of U2 display a diverse range of writing and compositional styles, when, as it were, being set free from 'being U2'.

Overall then, the U2 story can be regarded as a 'prodigal son' narrative: a journey from 'innocence' and righteousness to 'worldli-ness'/decadence and back again. Nonetheless a note of caution is warranted. As has been noted in review material, 2009's *No Line on the Horizon* does represent a hybrid of the band's early phase (particularly *October* and *Unforgettable Fire*) and the sonic experi-mentation of the *Achtung Baby/Zooropa* periods and is certainly more aesthetically adventurous than the two albums preceding it. Many, however, will miss the untutored energy of the band's early phase, of a band (and a nation) trying to 'stand up and find [its] feet' in the global noise.[73]

NOTES

1. John Lydon, *Rotten: No Irish, No Blacks, No Dogs* (London: Plexus, 1994), p.28.
2. Carmen Kuhling and Kieran Keohane, *Cosmopolitan Ireland: Globalisation and Quality of Life* (London: Pluto Press, 2007), p.14.
3. 'Zoo TV: Outside Broadcast', TV special directed by Kevin Godley, Initial Film and Television, 5 November 1992 on Channel 4 in the UK.
4. Shane Hegarty, 'The Sad Ballad of Bono and Bruce', *The Irish Times* (24 January 2009).
5. Niall Stokes, *U2 – Into the Heart: The Stories Behind Every Song* (London: Sevenoaks, 2006), p.84.
6. Ibid., p.86; Neil McCormick, *U2 By U2* (London: Harper, 2006), pp.211–12.
7. Lauren Onkey, 'Ray Charles on Hyndford Street: Van Morrison's Caledonian Soul', in Diane Negra (ed.), *The Irish in Us: Irishness, Performativity and Popular Culture* (London and Durham: Duke University Press, 2006), p.162.
8. Ibid., p.163.
9. Ibid.
10. Noel McLaughlin, 'Rattling Out Of Control: A Comparison of U2 and Joy Division on Film, *Film, Fashion and Consumption* 1, 1 (2012), pp.99–118.
11. Alison Landsberg, *Prosthetic Memory: The Transformation of American Remembrance in the Age of Mass Culture* (New York: Columbia University Press, 2004), p.2.
12. Gerry Smyth, *Space and the Irish Cultural Imagination* (Basingstoke: Palgrave, 2001), p.163.
13. Simon Reynolds, interview by Noel McLaughlin, 2009 (unpublished).
14. Reynolds, interview; Simon Reynolds and Joy Press, *The Sex Revolts: Gender, Rebellion, and Rock 'n' Roll* (London: Serpent's Tail, 1995), pp.76–83.
15. Tony Clayton-Lea and Richie Taylor, *Irish Rock: Where it's come from, where it's at, where it's going* (Dublin: Gill & Macmillan, 1992), p.88.
16. It is significant, though, that even the most visible and audible anti- or non-U2 bands still largely conformed to the organic paradigm and a rock 'seriousness'.
17. Colin Graham, 'Blame it on Maureen O'Hara': Ireland and the Trope of Authenticity', *Cultural Studies*, 15, 1 (January 2001), pp.71–5.
18. Jon Savage, *Time Travel: From The Sex Pistols to Nirvana* (London: Chatto & Windus, 1996), pp.266–7.

19. Gerry Smyth, *Noisy Island: A Short History of Irish Popular Music* (Cork: Cork University Press, 2005), pp.26–7.
20. Umberto Eco, *Travels in Hyper-Reality* (London: Harvest, 1986), pp.135–44.
21. Reynolds and Press, *Sex Revolts*, pp.82–3.
22. Bill Flanagan, *U2: At the End of the World* (London: Bantam Press, 1995).
23. Simon Reynolds, *Totally Wired: Post-Punk Interviews and Overviews* (London: Faber, 2009), pp.70–1.
24. Peter Hook in *Joy Division* (directed by Grant Gee, 2007), DVD Extras.
25. Reynolds, interview.
26. James Henke, 'U2: Here Comes the "Next Big Thing"', in *Rolling Stone* Editors, *U2: The* Rolling Stone *Files* (New York: Hyperion, 1994), p.2.
27. Flanagan, *U2: At the End of the World*. The author recalls how this track – which began life as simply 'The Real Thing' – was critiqued by Brian Eno, who berated the band for a lack of awareness of post-structuralist critiques of the real. This may of course have inspired the openly postmodern register of the song with its openly Baudrillardian 'sliding down the surface of things' refrain.
28. Brian Eno, 'Bringing Up Baby', in *Rolling Stone* Editors, *U2: The* Rolling Stone *Files*, p.170.
29. Smyth, *Space and the Irish*, p.169.
30. Ibid., p.170.
31. The band apparently took the title from a line in Mel Brooks's 1968 satirical comedy, *The Producers*, a reference that maintains, even amplifies, the ironic and playful mood.
32. Allan F. Moore, *Rock: The Primary Text – Developing a Musicology of Rock* (Farnham: Ashgate, 2001), pp.171–9.
33. Stokes, *U2 – Into the Heart*, p.102.
34. It would be wrong to claim that the album marked U2's first overtly synthesized tracks. Their cover of Cole Porter's 'Night and Day' (*Red, Hot and Blue*, 1990) has that distinction.
35. Richard Middleton, *Studying Popular Music* (Milton Keynes: Open University Press, 1990), p.90.
36. Eno, 'Bringing Up Baby', p.170. Eno's oxymorons do seem to predominate when seeking to describe the album: sincerely ironic, deeply superficial, authentically inauthentic and so forth.
37. Simon Frith, *Performing Rites: On the Value of Popular Music* (Oxford: Oxford University Press, 1996), p.159.
38. Quoted in Lynn Ramert, 'A Century Apart: The Personality Performances of Oscar Wilde in the 1890s and U2's Bono in the 1990s', *Popular Music and Society*, 32, 4 (2009), p.450.
39. Susan Fast 'Music, Context and Meaning in U2', in Walter Everett (ed.), *Expression in Rock-Pop Music: Critical and Analytical Essays*, 2nd ed. (New York: Routledge, 2008), p.187.
40. Richard Dyer, 'In Defence of Disco', in Richard Dyer, *Only Entertainment* (London: Routledge, 2002), pp.153–4.
41. Flanagan, *U2: At the End of the World*, p.36.
42. Sarah Thornton, *Club Cultures: Music, Media and Subcultural Capital* (Cambridge: Polity Press, 1995), p.38.
43. While U2 had used urban locations for videos prior to *Achtung*, this was infrequent and tended to support the pastoral. This was most evident in the use of Las Vegas in 'I Still Haven't Found What I'm Looking For' which offered an anti-materialist critique of the world of gambling and 'glamour'. The video work from the *Achtung Baby* went some way towards subverting previous iconographies. Two of the videos for 'One' were particularly striking in this

regard. Anton Corbijn's version – the first openly 'queer' iconography – featured the band in drag in Berlin. Mark Pellington's clip avoided the band and drew on the work of the late New York artist Mark Wojnarowicz, and offered grainy images of running buffalo, who tumble over a cliff at the track's conclusion. It is hard to think of imagery, or an ideology, further away from the a priori optimism of the past.

44. Simon Frith, 'Art versus Technology: The Strange Case of Popular Music', *Media, Culture and Society*, 8, 3 (1986), p.270.
45. Allan F. Moore, 'Looking for the Kingdom Come: Questioning Spirituality in U2', *Popular Musicology Online*, 2002 http://www.popular-musicology-online.com/issues/01/moore.html.
46. Smyth, *Noisy Island*, p.98.
47. Andrew Goodwin, *Dancing in the Distraction Factory: Music Television and Popular Culture* (London: Routledge, 1993), pp.101–4.
48. According to Bill Flanagan in *U2: At the End of the World*, p.6, Bono was fond of quoting Oscar Wilde in his preparation for the Fly character: 'Man is least himself when he talks in his own person, give him a mask and he will tell you the truth.' See Ramert, 'Century Apart', pp.447–60.
49. See Noel McLaughlin, 'Rock, Fashion and Performativity', in Stella Bruzzi and Pamela Church Gibson (eds), *Fashion Cultures: Theories, Explorations and Analysis* (London and New York: Routledge, 2000), pp.264–85.
50. Ramert, 'Century Apart', p.452.
51. Fast, 'Music, Context and Meaning', p.183.
52. Michka Assayas, *Bono on Bono: Conversations with Michka Assayas* (London: Hodder & Stoughton, 2005), p.39.
53. Mick Wall, *Bono: In the Name of Love* (London: Andre Deutsch, 2005), p.177.
54. McLaughlin, 'Rock, Fashion and Performativity'.
55. Simon Reynolds, *Rip It Up and Start Again: Post-Punk 1978–1984* (London: Faber, 2005)
56. Stan Hawkins, *The British Pop Dandy: Masculinity, Popular Music and Culture* (Farnham: Ashgate, 2009).
57. Simon Frith, *Performing Rites*, pp.224–5.
58. Ramert, 'Century Apart', p.452.
59. Helena Mulkearns, 'Review of Zoo TV', *Hot Press*, 16, 17 (September 1992), p.42.
60. Bill Graham, 'Achtung Station!', *Hot Press*, 16, 11 (May 1992).
61. Bill Graham, 'Zooropa: The Greatest Show on Earth?', *Hot Press*, 17, 18 (September 1993).
62. Ibid.
63. Helena Mulkearns, 'Zooropa: Concert Review', *Hot Press*, 17, 18 (1993).
64. John Waters, *Race of Angels: Ireland and the Genesis of U2* (Belfast: Blackstaff Press, 1994), p.126.
65. Milan Kundera, *The Book of Laughter and Forgetting* (London: Faber & Faber, 1996), p.3.
66. Assayas, *Bono on Bono*, p.33.
67. Bill Graham, *U2 – The Early Years: Another Time, Another Place* (London: Mandarin, 1989), p.8.
68. Sean Campbell, *Irish Blood, English Heart: Second-Generation Irish Musicians in England* (Cork: Cork University Press, 2011), p.57.
69. 'World in Action Special: U2', directed by Paul Greengrass et al., Granada Television, 1987, 27 July 1987. This hour-long 'special' was studded with the type of revelatory material the Hollywood concert film avoids and left them in

places looking exposed and naive.

70. Barry McIlheney, 'Review of *Nurse* by Therapy?', *Q*, 76 (January 1993), p.92.
71. Fast, 'Music, Context', pp.192–3.
72. Reynolds, interview.
73. This is a play on the opening line of 'Gloria' (October 1981), 'I try to sing this song/I try to stand up but I can't find my feet.' This is a track that easily lends itself to a reading in national-allegorical terms, with self, spirit and nation intertwining to powerful effect.

PART 3

After...

9

Crazy Diaspora: Sinéad O'Connor

...the outrage she generates is a precious thing. Name me another woman who can generate this kind of publicity without taking her clothes off. (Suzanne Moore)[1]

If the Virgin Mary were here today, she'd be ripping up pictures of the Pope. The Catholic Church have done [sic] such a lot against her as a symbol for all women. (Sinéad O'Connor)[2]

Crazy Baldhead. (Q)[3]

In the late 1980s and early 1990s Sinéad O'Connor was engaged in some key rearticulations of both musical form and the narratives of Irishness and stardom. As a highly controversial and visible performer, she has continually fulfilled one of the primary functions of being a pop star – not to be dull. Throughout her career she has offered, in the words of Campbell and Smyth, 'an aggressive and angst-laden antidote to the established array of Irish female imagery',[4] separating herself from the established paradigm of Irish female singer-songwriters (such as Mary and Francis Black, Dolores Keane and Eleanor McEvoy), with their more traditionally feminine iconographies and their association with home, family and the 'conventional' sphere of women's experience. In 1987 at the time of her international emergence she was significantly the most famous unmarried mother in modern Irish history.

She has expressed the most prominent opposition to the Vatican's position on reproductive rights and child abuse, which was crystallized in her notorious appearance on NBC's 'Saturday Night Live' on 3 October 1992. On performing the last line of an a cappella version of Bob Marley's 'War' – 'we have confidence in the victory of good over evil' – she produced a picture of Pope John Paul II from off camera and ripped it up. She then added the spoken line, 'fight the real enemy', and threw the shredded photograph at the camera, continuing 'there's only one liar and it's the Holy Roman Empire'. The impeccable theatrical timing and poise that underpinned the appearance of the photograph 'as if from nowhere' certainly exacerbated the surprise. Nobody applauded.

In fact, this was not an ill-considered and sporadic gesture. She had pre-primed the camera operator during the dress rehearsal to focus in on a photograph of an abuse victim at the song's conclusion.[5] The event became something of a diplomatic incident within international popular music. The singer was vilified, becoming a hate-figure in the United States. As Elizabeth Butler Cullingford has put it, 'few people in America understood what she was doing, though a lot of people knew they hated it. Outside the Irish context it looked like blasphemy.'[6] Less than two weeks later, O'Connor was due to perform 'I Believe in You' at the Thirtieth Anniversary Bob Dylan tribute concert in Madison Square Garden. After being introduced by Kris Kristofferson, she was jeered by a hostile audience for several minutes and prevented from singing the Dylan song. Though visibly distressed by this wall of abuse, she elected to stand her ground, silencing the band who on two occasions attempted to start the song. Kristofferson returned to the stage and embraced the singer at the microphone (indeed, he counselled her to 'not let the bastards grind her down'). In place of the Dylan song, she launched unaccompanied into a repeat performance of Marley's 'War', vehemently snarling out the words at those assembled – 'child abuse yeha...' – before leaving the stage in distress, accompanied by Kristofferson.

The controversies surrounding O'Connor do not end there. She refused to allow the playing of 'The Star Spangled Banner' at her concerts in protest against the censorship of rap artists, and has constantly criticized American foreign policy. In relation to the United States audience, O'Connor has been Bono's antithesis. If the young Bono's ambition was to embrace the United States, O'Connor has upset the relatively smooth Irish-American 'special relationship' more than any other Irish artist. Moreover, her support for the IRA in the later 1980s cut sharply against U2's condemnation of physical force Republicanism (especially evident in the performance of 'Sunday, Bloody Sunday' on the wake of the Enniskillen bombing from *Rattle and Hum*).

Her ambivalent star persona was put to provocative use when she played the Virgin Mary in *The Butcher Boy* (directed by Neil

Jordan, 1997). Not only could the Pope-ripping star's appearance in the role be construed as an affront to a conservative Catholic ethos, O'Connor's Virgin Mary was distinguished by consistently offering bad advice to the film's young protagonist and the routine spouting of profanities.[7] This, however, in no sense exhausts her association with the painful and the melodramatic. Years of childhood sexual abuse by her mother have been much commented on, as have her suicide attempts.[8] She also briefly 'came out' as lesbian and became ordained as a Catholic priest in the Latin Tridentine Church of Mater Dei, an obscure sect not sanctioned by the Vatican. And, like Madonna, she has a history of changing religion, announcing at different points in her career her conversion to Buddhism and Rastafarianism. Much has also been made of the singer's outspoken and at times wildly inconsistent views on a range of topics. In addition to her support for IRA/Sinn Féin she has, particularly in her early career, been vocal in her criticism of U2 – even going so far as to call Bono a 'turd'[9] – and remarking about the Edge, in response to his comments that the demos for her second album were too personal, that 'a guy who can't even call himself by his own name is obviously uncomfortable with his emotions'.[10] Therefore, in relation to discourses of Irishness, she has been extremely critical of two Irish institutions: the Catholic Church and U2. Indeed the core aspect of the wider press construction of the O'Connor persona has been her apparent 'craziness', mental instability and volatility.

Despite (or perhaps because of) this eventful and tumultuous career, in the international imagination O'Connor is now largely remembered for two high-profile events: the shredding of the photograph of the Pope and the related anti-Vatican rhetoric, and the 1990 hit single, 'Nothing Compares 2 U'. This cover of a lesser-known Prince song, promoted on MTV by John Maybury's striking tear-shedding video, made her a global superstar and was number one in Ireland, the United Kingdom and the United States. However, the reduction of her career to these two events (in addition to the overwhelming focus on the madness trope) is particularly regrettable as it has both diminished her musical achievement and prevented a more thoroughgoing assessment of her work. Given the controversies attending her career and the distinctive body of work she has produced, it is also surprising that she, as with U2, has been relatively under-explored in popular musical scholarship.[11] This is especially apparent if contrasted to the huge volume of work on

Madonna, which led Frith to coin the term 'the academic Madonna business'.[12]

What is particularly striking about O'Connor's early career is that she has easily matched Madonna for the amount of intrigue generated. As Suzanne Moore has observed, 'she didn't have to take her clothes off, nor engage in conventionally sexualised bodily display to make herself heard'.[13] Or, as Butler Cullingford has argued: 'O'Connor has a long history of confrontational political gestures that, unlike Madonna's ever-saleable masturbatory Catholicism, actually lessen her popularity.'[14] A profile of O'Connor in *The Guardian*, coinciding with the Pope's visit to the United Kingdom in 2010, argued that in tearing up the Pope's picture she had effectively committed career suicide[15] and she never again achieved the international visibility of the early 1990s (a point confirmed by her manager at the time, and in the current context, Fachtna O'Ceallaigh).[16] As has been the case with U2, the popular musical scholarship that has deigned to explore her work has been reluctant to engage with the singer's complex and fractious relationship to discourses of Irishness. While gender issues have been analysed, a grounded exploration of the relationship between gendered and national identities has been largely overlooked. This is particularly surprising. In Sheila Whiteley's study of female rock artists there are only a couple of references to O'Connor. Neither of these explore the singer's Irish identity nor engage with the Irish themes of her gender politics.[17] Emma Mayhew, in a useful discussion of the singer, focuses on her relationship to queer discourses and explores in some detail O'Connor's oscillation between defiance and vulnerability, yet it seems that Irishness is marginal to these issues.[18] This is particularly surprising, given that both the appearance on 'Saturday Night Live' and the Dylan tribute concert both announce a very specific meeting of Irishness and feminist politics on the world stage.

Keith Negus, in an otherwise careful and highly informative essay, makes passing reference to the singer's Irish identity, largely focusing on how she has deployed Irish signifiers as a part of broader syncretic strategies.[19] This is doubly odd, as Negus, in his own terms, seeks to explore the web of mediated discourses that together comprise the singer's overall star persona. If this is so, it is significant that questions of national identity are pushed some way down the interpretative hierarchy. This is unfortunate since O'Connor's work has been centrally concerned with Irish history and politics. As Butler Cullingford has argued, O'Connor 'constructs a coherent if slightly broad-brush postcolonial theoretical trajectory from the Catholic Church through imperialism to child abuse, historicising her antipathy to the Church by insisting on the intersection between religious and political colonisation'.[20]

SINÉAD AS ICON: HYBRIDITY AND CHALLENGE:
THE LION AND THE COBRA (1987)

O'Connor was born in Dublin in 1966 and grew up in the relatively affluent suburb of Glenageary in the south of the city. She was, by her own accounts, an unruly teenager:

> When I was a young girl, my mother – an abusive, less-than-perfect parent – encouraged me to shoplift. After being caught once too often, I spent 18 months in An Grianán Training Centre, an institution in Dublin for girls with behavioral problems, at the recommendation of a social worker. An Grianán was one of the now-infamous church-sponsored 'Magdalene laundries', which housed pregnant teenagers and uncooperative young women. We worked in the basement, washing priests' clothes in sinks with cold water and bars of soap. We studied math [sic] and typing. We had limited contact with our families. We earned no wages. One of the nuns, at least, was kind to me and gave me my first guitar.[21]

While studying piano at Dublin College of Music, she joined local band In Tua Nua as lead singer before fronting Ton Ton Macoute in 1985. She came to the attention of Nigel Grange, an executive from Ensign records in London. O'Connor collaborated with the Edge on the single for his soundtrack album *Captive* (Virgin, 1986), consolidating the potential Ensign saw in her. She moved to London and released her first album, *The Lion and the Cobra*, the following year.

This album has generated little in the way of academic discussion but is, however, an important album in the history of Irish rock and pop. It was also born of residing in the musical cosmopolitanism of late-1980s multicultural west London and drew heavily on the musico-cultural tapestry of that city. As O'Ceallaigh recollected:

> Sinéad when she came to London was a quiet and relatively inexperienced young woman who thought Mike Scott from the Waterboys was great and who liked Bob Dylan. When she came to London she

started listening to things I recommended to her – such as hip, hop, dub and reggae – but also a lot of different stuff that she dug out and discovered herself. She had this spark, this honesty. *The Lion and the Cobra* is a London-Irish, or Irish in London, album in many ways.[22]

It also made extensive and explicit use of ('delayed') punk and post-punk styles and musical forms (becoming the first commercially successful album produced by an Irish artist to do so). The result, which was significantly produced by the singer herself – and while heavily pregnant – was so successful that it sold well in excess of a million copies, was nominated for a Grammy award and made O'Connor an international star at the age of 21. She was, however, a star who developed a very distinctive iconography. The first significant aspect of this was her debt to punk's self-conscious and strategic use of the politics of 'semiotic appropriation'.[23] This was most apparent in her notorious appropriation of what Dick Hebdige has termed the 'aggressively proletarian and chauvinistic' iconography of the skinhead, the British subculture, the most dominant wing of which was both vehemently racist and devoutly masculine.[24] In the context of the late 1980s this look cut sharply against the prevailing rock zeitgeist in Britain and the United States. Just as it seemed that the 'centre' had moved beyond, or 'out-used' (or even got bored with) the rhetoric of re-signification, we find a novel and unexpected use of the strategy in O'Connor.

The irony here, as Hebdige has pointed out, is that the skinhead 'look' was itself an appropriation of aristocratic caricatures of the urban working-class and factory workers as 'all looking the same', de-individualized automatons, constructs of the industrial process.[25] There is, then, a double irony in O'Connor's appropriation of the skinhead iconography. It worked in the opposite direction, announcing her as an individualized and hence distinctive persona – what Negus has referred to as the creation of the star as a unique 'brand'.[26] However, the transposition of the skinhead 'uniform' – the shaven head, the fitted three-quarter-length jeans, the white tee shirt and the multi-eyelet Dr Martens boots – onto the body of a diminutive (and indeed conventionally attractive) Irish woman was also a radical gesture in political terms. It also suggested a cross-cultural alliance with other subordinated 'racial' groupings. In one sense, this gesture was a classic appropriation of 'thine enemy's clothes' and, as such, an attempt at neutralizing and destabilizing the skinhead aesthetic and what it represented; 'draining' the sign of its dominant meaning (machismo, racist aggression) and reinvesting it with different associations (the Irish, the feminine, anti-racism). Reciprocally, it also maintained and deployed the residue of the 'semiotic shock' (angry album/angry iconography), the transgressive and aggressive masculine aspects of the style, and thus attached them to the singer and to discourses of Irishness.

O'Connor, as Negus points out, has offered a variety of explanations for her distinctive choice of hair. These have ranged from claiming it was a therapeutic expression of childhood angst, to a later awareness of the look's more directly political and subcultural connotations. She has also said that she wanted to subvert the expectations of the male record executives at Ensign who, predictably enough, encouraged a more orthodox and glamorous (indeed 'sexy') female image.[27] At one level, her look at this point was about destroying conventional notions of 'beauty'; in fact the singer's iconography invokes the refrain from W.B. Yeats's 'Easter 1916', 'a terrible beauty is born'. As O'Connor put it in an early *Hot Press* interview:

> I like trousers but with the skinhead there's a danger of looking too much like a member of the National Front and understandably people get afraid. With the thin little party dresses I'm sweet in the middle which looks pretty good with the Docs. I'm aware this image mightn't go down so well in Ireland where people aren't used to skinheads, but I'll chance it.[28]

This is a revealing quote. The appropriation of the iconography of the skinhead was a versatile one that could be slotted into a number of narratives inviting a variety of readings in different sociocultural contexts. The skinhead dress code was abandoned after the first album and tour though the shaven head remained. Its meaning arguably shifted at this point, and as Negus has helpfully pointed out, the shaven head operated within 'a history of shaven heads'[29] and thus took on and foregrounded different connotations, such as the religious (as in Buddhism and Hinduism) – but also the close-cropped skull's connections to the abject, to history's 'victims': the concentration camps, asylum inmates, the infirm and the chronically ill,[30] as well as an index of the alien, the other-worldly. It is also significantly the iconography preferred by many lesbians, adding a performative and gender-indeterminate aspect to her persona. This oscillation between aggressor and victim, protestor and abused bisects her entire musical career in interesting ways.[31]

As an index of the transgressive power of the shaven-headed female in this context, the record company felt it expedient to tone down the 'aggressive' cover of *The Lion and the Cobra's* British and European releases for the US market, offering a 'softer' image of the singer.[32]

However, this is not an iconography that makes meaning in isolation, but one that is inflected by the music: by genre conventions, vocal stylings and performance modes. Negus has persuasively argued that the dynamic relationship between album covers and musical style is particularly important. 'The first two album covers', he argues, 'contain a mixture of the branded image of the pop star, combined with tangential images that comment upon and reinforce and work away from the music.'[33] The skinhead 'look' thus rubs against the conventions deployed on the first album. The skinhead subcultural style invokes the rhythms of ska, or the guitar thrash of Oi, and thus does not form an easy or direct fit with prevailing post-punk forms. While the connotations of anger and aggression suited the guitar-driven rock of 'Mandinka' and formed a fit with the shouted, swooping, angry vocals of the conclusion to the first single 'Troy', they did not sit smoothly alongside the more explicit post-punk stylings deployed on the album. These styles were especially important to *The Lion and the Cobra*. Marco Pirroni, the first Siouxsie and The Banshees guitarist, who later played with Bow Wow Wow and Adam and the Ants, was a post-punk musical veteran. His distinctive guitar style, through reference and allusion, drew upon post-punk's 'inventiveness', its simultaneous deconstruction and promotion of rock norms. The album also featured Ali McMordie, the bass player from Stiff Little Fingers, and Rob Dean, former guitarist with post-punk band Japan.[34] These post-punk stylings and the quest for continual reinvention were to sit uneasily alongside the connotations of 'Irishness' offered by O'Connor's voice with its confessional and intimate qualities. After all, post-punk was not associated with confessional singer-songwriters and rarely with solo artists. It was associated even less so with Irish artists and bands. O'Connor herself remarks about the album in progress: 'I admit it's a schizoid kind of sound...There'll be a couple of waltzes, a disco track and some heavy rock stuff mixed in with a Celtic sort of sound – operatic, you could even call it. It isn't shocking – it's emotional, heart-rending, exciting.'[35] As John

Reynolds, her drummer and partner at the time, has recalled, Prince's *Sign O' The Times* album (1987) and its eclectic inventiveness, its synthesis of rock, soul, funk and experimental synth-pop, was a seminal influence.[36] The album also clearly bears the influence of the metropolitan 'No Disco' or punk disco styles of the late 1970s and early 1980 and artists such as Material, Nona Hendryx and PiL. This was a sonic palette at some distance not just from both mainstream British and American rock sounds of the time but from Irish rock styles as well. The first album, therefore, was an uneasy hybrid of English post-punk styles and an extended and modernized Irish confessional mode.

'Troy' makes use of stringed orchestration, particularly a looped cello arpeggio reminiscent of Kate Bush's single 'Cloud Busting' (*The Hounds of Love*, 1986). But unlike Bush's more pastoral ambience, 'Troy' takes the style and renders it aggressive and punkish. The use of dynamic contrast in this track is extreme and O'Connor showcases a series of vocal techniques, from close-miked soothing whispers to long-sustained shrieks and howls. The track is the antithesis of easy listening; its extreme dynamic range was to become an O'Connor trademark, a sign of her distinctive vocal presence – what Katrina Irving has described as her ability to pull forth 'a gamut of timbres'.[37] However, the voice here is not simply offering a panoply of vocal techniques, held up, as it were, to be admired. Indeed the sense of anger conveyed by the 'female scream' on this track is palpable and is very far removed from the relative 'safety' and 'beauty' offered by established Irish female singer-songwriters. If the shrieking and howling owes something to post-punk female singers such as Siouxsie Sioux, the album deploys another aspect of post-punk: the movement's play with gender norms. These are articulated on the single, 'I Want Your (Hands on Me): Street Mix' (Ensign, 1988), and its accompanying video which received heavy rotation on MTV at the time. This version is significant as it reformulates the song as a duet with New York black female rapper M.C. Lyte. For Katrina Irving this is 'a song about sexual desire which plays both with transgression of the heterosexual norm (since it appears that the two women are singing the lyrics of desire to each other) and of the taboo against black/white sexuality'.[38] Thus, as early as 1988, O'Connor is articulating a self-consciousness about the cultural politics of 'race', gender and nationality.

Unlike U2's music where explicit references to Ireland are few, right from the beginning of her career O'Connor peppers her lyrics with references to Ireland and the Irish condition. Her first single 'Troy' announces the singer's place in Ireland in the opening line: 'I'll remember it/And Dublin in a rainstorm/And sitting in the long grass in summer keeping warm.' Indeed, 'Troy' is marked by a second, yet less explicit, reference to Irishness. Both title and chorus evoke Yeats's poem, 'No Second Troy', particularly its concluding line: 'Was there another Troy for her to burn'?

GLOBAL STARDOM: *I DO NOT WANT WHAT I HAVEN'T GOT*

O'Connor retained the shaved head for her second album, *I Do Not Want What I Haven't Got* (Ensign, 1990). However, here it causes something of a clash with the acoustic confessional styles which dominate that record and tracks such as 'Three Babies', 'The Last Day of Our Acquaintance' and 'Black Boys on Mopeds'. The intertwining of popular music, canonical poetry and feminist politics is maintained on 'Three Babies' which engages in critical dialogue with Seamus Heaney's 'Limbo'. This poem dramatizes the political and emotional traumas wrought on Irish womanhood by a conservative Catholic ideology. However, the reference to Heaney is not mere high cultural quotation. As Butler Cullingford has argued, 'Three Babies' offers a response to Heaney's poem and while the track shares 'Limbo's' feminist politics, it reverses 'the pessimistic conclusion of Heaney's poem . . . with its doctrine of limbo as a "cold glitter of souls" who will be forever unreachable and unredeemable'.[39] The track arrives at a pivotal point in a dialogue about gender politics in Ireland, especially in relation to abortion, divorce and Church–State relations in general. O'Connor joined this debate through her starring role in Derry Film and Video's *Hush-A-Bye Baby* (directed by Margo Harkin, 1989), the story of a 15-year-old teenager from nationalist Derry (Emer McCourt), who becomes entrapped by the repression of the Catholic community in which she lives when she becomes pregnant. The pro-abortion/pro-choice thrust of the film's narrative attracted O'Connor's support and she also contributed songs and other ambient material to the soundtrack. Significantly this film also further pursues the dialogue with 'Limbo', in the scene where the schoolgirls discuss the Heaney poem in the classroom.

The album's 'state-of-the-nation' track is 'Black Boys on Mopeds', a bare arrangement befitting the archetypal folk song mode. The vocal is close-miked, with connotations of intimacy, and is accompanied by a lightly strummed acoustic guitar in the key of B. The ballad is in 3/4 or waltz time, and moves through a simple chord progression beginning in D, moving to A and to G and then back to D again. The sparseness of the form serves to focus attention on the voice and the narrative offered by the lyric and therefore sets up a special place for the poetic and semantic property of the words, the modulations and inflections of the voice. This sparse arrangement pulls the listener into the dynamic interplay between the two: words as meaning and the presence of the voice as 'someone special' conveying that meaning. The slow air maintains the ongoing thread of the singer's diasporic concerns as the song (in the chorus especially) is ostensibly about images of Englishness. It uses the Irish ballad form to challenge representations of romantic English pastoralism, evident in the line 'England's not the mythical land of Madame George and roses.' This is extended in itself as the Irish ballad form has frequently romanticized rural Ireland, contrasting its beauty to the alienation of urban England. Here, the English pastoral tradition is being invoked, but also critiqued, with nostalgic rural nationalistic images replaced with a modern, urban and ultimately fractious multiculturalism. In the reference to 'Madame George' a complexity is introduced, as there is significantly no such character in English mythology (though there is, of course, the 'national saint', Saint George). The most famous Madame George is the eponymous figure in the song from Van Morrison's *Astral Weeks* and the song therefore begs the question: why does this reference intrude in a lament at the presence of racism in the English body politic? Is the singer accusing Morrison, albeit indirectly, of political quietism and invoking his fascination with the English Romantic poets in the face of harder, contemporary political Irish realities, or chiding him for ignoring the sectarianism of late 1960s Belfast in *Astral Weeks*?

The pastoral images frequently invoked in Irish folk song are replaced with urban images of a racially divided England where 'black boys' are the victims of police brutality and an endemic racism. The song refers to the tragic case of London teenager Colin Roach – whose parents are featured on the album artwork – who died in police custody from a gunshot.[40] It also draws upon a series of racially motivated attacks on black youth, both by police and by gangs of racist youth in England, that were prominent in the news media of the period. What is also interesting here, however, is the lyrical association of 'Irishness' and 'blackness' – in the interchange of 'black boys' and 'my boy' – which suggests solidarity through a common experience of racism in Britain. Thus, the concerns of the Irish traditional ballad narrative – the lament of a mother singing about her son and exile from Ireland – are intertwined, extended and given a contemporary political resonance. Similarly, the song takes the recurring Irish folk and traditional trope, that of being away from Ireland, and eschews the 'easy', or well-worn, sentimentalism associated with the genre and politicizes the narrative. 'Leaving', in this case, does not indicate a sentimental romantic yearning for a lost magical homeland as many Irish ballads do. The process of leaving is politicized as a desire for a place where racism is simply absent.

'Black Boys on Mopeds' draws together disparate discourses and musical forms – black, Irish, folk and narratives of home and displacement – and mobilizes them to unexpected political ends. As with 'Troy' (and unlike U2), references to place are specific, evident in the opening line: 'Margaret Thatcher on TV, shocked by the deaths in Beijing'. The singer's capacity to exploit extreme dynamic contrast is once again in evidence, especially on the change in vocal register; the move from quiet and confessional to holler and scream in the phrasing of 'RE-MEM-BEEEEER what I told you' stresses the importance of memory, a powerful vocal form of underlining and emphasis.

This type of critical reworking of song form is continued in a more musically ambitious fashion on 'I am Stretched on Your Grave'. This song featured prominently in music media at the time. It was released on two separate twelve-inch singles, one of which was the B-side of the single 'The Emperor's New Clothes'. O'Connor's idiomatically Irish vocal is in the *sean nós* (or old style) and the song itself was composed and set to music by Philip King for his band Scullion's first album (Mulligan Records, 1977). The original twelfth-century Gaelic poem, 'Táim sínte ar do thuama', on which the song is based, was translated by Frank O'Connor and expresses a man's grief for his deceased female lover. The poem is full of melodramatic imagery of the young man lying prostrate on the ground on his deceased lover's grave, unbeknown to his parents. However, this Irish Gothic imagery of yearning across the death divide is significantly re-gendered so that the original medieval lyric is restated as a postmodern gender-play in an Irish female context.

The track samples 'Funky Drummer' from James Brown's 1970 album, *In the Jungle Groove*. This, in itself, is not especially significant. Brown is perhaps the most heavily sampled artist in hip hop and rap and this track in particular had a long sampling history in the mid-to-late 1980s. Its highly recognizable shuffling rhythm 'break' (that part of a drum pattern that is selected and looped due to its danceability) was most prominently sampled by Public Enemy on several of their tracks, including the hit singles 'Rebel Without a Pause' (*It takes a Nation of Millions to Hold Us Back*, 1988), 'Bring The Noise' (*Less Than Zero*, 1987) and 'Fight The Power' from the soundtrack to Spike Lee's race-relations film, *Do The Right Thing* (1989). It was also deployed on the explicitly women-'dis-ing', 'She Watches Channel Zero?!' (*It takes a Nation of Millions to Hold Us Back*, 1988). The break has also significantly been appropriated by the seminal 'gangsta' rappers NWA (Niggaz with Attitude) on their controversial single 'Fuck the Police' and 'Quiet on Da Set' (*Straight Otta Compton*, 1988) and on L.L. Cool J's 'Mama Said Knock You Out' (*Mama Said Knock You Out*, 1990) amongst many others. Consequently it is one of the most recognized and easily spotted samples in a genre where sample sourcing, or sample literacy, is a central component of musical pleasure.

The sampling of James Brown records generally, and this track's distinctive break in particular, had become something of a bricoleur's cliché by 1990 (if not before), as sample-based artists began to source ever more obscure rhythmic material. However, its late and conspicuous use (the track, after all, begins with the rhythm in isolation for the first four bars) suggests wilful intent to make use of the break's connotations and for more than simply musical reasons. In invoking its original source, the rhythm track conveys a general 'funkiness', trawling up the rich history of African-American musical expression. These hybridization strategies, the rhythm combined with the traditional poem and melody, achieve a coming together of modern African-America and ancient rural Ireland in an imaginative musical fashion. Moreover, in the context of 1990, the connotations of the rhythm track invite particular expectations of what will follow: namely an African-American male voice and/or a high percussive and powerfully syncopated rap delivery. Instead the listener is greeted by O'Connor's distinctive vocal timbre which inflects the 'Funky Drummer' break with a melancholy. Therefore, the first aspect of the hybridization is aesthetic – the unexpected fusion in the novel mix of rhythm and vocal. Second, and perhaps more importantly, 'I am Stretched...', in sampling a rhythm associated with some of the most aggressive, masculinist and black nationalist rap records, is both referencing that history and invoking its legacy while simultaneously 'feminizing' it. The contrast with the expected muscular rap delivery is further heightened as the vocal is relatively recessed, reverberated and distant-miked.

It is a sparse track, comprised for most of its duration of just the drum break, O'Connor's vocals, and a synth bass playing the root note with synth-drums punctuating the wordless after-chorus. The voice does not dominate the other areas of the soundscape. This meeting of Ireland and the United States, of Black and Irish Atlantics,[41] is not the end of the story. It offers a vital re-contextualization of both the original poem and the virulent male-centric politics suggested by the drum sample. Musically they appear to merge seamlessly, but in terms of the politics of gender and identity they are held apart. As Negus has argued, 'O'Connor articulates a sexuality that problematises the naive macho stances... which rock performance began to acquire during the late 1960s and 1970s'[42] and which, evidently, were also a prominent feature of rap and hip hop. Thus, while the appropriation of the rhythm suggests solidarity with cultural forms heard and read as black and male, the synthesis of the forms in the manner described simultaneously invites a critique of racial, musical and sexual essentialism.

The conclusion of the track consolidates the drawing together of space/place/identity/history connections when Steve Wickham's traditional fiddle enters the mix. This is a moment of powerful affective change with the fiddle giving the impression that the tempo has accelerated. The introduction of the fiddle is supported by the addition of extra drums which accentuate the heavy downbeat of the first beat of each bar. This alters the thrust of the rhythm pattern, dragging it from its 'American', 'funk' and hip hop register to the 'Irish' and 'traditional'. Together the fiddle and the alternation of the drum pattern appear to reclaim the musical space for Irishness (while sounding contemporary and stylistically novel). In this sense, we would argue that 'I am Stretched...' is more than a 'daring fusion of techno and trad'.[43] The track anticipates the emergence of trip hop and the fusion of dub, reggae and hip hop that became synonymous with 'the Bristol sound' and associated with Massive Attack (with whom O'Connor went on to record), Tricky and Portishead and a whole host of later imitators.[44]

As a number of writers have observed, O'Connor makes use of the intimate, confessional style associated with more conventional Irish female singers which works alongside a second more confrontational and aggressive, even declamatory, mode.[45] The latter is less restrained, the timbre harder. Indeed, this is part of the singer's renowned vocal range, one that can 'jump from a whisper to a holler', and is often described as comprising a style of 'wailing' and as redolent of 'keening'. She thus makes ample use of the techniques of *melisma* and *morendo* in the dynamic between the voice-as-instrument and microphone-as-instrument, to construct a type of primitivist or hard primitivist sonic texture. In other words, the singer's highly distinctive and technically versatile voice is comprised of an interesting mix of punk 'freedoms' and traditional inflections. However, schematically, these two vocal modes may also be interpreted as articulating the key contradictions in her identity: the tension between aggressive assertion and vulnerability.

Sinéad O'Connor's relationship to Irish culture has been tumultuous. Both lyrically (as in 'Three Babies') and in political statements she has consistently made pro-abortion, pro-choice statements and has become infamous for vehement anti-Catholic Church rhetoric. This in itself does not mark her out as unique. Other rock and pop artists in Ireland, such as U2, Microdisney and Christy Moore, have lent support to pro-choice and pro-divorce movements in the form of fundraisers, benefit and awareness gigs. What marks O'Connor out as significant has been her consistent attempts to incorporate these issues into the main body of her work (against a perceived repression and/or silence, once again exploding many of the dominant myths of Irish womanhood). The vocal 'keening' style referred to earlier is another feature of the traditional, indigenous lexicon and, interestingly, she takes this motif and its primitivist associations and attaches them to areas of political life that many traditionalists may find uncomfortable. She uses traditional sounds politically and modernizes them, pulling sounds associated with one cultural and political context and transferring them to another, where they become challenging.

BLOWIN' IN THE WIND: O'CONNOR AT THE
BOB DYLAN TRIBUTE CONCERT

The situation of women within rock and pop protest is worth exploring as it contains more than a few ironies which are of interest to the discussion here. They foreground the problem of differential access of women in rock to notions of political protest and the right to speak unselfconsciously about certain issues and to take up particular platforms.[46] To return, therefore, to the Bob Dylan Tribute concert. If we consider the press material surrounding the event, the 'adult-orientated rock' magazine *Q*, in its review of the aftermath of the event,[47] ran with the headline 'Crazy Baldhead', taking and twisting the meaning of her iconography via Bob Marley's famous track and invoking its refrain about chasing 'those crazy baldheads out of town'. In this way, O'Connor's actions were collapsed into a discourse about irrationality and by implication about Irishness and women. In a similar vein, Neil Young, who was on the same canonical bill, ventured that O'Connor had come up against a good American audience who put 'her to the test and she just wasn't up to it'.[48] This 'almanac for the rites of passage for the aspiring protest singer' appeared to suggest that she should have 'been a man' and stood by what she believed, affirming a long rock ancestry announcing women as *different* and consolidating the notion that political protest is an essentially male preserve. This, of course, is but one instance in a long narrative where O'Connor has been deemed to be 'out of order', her politics attributed to her apparent 'craziness' and mental instability (and the aforementioned *Q* article even likened her to discredited television presenter-cum-religious cult-leader David Icke). In an interview in *Time Magazine* shortly after the event, the singer was asked if Dylan himself had said anything to her after the concert. Her reply is telling: 'That I should keep on doing what I'm doing. But it's no good saying that to me. Why doesn't he say it to them? I mean, why doesn't he take his responsibility?'[49]

We are less concerned here with assessing the respective merits (or otherwise) of O'Connor's pronouncements, as no doubt many of these have been prone to inconsistency and hyperbole. What is of interest is the discourse surrounding these and the thinly veiled sexism and inferred anti-Irish racism they reveal on occasion. After all, rock culture has not been short of male protest singers making wildly unsubstantiated, ill-informed and internally contradictory remarks on a variety of given topics (it would be unthinkable for the problematic remarks of, say, Mick Jagger or Liam Gallagher to be labelled as 'English' and 'male' in a similar manner). To a degree, the lambasting of Sinéad O'Connor has hinged on the trope about nature – and draws on the stereotype of the 'fiery Irish woman' and the surrounding connotations of unpredictability and instability. In relation to rock discourse it reveals the differential gendered access to the 'sacred mantle' of the protest singer and the ideological

18. 'Eclectic, difficult, radical and prescient' – Sinéad O'Connor in performance (Corbis)

assumption that access to the right to speak universally is a male prerogative. Thus it seems that even the sometime rock virtue of 'craziness' is gender biased – whereby 'wildness' has different ideological consequences for women. Masculine 'craziness' can be a rock virtue, whereas the madwoman has different and negative implications. It is a further irony that these tensions emerged at a retrospective tribute for *the* canonic protest singer and resulted in such a debacle.

However, O'Connor's performance on this show is actually quite extraordinary, even within the history of rock performances. Her four minutes on stage at Madison Square Garden subjectively seem a lot longer. It is an extremely powerful episode as she faces down a wall of boos. First, it shows the authority of her star-text – the 'what we know about her', in Frith's words – the weightiness of the ongoing master-narrative of Sinéad O'Connor. The event opens up a series of dramatic questions: what is happening, what will she do, what is she thinking, will she sing? It works in a similar fashion to John Cage's seminal '4.33' (where the orchestra is arranged in formal attire without a single note being played for four minutes and thirty-three seconds), in that a powerful performance doesn't necessarily require the singer to speak, let alone sing. These several minutes are held together in dramatic suspense by context, by the singer's biography, her well-established reputation for courting controversy. In this respect, the language of close-up allows us to register the minutia of every emotion on her face: the oscillation from vulnerability to defiance – and the look on her face is closer to Sissy Spacek's in the conclusion of the horror film *Carrie* (directed by Brian De Palma, 1976) or Isabelle Huppert after she stabs herself in the chest in the finale of *The Piano Teacher* (directed by Michael Haneke, 2001) – than to the male canon of rock performance (and it also carries the sense of internalized and repressed trauma, wrought by patriarchal forces articulated in two films). It also reveals something else: the apparent conservatism of the Dylan audience, its apparent lack of sympathy for feminist politics and/or its ignorance of the subjugation of women in the Irish context. As for Kris Kristofferson, he commemorated the event sympathetically with his song 'Sister Sinéad' from his 2009 album, *Closer to the Bone*. The song is strummed out on an acoustic guitar (ironically, with a harmonica break that the early Dylan would have recognized):

> I'm singin' this song for my sister Sinéad
> Concerning the godawful mess that she made
> When she told them her truth and just as hard as she could
> Her message profoundly was misunderstood.

And, of course, years later, we can see that she was right all along as the extent of child abuse by the clergy in Ireland became clear following the publication of the Ryan report in 2009. Most damning in the report was the extent to which this abuse was covered up by the Church itself, the very point that O'Connor was trying to make on 'Saturday Night Live'. Indeed, this may stand as another example of Jacques Attali's notion of *music-as-prophecy*, as presaging other areas of the social order.[50] As O'Connor herself reflected, in a self-penned article from 2010:

> Almost 18 years ago, I tore up a picture of Pope John Paul II on an episode of *Saturday Night Live*. Many people did not understand the protest – the next week, the show's guest host, actor Joe Pesci, commented that, had he been there, 'I would have gave her such a smack'. I knew my action would cause trouble, but I wanted to force

a conversation where there was a need for one; that is part of being an artist. All I regretted was that people assumed I didn't believe in God. That's not the case at all. I'm Catholic by birth and culture and would be the first at the church door if the Vatican offered sincere reconciliation.[51]

ANOTHER SORT OF HOMECOMING

Perhaps inevitably, within the discourse of Irish rock some of these complexities and contradictions are swept aside and Sinéad O'Connor is assigned a traditional place within discourses of nature and the natural. As Nuala O'Connor writes in *Bringing It All Back Home*, 'she has a strong true voice which needs neither accompaniment nor studio effects to show it off'.[52] Once again the importance of the organic – and the discourse of pre-industrial purity – is the primary means of conferring authenticity: 'While she publicly disavows any idea of Ireland as anything other than a modern twentieth century society, her choice of material and singing style belie this. The vocal influences, particularly the emphasis on the solo voice, [is] Irish and pre-pop ... [and] is frequently mistaken for "the real thing", an Irish Traditional song.'[53] She is praised for the apparent naturalness and purity of her voice and 'the absence of studio trickery' and other elements of the Sinéad O'Connor persona are filtered out, deemed irrelevant, as having no purchase on 'the music' and its 'pre-modern' power. This, of course, is a means of avoiding complication. We only have to hear the voice and we recognize it as Sinéad O'Connor; we get 'to know' her through the context of the recording. The validation of 'naturalness' is read onto, and not an intrinsic property of, her voice. It could be argued, just as persuasively, that Sinéad O'Connor's voice is 'unnatural' – hard, twisted and painful. As we have seen, like any other popular music vocalist she makes extensive use of studio techniques. Nuala O'Connor effectively quarantines the voice from its musical setting and production context (and she is also silent about the iconographic issues and gender politics). Conversely, what makes Sinéad O'Connor's work so interesting is the 'tensions' in the various textual material (and between text and context): between the voice, its associations and the way it recalls and articulates biography and political stance; the play on prior folk and traditional conventions and song narratives; the subversion of aspects of the lyrical confessional and the pulling together of disparate styles and genres. This does not prevent her from being co-opted to nostalgic, familiar and clichéd discourses of Irishness, as we have seen, but O'Connor and her music straddles the analytical division between the nationally-specific and nationalist.

Throughout her entire oeuvre she has doggedly focused on women's issues not normally discussed, both in the lyrical and thematic preoccupations of her music: miscarriage, abortion, domestic and sexual abuse, as well as the differential treatment of female artists within the music industry. In addition to this, Ireland has featured prominently in her work via the tropes of Ireland as 'the abused child of history', the 'feminine' Ireland as rape victim, as inseminated by the colonizer with violent and contradictory consequences. Unlike U2, for good or for ill, there is an attempt made at articulating a very specific kind of politics: broadly feminist, anti-colonialist and downright contrary. As Kristofferson speculates, 'Maybe she's crazy and maybe she ain't/But so was Picasso and so were the saints.'[54]

Her career, then, has been impressively polymorphous. She has composed, recorded and performed across a bewilderingly diverse range of genres: Irish folk and traditional music, hip hop, dub and reggae, 'world music', ambient electronica, big-band swing, country music, guitar-driven rock and dance music, pulling together an amalgamation of musical spaces, places and identities (Bristol, London, inner-city New York, Dublin, urban and rural Ireland, and the Caribbean). Indeed it is difficult to name another female artist who has been quite so eclectic. O'Connor's work represents an important space for the female artist to articulate a specific and valuable kind of politics on the world stage. As we have seen it is a strategy fraught with difficulties, as 'universal' speech and song have been easier to countenance.

In the broader narrative, 1992–93 was a high-profile period for Irish rock, with both U2 and Sinéad O'Connor in their very different ways creating controversy in the international arena.

NOTES

1. Suzanne Moore, 'Rock 'n' Roll Rebel with Too Many Causes', *The Guardian* (6 November 1992), quoted in Lucy O'Brien, 'An Inconvenient Woman: Sinéad O'Connor', *The Guardian* (26 April 1997).
2. Lucy O'Brien, 'An Inconvenient Woman'.
3. Adrian Deevoy, 'Crazy Baldhead', *Q*, 76 (January 1993), p.16.

4. Sean Campbell and Gerry Smyth, *Beautiful Day: Forty Years of Irish Rock* (Cork: Atrium Press, 2005), p.112.
5. Elizabeth Butler Cullingford, *Ireland's Others: Gender and Ethnicity in Irish Literature and Popular Culture* (Cork: Cork University Press/Field Day, 2001), p.249.
6. Ibid. It must be added that it looked a lot like blasphemy in the Irish context as well.
7. Martin McLoone, *Irish Film: The Emergence of a Contemporary Cinema* (London: BFI, 2000), pp.218–20.
8. See, for example, O'Brien, 'Inconvenient Woman'; Simon Hattenstone, 'The Vatican is a Nest of Devils', *Guardian*, 11 September 2010.
9. O'Brien, 'Inconvenient Woman'.
10. Ibid.
11. See Keith Negus, 'Sinéad O'Connor: Musical Mother', in Sheila Whiteley (ed.), *Sexing The Groove: Popular Music and Gender* (London: Routledge, 1997), pp.178–90; Noel McLaughlin and Martin McLoone, 'Hybridity and National Musics: The Case of Irish Rock', *Popular Music*, 19, 2 (2000), pp.181–99; Emma Mayhew, 'I am not in a box of any description: Sinéad O'Connor's Queer Outing', in Sheila Whiteley and Jennifer Rycenga (eds), *Queering the Popular Pitch* (New York and London: Routledge, 2006), pp.169–83; Michael Malouf, 'Feeling Eire(y): On Irish Caribbean Popular Culture', in Diane Negra (ed.), *The Irish in Us: Irishness, Performativity and Popular Culture* (London and Durham: Duke University Press, 2006), pp.318–353.
12. Simon Frith, *Performing Rites: On the Value of Popular Music* (Oxford: Oxford University Press, 1996), p.14.
13. Moore, 'Rock 'n' Roll Rebel'.
14. Butler Cullingford, *Ireland's Others*, p.248.
15. Hattenstone, 'Vatican'.
16. Fachtna O'Ceallaigh, interview by Noel McLaughlin, 2011 (unpublished).
17. Sheila Whiteley, *Women and Popular Music: Sexuality, Identity and Subjectivity* (London: Routledge, 2000), pp.122–3, 172.
18. Mayhew, 'I am not in a box'.
19. Negus, 'Sinéad O'Connor'.
20. Butler Cullingford, *Ireland's Others*, p.248. See Tony Purvis, ' "Ireland's Controversial Icon": A Study of the Work of Sinéad O'Connor', in Richard C. Allen and Stephen Regan (eds), *Irelands of the Mind: Memory and Identity in Modern Irish Culture* (Newcastle: Cambridge Scholars, 2008), pp.158–222. This insightful essay is one of the few in popular musical scholarship to engage (in an in-depth and non-essentialist fashion) with the nationally and culturally specific in relation to O'Connor's artistic work. In a similar vein, and equally insightful, is Emer Nolan's essay 'Sinéad O'Connor: The Story of a Voice', *Field Day Review*, 6 (2010), pp.52–69.
21. Sinéad O'Connor, 'The Pope's Apology for Sex Abuse in Ireland seems Hollow', *Washington Post*, 28 March 2010.
22. O'Ceallaigh, interview.
23. Dick Hebdige, *Subculture: The Meaning of Style* (London: Methuen, 1979).
24. Ibid., p.55.
25. Ibid.
26. Negus, 'Sinéad O'Connor', p.186.
27. Jimmy Guterman, *Sinéad: Her Life and Music* (Harmondsworth: Penguin, 1991); Negus, 'Sinéad O'Connor'.
28. Molly McAnally Burke, 'Sinéad O'Connor: The Bald Facts', *Hot Press* (November 1986).

29. Negus, 'Sinéad O'Connor', p.185.
30. Ibid.
31. Mayhew, 'I am not in a box', p.170–2.
32. Guterman, *Sinéad*, pp.33–5; Dermot Hayes, *Sinéad O'Connor: So Different* (London: Omnibus Press, 1991), pp.62–3.
33. Negus, 'Sinéad O'Connor', p.186.
34. Indeed, O'Connor can also boast an extensive and impressive list of such collaborations (some of which were drawn together on the 2005 album, *Collaborations*).
35. McAnally Burke, 'Sinéad O'Connor'.
36. John Reynolds, 'The Lion and the Cobra', *Hot Press* (November 2004).
37. Katrina Irving, ' "I Want Your Hands on Me": Building Equivalences through Rap Music', *Popular Music*, 12, 2 (1993), p.118.
38. Ibid., p.117.
39. Butler Cullingford, *Ireland's Others*, p.247.
40. Negus, 'Sinéad O'Connor', p.186.
41. See Paul Gilroy, *The Black Atlantic: Modernity and Double Consciousness* (London: Verso, 1993); Lauren Onkey, *Blackness and Transatlantic Irish Identity: Celtic Soul Brothers* (New York and London: Routledge, 2010); Malouf, 'Feeling Eire(y)'.
42. Negus, 'Sinéad O'Connor', p.186.
43. Campbell and Smyth, *Beautiful Day*, p.115.
44. Nabeel Zuberi, *Sounds English: Transnational Popular Music* (Chicago, IL: University of Illinois Press, 2001), pp.151–60.
45. See Negus, 'Sinéad O'Connor'; McLaughlin and McLoone, 'Hybridity and National Musics'; Campbell and Smyth, *Beautiful Day*; Mayhew, 'I am not in a box'.
46. Mavis Bayton, *Frock Rock: Women Performing Popular Music* (Oxford: Oxford University Press, 1998); Gillian Gaar, *She's a Rebel: The History of Women in Rock & Roll* (New York: Seal Press, 1993); Lucy O'Brien, *She Bop: The Definitive History of Women in Rock, Pop and Soul* (London: Continuum, 1995); Simon Reynolds and Joy Press, *The Sex Revolts: Gender, Rebellion, and Rock 'n' Roll* (London: Serpent's Tail, 1995); Whiteley, *Women in Popular Music*.
47. Deevoy, 'Crazy Baldhead', pp.16–17.
48. David Sinclair, 'Got a Problem, Pal', *Q*, January 1993, p.40.
49. Janice C. Simpson, 'People Need a Short, Sharp Shock: Sinéad O'Connor', *Time Magazine*, 9 November 1992, p.78.
50. Jacques Attali, *Noise: The Political Economy of Music* (Minneapolis, MN: University of Minnesota Press, 1985). p.11.
51. O'Connor, 'The Pope's Apology'.
52. Nuala O'Connor, *Bringing It All Back Home* (London: BBC Books, 1991), p.131.
53. Ibid.
54. In 2007 it emerged that the singer suffers from the depressive illness, bipolar disorder, casting the tabloid-style references to apparent instability in a different light (although O'Connor has more recently claimed that she was misdiagnosed).

10

Roads Not Taken?
Gregory Gray

Since the mid-nineteenth century a country's music has become a
political ideology by stressing national characteristics, appearing as
representative of the nation, and everywhere confirming the national
principle . . . Yet music . . . expresses the national principle's antimonies
as well. (Theodor Adorno)[1]

I left my home, so I could be myself,
I stumbled into town, trying to move ahead,
No fear of AIDS,
No fear of fame
1975 was a very different game. (Gregory Gray, 'Three Minute
Requiem')

Benedict Anderson has persuasively argued that the complex process
of creating the nation as an 'imagined community' is often at the
expense of representing the diversity of experience within its selective
affinities.[2] As has been suggested, Irish popular music is not only
framed within the hegemonic thrust of the national, but also by
broader international expectations of what 'good' Irish rock music
should be. The presence of neighbouring Britain has loomed large in
this regard, acting on the one hand as a benign, occasionally liberating and aspirational influence, and as something of a bête noire on
the other. The result has been to push out to the margins of Irish
popular music a range of styles and identities that don't neatly
conform to these centralized conceptions. The very notion of a
national music, when attempting to discuss nationality and rock/pop
together, is, therefore, frequently inflected by nationalist imperatives,
whether 'progressive', strategically essentialist or jingoistic.

In contrast to British popular music history where a relative
diversity of identities has been articulated in and by rock, pop and
dance genres, Irish popular music has, by contrast, been largely

dominated by a folk-inflected rock ideology and its attendant associations: a concern with authenticity and rock 'realism', authorial
expression, a preference for 'the organic' over the synthetic, and
music that constructs and represents 'community'. Even interiorized,
self-consciously authored and 'personal' rock may be mapped to,
and framed within, the national and hence read (heard) in allegorical terms. In this sense, Irish rock music has been indelibly marked
by an aesthetic that has ossified into cliché – the pastoral, the rural
as exotica – offered up in the recurrent images of wide, open,
windswept landscapes, traditional pubs and the 'mystical' aura of
the Celtic. This rock and folk-orientated culture, as we have seen,
also has a gendered aspect, and looked at through an alternative critical lens, the dominant narrative of Irish rock is an overwhelmingly
hetero-normative and even masculinist one. Indeed, Irish rock has
offered up fairly traditional, even stereotypical images of masculinity and femininity: with men, somewhat schematically, associated
with the public world of politics, and women with private, domestic
spaces (even though there are significant exceptions here, as we have
noted).

The hegemonic thrust of the national does not (and should not)
necessitate explicitly dealing with Irish themes, settings or preoccupations (although it may also do so). Nonetheless, even without the
overt signalling of these, Irish rock may play a role in marking out
territories, signposting differences and in consolidating gender
norms, in much the same way as folk and traditional musics have
done,[3] thus limiting the relative diversity of experience of Irish society and culture.

Coleraine-born singer-songwriter Gregory Gray is of major
significance here because he has attempted to extend the Irish pop
lexicon in important directions. Gray is also of interest as his music
has articulated the diverse aspects of gay identity/ies as well as
addressing gay audiences (though in no sense exclusively so). As far
as we are aware, Gray stands as Ireland's first pop/rock star to
acknowledge publicly his homosexual identity (from this vantage
point, he is something of a lone voice in an overwhelmingly hetero-
dox narrative). As the country's first 'out' gay pop performer, his
story is of further interest as he has been virtually erased from the
dominant discourse of Irish rock. Gray and Perfect Crime – the band
he formed and fronted in the early-to-mid 1980s – have been chronically under-profiled in *Hot Press*, for example. There is no mention
of the singer in the magazine's online archive and only a couple of

passing references to him and the band – two reviews – at the height of his local presence. However, a decade later in August 1996, perhaps ironically, Gray was the subject of a major *Hot Press* centre-spread retrospective, significantly entitled 'The Greatest Irish Rock Story Never Told'.[4]

This 'omission', however, is not exclusive to Ireland's major rock publication. Gray was also overlooked on the nationally broadcast 'So Hard to Beat', a 2009 BBC4 UK television documentary exploring four decades of rock and popular music in Northern Ireland (Friday 15 May 2009, rebroadcast Saturday 16 May). The programme, written and directed by former *NME* journalist Stuart Bailie, inexplicably included artists and bands of much lesser commercial and/or critical stature. Gray was, however, included in Ulster Television's earlier six-part documentary series 'Rockin' the North', broadcast regionally in 1994. This suggests that the creation of a Northern Irish rock and pop 'canon' may, to a degree, be an arbitrary process. Terri Hooley, the adviser, consultant and interviewer on the UTV series, reflecting on Gray's marginal place in the Irish rock narrative, claimed: 'I have always thought he was important. How could I not include him? There is nobody else like him...but some people don't like that. As for why Stuart Bailie didn't include him? You'd better ask.'[5] Moreover, in 1983, Channel 4's rock programme 'The Tube' broadcast a 'Tube special' from Belfast profiling the Northern Irish music scene (the same episode – 18 March – that featured U2 live in the studio). From the perspective of the Tube production team, at least, Perfect Crime were deemed worthy of inclusion (even if, due to contractual problems, Gray was the only band member to appear singing over a pre-recorded backing track).

As with the major BBC4 documentary, neither Gray nor Perfect Crime are mentioned in the two most prominent 'journalistic' histories of Irish rock.[6] Nor is band or solo artist namechecked in Gerry Smyth's *Noisy Island*, the first and only scholarly monograph on the subject.[7] They do not feature in Campbell and Smyth's detailed analysis of individual songs by a range of Irish performers, *Beautiful Day*, either.[8] This omission also extends to Sean O'Neill and Guy Telford's *It Makes You Want To Spit: The Definitive Guide to Punk in Northern Ireland 1977–1982*,[9] which, as the title implies, seeks to exhaustively catalogue the region's punk and post-punk bands. Again, what at first may appear simply as oversight becomes complicated in that Prendergast,[10] Clayton-Lea and Taylor[11] and Smyth[12] all offer comprehensive, even completist, catalogues and mini-biographies of commercially visible Irish artists.

Moreover, any selective criteria in operation here evidently does not work on the basis of citizenship as Gray was born, lived, performed and recorded for most of his career in Ireland (only leaving to live in London in the late 1990s). However, it is a crude fact that Gregory Gray and Perfect Crime are largely absent from the discourse of Irish rock. The reasons for this are interesting in terms of Irish rock and cultural identity, and discussion of these provides an opportunity finally to tell 'The Greatest Irish Rock Story Never Told'.

GREGORY GRAY: A BRIEF HISTORY

Gray is much more than a mere 'also-ran' in the history of Irish rock and pop. The singer has had a lengthy career, starting as rhythm guitarist Paul 'Flash' Lerwill in late-1970s teen-group Rosetta Stone (the band groomed by notorious Bay City Rollers' manager Tam Paton as the follow-up to that mid-1970s teen phenomenon). Throughout this thirty-something year oeuvre, he has signed deals with, and taken substantial advances from, four of the 'big five' major record companies: firstly with MCA in 1983, as lead singer/songwriter with the Portrush-based Perfect Crime. This pop/funk four-piece were a constant presence in the local live circuit (much like a precursor to The Frames in the 1990s). In this sense, they conformed to the rock cliché of 'paying one's dues' and establishing through 'grass-roots' live playing a reputation from the 'ground up'. Playing live in the period was also a major income stream and, in the period before the rise of cassette or computer-based 'home' studios, of financing recording. The band's pre-signing 'demo' recording, 'Fast Life Neon Ice', was played regularly on 'The Dave Fanning Show' and the band were also featured on Davy Simms' 'The Downtown Radio Sessions' (Northern Ireland's rough equivalent to 'The Dave Fanning Show') with 'Fast Life Neon Ice' released on an LP compilation, *Now in Session* (1982), featuring artists from the programme such as The Outcasts and Protex.

Even though the singer had not 'officially' 'come out' at this stage of his career and acknowledged his homosexuality publicly, his identity even at this early point was something of an open secret. Even those audience members unfamiliar with Gray's biographical details

19. 'The Greatest Irish Rock Story Never Told' – Gregory Gray

would have been left in little doubt of the singer's sexuality by witnessing Perfect Crime in performance (or hearing Gray in interview). Regular live tracks had titles such as 'The Bitch is On' – a percussive, disco-driven anthem – and 'Quentin', his ode to queer icon Quentin Crisp. Moreover, these were songs that in style, theme and performance couldn't be further from the prevailing residue of Northern Irish punk and sub-Undertones pastiche. Perfect Crime offered no songs about living in Northern Ireland at the height of the Troubles, nor owed much stylistically to guitar thrash or the rock realist aesthetic in the ascendancy at the time. In one sense, the invitation offered by the band was a camp version of the maxim, 'fuck the Troubles, let's dance' (even though, like The Undertones, Gray's lyrical address and accent was at times idiomatically Northern Irish; even north County Antrim).

As no playing opportunity in a limited small-venue circuit could be glibly turned down, this resulted in the band playing to less than 'gay-friendly' audiences. Gray also possessed a flamboyant and energetic performing style that sat in the hinterland between the authoritative masculine and camp display, which similarly left audiences in little doubt about his sexual identity. Many of these mid-Ulster performances could therefore be likened to a small-scale and local version of The Sex Pistols' notorious tour of the southern United States which resulted in confrontation between band and audience (and consequently Gray became particularly adept at sharp-witted camp put-downs to the routine and all-too-vocal hecklers). One possible source of antipathy towards Gray beyond out-and-out homophobia may emerge here: the risk of being interpreted as camping it up in a war zone (much as, from a rock-realist perspective, the New Romantics in Thatcher's Britain were condemned for appearing to celebrate materialism and conspicuous consumption in the face of a myriad of social and economic problems).

At the other end of the touring spectrum, away from the small provincial venues of rural Northern Ireland, the band supported Orchestral Manoeuvres in the Dark, Paul Young and The Royal Family, Eurythmics, Talking Heads and, more prominently, U2 on the European leg of their *War* tour in 1983. In fact, Gray's band was significantly the only other Irish act to play at U2's first major 'homecoming' festival in Dublin's Phoenix Park to 25,000 people on 14 August of that year (in a bill that included Steel Pulse, Big Country, Eurythmics and Simple Minds). The *Hot Press* reviewers made brief mention of the band's performance on that day:

> Perfect also were the Crime of the same name for their appointed role. Faced with the inevitable challenge of opening the proceedings, the Perfect Crime surmounted the difficulties, burgling the hearts and minds of many present and went away with a burgeoning reputation worth its weight in gold. On this showing they are destined to pull off the big one.[13]

Indeed they did and on signing to MCA Perfect Crime released two singles: 'Brave' (1983) and 'Feel like an Eskimo' (1984), both of which were heavily advertised and promoted (with the band performing 'Brave' on Saturday morning television in the United Kingdom). In the context of the Northern Ireland of the period, signing with a major record label was, in itself, a considerable achievement. Despite this rare mention in *Hot Press* and the commercial and artistic promise suggested, Perfect Crime disbanded sometime in 1984–85 with the singer subsequently beginning a career as a solo artist and signing with CBS in the United Kingdom (but maintaining his writing and recording base in an isolated farmhouse near the North Antrim coast).

Think of Swans, his debut album as Gregory Gray, was released on the imprint in 1986 and was produced by Walter Samuel, who has most famously engineered a number of Van Morrison albums. The album also featured the renowned double-bass virtuoso Danny Thompson, who had contributed to a wealth of critically lauded records, including albums by John Martyn, Nick Drake, Kate Bush and David Sylvian (among many others). 'Sensual' – featuring Thompson's distinctive style – and 'Books to Read Twice' were released as singles, with the former track amply supported by television appearances in the United Kingdom by both artist and accompanying music video. This included further slots on the 'youth'/pre-teen-orientated Saturday morning schedule, and the 'Sensual' video placed on rotation on MTV (as well as a prominent marketing campaign that encompassed the 'style' press, such as *The Face* magazine). Gray also toured the album in England and received positive reviews in the music press, particularly from Barry McIlheney in *Melody Maker*.[14]

Throughout this period of his career, he also maintained a high media profile in Ireland, with appearances on BBC NI's youth and current affairs programme, 'Channel One', and a lengthy prime-time profile on Ulster Television's magazine programme, 'Good Evening Ulster' (with Gray interviewed around the North Antrim coast by presenter Eamonn Holmes). He also routinely featured on Radio Ulster, Downtown Radio and RTÉ's Radio Two and was a studio guest on 'The Dave Fanning Show' a number of times. One of these appearances in particular is recalled fondly by show producer, Ian Wilson, due to the 'controversy' it caused in the form of listeners' complaints. When asked by Fanning if he liked the second Pogues' album, Gray responded by claiming that he knew 'more about rum, sodomy and the lash than those boys!'[15]

In 1990 Gray signed to Atco, a subsidiary of Polygram, and released the Davitt Sigerson-produced *Strong at Broken Places* in March of that year. The album was not released in the United Kingdom and was perhaps a sign that Gray had decided to focus on success in the world's largest record market. Sigerson is an auteur-producer who has worked with David and David and produced The Bangles' 1989 international number one single, 'Eternal Flame'. At the time of recording *Strong at Broken Places* he was simultaneously producing Tori Amos's debut album, *Little Earthquakes*, for release in 1992. Such was the faith and optimism placed in Gray's second album that Sigerson thought that it would be the 'overground' hit (with the debut Amos album the 'quirky', esoteric 'art' project).[16] History, of course, has shown that the opposite was the case and while Amos has flourished as an individual, esoteric talent, Gray has largely disappeared from view in the Irish context of the time. However, *Strong at Broken Places* was to be very favourably reviewed in *Rolling Stone*, *Billboard* and the *New York Times*, as well as receiving solid college radio play. A superficial sign of the desire for American success can be glimpsed in the album's sleeve and inlay photography that constructs the singer in a Michael Hutchence-style pose and what McIlheney[17] refers to as his 'Pre-Raphaelite curls' – and in fairly orthodox pop/rock star mode for the teen female gaze (conventionally good-looking and long-haired), thus downplaying any suggestion of homosexuality (in visual terms at least).

The singer was to switch major record companies one more time, following Sigerson to EMI America, where the producer took up an executive role as managing director. Gray recorded and released his last 'conventional' album to date in 1995, *Euroflake in Silverlake* (which, again like its predecessor, was not released in the United Kingdom but in the United States, Europe and the Far East). However, *Euroflake in Silverlake* differed from *Strong at Broken Places* in that the cover art, musical style and lyrical themes offered a more overt queer subtext, with Gray now sporting a close-cropped hairstyle. The album title also suggested a very different Irish-American/European-American relationship from the one explored thus far and one that directly references the infamous Silverlake gay district in Los Angeles.

While out-and-out high-profile or 'mainstream' visibility eluded him, Gray did achieve considerable commercial and critical success in Japan and in selective European territories, in addition to the substantial college radio following and (gay) 'subcultural' popularity in the United States. These, together with his prominent – if intermittent – appearances across various media in the United Kingdom and Ireland, clearly merit more than a mere mention.

From the late 1990s onwards, Gray 'reinvented' himself as 'Mary Cigarettes', releasing music on the Internet via streaming sites such as YouTube and SoundCloud, but also on social networking sites such as MySpace and FaceBook. His YouTube profile reveals thousands of hits, an internationally dispersed following and scores of pages of overwhelmingly favourable and enthusiastic comments. The singer has attempted to manage a complete severance from his musical past (few seem aware that Cigarettes is Gray), which makes the success of his current 'online' career all the more charged.

PERFORMANCE AND STYLE

Ultimately, what is of most importance is this artist's music and his idiosyncratic aesthetic in terms of performance and vocal style. His music can be described as wry and humorous, playing irreverently with pop conventions through the deployment of twisted narratives and unsettling musical juxtapositions. However, his work is not reducible to a clever use of irony and play, but is constantly changing register and can also be frequently moving and emotionally charged. This is, in part, a result of the eclectic and diverse range of influences underpinning his work. These swing from the pop of David Bowie, Marc Bolan, Grace Jones and George Michael to the folk and folk-rock of John Martyn and Nick Drake, through to the emotive – yet barbed and critical – soul of Millie Jackson, even powerfully covering the latter's 'Your Loving Arms' (*Still Caught Up*, 1974) as Mary Cigarettes on YouTube. One can also hear the influence of the 'torch songs' of Nina Simone and, in the contemporary context, Anthony and the Johnsons. In addition to this, Gray's work has been marked by an innovative and expressive use of electronic timbres and textures, inspired by the solo work of former Japan singer, David Sylvian, and other more overtly 'experimental' artists such as Brian Eno and Jon Hassell. While this list is extensive, it only scratches the surface of Gray's range of musical influences. His work, emerging out of the restless innovations of the post-punk period, has sat squarely in Ireland's largely unoccupied hinterland between rock and pop and is something of a hybrid of rock's emphasis on emotional affect and 'seriousness', and pop's 'plasticity' and anti-authenticating drives. In this sense, Gray sits in a 'queer' para-musical space, one that straddles the dialectic between acceptance/assimilation and resistance to 'mainstream' pop culture, of courting favour and announcing difference.[18]

'Who is Your Master', the B-side of the twelve-inch version of the debut Perfect Crime single 'Brave', intimated at the more mature Gray aesthetic, the track's propulsive bass-driven funk underpinning the lyrical themes of S&M and sexual power-play. It was also marked by the creative and expressive use of the studio – of the mixing desk and multitrack recording – as a musical instrument in its own right. Gray's voice on 'Who is Your Master' and throughout the first solo album was marked by an operatic tenor, which may be read as excessive, even 'over-the-top' in style. His work at this point moved away from the more generic pop/funk/disco of Perfect Crime. On his first album as a solo artist he had one foot in what Simon

Reynolds has termed 'the big music' associated largely with the post-punk of the Celtic periphery and artists such as Big Country, Simple Minds, The Waterboys, The Associates and, of course, U2.[19] In fact 'Sea Town', the singer's ode to the North Antrim coast from *Think of Swans* conforms to the epic soundscapes of the big music and conjures up windswept images and open landscapes. The singer's other 'foot' was in a 'camp' sensibility and marked by a shifting and ambivalent relationship to issues of meaning and 'sincerity' (as well as a more overt use of synthesizers than was customary with the 'big music'). His 'big' voice and the operatic stylings invoke the late Billy McKenzie of the Associates who is perhaps the nearest reference point vocally.[20]

Simon Frith has usefully argued that 'over-the-top' artists are enjoyable as they 'deliberately set gestures free from their appropriate setting' and thus 'don't so much enact emotional roles as hold their gestures up before us in fragments, so we can admire the shape of the gesture itself'.[21] Therefore, like many good 'queer' pop performers, Gray has

> ...grasped the camp point that the truth of a feeling is an aesthetic truth, not a moral one; it can only be judged formally, as a matter of gestural grace. 'Sincerity', in short, cannot be measured by searching for what lies *behind* a performance; if we are moved by a performer we are moved by what we *immediately* hear and see.[22]

In addition to the review of Perfect Crime at the U2 'homecoming' concert there is only one detailed reference to Gray in *Hot Press* in the 1980s: the 'favourable', yet strangely revealing, review of Gray's debut album. For the reviewer, *Think of Swans* 'evokes the aura of money and airbrush, big production' and, if that wasn't enough, 'big investment'. It continued in the same vein:

> Those of you who come seeking rough edges will be disappointed...it would be easy to dismiss *Think of Swans* as the product of another Thompson Twin or Pet Shop Boy...but through all the candy floss and peroxide rings the sound of a voice – funny, powerful, hurt and hurting. For all the producing, synthesizing and digital mastering, all the pomp and circumstance, all the heat-sealing is undermined by Gray's genuine talent...the passion shines through.[23]

Perhaps strangely, given the prose, the album achieved top marks on the ratings system. *Hot Press*, however, attempted to redeem the album via selective criteria – that despite all the apparent 'inauthenticity', 'technology' and (over) production and other markers of 'bad' music (such as money and 'candyfloss') there was an authentic human presence and real passion underneath. In other words, the album paradoxically succeeds in spite of itself. Despite owing something to the 'big music', clearly Gray's album does not easily fit into dominant conceptions of Irish rock, aesthetically, generically or indeed representationally. What therefore makes him significant in this context is the embrace of production techniques and a musical/performance aesthetic that tends towards the inauthentic: foregrounding studio 'artifice' and a conspicuously 'pop' sensibility. As many commentators have argued, music produced by 'gay' artists and musicians has frequently embraced the musical vocabularies of pop over and above the libidinal grind of rock (but of course this is not a necessary connection, nor the expression of the essence of gay masculinity).[24] What is clearly of further significance here, then, is the articulation of musical and performance modes that have strong gay/queer connotations into Irish rock and pop spaces.

This, however, is not to suggest that Gray's career thus far had been driven by a favouring of the centre – a clone of developments elsewhere – and was therefore decidedly un-Irish. For example, the album's opening track 'The Life of Reilly' clearly references the idiomatic Irish cliché of boundless leisure and 'an easy time'. It concludes with a lengthy monologue, in Gray's recognizably (and camp) Northern Irish accent (a feature that peppers the entire record).

'PEOPLE ARE HARD': *STRONG AT BROKEN PLACES*

In the mid-to-late 1980s when stars such as U2 were attaching themselves to signifiers of blackness by going in search of 'roots', and *The Commitments* was, in another way, attempting to conflate Irishness and blackness through notions of racial identity, Gray was playing with 'racialized' popular music forms in an altogether different way. *Strong at Broken Places* witnessed Gray dropping the operatic vocal styling for a more understated yet distinctive voice with a harder timbre. It was also, especially compared to its predecessor, a leaner album, more strongly pop and song orientated. Most significantly for the ongoing discussion, it returned Gray to urban dance rhythms (with Soul II Soul, The Pet Shop Boys, the Bristol sound of Massive

Attack and the sounds of Madchester clear contemporary influences, in addition to the funk and disco Gray was steeped in). For example, the second track on the album, 'People are Hard', utilizes a machine-driven dub reggae groove with a slippery staggered bass-line and a pop-song structure and melody. However, rather than sounding 'tripped out' and 'dubby' in a manner commensurate with the expectations of the genre (invoking, for example, the African-American or Afro-Caribbean English inner city), 'People are Hard' reorganizes the musical conventions to sound neurotic (a useful point of reference here might be Talking Head's David Byrne or post-punk nerds Devo jamming with Soul II Soul), with the vocal performance, melody and lyric contrasting sharply with the associations established by the rhythm section. While the vocal address and lyric are broad and general in their appeal, the vocal style and phrasing – concerned directly with the contradictory discontents of modern living – gives the impression of sounding 'unrelaxed'. It thus works against the conventional expectations offered by the bass and drum pattern. The associations of dub – its laidback or stoned euphoria – are taken and re-contextualized and with it the naturalized representational 'fit' of Irishness, blackness and the authenticity (and their attendant musical meanings) is unsettled (after all, this was the period – 1990–91 – when *Rattle and Hum* and *The Commitments* were in the Irish popular musical ascendancy).

Furthermore, a frequent strategy in Gray's work has been the subversion of the expectations of 'sincerity' associated with the confessional singer-songwriter.[25] At times, he avoided electronic textures altogether and a more 'natural' four-piece backing of guitar/acoustic guitar, bass and drums is deployed, such as on 'It's Easier Said Than Done':

> All of my friends have settled down
> They talk a foreign language now
> I'm not jealous when I see
> The way they've found security '...'
> And if someone kind and free
> Said she's going to wait for me
> Well it's easier, easier said than done.

Formally, 'Easier Said Than Done' is a 'classic' pop song comprising of the standard AABA (verse-chorus-verse-chorus-middle-eight-chorus) structure. In no sense could it be construed as formally innovative or stylistically novel. Lyrically the track is concerned with the recurring rock narrative of the problems of settling into domesticity and 'flight from bosom and hearth'. However, this trope of masculine outsidership is modified: first by the implied sexuality of the singer, and secondly by the manner in which the conventions employed are inhabited; the cues the vocal gives to suggest the singer's identity. Again, the different discourses that meet in this juncture are twisted to create novel tensions. The masculine protagonist/rural seer associated with the form and the narrative is taken and modified as the song progresses. Prior to the chorus the vocal inflection subtly shifts, the address and the timbre altering and becoming increasingly camp. This both undermines the 'authenticity' of the recurring, yet clichéd, narrative of escape from domestic entrapment but also 'queers' the narrative by dragging the song's meaning in a wholly different direction. This signals that the protagonist, the 'I' and the 'me' of the song, can't settle into the domesticity of heterosexual romance as his sexuality excludes him. The song can, of course, be enjoyed 'straight' or read via the vocal address, which destabilizes clichéd heterosexual assumptions about romance and outsidership. In fact, the track's spoken conclusion adds a further ironic twist to the narrative, wryly mocking the desire to escape the domestic, adopting and modifying the anti-consumerist position of much masculinist rock: 'Ain't got no house/Ain't got no refrigerator/Ain't got no Hoover/Ain't got no whatever'.

EUROFLAKE IN SILVERLAKE

The closest point of musico-stylistic comparison to Gray's work of the mid-1990s is The Pet Shop Boys, and indeed, the two artists shared renowned American producer Stephen Hague. Hague had developed a reputation as a producer of synth-pop in the 1980s and 1990s with artists such as New Order, Dubstar, Marc Almond and Holly Johnson. Specifically his name became associated with the type of flat and clean electronic soundscapes associated with and clearly audible in The Pet Shop Boys' work. However, it would be a mistake to suggest that Gray is merely a regionalized clone of Tennant and Lowe and their ilk. While the Hague-produced *Euroflake in Silverlake* shares what might be termed the anti-authenticating drives,[26] the wry cynicism and the overt pop sensibility synonymous with both producer and the artists he is associated with, there are important particularities to consider.

The first aspect of these is approaches to production. In interview, Gray described the production process of key tracks on the album and the occasional tension between himself and the producer. Hague wanted to, as it were, 'strengthen the sound' through the addition of reverbs and delay techniques to vocals, synth-pads and to the rhythm section. He also sought to record and 'double-up' with extra tracks in order to make the sound 'bigger, fatter and more powerful', whereas, by contrast, Gray fought to keep the sound, in his words, 'small and dry'.[27] This avoidance of production bombast was in no sense motivated by a desire to sound under-produced or 'raw' (as is often the case in rock). *Euroflake* in no sense sounds 'rough'. Rather, Gray's intention was to avoid any sense of 'epic' production by creating a sound that could be intimately connected with the music's meaning. And it seems that in this case, *small* sounds and thin textures were as much worth defending as 'big sounds' (or big music) and 'powerful' music was striven for in other contexts. While Gray writes, records and performs 'classic' pop songs, some of which are suitable for daytime radio play, he inhabits the generic conventions in a manner that could be described as 'perverse' (in a positive critical sense) and has the capacity to make audiences uncomfortable. Other tracks, however, are lyrically much more explicit, addressing more specifically gay concerns (stories of sexual encounters). Often the address is now explicitly camp, integrating classic pop songs with a knowing and barbed wit, yet expertly deployed use of the conventions of light entertainment and 'showbiz' culture.[28] With *Euroflake in Silverlake* Gray was less anxious to 'impress' than with previous albums and the result was a much 'smaller' and more coherent album.

Gray's musical vocabulary isn't limited to the wry Europop of The Pet Shop Boys, and the more overt camp address can be heard on *Euroflake in Silverlake's* opening track, first single and video, 'The Pope does not Smoke Dope'. Underneath the jokey chorus – 'Cut the crap, get real sweetheart/The pope does not smoke dope/ Even if he should' – the lyrics sharply explore and dissect the conceits of modern living (even incorporating a line from a local North Antrim farmer – 'it's just not sucking diesel out'). The album also included the artist's first generically 'gay' track, the Hi-NRG 'I'm Not Paranoid', but invests it with a knowing irony, in that it is a 'handbag' dance anthem about (chemically-induced) paranoia.

However, camp may also be a fraught strategy. It can often be taken to mean that the performer has gone too far or 'crossed the line'. As with Sinéad O'Connor, Gray can frequently be designated as 'out of order', regarded as 'perverse' or 'offensive'. As opposed to articulating an endless chain of 'already saids', Gray, through his use of uncomfortable lyrical juxtapositions and re-contextualization of performance and musical conventions, can reference the frequently unspoken. For example, he appeared on RTÉ television's 'The Gerry Ryan Show' in January 1997, performing naked from the waist up, with 'I love [as in the shape of a heart] Christy Moore' written in lipstick across his chest, thus co-opting Moore from his pre-eminent place in Irish folk discourse and his designated role as controversial and 'organic' Republican hero into an ambivalent (or is it ironic?) object of the homoerotic gaze. This discourse was also extended into the musical performance, as Gray delivered a characteristically Moore-style set – one man and his acoustic guitar – of folk ballad or 'story songs', performing 'The Pope does not Smoke Dope' in a stripped-down version that was adapted to the protest/folk singer mode. Thus, the form's 'natural' connotations became destabilized by the camp address and the accompanying queer playfulness.

Simon Frith has drawn attention to the way in which The Pet Shop Boys make use of music and performance meanings and associations to critique the norms of rock.[29] Here Neil Tennant's 'thin voice', the electronic sounds, the lack of 'passion', musically and in performance, works in a not dissimilar manner to Gregory Gray. In songs such as 'The Pope does not Smoke Dope' and 'People are Hard', we hear Gray, with The Pet Shop Boys in mind, gleefully mocking Irish rock norms, assumptions and residual authenticities, from a position of relative subordination and absence. This is in no sense to reduce these songs to being primarily about Ireland, as they have a much broader appeal (and the singer's manifest intentions may not recognize such a position). Nevertheless it would appear that Gray's music might be interpreted as offering an interesting musical micro-critique, one attuned and sensitive to the cultural specificity of Irish society and to the operation of hetero-normative structures of domination within it.

In common with Van Morrison, Gray's work combines the local and the international, except that this hybridity is both articulated and inhabited very differently. Unlike Morrison, Gray's work incorporates little or no recognizably Irish signifiers or place names (in fact, Morrison's legacy makes this very difficult to repeat), again revealing the limitations of not discriminating between different kinds of hybridity. In particular 'Scenes from a Madison Avenue Office' from *Euroflake in Silverlake* takes the synthesis of Irish and American musical elements and 'perverts' the orthodox hybrid, in an absurdist, even comical, manner. The track uses a reedy, thin machine-based 'soul' backing and the vocal is an excessive and (by Gray's own admission) incredibly poor imitation of a New York business executive (strategically poor mimicry?), eliciting sexual favours from his secretary.[30] Again in both production and interpretation the song utilizes an understanding of pop genre expectations and meanings, re-forging them to make exciting new critical connections.

In between his second and third albums, homosexuality was finally decriminalized in Ireland in 1993, much later than in neighbouring Britain (even though the conservative state was in no sense draconian in its attitude to gays and lesbians). This context perhaps grounds Gray's lyric from *Euroflake*'s concluding track: the slow, meditative and percussion-less 'Three Minute Requiem'. The period is also significant as it marks Gray's re-entry into the discourse of Irish rock. In that rare *Hot Press* centre-page, double-page feature interview with Stuart Clark in 1996 he seeks to counter the notion that being gay is the most important thing about him or his work, or that he is a representative of/for a gay/queer identity:

> There's a hollowness to selling out a club just because I'm gay. I really do object to the self-appointed guardians of the gay scene, deciding that the only music gay people should like is high-energy disco. Gay people like Metallica, The Stone Roses. They even like Andy fuckin' Williams. No one should ever have to apologise for their sexuality, but clearly some modes of performance and behaviour are more acceptable than others, if you want to avoid being shoved in the gay ghetto.[31]

Here, Gray seeks to displace the burden of representation – of being, by default, framed as spokesperson for gay culture. In so doing, in interview, as in his work, he addresses the related problems of ghettoization (breaking down stereotypical notions of what constitutes 'authentically' gay music and experience). This tension between the artist's elective affinities, the 'queer' aspects of his identity and dominant hetero-normative modes of pop/rock culture clearly inform Gray's performance. However, before we consider his performance we need to consider Gray's relationship to the discourse of Irish rock in more detail.

'The Greatest Irish Pop Story Never Told', which was part editorial, part interview and part *Euroflake* album review, noted Gray's virtual exclusion from the discourse of Irish rock. The irony here, of course, was that *Hot Press* was exposing the untold story and noting Gray's absence, even if, to a degree, it was (unwittingly) part of the exclusion process. The context for this major reappraisal merits some exploration. *Euroflake in Silverlake* initially had a US and mainland Europe only release and the magazine became involved in the story on discovering that EMI Ireland had taken the decision not to release the record in the domestic market.

It is worth pausing here. We are not suggesting that Gray is the victim of a homophobic conspiracy to erase his contribution from the 'official' narrative of Irish rock. Certainly, the doggedly left-liberal *Hot Press* would be rightly horrified by such a suggestion. Indeed the magazine, at this juncture, was concerned about a homophobic agenda on the part of EMI Ireland and the label's seemingly irrational reluctance to release the record. In fact, Stuart Clark uncovered a revealing and contradictory story (and one too detailed to explore here) that insinuated that Gray might be difficult to promote, again raising the issue that the singer's sexuality might be 'a problem'. Despite Clark's enthusiasm and praise for Gray's work and his surprise at his marginal place in Irish rock culture, one could countenance that anti-gay prejudice does not operate at the level of manifest attitudes alone and that homophobic discourse may inform tastes, shaping what is 'good' and 'bad' music, what is, and what is not, acceptable. Certainly there is much anecdotal evidence around the edges of (Northern) Irish rock culture in the 1980s that found Gray as a performer and personality to be 'out of order', 'over the top', alongside other more explicit and derogatory terms.

However, this is not to suggest that Gray's music has to be heard as gay music. When questioned directly about the problems of ghettoization by Stuart Clark, he responded:

> Thinking back to the 1980s, I still insisted in keeping one foot in the closet and I regret not 'coming out' sooner because by not coming clean I was inferring there was something wrong with me. I don't want to think of *Euroflake in Silverlake* as a 'gay record'. I prefer to think of it as a good pop record...In the past, record companies have been uncomfortable with aspects of me and my music, which could make for some unpleasantness: one A&R guy, an ex-public school

boy, kept giving me lectures on what he considered to be the 'real world' and what I had to tone down in order to survive. In the same office, another ex-public schoolboy confessed to me that he identified with my plight, which was just as difficult to cope with.[32]

MARY CIGARETTES

With the emergence of Mary Cigarettes and the singer's shift to internet platforms, his work has become more adventurous and extreme: musically, representationally and hence politically. Mary Cigarettes is an interesting name, not just for perverting fixed gender binaries, but because it economically mixes the sacred and the profane; the divine and the throwaway, the transcendent, blessed virgin and the cigarette: that mass produced and harmful yet plea-surable small object. In one sense it trawls up the related terms – 'Jesus' and 'Fags' – with 'fags', of course, being a well-known and pejorative synonym for gay and queer. The range of musical forms has also grown more extensive, although this has not resulted in esoteric abstraction (as in, say, the later work of Scott Walker) but is still wedded to a respect for and a deployment of the classic pop song. This, the latest period in Gray's career, has seen him collabo-rate as a guest vocalist with the Cork-based avant-house duo, Fish Go Deep ('Hard Times Lately' and 'Chemical God'), as well as embracing the sounds of 'underground' dance music: specifically, the type of minimalist techno and so-called 'broken beat' (an electronic style influenced by funk and jazz, marked by staggered beats and 'early' or delayed snare drum) associated with West London's Bugz in the Attic collective and Berlin's Jazzanova amongst others. This form is especially apparent in his 'A Movie Called Life' (2008) where these left-field electronic sounds meld with the verse-chorus struc-ture of the pop song, employing the type of wry and ambivalent lyrical address described previously.

SEIZING THE PHALLUS FROM COCK ROCK: RECLAIMING THE 'GOLDEN AGE'

In this stage of his oeuvre, there is little loyalty to any single genre (even if there is a dogged commitment to classic pop song form). 'Jimmy Page' (2009) successfully reproduces (and extends) the

1970's glam rock associated with Bowie, Bolan and The Sweet, even echoing the genre's distinctive multitracked 'Ah-Ahhhhhh' backing vocals (heard prominently on the latter's UK number one single, 1973's 'Blockbuster!'). 'Jimmy Page' not only economically employs and references glam rock, but lyrically turns the Led Zeppelin guitarist into both a commodity in a chain of musical transactions and also eroticizes the act of record purchase, turning Page into an object of the homoerotic gaze and/or queer aurality. The chorus repeats 'You're the one/You're the one/I want to spend my money on . . . / Jimmy Page/Jimmy Page', which is underscored and powerfully supported by glam rock's signature Ah-ahhhhhhs. These backing vocals, though, are not a mere recreation of the motif. Rather, the form is expressively extended, incorporating shifts in pitch at key moments in the song's narrative. The track builds into a soaring after-chorus, again making use of Gray's distinctive voice applied in harmonic layers, that lyrically twists the well-worn metaphor of rock music as nourishment for the 'head' and 'soul' and 'perverts' George Clinton's maxim of 'freeing your mind and your ass will follow' in an overtly queer direction, repeating the line: 'Feed my head, fill my hole' four times. 'Head' and 'hole' are evidently read within a sexualized subtext: head as the male member and hole as the anus, thus evoking the image of anal sex. Of course these 'puns' may be read 'straight' – with hole as 'whole' and hence heard 'innocently'. Therefore, the track takes the well-worn rock music 'n' sex connection and drags it in a queer direction. Thus the lines from the first verse invoke both the cliché of rock's transcendent power and link the form with sexual activity:

> Midnight at the window, smoking a joint,
> Listening to music I've never heard before,
> These gems will remain when you and I are dead and gone,
> These amazing things that kept us up all night . . .

The 'amazing things' are thus both musical and (queer) sexual. As with parts of Van Morrison's oeuvre, 'Jimmy Page' is ultimately concerned – in the musical, generic and lyrical conventions employed – with the liberating power of popular music at the periphery. Except here the respectful homage and its popular musical nostalgia – evident in the protagonist's regression to a musical past – is as much about queering that past and reclaiming its homoerotic potential than in simply uncritically celebrating that past. It is also important to note that the singer's Northern Irish accent is clearly audible, especially in 'smokin' a joint' and 'heard before', underlining the regionally-specific aspect of the song's meaning. The track concludes powerfully with 'you're the one...I want to spend my money on' backed by funk 'wah wah' guitar and a rising propulsive bass line.

Significantly, Gray has also branched into producing low-budget video clips to accompany his songs, with a high degree of success. The 'Jimmy Page' video extends the track's homage to English rock's 'golden age' of 1965–75, heightening its liberating possibilities in psychosexual terms in the midst of the conservatism of Northern Ireland. Set in a small independent record shop, it also something of a respectful homage to the power of the vinyl record, seven inch and album, as well as a paean to the 'indie' record shop. The video, which features Gray wearing a long wig that conceals his face, emphasizes the tactile qualities of vinyl, with slow motion and close-up shots revealing the luxuriant qualities and the physicality of the shiny black surface. This is accompanied by long, lingering shots of the classic album covers from the era that adorn the walls of the shop, hinting at the (homo)erotic qualities of the male stars featured (Cliff, Jagger, Bowie). The record shop's interior is offered as a dark and womb-like enclosed space, against the traffic outside. To accompany the track's 'you're the one...' refrain, the video breaks into a series of sexually charged close-ups of the protagonist's hand rubbing his thigh and suggestively pressing his rear against the racks of vinyl. A burst of colour against the fairly monochrome surroundings is provided by the introduction of the protagonist sporting a bright pink Gibson Les Paul guitar, the neck of which is caressed and polished in a similarly suggestive fashion.

The implications of this should be abundantly clear: the well-worn idea of the guitar as phallic instrument (and with it Page as icon) is being taken and wrenched from its moorings and homo-eroticized, claimed by queer discourse. It also echoes Gray's interview with Clark and his desire to break out of the 'gay ghetto' and the stereotypical association with Hi-NRG styles. The clip concludes to the powerful build-up of 'Feed my head/Fill my hole' with the unnamed protagonist, framed from a low angle and hence dominating his surroundings, wearing the 'erect' pink guitar, which occupies the centre of the composition. It is an imposing image. The video ends with a close-up of our hero's crotch and the opening of his trousers to reveal a pair of classic Y-fronts, hammering home its point. It is an interesting video and a creative use of low-budget production that deploys the power of glam rock in a fashion more innovative than Todd Haynes' cinematic meditation on the era, *Velvet Goldmine* (1998).

20. 'Seizing the Phallus from cock rock' – Mary Cigarettes

This is a singer with an incredibly rich, and yet strangely neglected, history. We will conclude with a brief mention of 'Burning Bridges That Never Really Mattered' (2009) and 'Bootcamp for the Broken Hearted' (2010). The videos for both songs are shot simply with one static camera, in one long unbroken take in the first, and two in the second. In the first, Gray appears in medium close-up for the entire duration of the track. Significantly, he sings into a hairbrush (with which he does his hair at the end). This draws attention to the 'feminized' world of pop and the teenage bedroom, of practising looks in the mirror and narcissistically 'becoming' one's favourite pop star. In his thick-rimmed glasses, V-neck tank-top and tie, the singer comes across as a mix of Brains (from the sci-fi puppet series 'Thunderbirds') and the neurotic David Byrne of *Stop Making Sense* (directed by Jonathan Demme, 1984). The nervous intensity of the performance, once again, has a complex relationship to the 'seriousness' of the sentiments expressed. He opens the track power-fully: 'Who cares if I'm faking it/So what if I lie'. Indeed.

Similarly, 'Bootcamp for the Broken Hearted', a down-tempo country-rock ballad, features the singer in medium close-up black-and-white, directly addressing the camera. However, in this video Gray literally mimes to playback without lip-synching (in the Marcel Marceau sense of the term). The simplicity of the shot grammar is echoed in his classic pinstriped suit and his look here is redolent of Charlie Chaplin and/or Robert Downey Jr (as many internet commentators have observed). The 'weightiness' of the song's lyrics are heightened by the direct address to camera, yet set in an odd semantic space by the mime. Any undercutting of emotional affect is heightened when, over the guitar solo at the song's conclusion, the singer polishes (rather than plays) his Gretsch guitar with a white handkerchief. This hybridization of the authentic – sincerity, depth and seriousness – and the inauthentic (subverting and unsettling the same performance modes) works to create an ambivalent and rich music experience.

Gregory Gray illustrates the importance of a regionalized popu-lar music culture in tension with, and even critical of, dominant notions of national identity. His music shows how hybrid texts can work to produce a new way of hearing (and looking). Clearly a simple celebration of hybrids for their own sake is problematic and cannot be validated purely on the basis of who produces or consumes them. However, forms of hybridity like those in Gray's work, which in some sense challenge residual and conservative musi-cal norms, are significant and of value for the manner in which they permit the articulation of identities and pleasures too often ignored at the centre.

NOTES

1. Adorno, quoted in Paul Gilroy, *The Black Atlantic: Modernity and Double Consciousness* (London: Verso, 1993), p.72.
2. Benedict Anderson, *Imagined Communities: Reflections on the Origin and Spread of Nationalism* (London: Verso, 1983).
3. Helen O'Shea, *The Making of Irish Traditional Music* (Cork: Cork University Press, 2008).

4. Stuart Clark, 'Gregory Gray: The Greatest Irish Rock Story Never Told', *Hot Press*, 20, 16 (August, 1996).
5. Terri Hooley, interview by Noel McLaughlin, 2009 (unpublished).
6. Mark J. Prendergast, *The Isle of Noises: Rock and Roll's Roots in Ireland* (Dublin: O'Brien Press, 1987); Tony Clayton-Lea and Richie Taylor, *Irish Rock: Where it's come from, where it's at, where it's going* (Dublin: Gill & Macmillan, 1992).
7. Gerry Smyth, *Noisy Island: A Short History of Irish Popular Music* (Cork: Cork University Press, 2005).
8. Sean Campbell and Gerry Smyth, *Beautiful Day: Forty Years of Irish Rock* (Cork: Atrium Press, 2005).
9. Sean O'Neill and Guy Telford, *It Makes You Want To Spit! The Definitive Guide to Punk in Northern Ireland 1977–1982* (Dublin: Reekus Music, 2003).
10. Prendergast, *Isle of Noises*.
11. Clayton-Lea and Taylor, *Irish Rock*.
12. Smyth, *Noisy Island*.
13. Chris Donovan, Bill Graham and Liam Mackey, 'Review of "A Day at the Races" ', *Hot Press*, 7, 6 (August 1983).
14. Barry McIlheney, interview by Noel McLaughlin, 2011 (unpublished). McIlheney wrote for *Melody Maker* in the 1980s and went on to become editor of *Smash Hits* and *Empire*.
15. Ian Wilson, interview by Noel McLaughlin, 1995 (unpublished).
16. Gregory Gray, interview by Noel McLaughlin, 1996 (unpublished).
17. McIlheney, interview by McLaughlin. For reviews of the album, see 'New and Noteworthy', *Billboard*, 24 March 1990, p.68; and James Hunter, 'Recent Releases', *New York Times*, 24 June 1990.
18. Stan Hawkins, 'On Male Queering in Mainstream Pop', in Sheila Whiteley and Jennifer Rycenga (eds), *Queering the Popular Pitch* (London: Routledge, 2006), p.279.
19. Simon Reynolds, *Rip It Up and Start Again: Post-Punk 1978–1984* (London: Faber, 2005), pp.439–54.
20. Billy McKenzie as a point of comparison is shared by Barry McIlheney, who has seen Gray, both as a solo performer and with Perfect Crime, several times. McIlheney, interview.
21. Simon Frith, *Performing Rites: On the Value of Popular Music* (Oxford: Oxford University Press, 1996), p.215.
22. Ibid.
23. *Hot Press*, 10, 7 (1986) (italics added).
24. Richard Dyer, 'In Defence of Disco', in Richard Dyer, *Only Entertainment* (London: Routledge, 2002), pp.153–4; Frith, *Performing Rites*; John Gill, *Queer Noises: Male and Female Homosexuality in Twentieth-century Music* (London: Continuum, 1995); Hawkins, 'On Male Queering'; and Stan Hawkins, *The British Pop Dandy: Masculinity, Popular Music and Culture* (Farnham: Ashgate, 2009).
25. Ian Biddle, ' "The Singsong of Undead Labor": Gender Nostalgia and the Vocal Fantasy of Intimacy in the "New" Singer/Songwriter', in Freya Jarman-Ivens (ed.), *Oh Boy! Masculinities and Popular Music* (New York: Routledge, 2007), pp.125–44.
26. Stan Hawkins, 'The Pet Shop Boys: Musicology, Masculinity, and Banality', in Sheila Whiteley (ed.), *Sexing the Groove: Popular Music and Gender* (London: Routledge, 1997) pp.118–33.
27. Gray, interview.
28. Dyer, 'In Defence of Disco'.

29. Frith, *Performing Rites*.
30. Gray, interview.
31. Clark, 'Gregory Gray'.
32. Ibid.

11

Non-stop Ecstatic Irish Dancing: Rave and its Legacies

The idea of Irish dance music brings up images of *Riverdance* and Michael Flatley with his painted-on pants. Well, this is Irish dance music of a different sort. This is BASIC, signed to Bono and the Edge from U2's Kitchen Recordings and their first single 'Greenback'. We love this here at 'Brand New' . . . (Zane Lowe)[1]

[Music] . . . brings compensations for the miseries of everydayness, for its deficiencies and failures. (Henri Lefebvre)[2]

Puritan Ireland in both its Protestant and Catholic manifestations has a long history of seeking to regulate, even prohibit, dancing, owing to its perceived associations with sexual behaviour and bodily pleasures (a legacy that goes back to the early days of the show-band). In fact the idea of Irish dance music still conjures up the image of traditional Irish dancing, in a way perhaps unthinkable with English or British dance music – such is the residual connection between Irishness, music and ethnicity. As superficial evidence of this, an online search using the 'master signifier's' keywords 'Irish', or 'Ireland', and 'dance' – or indeed 'Celtic' and 'dance' – will produce reams of traditional and folk compilation albums, but little in the way of dance music in the modern sense of the term. Yet again, the framing of Irish musical activity within a predominantly primitivist and rural imaginary has negative consequences, as it is hard to square this strong pastoral tradition with the overwhelmingly urban paradigm of (post)modern metropolitan dance cultures. Indeed, if historically dancing across many cultures has functioned as a sexual metaphor and played a role in courtship rituals, then the highly idiosyncratic, recognizable and disciplined posture of the body in Church and state-sponsored traditional Irish dancing – a

stiff upright torso, held rigid above the upper thigh – may be interpreted as nervousness about overt sexual display. It is of little
surprise, then, that the state authorities in Ireland, in the North and
the South, were nervous about the powerful connection between
repetitive electronic music, recreational drugs and mass dancing in
the immediate aftermath of the tabloid-generated moral panics
about 'rave' across the water.

As with the advent of punk a decade earlier, the arrival of dance
music in Ireland was marked by a slight time delay. The emergence
of dance music in Britain, of 'acid house' and 'rave', is, of course,
famously date-stamped by the much-mythologized 'second summer
of love' of 1988–89. Ireland, however, had to wait at least two years
for a large 'tribal' dance scene to crystallize into a mass movement
in an equivalent fashion.[3]

Before the advent of dance music in the period of 1990–91,
Dublin was a city with a highly centralized and visible rock culture.
In the local and international imagination Dublin was known as a
'rock' city – one dominated by a rock-as-folk ideology – and this
influence had spread outwards to regional cities and towns.[4] A
cursory glance at the capital's nightlife at the time would have
revealed the dominance of the pub and the pub backroom, which
functioned as makeshift rock venues. The ubiquitous image of a
band of hopefuls earnestly thrashing out their own compositions to
a mixture of friends, locals and the (often imagined) resident troop
of record company A&R personnel was a recurrent one. Similarly a
stroll along the former warehouse districts on Dublin's quays and
the pre-regeneration Temple Bar area at the turn of the decade
would have been soundtracked by the myriad sounds emerging from
the many rehearsal rooms that peppered these areas. In fact it is
these images of practising and performing which dominate one of
the most internationally known perceptions of contemporary Irish
popular music at the time – Alan Parker's 1991 film *The
Commitments*.

Certainly prior to the early 1990s, clubbing was synonymous
with the tacky clubs of Leeson Street and was – in musical terms at
least – a fairly impoverished affair. Unlike rave, where the notion of
dance as a route to sexual coupling was displaced onto the euphoria
of the musico-pharmacological experience, these clubs functioned
with reference to traditional gender relations – which is to say, men
leering at the female bodies on the dance floor. In fact, rave, as a
number of commentators have observed offered a more 'friendly'

space for women, where there was less emphasis on the construction of the body in terms of sexual objectification.[5]

The first dance club in Dublin conceived along contemporary British and US lines was called Sides and was located close to the city's Temple Bar district. Sides had opened in the mid-1980s as one of the city's first openly gay clubs and its increasing support for the new dance genres at the turn of the decade echoed the links between dance culture and homosexuality which had been such a crucial aspect of its emergence a few years earlier on the club scenes of New York and Chicago.[6] Many of the DJs who went on to become stalwarts of the Dublin club circuit, such as Johnny Moy and Billy Scurry, began their careers at the venue.[7] As the 1990s progressed, the image of Dublin as a rock city became less straightforward as the advent of dance music led to the disintegration of the mythical 'city of a thousand bands'. In common with many other European capitals, Dublin went through a rapid metamorphosis as a dance city.

The same developments were occurring in Belfast with the emergence of a number of clubs and club nights that have entered into Northern Ireland's dance musical folklore. One of the first clubs was Circus Circus in Banbridge, associated with DJs who, like their southern counterparts, were to become fixtures of the Belfast scene, such as Mark 'Jacko' Jackson and Eamon Beagon, who went on to become regulars at The Network Club. Belfast's Art College at the University of Ulster, in particular, became a venue associated with a dedicated clubbing crowd and is most remembered for the various nights hosted by David Holmes.

On one level, this transition from rock, and an infrastructure of live music performance, to dance and the dominance of the club and the DJ is, on the surface, unremarkable. In subcultural terms at least, dance music was displacing rock culture right across Western Europe and Ireland was no exception. What is interesting, however, is the significance of this transition, and its implications in the Irish context.

Leaving aside folk and 'traditional' music, Irish popular music, as we have seen, has become synonymous with rock (and a 'rock-as-folk' ideology) in the international imagination.[8] Indeed, rock music played a pivotal role in making Ireland visible in the global popular musical arena. As the 1980s progressed, highly successful artists came to figure prominently in both foreign and domestic perceptions of modern Irishness. As we have argued, the musical discourses that followed articulated and consolidated the notion of the Irish as an inherently musical 'race' and the notion that Irish identity is a 'natural', organic category. They have also associated Irishness with a familiar set of images, which include the pastoral, the spiritual, the pre-modern, the mystical, the Celtic and so forth. It is increasingly common to find a range of Irish rock artists from Horslips to U2 validated for the maintenance and/or modernization of these images. Of course, what Slavoj Žižek has termed the 'Nation-Thing' – one's libidinal and affective pleasures in the national, and especially national characterization and the stereotypes that attach themselves to such discourses – is one of the principal ways in which popular music is engaged with by consumers (whether they be fans, industry personnel, or scholars).

We can glimpse how deep-seated is the concept of natural, organic Irishness in the popular comedy series 'Father Ted', set on the fictitious Craggy Island off Ireland's 'mythical' western seaboard (the area of the nation regarded in nationalist discourse as the most authentically Irish). In the episode 'Think Fast, Father Ted' (broadcast in 1996) from the second series, the eponymous central character organizes some entertainment in the local village hall, ostensibly to raise money for repairs on the parish house. At one point in the proceedings he announces to the assembled throng that a few priest friends are going to perform a 'few tunes'. The manner of the introduction and the rural west of Ireland setting, as well as the dominant discourses of authentic Irishness, all conspire to suggest a performance in the folk or traditional mode. What the audience is treated to instead is a pastiche of early Kraftwerk, the famous pioneering electronic quartet from Dusseldorf, widely acknowledged in the many histories of dance music as a seminal influence on the form. The humour here resides in reversing the usual expressive repertoire of essential Irishness, and subverting its clichéd musical and performance markers – folk instrumentation, traditional songs, the past, the organic, the 'expressive' and the 'emotive' – to a cold electronic soundscape, with vocoded vocals in German and minimalist 'robotic' rhythms, and connotations of modernity, the synthetic and 'the future'. It may seem like a simple set of reversals, but this is progressive comedy. 'Father Ted' is attempting here to overturn stereotypes and expose the myth of folk authenticity and essential Irishness and upset the attendant critique of modern industrial society. It is also a tacit acknowledgement of the increased centrality of dance and electronic musics to both urban and rural Irish experience, which has been peripheralized in representations of Irish music culture across a range of media forms. The implicit 'in-joke' offered in this sketch is that the image of 'Oirishness' it seeks to undermine requires a certain stage-management; that it does not correspond to the many ways of performing and experiencing music in even peripheral west of Ireland settings.

Nonetheless, as we have seen, rock has also been important in Ireland due to the mobilization of ideologies of authenticity borrowed and carried forward from folk and traditional musics. Indeed, so intimately connected are Irishness and authenticity, we might say that authenticity functions for all intents and purposes as Irish rock culture's 'realism' (and in a sense standing in for the relative absence of a social realist tradition in film and television). The rock singer, as Jeremy Gilbert and Ewan Pearson have put it, must purvey 'the truth' and represent faithfully the values of 'community'.[10] Great emphasis is placed on the voice and lyrics – the importance in rock of what the song is taken to mean – but also on the type of instrumentation used. For example, synthesizers, samplers and computer-generated sounds have traditionally been regarded with greater or lesser degrees of suspicion in Irish musical discourse when compared to the 'expressive' instruments which comprise the classic rock format – guitar, bass and drums – or indeed with 'proper' folk instruments – such as the bodhran, fiddle, harp, pipes or flute. (And, as we have seen, things start to get complicated when synthesizers and samplers are utilized to convey a sense of the pre-modern or Celtic, as Clannad's *Magical Ring* album or U2's *Unforgettable Fire* illustrate, in their different ways.)

Music, therefore, actively signifies and represents dominant or preferred versions of Irishness, both at home and abroad. For instance, the 'mass rallies' of U2's Irish concerts in the 1980s articulated/represented the audiences' collective faith in the band and what they 'stood for'. Dance music 'represents' in different ways from classic rock and pop, however, and therefore needs to be interpreted differently. The absence of the singer as central focus, for example – indeed the assault upon traditional notions of 'the song' mounted by house and techno (just to mention two of the most influential subgenres) – presents major difficulties for conventional forms of interpretation. Its recalcitrance with regard to orthodox signifying and analytical discourses – the frequent absence of lyrics and lyrical meaning – has often led to dance music and dance culture being condemned as politically quietist, or indeed reactionary; its users imagined as Deleuzean bodies caught in the repetition of loops, mere 'desiring machines' on the road to who knows where. Thus, as Zuberi succinctly puts it, dance music 'says little in terms of language' and often 'doesn't necessarily say anything at all'.[11] But this nihilistic refusal of apparent sense-making and conventional representational politics may be regarded as positive in so far as it constitutes a potentially radical dissolution of essential Irishness and a possible end to the idea that music does, or should, somehow, represent, emanate from, or *belong to* a place. In this respect, the effects of rave, and the incursion of dance musics more broadly, were as profound as punk in witnessing a 'clearing of the decks'. What dance culture from rave onwards did was to sever the connection between Irishness, rock and folk and reconfigured the shape of musical production and consumption on the island. Dance culture, in other words, created new musical spaces such as the outdoor rave – the urban and rural 'superclubs' – but it also radically transformed existing rock performance spaces.

As we have argued earlier a key element in the range of stereotypes characteristically assigned to Ireland and the Irish has been their natural proclivity for music and songs.[12] The concept of Irish music both assumes and promotes an essential connection between music, people and place. The emergence of dance as a recognizable 'scene', subculture or tribal phenomenon in postmodern Ireland threatened this connection by contributing to the de-territorialization of contemporary culture, and with it displacing the discourse of the national in favour of opening up a whole series of transnational connections. Irish dance producers, DJs and clubbers were involved in the forging of a myriad of micro transnational musical routes: German artists remixed by Irish producers, Irish clubbers taking a weekend in Prague, Irish artists finding audiences in South American markets and so on. Irish dance music has not been recognizable by its Irish aspect. Successful dance acts have, in the main, tended to avoid foregrounding ethnicity, nationality or national identity. For example, the mid-to-late-1990s dance artists, The Dirty Beatniks (formerly Rootless) and Ceasefire (aka Derek Dahlarge), both signed to the 'uber-cool' London-based Wall of Sound label, hailed from Ireland, but neither musically nor in interview have they alluded to the fact. This may be, in part at least, because the dominant musical tropes of Irishness would have sat ill in the midst of drum samples, bass-lines and vocal snatches gleaned from 1960s and 1970s funk records that formed the mainstay of these artists' sounds. The images of the American inner city offered in these spliced-up and re-contextualized loops cut sharply against the dominant paradigm of Irish imagery. Ireland's two internationally known 'superstar' DJs – David Holmes and Robert 'Fergie' Ferguson – have drawn upon an eclectic repertoire of sounds and styles, few of which have any clear associations with Ireland/Northern Ireland. David Holmes, an artist with several commercially and critically successful albums to his name, including the Hollywood soundtracks for Stephen Soderbergh's *Out of Sight* (1998) *Ocean's Eleven* (2001) *Ocean's Twelve* (2004) and *Ocean's Thirteen* (2007) as well as Steve McQueen's *Hunger* (2008) amongst others, has engaged with the diverse range of genres and subgenres that have comprised the phenomenon of international dance music. Like his contemporaries in the international dance arena, Holmes possesses a good ear as a producer/bricoleur, weaving often-obscure 1960s soul samples into contemporary dance anthems. His hit club single 'My Mate Paul' appropriated the rhythm track of The Googie Rene Combo's 1966 obscurity, 'Smokey Jo's La La', and he also covered Les McCann's 'underground' and rare 1960s funk track, 'Compared To What?' on 2000's *Bow Down to the Exit Sign*.[13] Holmes has also developed his musical oeuvre as a bandleader of sorts on his *David Holmes Presents The Free Association* album (2003) and has even taken up the role of lead vocalist on the Kraut-rock inspired *The Holy Pictures* (2008). What is critically significant here is that Irishness is, in a sense, beside the point. Worse, it offers a potentially unusable, even reactionary, set of signifiers and associations – rock and folk song modes, the 'emotive' singer-songwriter, rural connotations, drinking and the traditional pub as well as the Celtic and the primordial – against which a modern, urban, multi-ethnic and futuristic (and exciting) dance culture may be measured. In one vital respect, despite belonging to different historical periods and seemingly inhabiting different musical cultures with contrasting approaches to production and composition, Holmes and Van Morrison share one important aspect: record capital (an enthusiasm and respect for records and the expressive musical repertoire they offer) – Morrison through his father's collection and Holmes via his own (although the latter has yet to explicitly weave recognizably Irish idioms into his hybrids in the way that Morrison has done with his brand of Celtic and Caledonian Soul).

For the dance music devotee, then, what is at issue is whether a particular set of sounds, styles and their related mythologies and meanings are 'cool' (or not); whether they, in that elusive term, 'work'. The dominant signifiers of Irishness do not graft onto the current trends of dance culture easily or particularly well. Dance music reconfigured the dialectic between place and placelessness, and did so in two ways. First, it discouraged the re-inscription of recognizably ethnic markers of Irishness and second, it offered sounds, pleasures and a type of politics that presented a challenge to the peculiar hegemony of rock and the intimate intertwining of rock and national authenticity. The 'difficulty' perhaps, from the perspective of the Irish dance music producer, was how to integrate and mobilize locally or nationally specific musical or cultural elements (or whether, indeed, it was even desirable to do so) that could be regarded as distinctive, or attractive, in the international marketplace (in the way that rock had done before it).

One (perhaps predictable) way out of this 'problem' has been addressed in the fusion of folk and traditional sounds with electronic dance rhythms, whether house, techno, drum 'n' bass or breakbeat. There are numerous examples of this type of hybridization: from the simple addition of samples of traditional sounds to existing dance styles genres, through to more 'serious' attempts to bring traditional rhythms, timings and melodies into complex syntheses with intricate drum 'n' bass patterns. The Afro Celt Sound System have fashioned a career based on the latter type of fusion, as well as combining traditional African and Irish sounds with other modern dance genres. The collective, built around British musician/producer Simon Emmerson, was signed to Peter Gabriel's world music label, Real World, releasing their first album, *Sound Magic Vol. 1* in 1996. 'Sure-As-Knot' from *Sound Magic* is a good example of this process. The track begins in a down-tempo or trip-hop style but, unusually, adds harp and melodic acoustic guitar to the form. As such, it manages to sound idiomatically Irish and yet modern. The latter half of the track 'doubles up' in timing into a drum 'n' bass rhythm, becoming increasingly complex in its interweaving of recognizably Irish melodies and timbres. The Afro Celts might be best described as a traditional group of floating transnational members of Irish, French and African origin, deploying a contemporary dance undercarriage with traditional Irish and African instruments and techniques. Or, as the music critic Tim Sheridan put it, 'the outcome is a sort of hip-hop jig and reel, like the Chieftains meet the Chemical Brothers'.[14] Indeed the nomenclature, 'sound system', invokes the world of Jamaican dub and reggae, the customizing of speaker systems and the creative use of the studio associated with that culture. However, despite the extensive range of dance styles and African and Irish instruments, and the creative synthesis it represents, the Afro Celts arguably create 'dance' music designed to be 'listened to'. Indeed, it is significant that the remixes the collective has released for the more visceral pleasures of the dance floor have been much more conventional and generic – conforming to the more orthodox blueprints of techno or house – and overt African and Irish rhythms, drones and melodies are downplayed.

Another area where traditional notions of Irishness and the Celtic have figured more prominently in dance culture broadly is in the area of so-called 'chill-out' music; a genre formed in the wake of Alex Patterson's Eno-inspired ambient night, 'The Chill-Out Room' at London's Land of Oz club.[15] As Zuberi has noted, the chill-out room permitted the playing of the types of sounds and styles frequently despised, or simply overlooked, in masculinist rock cultures – such as easy-listening artists Dean Martin and Tony Bennett, Hollywood and Bollywood soundtracks, the Hollywood musical, big-band swing, bossa nova and so forth. The range of musics so labelled owed something to the development of smaller back rooms in dance clubs/events where overheated dancers, or those on a pharmaceutical 'come-down', could relax away from the intensity of the main arena (the 'legendary' Cafe Del Mar in Ibiza and the range of compilations sporting its name is perhaps the most famous example of both the space and the format). Nevertheless, despite this extension of musical styles that dance culture helped to foster, the Celtic chill-out sub-genre did not penetrate the world of 'hip' clubbing terribly deeply (as an intensive trawl through the many 'trendy' down-tempo compilations would reveal). Rather, the meeting of the Celtic and modern down-tempo grooves became more firmly associated with ambient 'mood' music, a genre that was linked more to the world of polite and 'bourgeois' 'New Age' therapies and hence closer in style to Enya than to an 'oppositional' dance culture. But it is significant that once again Irishness is associated with relaxation and attached to tropes of exoticism and the fantasy of escape from urban industrial modernity. In this sense, music appears to work in support with broader, and more 'mainstream', tourist discourses constructing Ireland as a haven 'away from it all'.

As the case of Afro Celt Sound System and the 'laidback' Celtic sounds compilations demonstrates, a recognizable Irishness can be found in the interface of dance and world music. This is an area where dance music 'from' Ireland may differ from its British/English counterpart, for which country there are no recognizable 'ethnic' sounds conventions. However, this type of practice once again often risks accusations of exoticism, and the related problem of ghettoization, via the association of Irishness with the ethnic pre-modern. The opposite argument to this regards world music and world/dance fusions as preserving valuable musical forms by giving them new life – an 'organic' alternative to the packaged tastes of the dominant Anglo-American and western European nations. This is a complex debate and neither side has absolute purchase. What is apparent, however, is that despite the rhetoric of preservation involved in these debates, 'Irish-marked' or conspicuously 'ethnic' dance musics were not widely popular on Irish dance floors and the desire to retain or rearticulate a sense of Irishness in either its narrow or relaxed definitions is not something that occupied the majority of clubbers or producers in any part of the island. Even the major-label compilation *The Soundz of the Irish Underground* (1998) had no conventionally recognizable Irish sounds, in the notional and generally accepted sense of the term. In an entertaining and somewhat caustic article, John Hutnyk surveys the culture of the WOMAD festival and points to the politically problematic (and at times downright embarrassing) interface of 'cosmopolitan' dancers in search of a good time, whether hedonistic or vaguely 'spiritual', and the practices and belief systems of the performers present (such as dancing semi-naked and inappropriately in front of devotional singers, for example) and thus reducing the often complex traditions and practices to one 'big trip'. What Hutnyk exposes is the flattening out of discrete cultures, identities and ideologies, collapsing them into the desire for exotic experience with the musics of the 'world' reduced to an à la carte menu.[16]

Away from the world of rave and clubbing, rap and hip hop in Ireland did achieve a more successful synthesis of the 'traditional' and the 'modern'. As we have seen, this area achieved more high-profile success in the form of international visibility (as occasional tracks by Sinéad O'Connor and House of Pain illustrate). Less commercially successful artists such as Scary Eire, and former MC, Ri-Ra, Marxman and Creative Controle, made ample use of this type of hybridization, and significantly sidestepped the association with exoticism referred to earlier. This is in large part due to the agit-prop politics (and these artists' frequent articulation of Republican and explicitly anti-imperialist positions) and the more lyric-centred and confrontational performance practices associated with the form;

an Irish version of the Black Nationalist and hyper-masculine politics apparent in much of American rap. (In fact Marxman's 1993 single, 'Sad Affair', criticized the presence of British troops in Northern Ireland and, as a result, was banned by the BBC.[17]) As we have seen in the discussion of aspects of Sinéad O'Connor's work, the attempted solidarity between black and Irish idioms introduces complex questions about representation, aesthetics and politics. Interestingly, however, given rap's focus on poetic wordplay, many Irish hip hop MCs cite Irish poets and novelists as inspiration and many Irish towns possess strong hip hop and break-dancing scenes.

On a purely auditory level, there might not be any essential connection between a dance sound and a place, given that the origins of many sounds are machine/computer based and/or reconfigured via sampling. Yet such connections are routinely being remade, although in non-essentialist terms. As a matter of course, the rhetoric of place is used extensively in the dance music lexicon. Many emergent forms of dance music have been explicitly articulated to discourses about cities and nations, so in addition to Chicago and Detroit techno there are variations in German techno as well as 'the Bristol sound' (trip hop) of the late 1980s to mid-1990s, UK Garage (and most recently UK Grime), but also west London's broken beat and so forth. Claims have also been made for the specificity of French/Paris house and the minimalism of Berlin's techno variants, with both cities possessing not only distinctive styles but a roster of canonical dance producers/DJs and labels (Laurent Garnier, Dimitri from Paris, DJ Cam, Motorbass, La Funk Mob and Jazzanova and labels such as Yellow, Sonar Kollectiv and Tresor). Likewise, the elements that came together to form drum 'n' bass were particular to Britain – often, indeed, to specific parts of Britain. It is also evident in the number of Ibiza dance compilations, UK House collections or the placing of albums 'from' particular cities (such as Kruder and Dorfmeister's Vienna), or the *Sounds of* various cities/nations' *Underground* compilations (with *The Soundz of the Irish Underground*, unsurprisingly, a late offering in the series). Therefore, despite widespread claims that dance is the world's first truly international and 'placeless' popular music, it is clear that the music in fact trails (albeit in a modified form) the spatial discourses which emerged in relation to older rock and folk dispensations. These discourses are always attempting to drag the music back to specific national and/or metropolitan locations. And as with economic capital, some of these locations are more powerfully disposed to exploit, promote and develop their dance music, subcultural capital and related mythologies.

A further point emerges here. The cases of Paris and Berlin are of great significance to the discussion as throughout the period of Anglo-American rock's hegemony these nations – France and Germany – were regarded as 'rock and popular musical jokes' in the Anglo-American firmament. In a sense, the relative 'wordlessness' of dance music offered a challenge to the dominance of rock and the English language, allowing many nations less successful in popular music (even those that were politically and economically powerful) to become key figures in musical terms, contributing vital and exciting sounds and styles to the broader musical traffic of the global arena.

FIGHT (OR FLIGHT) FOR YOUR RIGHT TO . . . PARTY

Zuberi has argued that the increased regulation of dance culture in the rave aftermath, manifest in the British state's desire to control illegal parties, has resulted in dance and clubbing becoming a major part of the accepted fabric of city regeneration and a vital area of city identity and leisure tourism.[18] In this sense, Belfast (especially in the post-ceasefire period), Dublin and Cork were to become destinations for international clubbers taking advantage of the rise in budget air travel and so-called city breaks. In fact, the role of relatively cheap flights cannot be underestimated in underpinning dance's transnational connections as it became conventional wisdom for many clubbers that travel from one European city to another was no less expensive (and often cheaper) than, say, intercity travel within the United Kingdom. While dance music produced in Ireland may not have been distinctive – after all, the island has not bequeathed a specific genre, nor become associated with one, in the history of the form in the manner just described – but the dance floors themselves evidently held promise for both local and visiting participants. Thus, like other major cities, Dublin, Belfast and Cork could offer a variety of visiting internationally known 'name' DJs working alongside local producers. These scenes arguably became increasingly rich and diverse as the 1990s progressed and as the influence of 'rave' and acid house waned, with the initial homogeneity of musical style fragmenting into a series of ever-proliferating sub-genres and drawing upon a range of globally (and historically) dispersed musical styles. Whether this break-up of dance as an imagined oppositional, 'tribal' culture into a more diversified field is a good or a bad thing is a moot point. However, it certainly introduced the notional listener/dancer to a huge range of musics, both contemporary and historical, that would have been concealed if the rock and pop hegemony had held sway. Moreover, dance music, in the broad sense of the term, also filtered into daytime, non-club locations: into coffee shops and bars, with the DJ becoming a presence in many pubs as well. Indeed, part of hidden history of Irish clubbing is the transformation of the traditional pub into a club venue in rural locations, some of which could boast visiting celebrity DJs, offering images at least as incongruous as the 'Father Ted' example referred to earlier (such as jungle/drum 'n' bass luminary Goldie's DJ set in the Anchor Bar in the small coastal town of Portstewart). This is to say that dance music permeated the entire leisure fabric of towns and cities and its history is in no sense quarantined to dancing and to club spaces.

PRODUCTION AND POLITICS

We wanna' be free. We wanna' get loaded and have a good time. (Primal Scream)[19]

In Northern Ireland, Ecstasy encouraged fraternization across Catholic–Protestant lines, at least at non-sectarian raves and clubs; this may be one reason why the paramilitaries (who control the drug trade) have been cracking down on dealers. Generally speaking, Ecstasy seems to promote tolerance. (Simon Reynolds)[20]

During the 1990s, Ireland, as with every other developed nation, benefitted from the increasing affordability of the means of musical production and access to the transnational musical networks via the Web and saw a concomitant rise in the petit-bourgeois entrepreneurialism that was a feature of punk before it. Ireland became a culture characterized by a plethora of 'invisible' bedroom recording studios operating programmes such as Cubase and Cakewalk and cheap or 'cracked' plug-ins and so-called 'soft-synths' (which, unlike the 'hard' synthesizers on which they were based, were not prohibitively expensive). These home studios can produce a finished recording in a variety of formats to a highly professional standard, allowing producers to promote and sell (or even give away) their work on a 'press-as-required' basis. This type of practice has been extended through the development of peer-to-peer websites such as MySpace, YouTube and FaceBook. While potentially radical in its consequences, a note of caution is warranted. Economic power still resided overwhelmingly with the record industry and its existing patterns of promotion and distribution, and as many commentators have observed, the record companies adapted relatively quickly to dance music's modes of promotion and dissemination.[21]

Alas, a great deal of home-produced dance music formed a part of the huge bulk of music that failed to find an audience outside the producers, their friends and immediate social milieu. However, dance culture juggled the twin poles of 'selling out' and 'making it' in a different fashion to rock. Many dance 'subcultures' actively courted, and were based on, ideologies of exclusivity, fetishizing the rarity of their recorded work (as the vogue for the 'white label' twelve-inch single attests). Much work, while produced with broader 'mainstream' genres in mind, may have largely bypassed the commodity circuits of record capitalism entirely. In this sense, dance culture took the do-it-yourself ethos of punk and managed to sustain it for a longer period. Moreover, dance broke with the desire to achieve success in traditional media and was often more focused on making and sustaining these types of micro transnational connections. Once again, dance in Ireland's hidden history is littered with figures who may have not achieved popular renown, but nonetheless made a sometimes lucrative living DJ-ing in clubs both at home and abroad, and/or licensing tracks to compilations on small labels; or just playing their own unreleased tracks in clubs or house parties (in the conventional, 'old-fashioned', sense of the term).

This lower cost of production enabled some of Ireland's clubs to form record label offshoots. Unlike punk, which revelled in the demystification of the production process, dance revelled in the banal availability of the means of musical production. In addition to David Holmes, a DJ such as Phil Keiran (one-time resident at Belfast super-club Shine) was able to record not only for his own club's label, but also to sign to and record and remix for Skint Records in Brighton, owned by one of the world's most famous DJ/producers, Norman Cook, aka Fatboy Slim (who himself illustrated that dance production, with its apparent anonymity, permitted the releasing of records under a variety of aliases). Likewise, Dublin had a thriving (if small) dance-related industry, with labels such as Baby Doll, Psychonavigation and D1 producing music in a wide variety of genres to cater for the many different (and often antagonistic) tastes which comprised the city's dance music audience.

Even Bono and the Edge from U2 got into the act. Following on from their enthusiasm for aspects of dance culture in the early 1990s, and the opening of their Kitchen Nightclub in 1994, they extended their dance franchise with the label Kitchen Recordings in 1997–98. The Kitchen Club was an interesting space. Located in the basement of their Clarence Hotel, the club's architecture was based on the Mos Eisley Cantina – the little bar full of aliens and freaks – in the first *Star Wars* film and was a relatively small and intimate venue (and, as such, an interesting meeting of the 'local Dublin' and the 'cinematic global'). As the head of Kitchen Recordings, Reggie Manuel (a school friend of the band and one-time member of Lypton Village) recalls:

> The Kitchen nightclub had its heyday in the mid-1990s with full to the brim nights of sweaty happy punters. It was clear that the international DJs were keeping the club full, but young Irish DJs and music producers were doing it too. Francois, Podge, Greg O'Hanlon and Rob Rowland were some of the Irish acts that could draw big crowds and yet had no significant outlet for their music internationally. A step-up to a bigger stage for these artists through a record label using the club name and Bono and Edge's involvement seemed like a plan that could work.[22]

Kitchen's main signing was the electronic duo BASIC, whose 'Greenback/Flashcars' became the label's second twelve-inch release in July 1999. This track also benefitted from the lower cost of the means of production in video and had an accompanying experimental promo that secured the track a place on the requisite slots on MTV (including the prime-time 'Brand New'), Sky and RTÉ.

BASIC were somewhat unusual in the Irish context for a number of reasons. They began their career playing dance music 'live' with a mix of cheap, second-hand keyboards, samplers and tape-machines (something of a lo-fi version of English electronic duos Orbital and The Chemical Brothers) to audiences in Belfast and Dublin. Playing live was, in part, a reaction to the prohibitive cost of vinyl and a way around the competition for DJ slots. They also performed their own compositions in a set-up as mobile as any DJ. Like other acts discussed, BASIC offered no recognizably Irish signifiers. However, this did not prevent local music press reportage in looking to map their sound and performance to more explicitly political meanings

and returns us to the issue of dance music's recalcitrance to orthodox interpretative strategies. BASIC's Eamonn Creen is a classically
trained flautist and the concert flute was frequently deployed in early
performances. This prompted one reviewer for *Hot Press* to write:

> Live there's some startling symbolism going on as Eamonn whips out
> a flute, the national instrument of Northern Ireland, generally associ-
> ated with sectarian tradition. But in the BASIC scheme of things, the
> instrument's tones are chopped and recycled, making for a glorious
> reconstitution. The mission to reroute the flute has been accom-
> plished, even if many observers haven't been sure how to deal with the
> in-concert experience.[23]

What is interesting here is the attempt to find political 'meaning'
(somewhere) *in* the performance against its absence, to draw upon
older modes of interpretation and force some kind of fit between
aesthetics and meaning that is difficult to sustain. Of course, this –
and the elision of the *marching* flute with the *concert* flute – understandably irritated the duo, with the result that the instrument was
never deployed in live performance subsequently. As Creen put it in
interview: 'I spent my teens in cross-community youth orchestras, so
the thought of being painted, even in one article, as some kind of
posturing, classically trained Dave Spart figure was too trite to live
down.'[24]

Rather, against this blatant attempt to recruit them to a type of
agitprop more appropriate to Northern Irish punk in the late-1970s,
BASIC were interesting for altogether different reasons. The duo
forged together an eclectic range of styles: from hip hop and funk, to
left-field house and drum 'n' bass. They also played with – and
twisted to their purposes – Bollywood soundtracks, Bhangra
rhythms and other sounds associated with the so-called Asian underground in Britain.[25] The rampant and playful fusion offered by the
work of Bradford's Black Star Liner was a particular influence and
one that was comparatively rare in the Irish context (and indeed
BASIC supported the Bradford collective on their Irish dates in
1998).

While BASIC's sound was in no sense uniquely Irish, one could
argue that the meeting of the disparate sounds and styles they yoked
together was specific to its production location. It may trawl up
accusations of orientalism and exoticism, but for BASIC these may
have been points of symbolic solidarity and hence driven by a
respectful, yet playful, homage. In one sense, perhaps tacitly, BASIC

could identify with the not dissimilar difficulties that many British-Asian dance producers felt in attempting to fashion an attractive image/mythology beyond the stereotypes of Asian deference, of quiet 'hard work', of Asians as passive and middle class (identities at some distance from the type of militant and earthy proletarianism of 'outlaw' black masculinity that has been a source of fascination and symbolic solidarity for some areas of white dance and hip hop Bohemia). Indeed it is worth noting here that British-Asian dance producers were much more successful than their Irish counterparts in adapting the rubric of musical ethnicity, of 'sounding' and 'looking' Asian, of hybridizing Asian sounds and rhythms with dance styles in ways that could frequently circumvent exoticist positions. In other words, while creative synthesis and borrowing was routine in Irish dance music production, the actual forms mixed in BASIC's case were not. In fact, the duo also pre-empted the later sub-genre known as 'punk-funk' (with their track, 'P-DAT-MOTE'), which, as the name implies, mixed the aggression of punk with dance beats, and was a sign that dance producers in Ireland were not always doomed to lag behind trends (even if these producers rarely found themselves in the few opportune spaces for this to be widely acknowledged).

Even though BASIC displayed that do-it-yourself electronics could compete with the DJ and attract the attention, and support, of two members of Ireland's premier rock super-group, the association with U2 was, predictably enough, to have ambiguous consequences. On the one hand, it precipitated a certain subcultural 'kiss-of-death' through being connected with the wider world of alleged corporate rock, and with it a certain amount of local jealousy (an echo, ironically, of what U2 themselves experienced at points in their early career). Despite the involvement of left-field DJ/producer Howie B in the label, BASIC's connection with Kitchen frequently offended a dance cultural sensibility based on elitism, exclusivity and the imagined authenticity of the underground. On the other hand, the attachment to the label brought the duo some attention from outside of Ireland, some of it from U2's existing fan base, evidently curious about the Kitchen Club and the new label and thus bringing a range of sounds perhaps unfamiliar to that audience. Whichever way, this contradictory inclusivity/exclusivity dialectic was routine in dance music production and evaluation.

Ultimately the gradual de-centring of dance and the general decline of records sales (but particularly dance sales) in the wake of downloading as the noughties progressed was accompanied by the closure of many clubs, club nights, labels, magazines and dance festivals. The Kitchen label folded in 2001, followed by the closure of the Kitchen Club in May 2002. Many reports of the time document the reconfiguration of the Dublin's after-hours leisure economy. The label had to abandon its release schedule, leaving behind a number of planned twelve-inch singles and an unreleased BASIC album. As the label boss has described it:

> The more we moved slowly forward, the more things changed and the more I saw difficulty in making a return on investments. Evidently not a problem for the multimillionaire rock stars – actually they wanted to keep going – but I just saw their money going up in smoke. I look back on it – the amazing dance music and creativity – but regret raising hopes in young talented musicians.[26]

Despite the Kitchen label's desire to stand on its own economic feet, and to rely on the quality of its signings, and only draw upon the (albeit ambivalent) cultural capital of its owners, this (with the luxury afforded by hindsight) was clearly insufficient. A number of political-economic, cultural and aesthetic forces were accruing that would dethrone dance music in time.

FIGHT FOR YOUR RIGHT TO PARTY:
THE 'TROUBLE(S)' WITH DANCE MUSIC

An important addition to the master narrative of dance music that prevents 'rave' in Northern Ireland from being nothing more than a pale echo of the more extensive and elaborate culture that existed in Britain is the province's relationship to 'the Troubles' and an endemic culture of sectarian strife. A number of writers have already comprehensively covered the way in which Britain's dance culture articulated a certain kind of anti-Thatcherite politics, with the development of the free-party movement and its challenge to public order legislation.[27] Dance culture in the United Kingdom became politicized when forced to fight for its survival in the wake of 1994's Criminal Justice and Public Order Act which gave the police power to close any event where 'noise' – principally 'repetitive beats' – disturbed residents. It also included sections specific to 'public trespass' targeted at ravers, but also severely curtailed the right to free assembly. Indeed this area had its Irish and Northern Irish equivalents. Northern Ireland was well accustomed to draconian public legislation and, of course, The Prevention of Terrorism Act was highly adaptable to curtailing 'mass' gatherings that the state was nervous of.

Not only was dance music's arrival in Ireland marked by a time delay but it seems, in the North in particular, that the type of tabloid invective against the evils of Ecstasy and the culture surrounding it was similarly marked. Brian Hollywood has argued that the paramilitary ceasefires of mid-to-late 1994 had the odd effect of compelling the state and Northern Ireland media to find 'a new adversary'. Thus, the war on drugs and rave was to replace *the* war, with the 'evils' of Ecstasy and rave culture filling the void left after years of routinized media reportage of the armed conflict.[28] Indeed, this anti-rave discourse was to make the scene more attractive to younger people, conveying a sense of excitement, danger and outsidership that have been a feature of many subcultures before it. It was also another opportunity to say 'fuck the Troubles, let's dance' on a larger scale.

Not since punk had a scene or subculture (in Hebdige's sense of the term, with its connotations of refusal, resistance and opposition) impacted on the Northern Irish body politic so forcibly. Many clubbers in the North were seemingly united in their hostility to a Unionist regime that was widely regarded as 'anti-fun'. Two broad perspectives framed public discussion in the North. First, following the Ecstasy death of teenager Leah Betts in 1995, a specific spin on the discourse of the evils of drugs emerged, followed by a tabloid-led moral panic. Second, in addition to these well-documented fears about the drug itself, in the context of Northern Ireland a great deal of commentary centred on the control of the drug trade by paramilitaries on either side of the sectarian divide. At one level this was an attempt to undermine the very real pleasures offered by rave and dance culture, a way of delegitimating its opening up of non-sectarian spaces, through the creation of a very Northern Ireland-specific 'folk-devil' – the paramilitary drug baron. Thus, in addition to the endemic discourse about the dangers of drugs, the suggestion that sales of 'E' were financing paramilitary activity cut sharply against the 'loved-up' lived experience and ideology inhabited by many participants. The schism between the apparent political economy of drug culture and the semiotics of that culture was one that was foregrounded on occasion in the Northern Irish press, constructing dance culture as one shot through by a fundamental hypocrisy.

The contrasting narrative (and one, predictably enough, less told in mainstream media) was the more utopian story that rave's chemical euphoria was not only challenging the hegemony of rock but actively breaking down the entrenched sectarian tribalism of Northern Irish society. Many clubbers in the province have their tales of seeing known paramilitaries from opposing sides of the sectarian divide hugging on the dance floor, or glimpsing the image of a painted rainbow and/or a smiley insignia on the 'You are now entering Free Derry' mural at the entrance to the city's Bogside. Of course, these may be the urban myths common to any subcultural Bohemia, but they provide both a sense of the optimism that dance culture generated, however fleetingly. They also signal the types of bravado, hyperbole and myth-making that have been a feature of rave culture and discourse (with its macho and competitive tales of heroic drug consumption – the 'chemical pornography' – and the detailed recounting of the duration of one's exploits). In fact, the notion that the combined pleasures of Ecstasy, music and dancing were a 'cure' for sectarian hatred controversially entered (albeit as a footnote) the master narrative of dance music when the dance correspondent at the *NME*, Jack Barron, claimed that the drug could bring to an end the seemingly intractable paramilitary feuding.[29] Indeed, however naive, the spirit of Barron's comments was common among many Northern Irish clubbers. Perhaps more significantly this nexus of drugs and war may even be Ireland's only mention in the story of urban dance music. In this sense, rave and dance reignited many of the myths of outlaw masculinity that have been a feature of rock culture. Dance culture seemed to provide, a decade after punk, the second great flourishing of utopian cross-community solidarity to emerge from a youth subculture which had set its face against the sectarianism of the parent culture.

Dance culture, however, was largely devoid of the political sloganeering of punk and it was thus able to sidestep many of the moral pieties and the lack of lyrical insight that marked Irish rock's engagement with Northern Irish politics – from Stiff Little Fingers' 'Alternative Ulster' to The Cranberries' 'Zombie' (arguably more conservative than British media representations of the Troubles at their height).[30] Thus a non-verbal, non-representational musical form could be appealing, given rock's seeming inability to construct a position on the Troubles terribly different from mainstream media. It was not altogether surprising that the relatively 'blank' semiotic of dance might be appealing in a culture where political symbolism and representational forms had assumed such force. Indeed, it is one of the ironies of dance culture that a seemingly apolitical hedonism could be mapped to political opposition. Certainly when compared to Northern Irish rock in the 1980s, dance 'meant' more in terms of the change it effected (even if, unlike rock, it wasn't ostensibly concerned with 'meaning' or 'message' or political engagement). At the same time, this radical potential, even when interpreted with the utmost optimism, does not have the weight (either material or discursive) to greatly challenge the entrenched political structures of a deeply divided body politic and one could ask if it is appropriate to burden dance culture with such an expectation. Escaping into the trance offered by dance music, of 'getting out of it', is a type of interiorized politics that has no necessary connection to concrete political change. As Jeremy Gilbert and Ewan Pearson put it:

> What if the ecstasy, the liberatory jouissance to which rave grants us access, is nothing but an empty space from which no political position as such can possibly be articulated? Ecstatic dancing...can be a tremendously liberating experience. Liberation is not the same thing as transformation, however. Escape – especially if only temporary – is not the same thing as political change...when we get back from the party, have we left all those structures as intact as they were before.[31]

As David Holmes put it in interview in the BBC Northern Ireland television profile *Gritty Shaker*: 'there are people at my club from Poleglass [nationalist housing estate in west Belfast] dancing alongside people from Rathcoole [loyalist estate on the north-eastern fringe of the city] and they don't give a stuff about all that crap we have to deal with'. One might suggest, in order to counter the optimism of Holmes's interpretation, that any manifest sectarianism was 'checked in', as it were, at the cloakroom like a holdall on entrance to the club and collected again on the way out.

While dance music and the experience of club culture offers no guarantee on how people will behave once the party is over, it has been pressed into service as a harbinger of non-sectarian spaces and in offering an alternative imaginary – and again, dance's similarity to punk in this regard should be noted. And evidently, a loved-up, pharmaceutically driven culture, with real or imagined strangers embracing across the divide, is obviously preferable to embedded sectarian hatred.

However, once again a note of caution is warranted. Claims made about dance's post-national, post-gender, post-class and, in Northern

Ireland, post- or anti-sectarian status need to be qualified. Many urban participants heading off to gatherings in remote countryside locations in similar fashion to those who attended the secret London orbital or M25 parties in England were often understandably nervous about whose territory they were entering; that is, which side was either controlling or in the majority at the event? Thus, once again, the oft-noted fear of being asked one's name, or where one is 'from', intruded into dance's imagined utopian spaces. Thus, both raving and clubbing in Northern Ireland were as much structured by the sectarian body politic as they could also be said to have extended non-sectarian spaces. Indeed, many raves and clubs operated along the lines of existing territory/identity politics. For example, west Belfast's Ta's nightclub is virtually exclusively nationalist. Moreover, many in the nationalist community were suspicious of rave's perceived Englishness, its status as a point in a long line of British/English popular cultural imports, thus placing rave in a contradictory position. On the one hand, rave was yet another symptom of English-led cultural imperialism; on the other, rave could be articulated to an anti-State, anti-Unionist politics, and a riposte to its scripture-driven veto on fun. Whichever way: many raves and club events were organized along existing lines of sectarian stratification: that is, for Protestants or Catholics only. Moreover, the paramilitaries' position on rave and dance parties was starkly Janus-faced. As Hollywood has pointed out, while paramilitaries were involved in 'doling out justice' to known dealers and users in the form of punishment beatings, and breaking up illegal dance events and seizing or smashing equipment (with the often vocal support from non-raving members of the community), they simultaneously sought to control and profit from the drug economy.[32] Republican paramilitaries, for example, were in the complex position of having to be seen to take a moral stand on drugs, policing rave culture and responding to the nationalist community's sense of rave as a menace, a nuisance and an import, while simultaneously playing the alternating roles of pusher, profiteer and participant. This is a way of signalling caution at the hyperbole and the oft-recycled subcultural narrative that stresses dance culture's actual and symbolic opposition to the parent culture and its sectarianism. While dance, undoubtedly, did play a role in extending non-sectarian spaces and offering momentary spaces for chemical-fuelled jouissance, it did not do so on anything like the scale that its subcultural devotees – and their more considered academic and theoretical adherents – have claimed. In this sense, dance music in Northern Ireland was perhaps less *Human Traffic* (Kerrigan, 1999) and a little more akin to the territory wars and complex drug politics of *The Wire* (HBO, 2002–08).

The explicit avoidance of politics in the bulk of locally produced dance music does not imply that a political position has been entirely absent in the music itself. Against the grain of much dance music, the art of sampling has been deployed in a situationist fashion to make fairly forceful political statements. 'Wasp in the Jungle' by Earwhacz is such an example. This track sampled Ian Paisley – the fundamentalist Unionist politician who would go on to become Northern Ireland's First Minister – to comic effect. A Paisley speech about impending Armageddon is turned into a rap over a frenetic breakbeat. Here dance music, as with punk previously, is being pressed into the service of undermining some of the more conservative aspects of Northern Irish society via a cut 'n' paste strategy. There are many more similar examples but the transience of some dance styles, combined with limited distribution and the subcultural 'insiderism' endemic to some areas of dance culture, makes tracking every example difficult.

Initially, however, dance was an imagined community in subcultural discourse marked by deep horizontal comradeship, its participants united in oneness, whether against the mainstream, the repressive aspects of the State, or leading the charge against incorporation into the parent culture, either in its bourgeois-capitalist or sectarian guises. However, in more narrowly musical terms, its relentless quest for innovation cannot be easily dismissed, especially when compared to the relative homogeneity of rock. This is not to idealize dance culture. As Sarah Thornton[33] has argued, drawing on the work of Pierre Bourdieu,[34] oppositionality and resistance, and aesthetic innovation, in dance culture has often been linked to the acquisition and display of 'subcultural capital' and the remaking of hierarchies of cultural knowledge and the reinforcing of taste distinctions *within* dance culture. As with other scenes and subcultures in their day, dance is shot through with elitism and stratification and a myriad of competing truth claims. The constant drive to 'keep it real' creates constantly evolving (and transient) hierarchical communities of knowledge and taste. Also, the history of dance in Ireland is shot through with competing claims as to who deserves to be included in the canon and who does not. The question arises as to whether dance cultures were – or ever can be – really anti-capitalist and oppositional, or whether they are always doomed to reproduce existing patterns of social inequality?

Indeed, as the 1990s progressed, dance culture moved from being a relatively unified 'mass' or 'tribal' movement to a post-rave (or 'institutionalized') dance culture splintered into a series of ever-evolving sub-genres with their attendant devotees and detractors. This was to create a long list of forms and styles: the many variations on house, techno and trance (happy, hard, progressive, minimal, acid and psychedelic, as well those styles articulated to place – Detroit, Chicago, Berlin and Goa and so) but also the different schools of hip hop, drum 'n' bass, garage, breakbeat, nu-school breaks, broken beats and big beats. Therefore, dance music culture in Ireland, as elsewhere, included a wide variety of practices under its umbrella. What is most interesting is that in terms of production none of these styles were articulated to local spaces and places, and while Belfast had a reputation as a hard techno city (to correspond with its 'hard' industrial and 'troubled' image, its raw rhythm and blues of an earlier era), the city never produced nor coined such a genre, where 'Belfast techno' circulated as a discrete category/genre in specialist record shops. This is not to suggest that Irish dance producers were doomed to the role of mere sideline participants, forced into playing Lear's fool to the great global trends begat elsewhere. As we have seen, that would clearly be a disservice to the many scenes, stories and the often-innovative music the island has produced. Nonetheless, figures such as David Holmes, or Cork's Fish Go Deep and the other long-standing producers and DJ residents, have largely worked *within* existing dance genres, inhabiting these successfully and even bending generic conventions to suit their purposes, becoming respected figures internationally in the process. But this is not the same as *being there* and being known to be present at the birth of a genre, style or movement and forging that powerful music-press connection in subcultural terms and beyond.

SHUT UP AND DANCE!

From the perspective of the romantic discourse of authorship, Ireland occupies a peripheral place in the story of modern electronic club-orientated dance music. To the master narrative it contributes no canonical figures, with the possible exception of David Holmes, but even he, though highly regarded in critical terms, was not there when the party started, nor did he spearhead a genre or style. Thus

Ireland offers no significant moments, no pioneers or innovators to the broader story. In fact, as with punk before it, rave in Northern Ireland is dominated by, and often reduced to, subcultural discourse and the assessment of rave's progressive (or otherwise) effects on sectarian strife. Oddly, the most famous mention of Ireland in dance *music* itself perhaps comes from innovative English techno duo Orbital, in their vocal-less track 'Belfast', an uplifting and gentle piece of ambient techno that cuts sharply against the dominant image of the troubled city. Of course, an irony in the cinematic representation of dance culture is that this track, with its location-specific title, was to soundtrack a scene showing Cardiff awakening in the dawn of 'the morning after many nights before' in *Human Traffic* (and, in so doing, suggested the transnational nature of dance culture).

As dance music has been so closely associated with the idea of the modern metropolis, Ireland has not been very well placed to inhabit the form, with its location on Europe's periphery, its relatively small population and limited urban areas. Again, the dominant images of Ireland, from folk and traditional music to its convivial pub culture, do not lend themselves well to the creation of an internationally exportable dance music mythology (and clubbing, just like rock before it, was framed by existing discourses present in the cultural arena). In this sense, dance culture tended to reproduce existing space/place power relations in representational terms. And it is little surprise that the capitals and/or the largest cities of the world's dominant nations – London, Manchester, New York, Chicago, Paris, Berlin and so forth – became the most visible and most mythologized dance locations in the global imaginary. Even Dublin, as the largest urban area on the island, has had a cantankerous relationship with the orthodox blueprint of the modern European or American city. However, dance music did find a home in some non-metropolitan, out-of-the-way locations. One of the country's super-clubs, Lush, is such an example, located on the sparsely populated North Antrim coast in the small town of Portrush. Perhaps we are returning to the culture of the showbands at the beginning of Ireland's engagement with international popular music culture where this type of peripheral club provided a hedonistic outlet otherwise unavailable, perhaps compensating for the lack of other pleasures.

In dance culture, we glimpse the contradictions involved in Ireland's orientation towards global cosmopolitanism and the difficulties involved in adapting its colonial past to modern metropolitan forms in a fashion that retains a sense of local/national distinction. Most clubbers would claim, with some justification, that modern Irish dance music is simply dance music made by Irish producers; nor, one could assume, would they make any claims for the form being Irish, nor bring the national dimension to bear on listening/dancing pleasures.[35] In this sense, the many Irish producers, remixers, DJs, promoters and entrepreneurs form a hidden history (which maybe even defies being woven into a single story, such is the de-centred and fragmented nature of the field). One point can be made with some certainty. Some global places and spaces were better positioned to exploit and adapt their rubrics of place, and the attendant mythologies trailing in their wake, in a way that Ireland has not. One need only think of the way in which 'British'/'English' and 'dance' are not mutually exclusive categories and how post-war urban discourses and images – increased immigration and multiculturalism, regeneration, the politics of Thatcherism and the opposition to the Criminal Justice Bill, among other things – have contributed in forging a relatively coherent urban cultural tapestry that can be re-spun, rewound and remixed – in short, mobilized into discrete genres and styles to energizing effect. Against such an elaborated and urbanized cluster of tropes – which exist free from the ghettoizing shackles of the ethnically framed, primitivist and exoticist positions within which post-colonial Ireland has been framed – Irish dance culture cannot help but look like an anonymous, even fairly undistinguished, region of the United Kingdom, a weak reverberation of developments at the centre. One of the most interesting aspects of dance music in the Irish context was that the type of libidinal investment that Žižek[36] regards as a central component of the Nation-Thing was displaced outwards, as it were, away from the geopolitical space of the island-nation and onto other musical spaces/places, whether actual or virtual. In Northern Ireland, arguably, once again there was good reason to (in Frith's words) reject ethnic sounds for the sounds of international 'corruption'.

However, with the return of rock and indie in the mid-to-late noughties, dance music now possessed a bounded history (in Ireland from 1990–91 to the mid-noughties), and one might then have concluded that the space/place mythologies generated in the rave aftermath may have presided over the further peripheralization of recognizably Irish, or Ireland-specific, idioms.

NOTES

1. Zane Lowe, 'Brand New', MTV, September 1999.
2. Henri Lefebvre, *Rhythmanalysis: Space, Time and Everyday Life*, trans. Stuart Elden and Gerald Moore (London: Continuum, 2004), p.66.
3. John Braine, 'A History of Dublin Clubbing', *DUBfly*, September 2000; Jeremy Gilbert and Ewan Pearson, *Discographies: Dance Music, Culture and the Politics of Sound* (London: Routledge, 1999); Steve Redhead, *The End of the Century Party: Youth and Pop towards 2000* (Manchester: Manchester University Press, 1990).
4. Tony Clayton-Lea and Richie Taylor, *Irish Rock: Where it's come from, where it's at, where it's going* (Dublin: Gill & Macmillan, 1992); Mark J. Prendergast, *The Isle of Noises: Rock and Roll's Roots in Ireland* (Dublin: O'Brien Press, 1987); Gerry Smyth, *Noisy Island: A Short History of Irish Popular Music* (Cork: Cork University Press, 2005).
5. Gilbert and Pearson, *Discographies*; Sarah Thornton, *Club Cultures: Music, Media and Subcultural Capital* (Cambridge: Polity Press, 1995); Nabeel Zuberi, *Sounds English: Transnational Popular Music* (Chicago, IL: University of Illinois Press, 2001).
6. John Bidder, *Pump up the Volume: A History of House* (London: Channel 4, 2001); Bill Brewster and Frank Broughton, *Last Night a DJ Saved My Life: The History of the DJ* (London: Headline, 1999); Simon Reynolds, *Energy Flash: A Journey through Rave and Dance Culture* (London: Picador, 1998).
7. Braine, 'History of Dublin Clubbing'.
8. Noel McLaughlin and Martin McLoone, 'Hybridity and National Musics: The Case of Irish Rock', *Popular Music*, 19, 2 (2000), pp.181–99.
9. Slavoj Žižek, *Tarrying with the Negative: Kant, Hegel, and the Critique of Ideology* (Durham: Duke University Press, 1993), p.201.
10. Gilbert and Pearson, *Discographies*, p.184.
11. Zuberi, *Sounds English*, p.109.
12. McLaughlin and McLoone, 'Hybridity and National Musics', p.181.
13. This is a song that significantly can be read as an African-American challenge to the ideologies of musical and racial authenticity which underpinned white Bohemia's fascination with blackness. The chorus succinctly invokes the dilemma: 'Tried to keep it real, but compared to what?'
14. Tim Sheridan, 'Afro-Celt Sound System', in Tim Sheridan, *All Music Guide: The Definitive Guide to Popular Music* (Enfield: Backbeat Boots, 2001), p.950.
15. Zuberi, *Sounds English*, p.118.
16. John Hutnyk, 'Adorno at Womad: South Asian Crossovers and the Limits of Hybridity-Talk', in Pnina Werbner and Tariq Modood (eds), *Debating Cultural Hybridity: Multi-Cultural Identities and The Politics of Anti-Racism* (London: Zed Books, 1997), pp.106–36.
17. Johnny Caldwell, 'Troubles Tunes Which Annoyed Auntie', BBC News, 1998, http://news.bbc.co.uk/1/hi/northern_ireland/7464668.stm.
18. Zuberi, *Sounds English*, pp.104–5.
19. Primal Scream, 'Loaded', *Screamadelica* (1991).
20. Reynolds, *Energy Flash*, p.404.
21. Gilbert and Pearson, *Discographies*; Zuberi, *Sounds English*.
22. Reggie Manuel, interview by Noel McLaughlin, 2011 (unpublished).
23. Stuart Bailie, 'Over Under Sideways Down', *Hot Press* (August 1998).
24. Eamonn Creen, interview by Noel McLaughlin, 2011 (unpublished). BASIC did fight political battles, though of a different sort. The duo sampled a

comment made by David Holmes: 'I think it's a bit embarrassing ... that there isn't [sic] more people on my level ... making electronic-based music. I think that's a bit ... sad.'

25. Zuberi, *Sounds English*, pp.181–241; Sanjay Sharma, John Hutnyk and Ashwani Sharma (eds), *Dis-Orienting Rhythm: Politics of the New Asian Dance Music* (London: Zed Books, 1996); David Hesmondhalgh, 'International Times: Fusions, Exoticism, and Antiracism in Electronic Dance Music', in Georgina Born and David Hesmondhalgh (eds), *Western Music and Its Others: Difference, Representation, and Appropriation in Music* (Berkeley and Los Angeles, CA: University of California Press, 2000), pp.280–304.
26. Manuel, interview.
27. Matthew Collin, *Altered State: The Story of Ecstasy Culture and Acid House* (London: Serpent's Tail, 1997); Gilbert and Pearson, *Discographies*; Reynolds, *Energy Flash*; Thornton, *Club Cultures*.
28. Brian Hollywood, 'Dancing in the Dark: Ecstasy, the Dance Culture, and Moral Panic in Post-Ceasefire Northern Ireland', *Critical Criminology*, 8, 1 (Spring 1997), pp.62–3.
29. Gilbert and Pearson, *Discographies*, p.4.
30. Bill Rolston, ' "This is Not a Rebel Song": The Irish Conflict and Popular Music', *Race and Class*, 42, 3 (2001), pp.49–67; Sean Campbell and Gerry Smyth, 'From Shellshock Rock to Ceasefire Sounds: Popular Music', in Colin Coulter and Michael Murray (eds), *Northern Ireland after the Troubles: A Society in Transition* (Manchester: Manchester University Press, 2008), pp.235–42.
31. Gilbert and Pearson, *Discographies*, p.164.
32. Hollywood, 'Dancing in the Dark', pp.68–70.
33. Thornton, *Club Cultures*, p.116.
34. Pierre Bourdieu, *Distinction: A Social Critique of the Judgement of Taste* (London: Routledge, 1984), p.39.
35. John O'Flynn, *The Irishness of Irish Music* (Farnham: Ashgate, 2009).
36. Žižek, *Tarrying with the Negative*, pp.201–2.

12

Cabaret Ireland

One distinctive aspect of Irish popular music in the 2000s has been the emergence and the increased centralization of the cabaret song or European musical theatre (*Schlager*) tradition associated with Weimar Germany in the 1920s and early 1930s, and in particular with German composer Kurt Weill. A related yet equally strong influence from a different period and context has been the music, writing and performance styles of Belgian Francophone songwriter and performer Jacques Brel. This is a popular music seam that has, of course, been explored previously in English rock and pop by artists such as David Bowie, Marc Almond, P.J. Harvey and Marianne Faithful among others (Bowie has covered both Weill and Brel, and Marc Almond had a hit with Brel's 'Jackie'). Indeed both Brel and Weill formed something of an alternative and self-consciously 'European' canon for a range of performative English rock artists, and it is very common in review material to see the two names (and contexts) yoked together.[1]

However, this embracing of cabaret song in Irish popular music culture has a longer, if marginal, history than the last decade. Its flavour permeates the work of post-Virgin Prunes Gavin Friday and can be heard on his three collaboration albums with Maurice Seezer, *Each Man Kills the Thing He Loves* (1989), *Adam 'n' Eve* (1992) and *Shag Tobacco* (1995). In a lighter, more whimsical (and less performative) vein it also informs Neil Hannon and The Divine Comedy's oeuvre in the mid-to-late 1990s. In both of these cases the Brel/Weill influence is hybridized with other musical styles, from – in the case of Gavin Friday – the glam rock of T-Rex and Bowie with its attendant gender-play, and – in Hannon's case – the use of Scott Walker, Noel Coward and more 'mainstream' pop and rock traditions.

What marks out post-millennial Irish popular music is that these influences have become increasingly popular and visible in a number of performers, most notably in Jack Lukeman, or Jack L (a play on

Jacques Brel, no less), Camille O'Sullivan and Duke Special. All three artists have made high-profile appearances on terrestrial television in the United Kingdom and Ireland (with O'Sullivan and Duke Special appearing on different episodes of 'Later with Jools Holland', the BBC's most high-profile live popular music programme).

Lukeman has covered Brel right throughout his career, most notably on *Chez Jack L: Love, Sex, Death and Brel*, a live DVD of Brel songs recorded in Dublin's Spirit Club in 2003, which in turn became a sell-out tour in Ireland. The Brel/Weill and Weimar influence is perhaps even stronger in O'Sullivan's work, with the artist openly namechecking in her publicity material the influence of Weimar composers such as Hanns Eisler and Freidrich Höllander as well as Weill. She describes her love of the form, noting its exploration 'of politics, sexuality, life's degenerates…the seedier side of life, desolate love'.[2] Both Lukeman and O'Sullivan have lived in Europe: Lukeman ran away from his job as an apprentice mechanic to busk around the continent,[3] and Franco-Irish O'Sullivan (French mother and Irish father) resided in Berlin for a time. They both inhabit the cabaret song tradition in an expert fashion. Lukeman's adaptation of Brel's 'Lockman' from *Chez Jack L* is particularly impressive. The track begins quietly, the emphasis on atmosphere, with Lukeman's close-miked voice no more than a whisper and bathed in echo. This is Brel reconfigured through a familiar, vaguely Celtic ethereality (that should be familiar to the Irish rock fan). It builds gradually into a great wash of sound, with Lukeman's strong baritone emerging in increments into his fully blown operatic tenor. In operatic fashion he holds long sustained wordless notes which slide down the scale to bring the track to its powerful conclusion. The rising plea of the chorus's powerful double negative – 'it's not nothing, being a lockman' – should have a resonance in the Irish context of the time where success, status and acquisition were increasingly lauded.

However, the operatic tenor aside, the track is greatly indebted to Irish rock styles – to early U2 and Sinéad O'Connor in particular with its use of extreme dynamic contrast – as it does to Brel and the cabaret song tradition. What is interesting, however, is the critical significance of this increased centralization of musical styles. Is it simply a case of aesthetic novelty, of Irish artists and producers looking for a language outside of the dominant folk-authenticity paradigm? On a rudimentary level the answer is, of course, yes; but this is to leave aside the possible reasons for this embrace of these very particular periods of European song and performance. Given the range of historically and spatially dispersed musics that exist in the current audioscape ripe for plundering, it is interesting that popular Irish music should witness this quite specific 'turn to Europe'.

The first and perhaps obvious connection is the way in which the cabaret tradition and its particular cluster of mythologies could be articulated to Irish and Northern Irish contexts. This was, after all, the period when Ireland, North and South, underwent fundamental changes. With the advent of the so-called Celtic Tiger, the Republic and especially Dublin moved from being one of the poorest economies in western Europe to perhaps the most affluent. Similarly, in the years after the paramilitary ceasefires, Belfast morphed into a cosmopolitan and confident city full of award-winning restaurants, clubs and bars – in short, all of the amenities of a wealthy European capital. In other words, both cities, like their counterparts in Britain, had to face the ambivalent effects of regeneration, the so-called 'turn to culture' and the emergence of 'the new individualism' in the Irish context.[4] In this sense, both Dublin and Belfast may have eerie parallels with Weimar Germany and Berlin in the interwar years: the ecstatic release from armed conflict and austerity and the contradictory experience of affluence in the aftermath of economic and political difficulties. The work of Brel and Weill was to provide a template for both dramatizing and analysing the contradictions born of affluence and was, thus, a style that could be articulated to the Irish context. Like the Irish folk tradition and the confessional singer-songwriter, the cabaret tradition made a special case for the importance of words and meaning. Even though the style, and the spaces it invokes and is performed in, are markedly different from folk and from rock, its shared emphasis on the semantic – on 'meaning' and 'message' – makes it amenable to those audiences.

Schlager also has a rich cinematic heritage and is associated with images of Marlene Dietrich in Josef Von Sternberg films and, of course, with Bob Fosse's film *Cabaret* (1972). It conjures up images of gender indeterminacy, sexual excess and bruised low-life, of characters who have lost their way through drugs and alcohol, images that could easily be articulated to a more general post-millennial ennui. In this sense, cabaret, as a particular type of popular musical theatre, sat in an ambivalent relationship to the process of regeneration. It was a symbol of a sophisticated, cosmopolitan and urban culture, and (trailing the legacy of Brecht and Weill) could offer a focus on those excluded by regeneration initiatives; a musical poetics about the marginalized of sorts. It was therefore a form addressed to a mix of Bohemian and 'bourgeois' audiences that simultaneously offered a critique of middle-class complacency. Despite sharing with folk and rock a focus on meaning and message, the iconographies and performance spaces involved were also at some distance from organic folk and folk-rock styles. Cabaret is, of course, centrally concerned with 'dressing up', and costume is of great significance, offering a heady mix of urbane sophistication and bawdy theatricality. Performers such as Lukeman and O'Sullivan exemplify this in the conspicuous use of colour, of silks and satins, brilliantine and basques and fishnet stockings (although in the Irish context there was little overt mixing of clothing across orthodox gender lines). This is an appropriate place to discuss Duke Special, the stage name for Northern Ireland's Peter Wilson, as he differs in important ways from Lukeman and O'Sullivan. While Duke Special has covered songs by the auteurs of the cabaret song tradition, his engagement with the form has had greater penetration into the world of high culture. He wrote the music for the National Theatre's production of Brecht's *Mother Courage and Her Children* in 2009 (in fact, his adaptations of Brecht and Weill even received the endorsement of the Kurt Weill Foundation), but he differs in three vital respects from Lukeman and O'Sullivan. First, a higher proportion of his recorded output is self-penned and he clearly is enjoyed and interpreted, in part, within the discourse of the 'serious' singer-songwriter. Second, he departs from the 'orthodox' and 'glitzy' cabaret iconography, and while he performs in similar venues to the other artists, his image runs against the grain. Thus the cabaret sound and influence is hybridized with subcultural styles that are not usually associated with the form. Wilson sports a mix of dreadlocks, eyeliner and a clothing style that invokes a range of images, from Woody Guthrie to Victorian London to the cinema of Tim Burton (in a sense, 'Crusty', Goth, Berlin cabaret) that serves to mark him out as distinct from the sensitive singer-songwriter. Thirdly, and in addition to this wilful perversion of subcultural styles and genres, Wilson obstinately foregrounds his local accent in a manner distinct from Lukeman and O'Sullivan. This stressing of his vocal idiolect has been remarked upon by Campbell and Smyth: 'Not since the emergence of Scottish folk band The Proclaimers has a singer insisted on the validity of his own accent with such charming insouciance.'[5]

Recourse to the cabaret tradition also, of course, introduces the problem of nostalgia, whether simple or reflexive, and the issue of whether the fetish for the form – and the cultural mythologies that trail in its wake – represents a retreat into the past as a respite from the problems of the present (a type of contemporary 'cabaret light', as opposed to historical 'cabaret heavy', as it were). While it is difficult to circumvent accusations of nostalgia (and the conservatism it implies), arguably the meanings dredged up by the form offer liberating possibilities (especially in the Irish context). Unlike folk music and its related performance spaces – the 'elaborate construction of informality',[6] the destruction of glamour, and the rules that do not appear to be rules – Anno Mungen argues that in cabaret there is 'an implied opposition to the "real world" ' and a potential 'artistic space for gender crossing'[7] (and if not explicit gender crossing, for challenging the codes of folk authenticity and articulating in performance very different ideas and meanings). In short, like Mikhail Bakhtin's concept of the carnivalesque, a special space is created in cabaret where the normal rules of society are temporarily suspended: an interruption and opposition to the 'everyday' structures of authority.[8] Of course this 'performative' space could be inhabited in a manner that ran from the mildly risqué right across to the more self-consciously avant-garde and subversive. Certainly in Dublin and Belfast at the turn of the 1990s many venues emerged that catered for the form.

While cabaret may have radical potential, there was a sense too that this performance mode and its related settings had become conventionalized. For example, in its review of Camille O'Sullivan's run of concerts at London's Apollo Theatre, *The Guardian* complained that the singer was hampered by 'the usual alternative-cabaret offerings' (even if the same reviewer noted the power of the performance and the singer's capacity to command such a large venue).[9] It was common for performers such as Jack L and O'Sullivan to mix Brel and Weill with earlier rock artists inspired by the form. Hence O'Sullivan covers songs by Nick Cave and David Bowie (as well as singers adaptable to the form, such as Johnny Cash). Part of the pleasure, therefore, was as much to do with popular music nostalgia and the cover version, of hearing well-known pop and rock songs transposed to the cabaret style and context.

The appropriation of the cabaret song form runs another risk: the dissolution of quite distinct traditions into a more generalized, vaguely decadent and non-specific interwar European milieu.

21. Cabaret Ireland in action – Camille O'Sullivan (Corbis)

Clearly there are important historical, aesthetic and political differences between Weill, Brel, cabaret song and chanson which are rendered merely academic in this more nebulous appeal to, and invention of, a more generalized 'European' cabaret tradition. In this sense disparate styles are amalgamated; a low life, lost loves and a general sleaziness are all foregrounded and historical specificities are left to one side. Any borrowing and referencing is selective, driven by the needs of the current context. There is, for example, little of the pointed class critique of Weill, Brecht and the other Weimar composers in the work of the artists discussed. (If Weill famously complained to Brecht that he could not set *The Communist Manifesto* to music, then perhaps in the Irish context he would have settled for at least some class awareness.) There was, then, a certain sanitization of both the performative and political radicalism of the work referenced in favour of lauding the forms as an aesthetic, as a marker of a general decadence and a token of cosmopolitan sophistication, over animating a critique that might resonate with the present: in short, a postmodern cabaret, and one informed, in part, by rock norms (and in review material even regarded as soft rock).

However, this work in the context of Irish rock and pop is important. Firstly it broke with rock's hegemony and occupied an
interesting space in the rock/pop hinterland, between the 'serious'
and the 'trivial', the authentic and the inauthentic, between 'sincerity' and show business. As we have seen, there has been a degree of
suspicion of overt theatricality – and the stage management it
implies – by Irish rock culture. Thus while much of this work falls
short of the heroic class critique of Weill, this is perhaps too much
to expect. It is just a pity that the method was not more widely
adopted than the style replicated. In other words, the mixture of
rock and its concern with affect, of being judged by its power to
move, was to overwhelm the contrary drives of the cabaret song
tradition – which not only sought to *move* the audience, to invite
them to sing along in the chorus, but also to upset, discomfort,
confuse and question. Aspects of rock had found a new home in
cabaret, even if in its noughties guise this was at some distance from
the more experimental engagement with the form evident in Friday
and Seezer. But it was also at some distance from mainstream rock
and pop, the music that continued to sell and dominate in and out
of Ireland, and for this alone it deserves mention.

NOTES

1. Simon Frith, *Performing Rites: On the Value of Popular Music* (Oxford:
    Oxford University Press, 1996), pp.170–1.
2. http://www.camilleosullivan.com/profile.htm.
3. Alan Swan, *From the Cradle to the Stage: Irish Music Greats, A Chronicle of
    the Early Years* (Dublin: Poolbeg Press, 2003), p.151.
4. See for example, Anthony Elliot and Charles C. Lemert, *The New
    Individualism: The Emotional Costs of Globalization* (New York and
    Abingdon: Routledge, 2009); Carmen Kuhling and Keiran Keohane,
    Cosmopolitan Ireland: Globalisation and Quality of Life (London: Pluto Press,
    2007); Slavoj Žižek, *Living in the End Times* (London: Verso, 2010).
5. Sean Campbell and Gerry Smyth, 'From Shellshock Rock to Ceasefire Sounds:
    Popular Music', in Colin Coulter and Michael Murray (eds), *Northern Ireland
    after the Troubles: A Society in Transition* (Manchester: Manchester University
    Press, 2008), p.248.
6. Niall Mackinnon, *The British Folk Scene* (Milton Keynes: Open University
    Press, 1993), p.81.
7. Anno Mungen, '"Anders als die Anderen": Or Queering the Song
    Construction and Representation of Homosexuality in German Cabaret Song
    Recordings before 1933', in Sheila Whiteley and Jennifer Rycenga (eds),
    Queering the Popular Pitch (New York and London: Routledge, 2006), p.68.

8. Mikhail Bakhtin, *Rabelais and His World*, trans. Helene Iswolsky (Bloomington, IN: Indiana University Press), pp.4–11.
9. Maddy Costa, 'Review of The Dark Angel: Camille O'Sullivan at the Apollo Theatre', *Guardian*, 4 January 2010, p.32.

Conclusion: Irish Popular Music in the New Millennium

On today's market, we find a whole series of products deprived of their malignant property: coffee without caffeine, cream without fat, beer without alcohol . . . This leads us to today's tolerant liberal multi-culturalism as an experience of the Other deprived of its Otherness – the decaffeinated Other. (Slavoj Žižek)[1]

. . . the notion of the 'hybrid' can become as fixed a category as its essentialist nemesis. A politics of identity may not necessarily translate from the subjective to the collective, and hybridity can be as regressive as any other normative identity, as well as an ideological tool for glob-alized capitalism. (Nubeel Zuberi)[2]

We began this book with The Beatles' arrival in Ireland in 1963 and explored the implications of this visit to the interrelation-ship of popular music and Irishness. If this marked the starting point of a narrative, then U2's appearance alongside Paul McCartney at 2005's Live 8 forms a postscript of sorts. This was not just a meet-ing of two of the most famous acts in popular music history (though in the case of Bono, some have complained that yet again he was merely staking a claim to stand alongside a 'true' rock legend). It also symbolized the twin arcs of the Irish (popular music) diasporic experience and the 'in-between-ness' that the two groups, in their differing ways, symbolize: the second/later generation Irish in England and the British in Ireland (both actual and musi-cal/cultural). Indeed both of these 'biggest groups in the world' encapsulate a time when music was a mass tribal phenomenon – The Beatles 'saving the world from boredom'; U2 saving rock 'n' roll from sex 'n' drugs. Both groups, in their different eras, made their respective countries of origin renowned centres for popular music production in the international imagination.

More generally, the event also marked an increased postmodern incursion of the popular music of the past into the musical landscape of the present. Indeed the majority of artists and bands discussed throughout this book were, and are, still producing music in the noughties. U2 have a new album imminent in 2012 and are still involved in lengthy global tours that promote their new material as well as drawing upon (and selling) their extensive back catalogue (and anniversary special issues). Significantly, their U2 360° tour of 2009 announced a key change in the political economy of popular music, as the revenue stream from live performance was no longer in the service of 'promoting' new music but was increasingly funda-mental to group monies.

Van Morrison and Christy Moore, similarly, continue to release new material and to tour. Sinéad O'Connor is another artist with an album due for release in late 2011, which has been described by producer/drummer and former partner, John Reynolds, as 'one of the two best albums I have ever worked on',[3] and a sign that the artist's best work may not be in the past. Bob Geldof also released a new album in 2011, *How To Compose Popular Songs That Will Sell*, his first in a decade. Northern Irish DJ/producer David Holmes maintained his pattern of releasing an album every two to three years with 2008's *The Holy Pictures* (broadening his already catholic sonic envelope, especially evident in that album's embrace of Kraut-rock) and in 2010 he cemented his established position with a compilation of past work, *The Dogs are Parading*. Away from these canonical figures, many Irish dance and hip hop producers continue to DJ and record, releasing music on the internet via YouTube and other social media sites: a sign that these forms have not disappeared despite the decentring of dance in the past decade (and that musi-cians do not simply give up because they are not signed nor releasing 'records' in the conventional sense). Moreover, many highly regarded groups from the past have reformed, to promote new mate-rial, or to offer audiences a chance to recapture former glories, or to provide young devotees with a chance to experience their live show. Thus, Horslips, The Bothy Band, Moving Hearts, Stiff Little Fingers and The Undertones have all engaged in reunion activities, in either original or augmented line-ups. An informal industry of sorts has also clustered around the figure of Terri Hooley and the legacy of Northern Irish punk and Good Vibrations Records. This was consolidated in the publication of the former label boss's memoirs, and rumours of a feature biopic continue to circulate.[4]

If U2 possess an extensive back catalogue (demonstrated effectively in their 'greatest hits' set at the 2011 Glastonbury festival) Irish rock generally now has a considerable legacy and certainly no writer could claim Dublin or Belfast as 'blank slates', as was common in the past. This legacy, and its intrusion on the present, makes itself felt in a number of ways. It shapes the ongoing discourse of Irish rock and pop with the 'past tense' becoming ever more prominent. *Hot Press*, for instance, regularly features items such as 'Best Irish album ever made' lists and retrospectives of key moments in Irish rock's history, such as features and tributes to the late Phil Lynott, Gary Moore and Rory Gallagher. Moreover, this journalistic and discursive self-consciousness about 'heritage' is consolidated in the broader public arena, in rock tours of both Belfast and Dublin: to Hyndford Street, Cyprus Avenue and the site of the former Maritime Club in Belfast; and Windmill Lane, The Baggott Inn and McGonagles in Dublin. The customary blue plaques adorn key sites (such as The Maritime) and statues have been erected to commemorate pivotal figures who died young, like Rory Gallagher and Phil Lynott. Institutions such as the (now closed) *Hot Press* Irish Music Hall of Fame are examples of this process and in hot.press.ie's online cuttings archive the possibilities for nostalgia and recall of Irish rock's past extends to the realm of cyberspace.

The last decade also witnessed the emergence of Irish popular music studies in the academy, beginning with 'Hybridity and National Musics: The Case of Irish Rock'[5] in the most prominent academic journal in the field, *Popular Music*, in 2000, which sought to build on the pioneering lone voice of Barbara Bradby in the 1980s.[6] This continued a year later in the final chapter of Gerry Smyth's *Space and the Irish Cultural Imagination*[7] and in a Smyth-edited special edition on Irish popular music in the main Irish Studies journal in Britain, *Irish Studies Review*, which included articles on folk, rock, punk and dance musics on the island.[8] However, 2005 was perhaps the pivotal year for Irish popular music studies, as it marked the appearance of the first two scholarly monographs on the subject: Sean Campbell and Gerry Smyth's *Beautiful Day: Forty Years of Irish Rock* and Smyth's *Noisy Island: A Short History of Irish Popular Music*.[9] This momentum has been maintained in the decade's latter half with the publication of John O'Flynn's *The Irishness of Irish Music*[10] and Smyth's *Music in Irish Cultural History*[11] in 2009, Lauren Onkey's *Blackness and Transatlantic Irish Identity: Celtic Soul Brothers* in 2010, and Sean Campbell's *Irish*

Blood, English Heart: Second-Generation Irish Musicians in England in 2011.[12] This impressive body of work has also been supported by numerous stand-alone articles in peer-reviewed journals and book chapters across a variety of disciplines (media and cultural studies, musicology, sociology, and cultural history). It is also driven by an eclecticism of theoretical means (post-colonial, postmodern, Marxist and so forth) and has offered an important counterweight to the more journalistic and advertorial writing on Irish music which has dominated the field.

A further distinctive aspect of the last decade has been the emergence of state-sponsored and private/public funding initiatives and their role in the formation of institutions such as Belfast's Oh Yeah! Centre, The Nerve Centre in Derry and Temple Bar Music Centre in Dublin's 'Bohemian' quarter. These 'centres' offer a mix of recording studios, rehearsal rooms and performance spaces as well as running courses on various aspects of popular music production. These range from the vocational courses – musical and technical skills, music business management and law – to the more academic programmes on rock and pop history (and in this sense they complement the concomitant rise of similar programmes in further and higher education). They also draw on the considerable local expertise accrued in the area: technical and legal, practical and journalistic (with former assistant editor at the *NME*, Stuart Bailie, and Undertone Sean O'Neill both centrally involved in Oh Yeah! and the Nerve Centre respectively). Smyth argues that for good or for ill, this move from rock as an informal and 'marginal' activity to a 'set of codes and practices formalized within the mainstream economy' at least engages with rock for what it always has been (and frequently pretended not to be): a business.[13] And, if nothing else, these centres and the type of advice they offer may prevent those young artists and bands fortunate enough to sign a deal with the broader industry from being 'ripped off' (thus there may be no more need in the future for interminable songs about the great deception of the music industry). In fact, cultural, subcultural and musical 'capital' has always been important to musicians, whether it has emerged from 'official' or 'unofficial' sources (and one need only think of the importance of the Art School and Art School ideas to British rock and pop for figures such as Brian Eno, Bryan Ferry and Westwood and McLaren,[14] or the record capital accrued from American GIs and his father's record collection in the case of Van Morrison). As Smyth notes, whatever the changes in the sector, only a tiny proportion of musicians and bands will 'make it', and whether the music is produced inside or outside of educational, or 'fame academy'-type structures, neither production base will guarantee whether the music is, in that elusive term, 'any good' in either an aesthetic or sociological sense (or indeed if it will find a broader audience).

The presence of the music of the past in the present, the foregrounding of Irish rock's legacy and the broader 'flattening out' of historically, geographically and aesthetically dispersed musics in the current context has other consequences to do with representation and meaning. A greater range of styles is now available for plundering than ever before, as 'off-the-peg' clothes, as it were, to try on for size. It is perhaps more difficult to identify a governing Irish rock or pop aesthetic in the last decade, especially one that animates or articulates specifically Irish or Northern Irish themes (and whether or not these terms are relevant in what many analysts describe as a postnational context). However, particular forms and modes have remained remarkably durable. The 'sensitive' singer-songwriter is such a long-standing tradition that it has almost become synonymous with Irish music more broadly. The 'superabundance' of this mode noted by Smyth, has, if anything, become even more highprofile in the noughties in a host of artists such as Iain Archer, Damien Dempsey, Lisa Hannigan, Gemma Hayes, Nina Hynes, David Kitt, Mundy, Damien O'Rourke, Foy Vance and many others. As Smyth has argued, 'A range of factors have contributed to the rise of the modern singer-songwriting scene . . . the greater availability of cheap computer technology and the consequent growth in home recording. All you need is a quietish room, a microphone and a computer with studio software and you are ready to make your own "album".'[15] While this may be so, it leaves aside the why? Why has this new affordable means of production been put towards the uses it has been? Despite the importance of *Zoo TV*-era U2 and the work of The Virgin Prunes in detonating or wilfully perverting and extending Irish music idioms, in terms of music production these interventions might as well not have happened. However innovative the range of 'new' singer-songwriters has been, they still broadly associate Ireland and Irish music with the 'warm', the 'sincere' and the organic: in short, a certain casual folksiness. The expectation appears to be that the Irish should emote. In fact, the island's music production is still, post-2000, relatively bereft of the extensive range of forms that can be grouped under the 'plastic' and the 'cold', with the modernist, the performative and self-consciously experimental still conspicuous by their absence. It still seems as if this range of forms is regarded as somehow essentially un-Irish.

The work of the singer-songwriters in the noughties has been marked in general terms by a certain interiorization – a textualizing of the inner self – or a projecting outward of private concerns in musical form. Of course this interiorization has different, and important, consequences with regard to gender and, indeed, the post-millennial period has (at last) witnessed the rise in the number of prominent female exponents of the form (there are now many more prominent Irish female artists than at any point previously). A number of writers have explored the form's appropriateness to women,[16] but if a female singer-songwriter lineage from Joni Mitchell to Sinéad O'Connor has been influential, this more recent work has deployed the confessional and aesthetic aspects of these vocalists oeuvres rather than the more confrontational, public and political aspects. Many of the female singer-songwriters are, of course, highly regarded and successful internationally. For example, at a star-studded tribute to the renowned English folk singer, the late Nick Drake, held at London's Barbican centre in January 2010 (and televised on BBC4), Lisa Hannigan stole the show with a radical reworking of Drake's 'Black Eyed Dog'. It is significant that the tribute was to the quintessential confessional singer-songwriter with his tortured persona and deeply personal songs and in many ways, he stands as the model of the new breed of troubadour. Despite the manifest lack of politics and the apparent absence of courting controversy that we have noted, many of the noughties crop of Irish female singer-writers inhabit the form, like Drake, in a musically ambitious and emotionally powerful manner.

Of the male artists, Damien Rice is the most widely known. His work differs in vital respects from earlier male Irish singer-songwriters. This most pronounced in approaches to style. Rice's work is more self-consciously *designed* and overtly sculpted and, as such, owes as much to *art* as to *folk* music, emphasizing space and quietness and foregrounding quite specific textures and timbres. The clean, crafted and sparse sound, the creation of a distinctive 'signature' audioscape, owes as much to groups such as Scotland's The Blue Nile or to the solo work of David Sylvian as it does to Irish folk confessional styles. This sonic signature is also intimately connected to the recurring lyrical themes of loss, vulnerability, emotional insecurity and the highs and lows of romantic coupling. In analysing the new, 'sensitive', male singer-songwriter, Ian Biddle notes some of the ideological problems with the form: the fetishization of male angst and a re-centring of the masculine self which may be a response to the gains made by feminism and the uncertainties for male subjectivities in the post-Fordist era.[17] Damien Dempsey, on the other hand, likes to ground his music in the realities of contemporary Ireland, and his voice, railing against the disparity of wealth and opportunity, was one of the few politically motivated 'begrudgers' of the Celtic Tiger era.

22. New Generation female singer-songwriter, Lisa Hannigan (Corbis)

With regard to Irishness specifically, Smyth argues that there is little in these artists' oeuvres that marks them as Irish (in the notionally accepted sense of the term), aside from foreknowledge that they are. Aside from the form's commensurability with Irish identity that we noted earlier, much of this work has eerie parallels with the cinema of the Celtic Tiger in the Republic and post-ceasefire cinema in the North, and the forging of an image of the island as a 'place much like anywhere else'. Moreover, this address to more 'universal' and 'interiorized' concerns can also be detected in the main rock bands of the decade, in Snow Patrol, JJ72 and others. Whatever their achievements and successes the question still remains of how popular musical forms might engage with local/national circumstances, whether the local is either marketable or a barrier to broader acceptance. Has the mobilization of musical and lyrical tropes of place and identity any critical or ideological validity?

One of the consequences of increased yet uneven cosmopolitanism appears to be a form of severance from the past, making it difficult to mobilize the aesthetics of otherness: whether as victim or in ethnic, colonial, aggressive or 'troubled' terms. This is not to romanticize the past, nor to reduce it to mere currency in a popular music marketplace, hungry for difference, but affluent cosmopolitanism clearly does have consequences for music and perhaps Campbell and Smyth are correct in their analysis that post-ceasefire Northern Irish rock possesses a certain 'weightlessness'.[18] Or, to borrow from Žižek, are we at a point where Irish music is now deprived of its Irishness – not in essentialist terms, but in a nationally or culturally specific sense, in being able to animate the salient contradictions of the experience of life on the island (and being able to do so in a fashion that is of interest to the global music market)?

The contemporary problem (if indeed it is one for many musicians and listeners) is a familiar one: how to forge a mythology that is attractive to the international popular music imaginary from a space on the periphery with its own strong markers of identity. The issue is whether place-bound tropes have any currency in the global popular music economy. One could argue that many of the types of hybridity we have been exploring are now overly familiar and, given Irish popular music's long and successful history, there is a question of how many of them can continue to be exploited for commercially successful ends. In reviewing the noughties, Smyth regards the demise of the London Fleadh in 2003 as marking a symbolic turning point and as announcing the declining fortunes of overtly ethnic Irish rock music in the broader international arena.[19] Certainly, the vogue for Irish sounds and styles, whether the raucous performances of The Pogues or the Celtic Soul of Van Morrison, did seem somewhat passé by the mid-2000s. This, perhaps, coincided with the collapse of the Irish economy in 2008 when images of the Celtic Tiger and its conspicuous consumption were replaced by a return to the age-old narrative of economic hardship.

However, like economic booms and busts, this itself may prove to be a temporary aberration. The enduring power and appeal of the organic paradigm in Irish rock and popular music was evident in the rebirth of the London Fleadh in 2011 as the London Feis. Under the rubric 'Irish in flavour, international in reach' the Feis line-up, headed by Bob Dylan and Van Morrison, represented the cream of 'authentic' folk-inflected rock. The core of the festival consisted of performers from every decade of the rock era from the 1960s to the present. The line-up did include Camille O'Sullivan and the Afro Celt Sound system but, for the rest, it was dominated by those artists from Irish rock's past who comfortably conformed to the dominant folk aesthetic. This was a considerable demonstration of the durability of Irish rock nostalgia and its underlying ideologies. The result is, once again, the near omission of the plastic arts and its pop equivalent which we have identified as a major absence in Irish popular music culture generally.

Neil Jordan's 2005 film *Breakfast on Pluto* is one of the few areas of Irish culture where this absence has been addressed. The film revisits and explores glam rock and the liberating aspects of its gender play and does so via the legacy of the showband. Indeed it is significant that Gavin Friday plays the role of sexually ambivalent and glam-influenced showband leader Billy Hatchet. It captures some of the surreal aspects of showband performance and the often-overlooked 'progressive' possibilities of the form. The musical performances are unsettling, their sense of unease generated by the extremes of their gender play and their mixing of show biz conventions and pop music schmaltz. (Indeed, one example of the power of performative pop from the film is the extraordinary performance of Lee Hazelwood's 'Sand' – with Hatchet and Cillian Murphy's Kitten standing in for Hazelwood and Nancy Sinatra – in front of a hostile audience at a benefit gig for Republican prisoners.) The film hints at an alternative and subversive narrative of Irish popular music history, one that would have been familiar to both Gregory Gray and The Virgin Prunes (and perhaps even to Sinéad O'Connor).

Nick Hamm's *Killing Bono* (2011) also addresses an interesting part of the overall narrative of Irish rock (and indeed of rock music everywhere) in that it acknowledges, celebrates and makes capital out of *failure*. In one sense, both the film and the memoir on which it is based, Neil McCormick's *I was Bono's Doppelganger* (2005), represent the majority Irish music-making experience, that of *not* securing a deal; and if successful in signing, of *not* finding an audience (of not 'making it', like the many talented and adventurous acts in the past that have already been discussed). The film, in darkly satirical terms, also conveys a sense of how Bono and U2 hover over

Irish popular music as a spectre, as the dominant Irish rock success story. Neil McCormick's close proximity to the band is, of course, not representative of the majority experience but it does allow the film to underscore the contradictory mix of celebration, wonder, adoration, jealousy, criticism and antipathy that U2 have elicited from aspiring Irish rock musicians and fans over the years (more often than not within the same individual). *Killing Bono* is a universal story, no doubt, but it is one that can clearly be read in national allegorical terms. As such it conveys some of the salient contradictions in Irish rock music: that between local register and global reach; between national idioms and international rhythms; between spectacular success and (sometimes not so) noble failure; between authenticity and hybridity; between rootedness and transcendence; and between nation and aspiration.

This book, then, has sought to challenge some of the orthodoxies of the Irish rock narrative and to question some of the ways in which the dominant discourse of Irish rock has been organized: hence the desire to offer at least the beginnings of a revision of the showband legacy. In doing so, the book has also noted the absence of the performative and gender play, such a central aspect of popular music in Britain and Europe. We have also been keen to highlight the importance of Irish rock in exile and to note important market failures: acts that in themselves construct an alternative narrative to the dominant discourse and indicate some of the roads not taken (or not chosen). The book has also tried to give an emphasis to other less well-known aspects of Irish rock, like its vibrant dance music scene and the genuinely surprising cabaret tradition.

The discourses of recovery, retrieval and reclamation have been central to the history of Irish rock. If there has been anything futuristic, it has paradoxically been its very saturation in nostalgia, its 'rear-view mirrorism'; hence its long-standing association with folk and traditional musics via numerous folk-rock hybrids and its concomitant links with the ethnic, the pastoral and the primitive. In this sense, Irish rock has been perversely forward-looking in anticipating the widespread retromania which dominates contemporary popular music culture as described by Simon Reynolds.[20] Indeed Irish retro, *pace* Reynolds, has functioned to represent the nation (yet again) as a haven away from it all, acting as a conspicuous *other* to the world of rampant consumption and 'the abyss of plenty'[21] promised by the streaming of music on the Internet where it is possible to procure all of the popular music in history by the click of a mouse (if one knows where to look). In other words the 'Utopia of plenty' offered by our current musical context is riven with problems and dangers: the lack of investment in any particular sound or style and the risk of being cast adrift in musical overload. In the current context, Irish music is not unlike John Ford's *The Quiet Man* (1952), representing a simpler world – a rural Utopia – defined in opposition to the perils of (hyper-)modernity. As Reynolds observes drawing upon the work of Frederic Jameson, 'there is actually another literary tradition of utopias that are about seclusion and serenity: withdrawal from promiscuous bustle and hyper-stimulation in favour of pastoral stasis. A utopia that is not about wanting *for* nothing, but about wanting *nothing*.'[22] However, as we have seen, in the Irish context this ideology is both an advantage (and a unique selling point) *and* something of a representational prison. In one sense, this book shares the nostalgic and utopian impulse of much Irish music, but ours is a nostalgia for the possibilities born of the co-mingling of rock, pop and nation; for a time when music was scarce, tribal and subcultural, when music and its pleasures and meanings were heavily invested in and when music had the related capacity to subvert, surprise, challenge and change – in short, nostalgia for imagining a better future, a better politics and other ways of being.

NOTES

1. Slavoj Žižek, 'Liberal Multiculturalism Masks an Old Barbarism with a Human Face', *Guardian*, 3 October 2010.
2. Nabeel Zuberi, *Sounds English: Transnational Popular Music* (Chicago, IL: University of Illinois Press, 2001), pp.239–40.
3. John Reynolds, interview by Noel McLaughlin, 2011 (unpublished).
4. Terri Hooley and Richard Sullivan, *Hooleygan: Music, Mayhem, Good Vibrations* (Belfast: Blackstaff Press, 2010). A number of press reports have alluded to a biopic of Hooley's life for quite some time, provisionally entitled *Good Vibrations*. Figures connected to the project include David Holmes and Gary Lightbody, lead singer of Snow Patrol, who are presumed to be co-producing the film. Holmes' sleeve designer, Glen Leyburn, is also reputed to be involved. Filming finally got underway in August 2011, with actor Richard Dormer playing Terri Hooley.
5. Noel McLaughlin and Martin McLoone, 'Hybridity and National Musics: The Case of Irish Rock', *Popular Music*, 19, 2 (2000), pp.181–99.
6. Barbara Bradby, 'God's Gift to the Suburbs? A Review of *Unforgettable Fire: The Story of U2* by Eamon Dunphy', *Popular Music*, 8, 1 (1989), pp.109–16; and Barbara Bradby and Brian Torode, 'To Whom do U2 Appeal?', *Crane Bag*, 8, 1 (1985), pp.73–8. These were the only significant academic articles on Irish rock and popular music in the 1980s.

7. Gerry Smyth, *Space and the Irish Cultural Imagination* (Basingstoke: Palgrave, 2001).
8. *Irish Studies Review*, 12, 1 (2004).
9. Sean Campbell and Gerry Smyth, *Beautiful Day: Forty Years of Irish Rock* (Cork: Atrium Press, 2005); Gerry Smyth, *Noisy Island: A Short History of Irish Popular Music* (Cork: Cork University Press, 2005).
10. John O'Flynn, *The Irishness of Irish Music* (Farnham: Ashgate, 2009).
11. Gerry Smyth, *Music in Irish Cultural History* (Dublin: Irish Academic Press, 2009).
12. Lauren Onkey, *Blackness and Transatlantic Irish Identity: Celtic Soul Brothers* (New York and London: Routledge, 2010); Sean Campbell, *Irish Blood, English Heart: Second-Generation Irish Musicians in England* (Cork: Cork University Press, 2011).
13. Smyth, *Noisy Island*, p.134.
14. Simon Frith and Howard Horne, *Art into Pop* (London and New York: Methuen, 1987).
15. Smyth, *Noisy Island*, p.125.
16. Sheila Whiteley, *Women and Popular Music: Sexuality, Identity and Subjectivity* (London: Routledge, 2000), pp.72–94; Susan McClary, *Feminine Endings: Music, Gender and Sexuality* (Minneapolis, MN: University of Minnesota Press, 2002); Smyth, *Noisy Island*, pp.122–7.
17. Ian Biddle, '"The Singsong of Undead Labor": Gender Nostalgia and the Vocal Fantasy of Intimacy in the "New" Singer/Songwriter', in Freya Jarman-Ivens (ed.), *Oh Boy! Masculinities and Popular Music* (New York: Routledge, 2007), pp.125–44.
18. Sean Campbell and Gerry Smyth, 'From Shellshock Rock to Ceasefire Sounds: Popular Music', in Colin Coulter and Michael Murray (eds), *Northern Ireland After the Troubles: A Society in Transition* (Manchester: Manchester University Press, 2008).
19. Smyth, *Noisy Island*, p.133.
20. Simon Reynolds, *Retromania: Pop Culture's Addiction To Its Own Past* (London: Faber, 2011).
21. Ibid., p.127.
22. Ibid., p.128.

Select bibliography

Appiah, K.A., 'Rooted Cosmopolitanism', in K.A. Appiah, *The Ethics of Identity* (Princeton, NJ: Princeton University Press, 2005).

Assayas, Michka, *Bono on Bono: Conversations with Michka Assayas* (London: Hodder & Stoughton, 2005).

Attali, Jacques, *Noise: The Political Economy of Music* (Minneapolis, MN: University of Minnesota Press, 1985).

Bakhtin, Mikhail, *Rabelais and his World*, trans. Hélène Iswolsky (Bloomington, IN: Indiana University Press, 2009).

Barker, Hugh and Taylor, Yuval, *Faking It: The Quest for Authenticity in Popular Music* (London: Faber, 2007).

Bayton, Mavis, *Frock Rock: Women Performing Popular Music* (Oxford: Oxford University Press, 1998).

Bennett, Andy and Stratton, Jon (eds), *Britpop and the English Music Tradition* (Farnham: Ashgate, 2010).

Bidder, John, *Pump up the Volume: A History of House* (London: Channel 4, 2001).

Biddle, Ian and Knights, Vanessa (eds), *Music, National Identity and the Politics of Location: Between the Local and the Global* (Farnham: Ashgate, 2007).

Bordowitz, Hank (ed.), *The U2 Reader: A Quarter Century of Commentary, Criticism and Reviews* (Milwaukee, WI: Hal Leonard, 2003).

Born, Georgina and Hesmondhalgh, David (eds), *Western Music and Its Others: Difference, Representation, and Appropriation in Music* (Berkeley and Los Angeles, CA: University of California Press, 2000).

Bourdieu, Pierre, *Distinction: A Social Critique of the Judgment of Taste* (London: Routledge, 1984).

Bowler, David and Dray, Brian, *U2: A Conspiracy of Hope* (Philadelphia, PA: Trans-Atlantic Publications, 1993).

Bradby, Barbara and Torode, Brian, 'To Whom Do U2 Appeal?', *Crane Bag*, 8, 1 (1985).

Bradby, Barbara, 'God's Gift to the Suburbs? A Review of *Unforgettable Fire: The Story of U2* by Eamon Dunphy', *Popular Music*, 8, 1 (1989), pp.109–16.

Brewster, B. and Broughton, F., *Last Night a DJ Saved My Life: The History of the DJ* (London: Headline, 1999).

Butler Cullingford, Elizabeth, *Ireland's Others: Gender and Ethnicity in Irish Literature and Popular Culture* (Cork: Cork University Press/Field Day, 2001).

Cambrensis, Giraldus, *The History and Topography of Ireland*, edited by Thomas Wright, translated by Thomas Forester (London: H.G. Bohn, 1863).

Campbell, Sean, '"What's the Story?": Rock Biography, Musical "Routes" and Second-Generation Irish in England, *Irish Studies Review*, 12, 1 (2004), pp.63–75.

Campbell, Sean, 'Ethnicity and Cultural Criticism: Evocations and Elisions of Irishness in the British Music Press', *Celtic Cultural Studies: An Interdisciplinary Online Journal* (2007).

Campbell, Sean, *Irish Blood, English Heart: Second-Generation Irish Musicians in England* (Cork: Cork University Press, 2011).

Campbell, Sean and Smyth, Gerry, *Beautiful Day: Forty Years of Irish Rock* (Cork: Atrium Press, 2005).

Campbell, Sean and Smyth, Gerry, 'From Shellshock Rock to Ceasefire Sounds: Popular Music', in Coulter and Murray (eds), *Northern Ireland After the Troubles: A Society in Transition* (Manchester, Manchester University Press, 2008).

Carby, Hazel, 'What is this Black in Irish Popular Culture?', *European Journal of Cultural Studies*, 4, 3 (2001), pp.325–49.

Cashman, Lola, *Inside the Zoo with U2: My Life with World's Biggest Rock Band* (London: John Blake, 2003).

Chambers, Iain, *Urban Rhythms: Pop Music and Popular Culture* (Basingstoke: Macmillan, 1985).

Chambers, Iain, *Border Dialogues: Journeys in Postmodernity* (London: Routledge, 1990).

Chambers, Iain, *Migrancy, Culture, Identity* (London: Routledge, 1993).

Chatterton, Mark, *U2: The Complete Encyclopedia* (London: Firefly, 2001).

Clayton-Lea, Tony and Taylor, Richie, *Irish Rock: Where it's come from, where it's at, where it's going* (Dublin: Gill & Macmillan, 1992).

Cloonan, Martin, 'State of the Nation: "Englishness", Pop and Politics in the Mid-1990s', *Popular Music and Society*, 21, 2 (1997), pp.47–71.

Cloonan, Martin, 'Pop and the Nation-State: Towards a Theorisation', *Popular Music*, 18, 2 (1999), pp.193–207.

Cobley, Paul, 'Leave the Capitol', in Sabin (ed.), *Punk Rock: So What?* (1999), pp.170–85.

Cogan, Visjna, *U2: An Irish Phenomenon* (Cork: Collins Press, 2006).

Cohen, Robin, *Global Diasporas: An Introduction* (London: Routledge, 1997).

Collin, Matthew, *Altered State: The Story of Ecstasy Culture and Acid House* (London: Serpent's Tail, 1997).

Collis, John, *Van Morrison: Inarticulate Speech of the Heart* (London: Little, Brown & Co, 1996).

Coulter, Colin and Murray, Michael (eds), *Northern Ireland After the Troubles: A Society in Transition* (Manchester: Manchester University Press, 2008).

Dalton, Stephen, 'In the Name of Love: U2 – The Untold Story', *Uncut*, December 1999, pp.40–62.

Dowling, Martin, *Folk and Traditional Music and the Conflict in Northern Ireland: A Troubles Archive Essay* (Belfast: Arts Council of Northern Ireland, 2009).

Dunphy, Eamon, *Unforgettable Fire: The Story of U2* (London: Penguin, 1987).

Dyer, Richard, 'In Defence of Disco', in Richard Dyer, *Only Entertainment* (London: Routledge, 2002), pp.149–58.

Dylan, Bob, *Chronicles, Volume 1* (London: Simon & Schuster, 2004).

Eno, Brian, 'Bringing Up Baby', in *Rolling Stone* Editors, *U2: The* Rolling Stone *Files* (New York: Hyperion, 1994), pp.165–70.

Fast, Susan, *In the Houses of the Holy: Led Zeppelin and the Power of Rock Music* (Oxford: Oxford University Press, 2001).

Fast, Susan, 'Music, Context and Meaning in U2', in Walter Everett (ed.), *Expression in Rock-Pop Music: Critical and Analytical Essays*, 2nd ed. (New York: Routledge, 2008), pp.175–97.

Flanagan, Bill, *U2: At the End of the World* (London: Bantam Press, 1995).

Frith, Simon, 'Art versus Technology: The Strange Case of Popular Music', *Media, Culture and Society*, 8, 3 (1986), pp.263–79.

Frith, Simon, 'Critical Response', in Robinson, Buck and Cuthbert, *Music at the Margins* (1991), pp.280–87.

Frith, Simon, *Performing Rites: On the Value of Popular Music* (Oxford: Oxford University Press, 1996).

Frith, Simon, 'The Discourse of World Music', in Born and Hesmondhalgh (eds), *Western Music and Its Others* (2000), pp.305–22.

Frith, Simon, 'Does British Music Still Matter?: A Reflection on the Changing Status of British Popular Music in the Global Music Market', *European Journal of Cultural Studies*, 7, 1 (2004), pp.43–58.

Frith, Simon and Horne, Howard, *Art into Pop* (London and New York: Methuen, 1987).

Frith, Simon and McRobbie, Angela, 'Rock and Sexuality', *Screen Education*, 29 (Winter 1978/79), pp.3–19.

Gaar, Gillian, *She's a Rebel: The History of Women in Rock & Roll* (New York: Seal Press, 1993).

Geldof, Bob, *Is That It?* (Harmondsworth: Penguin, 1986).

Gibbons, Luke, *Edmund Burke and Ireland* (Cambridge: Cambridge University Press, 2003).

Gilbert, Jeremy and Pearson, Ewan, *Discographies: Dance Music, Culture and the Politics of Sound* (London: Routledge, 1999).

Gill, John, *Queer Noises: Male and Female Homosexuality in Twentieth-Century Music* (Minneapolis, MN: University of Minnesota Press, 1995).

Gilroy, Paul, *The Black Atlantic: Modernity and Double Consciousness* (London: Verso, 1993).

Gilroy, Paul, *After Empire: Melancholia or Convivial Culture?* (London: Routledge, 2004).

Gilroy, Paul, *Darker than Blue: On the Moral Economies of Black Atlantic Culture* (Cambridge, MA: Harvard University Press, 2010).

Glatt, John, *The Chieftains: The Authorised Biography* (New York: St Martins Press, 1997).

Goodwin, Andrew, *Dancing in the Distraction Factory: Music Television and Popular Culture* (London: Routledge, 1993).

Gracyk, Theodore, 'To Find a Song that I Can Sing: What Philosophy of Language Can Tell Us about Popular Success', in Wrathall (ed.), *U2 and Philosophy* (2006), pp.163–76.

Graham, Bill, *U2 – The Early Years: Another Time, Another Place* (London: Mandarin, 1989).

Graham, Bill and van Oosten de Boer, Caroline, *U2: The Complete Guide to their Music* (London: Omnibus Press, 2004).

Graham, Colin, '"Liminal Spaces": Post-Colonial Themes of Irish Culture', *Irish Review*, 16 (1994).

Graham, Colin, 'Blame it on Maureen O'Hara: Ireland and the Trope of Authenticity', *Cultural Studies*, 15, 1 (January 2001), pp.58–75.

Graham, Colin, *Deconstructing Ireland: Identity, Theory, Culture* (Edinburgh: Edinburgh University Press, 2001).

Guterman, Jimmy, *Sinéad: Her Life and Music* (Harmondsworth: Penguin, 1991).

Harper, Colin and Hodgett, Trevor, *Irish Folk, Trad and Blues: A Secret History* (Cork: Collins Press, 2004).

Harrison, Melissa (ed.), *High Society: The Real Voices of Club Culture* (London: Piatkus Books, 1998).

Hast, Dorothea E. and Scott, Stanley, *Music in Ireland: Experiencing Music, Expressing Culture* (New York and Oxford: Oxford University Press, 2004).

Hawkins, Stan, 'On Male Queering in Mainstream Pop', in Whiteley and Rycenga (eds), *Queering the Popular Pitch* (2006), pp.279–94.

Hawkins, Stan, *The British Pop Dandy: Masculinity, Popular Music and Culture* (Farnham: Ashgate, 2009).

Hayes, Dermot, *Sinéad O'Connor: So Different* (London: Omnibus Press, 1991).

Hebdige, Dick, *Subculture: The Meaning of Style* (London: Methuen, 1979).

Henke, James, 'U2: Here Comes the "Next Big Thing",' *Rolling Stone, U2: The Rolling Stone Files* (New York: Hyperion, 1994), pp.1–2.

Hesmondhalgh, David, 'International Times: Fusions, Exoticism, and Antiracism in Electronic Dance Music', in Born and Hesmondhalgh (eds), *Western Music and Its Others* (2000), pp.280–304.

Hesmondhalgh, David, 'British Popular Music and National Identity', in David Morley and Kevin Robins (eds), *British Cultural Studies* (Oxford and New York: Oxford University Press, 2001), pp.273–86.

Heylin, Clinton, *Dylan: Behind the Shades* (Harmondsworth: Penguin, 1991).

Heylin, Clinton, *Can You Feel the Silence? Van Morrison: A New Biography* (Harmondsworth: Penguin, 2002).

Hinton, Brian, *Celtic Crossroads: The Art of Van Morrison* (London: Sanctuary, 1997).

Hollywood, Brian, 'Dancing in the Dark: Ecstasy, the Dance Culture, and Moral Panic in Post-Ceasefire Northern Ireland', *Critical Criminology*, 8, 1 (Spring 1997).

Hooley, Terri and Sullivan, Richard, *Hooleygan: Music, Mayhem, Good Vibrations* (Belfast: Blackstaff Press, 2010).

Hutnyk, John, 'Adorno at Womad: South Asian Crossovers and the Limits of Hybridity-Talk', in Pnina Werbner and Tariq Modood (eds), *Debating Cultural Hybridity: Multi-Cultural Identities and The Politics of Anti-Racism* (London: Zed Books, 1997), pp.106–36.

Irving, Katrina, ' "I Want Your Hands on Me": Building Equivalences through Rap Music', *Popular Music*, 12, 2 (1993), pp.105–21.

Jal de al Parra, Pimm, *U2 Live: A Concert Documentary* (London: Omnibus Press, 1994).

Jarman-Ivens, Freya (ed.), *Oh Boy! Masculinities and Popular Music* (New York: Routledge, 2007).

Kuhling, Carmen and Keohane, Kieran, *Cosmopolitan Ireland: Globalisation and Quality of Life* (London: Pluto Press, 2007).

Laing, Dave, *One Chord Wonders: Power and Meaning in Punk Rock* (Milton Keynes: Open University Press, 1985).

Landsberg, Alison, *Prosthetic Memory: The Transformation of American Remembrance in the Age of Mass Culture* (New York: Columbia University Press, 2004).

Lefebvre, Henri, *Rhythmanalysis: Space, Time and Everyday Life*, trans. Stuart Elden and Gerald Moore (London: Continuum, 2004).

Lloyd, David, *Anomalous States: Irish Writing and the Post-Colonial Moment* (Durham and London: Duke University Press, 1993).

Lydon, John, *Rotten: No Irish, No Blacks, No Dogs* (London: Plexus, 1994).

Lynch, Michael and Smyth, Damian, *The Beatles and Ireland* (Cork: Collins Press, 2008).

Mackinnon, Niall, *The British Folk Scene* (Milton Keynes: Open University Press, 1993).

Malouf, Michael, 'Feeling Eire(y): On Irish Caribbean Popular Culture', in Negra (ed.), *Irish in Us* (2006), pp.318–53.

Marcus, Greil, *Listening to Van Morrison* (London: Faber & Faber, 2010).

Mayhew, Emma, 'I am not in a box of any description: Sinéad O'Connor's Queer Outing', in Whiteley and Rycenga (eds), *Queering the Popular Pitch* (2006), pp.169–83.

McClary, Susan, *Feminine Endings: Music, Gender and Sexuality* (Minneapolis, MN: University of Minnesota Press, 2002).

McClintock, Anne, *Imperial Leather: Race, Gender and Sexuality in the Colonial Conquest* (New York: Routledge, 1995).

McCormick, Neil, *I was Bono's Doppelgänger: A Life in the Shadows of Superstardom* (London: Penguin, 2005).

McCormick, Neil, *U2 by U2* (London: Harper, 2006).

McGee, Matt, *U2: A Diary* (London: Omnibus Press, 2008).

McLaughlin, Noel, 'Rock, Fashion and Performativity', in Stella Bruzzi and Pamela Church Gibson (eds), *Fashion Cultures: Theories, Explorations and Analysis* (New York and London: Routledge, 2000), pp.264–85.

McLaughlin, Noel, 'Bodies Swayed to Music: Dance Music in Ireland', *Irish Studies Review*, 12, 1 (2004), pp.77–85.

McLaughlin, Noel, 'Bono! Do you ever take those wretched sunglasses off? U2 and the Performance of Irishness', *Popular Music History*, 4, 3 (2009), pp.309–31.

McLaughlin, Noel, 'Post-Punk Industrial Cyber Opera? The Ambivalent and Disruptive Hybridity of Early '90s U2', in John O'Flynn and Mark Fitzgerald (eds), *Music and Identity in Ireland* (Farnham: Ashgate, 2012, forthcoming).

McLaughlin, Noel, 'Rattling Out Of Control: A Comparison of U2 and Joy Division on Film', *Film, Fashion and Consumption*, 1, 1 (2012), pp.99–118.

McLaughlin, Noel and McLoone, Martin, 'Hybridity and National Musics: The Case of Irish Rock', *Popular Music*, 19, 2 (2000), pp.181–99.

McLoone, Martin, *Irish Film: The Emergence of a Contemporary Cinema* (London: BFI, 2000).

McLoone, Martin, *Film, Media and Popular Culture in Ireland: Cityscapes, Landscapes, Soundscapes* (Dublin: Irish Academic Press, 2008).

McNamee, Peter (ed.), *Traditional Music: Whose Music?* (Belfast: Institute of Irish Studies, 1991).

Memmi, Albert, *The Colonizer and the Colonized* (Boston, MA: Beacon Press, 1957).

Mercer, Kobena, *Welcome to the Jungle: New Positions in Black Cultural Studies* (London: Routledge, 1994).

Middleton, Richard, *Studying Popular Music* (Milton Keynes: Open University Press, 1990).

Middleton, Richard, 'The Real Thing? The Specter of Authenticity', in Richard Middleton, *Voicing The Popular: On the Subjects of Popular Music* (New York and London: Routledge, 2006), pp.199–246.

Mills, Peter, *Hymns to the Silence: Inside the Words and Music of Van Morrison* (London: Continuum, 2010).

Moloney, Mick, *Far From the Shamrock Shore* (Cork: Collins Press, 2002).

Moore, Allan F., *Rock: The Primary Text – Developing a Musicology of Rock* (Farnham: Ashgate, 2001).

Moore, Allan F., 'Authenticity as Authentication', *Popular Music*, 21, 2 (2002), pp.209–23.

Moore, Allan F., 'Looking for the Kingdom Come: Questioning Spirituality in U2', *Popular Musicology Online*, 2002 (ISSN 1357-0951).

Mungen, Anno, '"Anders als die Anderen": Or Queering the Song Construction and Representation of Homosexuality in German Cabaret Song Recordings before 1933', in Whiteley and Rycenga (eds), *Queering the Popular Pitch* (2006), pp.67–80.

Nederveen Pieterse, Jan, 'Hybridity, So What? The Anti-Hybridity Backlash and the Riddles of Recognition', *Theory, Culture and Society*, 18, 2–3 (2001), pp.219–45.

Negra, Diane (ed.), *The Irish in Us: Irishness, Performativity and Popular Culture* (London and Durham: Duke University Press, 2006), pp. 318–53.

Negus, Keith, 'Sinéad O'Connor: Musical Mother', in Whiteley (ed.), *Sexing The Groove* (1997), pp.178–90.

Nehring, Neil, ' "Everyone's Given Up and Just Wants to Go Dancing": From Punk to Rave in the Thatcher Era', *Popular Music and Society*, 30, 1 (2007), pp.1–18.

O'Brien, Lucy, *She Bop: The Definitive History of Women in Rock, Pop and Soul* (London: Continuum, 1995).

O'Connor, Nuala, *Bringing It All Back Home: The Influence of Irish Music* (London: BBC Books, 1991).

O'Flynn, John, 'National Identity and Music in Transition: Issues of Authenticity in a Global Setting', in Biddle and Knights (eds), *Music, National Identity and the Politics of Location* (2007), pp.19–38.

O'Flynn, John, *The Irishness of Irish Music* (Farnham: Ashgate, 2009).

O'Halloran, Daragh, *Green Beat: The Forgotten Era of Irish Rock* (Belfast: Brehon Press, 2006).

O'Neill, Sean and Telford, Guy, *It Makes You Want To Spit! The Definitive Guide to Punk in Northern Ireland 1977–1982* (Dublin: Reekus Music, 2003).

Onkey, Lauren, 'Ray Charles on Hyndford Street: Van Morrison's Caledonian Soul', in Negra (ed.), *Irish in Us* (2006), pp.161–95.

Onkey, Lauren, *Blackness and Transatlantic Irish Identity: Celtic Soul Brothers* (New York and London: Routledge, 2010).

O'Riada, Seán, *Our Musical Heritage* (Portlaoise: Dolmen Press, 1982).

Power, Vincent, *Send 'Em Home Sweatin': The Showbands' Story* (Dublin: Kildanore Press, 1990).

Prendergast, Mark J., *The Isle of Noises: Rock and Roll's Roots in Ireland* (Dublin: O'Brien Press, 1987).

Purvis, Tony, '"Ireland's Controversial Icon": A Study of the Work of Sinéad O'Connor', in Richard C. Allen and Stephen Regan (eds), *Irelands of the Mind: Memory and Identity in Modern Irish Culture* (Newcastle: Cambridge Scholars, 2008), pp.158–222.

Ramert, Lynn, 'A Century Apart: The Personality Performances of Oscar Wilde in the 1890s and U2's Bono in the 1990s', *Popular Music and Society*, 32, 4 (2009), pp.447–60.

Redhead, Steve, *The End of the Century Party: Youth and Pop towards 2000* (Manchester: Manchester University Press, 1990).

Reynolds, Simon, *Energy Flash: A Journey through Rave and Dance Culture* (London: Picador, 1998).

Reynolds, Simon, *Rip It Up And Start Again: Post-Punk 1978–1984* (London: Faber, 2005).

Reynolds, Simon, *Totally Wired: Post-Punk Interviews and Overviews* (London: Faber, 2009).

Reynolds, Simon, *Retromania: Pop Culture's Addiction To Its Own Past* (London: Faber, 2011).

Reynolds, Simon and Press, Joy, *The Sex Revolts: Gender, Rebellion, and Rock 'n' Roll* (London: Serpent's Tail, 1995).

Robinson, Deanna Campbell, Buck, Elizabeth and Cuthbert, Marlene, *Music at the Margins: Popular Music and Global Cultural Diversity* (London: Sage, 1991).

Rogan, Johnny, *Van Morrison: No Surrender* (London: Vintage, 2005).

Rolston, Bill, ' "This is Not a Rebel Song": The Irish Conflict and Popular Music', *Race and Class*, 42, 3 (2001), pp.49–67.

Sabin, Roger (ed.), *Punk Rock: So What? The Cultural Legacy of Punk* (London: Routledge, 1999).

Savage, Jon, *England's Dreaming: Sex Pistols and Punk Rock* (London: Faber & Faber, 1991).

Savage, Jon, *Time Travel: From The Sex Pistols to Nirvana* (London: Chatto & Windus, 1996).

Sharma, Sanjay, Hutnyk, John and Sharma, Ashwani (eds), *Dis-Orienting Rhythm: Politics of the New Asian Dance Music* (London: Zed Books, 1996).

Shohat, Ella and Stam, Robert, *Unthinking Eurocentrism: Multiculturalism and the Media* (London and New York: Routledge, 1994).

Smyth, Gerry, *Space and the Irish Cultural Imagination* (Basingstoke: Palgrave, 2001).

Smyth, Gerry, *Noisy Island: A Short History of Irish Popular Music* (Cork: Cork University Press, 2005).

Smyth, Gerry, *Music in Irish Cultural History* (Dublin: Irish Academic Press, 2009).

Steward, Sue and Garratt, Sheryl, *Signed, Sealed and Delivered: True Life Stories of Women in Pop* (London: Pluto Press, 1984).

Stockman, Steve, *Walk On: The Spiritual Journey of U2* (Orlando, FL: Relevant Media Group, 2001).

Stokes, Martin (ed.), *Ethnicity, Identity and Music* (Oxford: Berg, 1994).

Stokes, Niall, *U2 – Into the Heart: The Stories Behind Every Song* (London: Sevenoaks, 2006).

Strachan, Rob and Leonard, Marion, 'A Musical Nation: Protection, Investment and Branding in the Irish Music Industry', *Irish Studies Review*, 12, 1 (April 2004), pp.39–49.

Street, John, *Rebel Rock: The Politics of Popular Music* (Oxford: Blackwell, 1986).

Swan, Alan, *From the Cradle to the Stage: Irish Music Greats, A Chronicle of the Early Years* (Dublin: Poolbeg Press, 2003).

Taylor, Gavin, 'Director's Commentary', DVD Extras, *Under a Blood Red Sky* (2009).

Taylor, Timothy D., *Global Pop: World Musics, World Markets* (New York and London: Routledge, 1997).

Thornton, Sarah, *Club Cultures: Music, Media and Subcultural Capital* (Cambridge: Polity Press, 1995).

Tobin, Fergal, *The Best of Decades: Ireland in the 1960s* (Dublin: Gill & Macmillan, 1984).

Toynbee, Jason, 'Policing Bohemia, Pinning Up Grunge: The Music Press and Generic Change in British Rock and Pop', *Popular Music*, 12, 3 (1993), pp.289–300.

Wall, Mick, *Bono: In the Name of Love* (London: Andre Deutsch, 2005).

Washburn, Kim, *Breaking Through by Grace: The Bono Story* (Grand Rapids: Zondervan, 2010).

Waters, John, *Race of Angels: Ireland and the Genesis of U2* (Belfast: Blackstaff Press, 1994).

Werbner, Pnina and Modood, Tariq (eds), *Debating Cultural Hybridity: Multi-Cultural Identities and the Politics of Anti-Racism* (London: Zed Books, 1997).

Whiteley, Sheila, *The Space Between the Notes: Rock and the Counter-Culture* (London: Routledge, 1994).

Whiteley, Sheila (ed.), *Sexing The Groove: Popular Music and Gender* (London: Routledge, 1997).

Whiteley, Sheila, *Women and Popular Music: Sexuality, Identity and Subjectivity* (London: Routledge, 2000).

Whiteley, Sheila and Rycenga, Jennifer (eds), *Queering the Popular Pitch* (New York and London: Routledge, 2006).

Wrathall, Mark A. (ed.), *U2 and Philosophy: How to Dismantle an Atomic Band* (Chicago, IL: Open Court, 2006).

Yorke, Ritchie, *Van Morrison: Into the Music* (London: Charisma, 1975).

Young, Robert J.C., *Colonial Desire: Hybridity in Theory, Culture and Race* (London: Routledge, 1994).

Žižek, Slavoj, *Tarrying with the Negative: Kant, Hegel, and the Critique of Ideology* (Durham: Duke University Press, 1993).

Žižek, Slavoj, *Living in the End Times* (London: Verso, 2010).

Zuberi, Nabeel, *Sounds English: Transnational Popular Music* (Chicago, IL: University of Illinois Press, 2001).

Index